# Children and War

# Children and War

## *A Historical Anthology*

EDITED BY

*James Marten*

*Foreword by Robert Coles*

*New York University Press*

NEW YORK AND LONDON

NEW YORK UNIVERSITY PRESS
New York and London

Library of Congress Cataloging-in-Publication Data
Children and war : a historical anthology / edited by James Marten.
p. cm.
Includes bibliographical references and index.
ISBN 0-8147-5666-2 (cloth : alk. paper)
ISBN 0-8147-5667-0 (paper : alk. paper)
1. Children and war.   I. Marten, James Alan.
HQ784.W3 C53 2002
303.6'6'083—dc21          2002004989

*To the children, and to the fathers and mothers, brothers and sisters,
aunts and uncles, who died in New York, Washington, and Pennsylvania
on September 11, 2001.*

*And to Lauren and Eli Marten,
that they may never become children of war.*

# Contents

# Foreword

## *Robert Coles*

The past century has told us much about the inner life of children—their desires and worries, their attachments and aspirations for the future. By now we understand the home life of children, as well as their struggles within the family and on the streets and playing grounds of the neighborhoods which they have come to know as their very own. We also observe schoolchildren with increasing sensitivity and assurance, hence the substantial number of clinical workers who help teachers and parents to view the youngsters in their charge with a kind of confident sophistication and subtlety denied earlier generations of mothers and fathers, as well as classroom instructors. Moreover, as the child psychoanalyst, Erik Erikson, so wisely reminded us, we can learn about the world through the eyes and ears of children: What they notice and remember hearing gives us a good idea of what is out there, waiting for them to attend. Note the title of Erikson's first and seminal book, *Childhood and Society*—its author is at pains to insist that even as the young are shaped by the world around them, that holds as well for their grown-up guardians, at home or in the classroom. "So often," Erikson once remarked to a group of his colleagues,

> we want to explain a child's behavior by looking at the "social rules of the game," the values and norms that affect a boy, a girl, who grows up in a country, in a class or race or religion that is part of that country's life. But there is another side of that coin: children require our care, our constant concern, and so their presence among us exerts a strong influence upon us, to the point we become the beneficiaries of their requirements (and once in a while, I suppose it can be said, the victims—since some children can drive some of us, as we all know to say, "to distraction."

A subtly knowing and seasoned clinician was remarking upon the young, as they prod and stir us, especially at a time, these days, when we are so aware of their complex psychology, so interested in knowing about their yearnings and apprehensions, their secrets, their daytime thoughts and evening experiences (the passing dreams and nightmares that come upon them once they have gone to bed, shut their eyes, entered the oblivion of sleep, until the morning call of daytime action asserts itself and gets heard). Of course, the ordinary childhood of family and neighborhood life can abruptly and threateningly give way to the felt urgencies and fears, the shared social jeopardy, of war, as it travels well beyond the confines of battlefields into the cities and towns "behind the scenes" of conflict. Airplanes bring destructive danger; radios and televisions tell of what is happening far away, but also of what can, alas, in an instant become all too dangerously near at hand. Once war involves a child's ongoing psychological life, all sorts of consequences ensue, as this book's many essays make quite clear: yes, the inner emotional turmoil, but also the suffering, the constant jeopardy and vulnerability, which in their sum become an all too evident and overbearing presence, prompting nervous irritability and fearfulness, needless to say. But as we learn in the pages that follow, the consequences of war prompt other responses, too, including a combative desire (on the part of certain children) to take part in the very violence visited upon them and their families or neighbors. Indeed, the heart of this anthology is its comprehensive and telling account of war as it has become a critical aspect of the lives of children across the continents.

As I read these accounts, I kept thinking of the photographer Robert Capa's collection of images, published many years ago as *Children of War, Children of Peace*. Those visual images in their own way spoke volumes of what befalls the young as violence and hatred come to rule every day's experiences (words heard, deeds and sights seen). I also took note of the words of this anthology's editor—his fine introductory assist to us readers, which helps carry us through this extraordinary volume, a repository of history and psychology and sociology as those disciplines can be fathomed (and narrated) by recourse to children as witnesses, and even antagonists, or protagonists, in what takes place during certain wars. Once, ruminating on "war and children" as she observed boys and girls in London during the Nazi air blitz days of the early 1940s, Anna Freud (who appears in this book) fell into a spoken memory as she conversed with a few of us lucky to be in her presence (New Haven, 1972):

We were trying so hard to be of psychological assistance to those children, but I have to say, they were of great assistance to us—I mean [by that] there was so much for us to learn from them. We learned about the stresses placed on the young by war, but we also learned about the agility and resourcefulness of children, how they become fighters as well as hurt ones (I mean, how they responded in a difficult time, became solid citizens of a country gravely embattled). A remarkable time for the boys and girls, but a remarkable time for us—we became, in a way, their interested, always alert students as well as their adult guardians!

This anthology will help many of us, yet again, to learn from (and certainly, about) children—as did Anna Freud and others. Now, courtesy of one essay after another, and an editor's knowing, thoughtful diligence, we readers will be able to comprehend human possibility and variousness as they affirm themselves in young people whose lives become connected to war (hurt by it, or stirred toward involvement in it)—children, in a sense, at war during war (within their minds, or within their bodies).

# Acknowledgments

Like all anthologies, *Children and War* is truly the product of the work of many different people coming together to tell the often sad, sometimes inspiring, but always important stories of the ways children have been and are affected by war. This particular team came together when, at the invitation of Jennifer Hammer of NYU Press, I issued a call via H-Net for essays on children and war. Well over forty scholars responded. Indeed, one of the most difficult parts of editing this volume was cutting the number of proposals down to a workable one. I was aided in that task by the comments of three anonymous readers of the book proposal—which still included over thirty ideas for essays—who, in addition to advising me on which essays would and would not fit, also helped guide my own thinking about how to frame the essays in my introductions. I would also like to thank Jeanine Graham and Tom Cardoza for offering suggestions on how to improve the general introduction.

In order to include a greater variety of pieces, Jennifer and I determined to include as many of the original proposals as possible, which meant that authors would have to write essays somewhat shorter than those found in most collections and with rather less room for citations and other scholarly equipage. This choice created countless dilemmas for the authors, who had to endure a brutal word limit and a sometimes ruthless editor in choosing which snippets of prose, which points of analysis, which pieces of evidence to omit. For their unfailingly cheerful acceptance of this challenge I extend a hearty thanks. The shared determination of these junior and senior scholars, who hail from five countries, several disciplines, and numerous subspecialties, allowed us to create a lean, useful anthology that was sent to the publisher only a couple of months late!

Robert Coles, whose work on children in conflict and in crisis has inspired and informed scholars in so many disciplines, deserves special thanks for taking the time to read the manuscript and to write the moving and thoughtful foreword.

At NYU Press, I'd like to thank Jennifer Hammer for asking me to do this book, for her insights on managing the process, and for her suggestions on the introductions, as well as Despina Papazoglou Gimbel and the rest of the staff for smoothing the production process.

Even as this book goes to press in late October 2001, thousands of children and their parents, siblings, relatives, and friends have become victims of terrorist attacks on the United States, attacks that reflect the crumbling distinction between home front and battle front, attacks that remind Americans that war in the twenty-first century ignores national boundaries as well as victims' ages and economic status. In the days after the attacks, broadcast reports and articles in the print media frequently referred to the necessity of explaining the events of September 11 to children, acknowledging that even those children living far from the disaster, called an "act of war" by the nation's political and military leaders, would be frightened and enraged, mobilized and depressed, confused and focused by the events that changed their worlds forever.

As the opening of the beloved children's play and story, *Peter Pan*, goes, "All this has happened before. And all this will happen again." In the context of the Darling children's bittersweet journey to Neverland, that possibility is a little haunting, a little exciting, but ultimately comforting. That it can also be applied to the pain and suffering and dislocation inflicted on children around the world by war is no fairy tale, but a stark fact, unfortunately, of so many children's lives.

# Children and War

# Introduction

## *James Marten*

Autumn 2000: An outburst of Palestinian-Israeli violence in Gaza pins down a Palestinian father and his twelve-year-old son; a French film crew catches the horror in the boy's eyes—and his death a moment later as bullets rip into him and his father.[1]

1989: Dozens of young Iranian soldiers while away their time in a dreary Iraqi prisoner-of-war camp; although they are now in their late teens or early twenties, they have been in prison for at least four years. They are some of the survivors from among the tens of thousands of soldiers under the age of fifteen who fought against Iraq during the massive Iran-Iraq conflagration of the 1980s.[2]

1918: Hundreds of thousands of American children take part in the U.S. School Garden Armies, planting gardens to offset food shortages and imbibing patriotism through their participation in the home front war effort.[3]

1864: Children whose fathers and brothers and neighbors are fighting to the save the Union in the American Civil War can purchase *The Union ABC*, a picture book whose alphabet is illustrated by images of patriotism and war. It includes phrases like "A is America, land of the free, B is a battle, our soldiers did see"; "G is a Gun, that is used in the war, H is for Hardtack, you scarcely can gnaw"; and "S is a Sailor, who respected will be, T is a Traitor, that was hung on a tree."[4]

These images and vignettes are part of the vast collage of words and pictures portraying the experiences of children in nineteenth- and twentieth-century wars. They join the iconic photographs of the doomed Anne Frank and of the badly burned girl fleeing down a Vietnamese road after a napalm attack, as well as the charming, heartbreaking words of the famous Bosnian diarist Vladia Filopovic. Clearly, the last two centuries of global history have too often been illustrated by visions of children and war.

*Children and War: A Historical Anthology* seeks to describe and to explain the ancient and modern, awful and inevitable connection between children and war. The chapters are divided into three broad categories: Memory and Meaning, Lessons and Literature, and Actors and Victims. In this book, children are pulled kicking and screaming—literally—into wars, but they also become willing participants in them. The timeliness of a volume such as this, one that places such a "hot topic" in its historic contexts, is obvious. Although this is a work of historical analysis, part of the impetus for publishing it is the increasing awareness of the effects of war on children and of children's roles in warfare. Over the last several years, newspapers, magazines, television programs, and Websites have shown the extent to which the lives of children have increasingly been shadowed by war:

## As Casualties

The United Nations claims that, while civilians comprised 10 percent of all casualties in the First World War and 45 percent during the Second World War, they now make up as much as 90 percent of casualties caused by wars—and many of those casualties are children. In the 1990s, an estimated 1.5 million children were killed and another 4 million were injured by warfare, while 12 million became refugees.[5]

## As Soldiers

An unfortunate truth behind the military use of children is that they make good soldiers. They can easily handle lightweight modern weapons; they are easily motivated and natural "joiners," willing to take risks; and, ironically, they can often infiltrate enemy positions and territory because most adult soldiers are reluctant to fire on children. Youth Advocate Program International believes that boys and girls under the age of fifteen are participants in conflicts in well over three dozen countries, on behalf of governments, opposition forces, or both. The countries in which these child soldiers fight range from Afghanistan and India to South Africa and Angola to Northern Ireland and Turkey, to Guatemala and Colombia. The U.S. Coalition to Stop the Use of Child Soldiers believes that an estimated 300,000 minors living on nearly every continent were engaged in combat at the end of the twentieth century.[6]

A series of *Newsday* articles in October 1999 painted a horrific picture of the incorporation of children into brutal revolutionary and ethnic struggles in third world countries. The Lord's Liberation Army, for example, a rebel organization fighting against the Ugandan government, has kidnapped over 8,000 children and forced them to be soldiers, menial laborers, and, in some cases, sex slaves; when they disobey their captors or are hurt or injured, they are simply killed on the spot. Over and above the dangers of actual combat, the effects on children of military service can be devastating. The rigors of hard marching with heavy packs can deform young spines, the uncertain availability of rations can lead to malnutrition, exposure to all kinds of weather can cause skin diseases and respiratory infections, and taking part in forced or consensual sex with other, often much older, soldiers, can lead to sexually transmitted diseases.[7]

The use of child soldiers has not gone unchallenged; indeed, much of the media's interest in children and war confronts the practice directly. It has also become a political issue, with the public outcry against the use of child soldiers led by the United Nations, UNICEF, and a number of other children's rights and humanitarian organizations. The Convention on the Rights of the Child, a document created by a committee of the United Nations, has been signed by 191 states. It seeks to establish moral and political guidelines for treating the child victims of warfare and to raise the minimum age of combat soldiers from fifteen to eighteen. This second initiative is opposed by the U.S. government, which allows seventeen-year-olds to volunteer for its armed forces but promises not to send them into battle. Yet even the current world standard of fifteen is regularly ignored by armies and rebels around the world.[8]

## As Survivors and Veterans

The long-term impact of war experiences as both victims and combatants has occupied journalists, scholars, and health care professionals. A journalist visiting a Sri Lankan rehabilitation camp for former child soldiers noted that during a game of charades, young boys frequently could come up with only combat-related imagery. When one child seemed, in the eyes of the reporter, to be miming the plowing of a field, one boy guessed, "He is digging a mass grave." Another disagreed; he was "bayoneting half-dead soldiers." Child soldiers and victims frequently draw pictures and tell stories haunted by images of death, devastation, and violence. The few kidnapped children who manage to escape from the Lord's Resistance Army in Uganda are treated in trauma centers by psychologists and social workers who confront the rapes and unwanted babies, the effects of constant abuse and threat of instant death, the numbness that rises in the face of casual violence and harsh discipline.[9]

Not surprisingly, even children who have not been forced to serve in the military suffer when they confront war. A number of researchers have found evidence of post-traumatic stress disorders in children who have witnessed or been the victim of atrocities, dislocation, and other facets of warfare. Few Belfast children living near the scenes of riots in the early 1970s escaped displaying at least one symptom of acute anxiety, which include sleep disorders, fears of separation, loss of appetite, urinary and gastric infections, and headaches.[10]

Experts and journalists agree that these young victims, especially those forced into military service, "are the lost generation of protracted civil wars," especially "in nations where the three things that are most plentiful are children, poverty and violence." Worse, because they are seized and indoctrinated before their moral values are fully formed, they become thoughtless killers; ironically, some of the worst atrocities carried out against children are committed by children. One child-development expert with UNICEF believes that among the worst effects of the use of child soldiers are the brutality that they internalize and the independence that they learn. "These guys are loose cannons in a way. They're so used to being on their own, that they're basically just little, early adults." There may be tiny silver linings to the horror; with rehabilitation, counseling, and a return to normality, such as it is, child soldiers often seem to recover fairly quickly. Officials at a World Vision rehabilitation camp in Uganda assert that they know of no children who returned willingly to the rebel army out of the nearly 4,700 who have been treated.[11]

Cataloguing the perils of being a child in this war-torn world hardly explains the meaning of conflict in their lives or the meanings they take from war. At one level, it is presumptuous of adults, including scholars, to impose their own fears and assumptions on the children of war. Clearly, children have not simply been victims of modern wars or of wars from any era. Although the notion that children can accept war—enthusiastically, in fact—may seem counter-intuitive to many, it is well grounded in psychological theory. Anna Freud and Dorothy Burlingame, in their path-breaking study of children's reactions to the German bombing campaign against Britain during the Second World War, suggested that, far from being frightened by the destruction of war, children were engaged by "primitive excitement," joyfully playing amidst wreckage and debris and actually becoming rather heedlessly destructive themselves. Robert Coles has shown that girls and boys around the world constantly think in terms of their own and their families' place in the political world and that they clearly understand what is at stake in the religious and political conflicts in which their countrymen and women fight.[12]

Indeed, youngsters seem to understand war more instinctively than they do peace. They can conjure up images of the former much more readily and concretely than the latter; peace remains an abstract idea reflecting an inner state rather than relationships among groups. For many, according to a psychologist who studied Israeli and Palestinian children, war is not an external event, but "an integral part of [their] psyche and mental life. War . . . is transferred as feelings, symbols and models to a child's emotional life," replacing, in some ways, the normal traumas and conflicts that all children experience.[13]

The story of Johnny and Luther Htoo, the diminutive twins who led a band of Karen rebels called "God's Army" against the government of Myanmar for two years, recently helped focus the Western world's attention on the fact that children sometimes become willing participants in armed conflict. According to the legend that quickly grew around them, the brothers demonstrated mystical powers when they allegedly led a successful counterattack when government forces raided their village. Yet they retained a certain childishness; when they finally surrendered to Thai officials early in 2001, the boys looked much younger than the thirteen or fourteen years old they were supposed to be; they claimed that they simply wanted to find their mother, rumored to be living in a refugee camp.[14]

In the violence that rumbled through the Gaza Strip in late 2000 and 2001, Palestinian children clearly chose to participate in the protests against Israel. In a "Day of Rage" rally in March 2001, boys waved assault rifles while riding on their fathers' shoulders, and fifteen children under the age of ten performed a play in which a suicide bombing of an Israeli target was acted out to the accompaniment of the children chanting, "We die for the sake of God." The Associated Press quoted a leader of the Islamic Jihad, sponsor of the rally: "The Islamic nation and the Palestinian nation, from the small children to the old men, are ready to sacrifice for this land." In the half year of fighting between Palestinians and Jewish soldiers after September 2000, 66 of the 352 Palestinians killed were under the age of eighteen; almost a fifth of the ten thousand Palestinians injured in the protests were minors. As if to prove the point, a fourteen-year-old victim of Israeli gunfire, Wael Imad, had eagerly joined a rock-throwing attack against an Israeli outpost, telling the friend with whom he shared a taxi ride to the scene of that day's riot, "I need to go only one way, I'll come back in an ambulance." He was struck in the forehead by a "rubber bullet" and killed instantly.[15]

That not all children go to war against their will is as true now as it was in 1212, when French and German children mounted the "Children's Crusade," which ended in disaster but, through an uncertain haze of religious myth and legend, inspired the world; or in 1861, when ten-year-old John Clem ran away from home to be a drummer boy for the Union army, but within a year traded his drum for a rifle to become a front-line soldier; or in countless other countries and colonies where indigenous boys and girls became—and become—men and women before their time to fight invaders, colonists, and oppressors. Even today, Burmese children are raised on stories of heroes like General Aung San, who helped to liberate the country from Britain and Japan, and of the famous warriors of the nation's diverse ethnic groups. As in many societies, becoming a soldier is a sign of manhood, accompanied by prestige and honor. This "pull" effect is complemented by an equally strong "push": Many Burmese children already work long, hard hours in fields or shops. Entering the military is not necessarily a matter of leaving behind childhood, but of exchanging different modes of premature adulthood. Similar economic distress caused children in Sierra Leone to volunteer for military service; others enlisted because family members were already participating in the conflict and because "it often seemed better to become a soldier than to sit at home, frightened and helpless."[16]

Of course, there are many other ways for war and conflict to enter the lives of children. Even in the face of daily violence and danger, children play war—employing "an instinctual form for understanding the absurd and accommodating the irrational," according to a scholar of the play of Jewish children in concentration camps—and participate in the political movements that accompany the war. During "the Troubles" in Northern Ireland, boys played "soldiers and terrorists," "Bobby Sands" (the IRA martyr), and "riot"—complete with tomato sauce blood. They also marched at the front of funeral processions where, in the words of Roger Rosenblatt, they lent "moral authority to [the] cause."[17]

There is another level of children's participation in war, best represented but certainly not restricted to the United States during the Second World War. Although American children were safe from the actual fighting, they nevertheless plunged into the war spirit that infused almost every aspect of their lives. The media fed their hunger for information through newsreels, radio programs, comics, movies, and children's magazines; schools rewarded scholastic achievement with military ranks and held military-style inspections; boys and girls focused intensely on war news and on details related to the warlike uniforms and military technology; and, of course, they participated widely in civil defense exercises and home front efforts like collecting scrap iron, rubber, and newspaper. American children and youngsters in countless other countries had experienced many of these elements of war on the home front, but the Second World War focused the attention of a generation of children—the offspring of "The Greatest Generation"—more than any other before or, perhaps, since.[18]

Children are rarely left to interpret the causes and meanings and ramifications of wars completely on their own, and such efforts comprise another element of this anthology. Children's experiences during wartime cannot be separated from larger efforts by families, governments, schools, and other institutions and organizations to shape the responses and even memories of children. British policies regarding the evacuation of children from urban areas during the Blitz helped determine the way several hundred thousand boys and girls sent out to the country recalled the war; indeed, their notions about class and region—even their personalities, according to Ruth Inglis—were deeply affected by the evacuation. French children living in Vichy, France became part of an attempt to reconfigure French society through neofascist institutions modeled after Germany's Hitler Youth. Even a so-called "cold war" needs to be packaged by governments and political parties and in schoolbooks; such was certainly the case during uneasy conflict on both sides of the Berlin Wall after the Second World War, and even in such benign American publications as *My Weekly Reader*.[19]

The preceding only scratches the surface of the large journalistic and historical literature that addresses issues that emerge from the study of children and war, many of which appear in one form or another in the following chapters. The authors explore the circumstances affecting children during world wars, civil wars, cold wars, total wars, and limited wars, as well as during the periods leading up to wars and in the aftermaths of wars. Obviously, there can be no single definition of "war" for a volume such as this, just as there is no single definition of "child." The pieces deal with cultures in which children come of age at quite different times, in which adults maintain very different expectations for their offspring, and in which gender roles may vary dramatically.

But a pair of assumptions provide the main structure to the volume: (1) Children have been and are deeply engaged in every facet of war—not simply as victims; (2) Children become a part of the "meaning" of war through their own responses and by the way in which societies use children as symbols of virtue, sacrifice, patriotism, and any number of other characteristics.

Children will certainly play the role of victims in *Children and War*, but the authors also show that youngsters of all ages have often sought to incorporate armed conflict into their lives and have responded in surprisingly positive and multi-layered ways to grown-ups' attempts to explain war to them. Taken together, the essays address a number of questions: How do children embrace or endure warfare? How do societies, governments, and institutions manage the effects and the lessons of war? How do gender, class, and ethnicity influence the impact of war on children and the response of children to war? The authors place war, in the field and in the home, in a number of contexts: from entertainment and play to work and responsibility, from child rearing and education to propaganda and socialization, from race and ethnicity to constructs of femininity and masculinity, and from experience and participation to memory and commemoration.

A number of points of view emerge from these case studies of children and war over the last two centuries, and authors describe several levels of participation by children in war. Tensions appear between what children think about war and what society wants them to think. Adults study the effects of war on children; children accept war as a "normal" part of their lives. Schools and patriotic organizations attempt to socialize children to their appropriate roles and responsibilities; children internalize martial values and become politicized, sometimes despite the best efforts of adults and governments. We must not forget that these are children and that the business of growing up continues even as conflict impedes and scrambles common assumptions and values.

In the early 1990s, a teenaged girl wrote an American pen pal from Sarajevo that "worst things are happening, which you couldn't imagine, there in the paradise." Walt Whitman had made a similar assertion about the American Civil War a century-and-a-third earlier, claiming that "the real war will never get in the books." He went on: "In the mushy influences of current times . . . the fervid atmosphere and typical events of those years are in danger of being totally forgotten." Whitman doubted that the patriotism, pride, and short memories of Americans would allow them to understand the nature of the Civil War, to comprehend fully the blood and sacrifice and squalor of the battlefields and hospitals he witnessed. The scholars who contributed to *Children and War* may or may not have gotten the "real" children's war into their chapters, but they have studied a diverse set of factors and experiences in locations from all around the world. And, by awakening readers' imaginations to the myriad ways in which war shapes the lives of children, they have helped to ensure that the stories of children of war are not forgotten.[20]

NOTES

1. Among the many articles inspired by the photograph of the death of Mohammed al-Durrah is Julian Borger's column, "A photo often goes to the very heart of the matter," which appeared in the *Milwaukee Journal Sentinel* on October 8, 2000.

2. Brown, *Khomeini's Forgotten Sons.* Complete citations for key secondary sources related to children and war in this and all other chapters can be found in the Bibliography.

3. O. L. Davis, Jr., "School Gardens and National Purpose During World War I," *Journal of the Midwest History of Education Society* 22 (1995): 115–126.

4. *The Union ABC* (Boston: Degen, Estes & Company, 1864), n.p.

5. Tina Susman and Geoffrey Mohari, "A Generation Lost to War," *Newsday* (October 10, 1999), A54; "Caution: Children at War: Child Soldiers Fact Sheet," Amnesty International USA, www.amnestyusa.org.

6. Rohan Gunaratna, "Tiger Cubs and Childhood Fall as Casualties in Sri Lanka," *Jane's Intelligence Review* 10 (July 1, 1998), 32–37; Susman and Mohari, "A Generation Lost to War," A54; "Child Soldiers Fact Sheet."

7. Tina Susman, "Dual Captivity: Rebel Groups Force Girls into Soldiering and Sex," *Newsday* (October 11, 1999), A5, A20, A22; "Child Soldiers of Sierra Leone," *World Press Review* 46 (December 1999), 45.

8. Francesco Paolo Fulci, "Massacre of the Innocents," *UN Chronicle* 35:4 (1998), 26–27; Shannon McManimon, "Protecting Children from War: What the New International Agreement Really Means," *Peacework* 27 (May 2000), 14–15. Perhaps 1,000–2,000 soldiers under the age of seventeen serve in U.S. military units that may be ordered into combat. "A Fight over Child Soldiers," *U.S. News & World Report* 128 (January 24, 2000), 8.

9. Associated Press, *Milwaukee Journal Sentinel,* September 10, 2000; Higgins and Ross, *Fractured Identities*; Catholic Archdiocese of Monrovia, *The Liberian Civil War through the Eyes of Children*; Susman, "Dual Captivity," A5, A20, A22.

10. Dodge and Raundalen, *Reaching Children in War,* 28–32; Fraser, *Children in Conflict,* 61. J. J. Harbison and others have suggested that the long-term psycholog-

ical effects of "the Troubles" are relatively minor. Harbison, ed., *Children of the Troubles.*

11. Susman and Mohari, "A Generation Lost to War," A7, A60; Paul Harris, "Uganda's Civil War: Bloody, Brutal and Bereft of Morality," *Jane's Intelligence Review* 10 (February 1, 1999), 45.

12. Freud and Burlingame, *War and Children*, 23–24; Coles, *The Political Life of Children.*

13. R. L. Punamaki, "Childhood in the Shadow of War: A Psychological Study on Attitudes and Emotional Life of Israeli and Palestinian Children," *Current Research on Peace and Violence* 5:1 (1982), 28; Daniel Glaser, "Violence in the Society," in *Violence in the Home: Interdisciplinary Perspectives*, ed. Mary Lystad (New York: Brunner/MazeL 1986), 18–21.

14. Associated Press, *Milwaukee Journal Sentinel*, January 18, 2001.

15. *Milwaukee Journal Sentinel*, March 17, 2001; Matt Rees, "Fields of Fire," *Time* 156 (December 18, 2000), 55.

16. "No Childhood at All": A Report about Child Soldiers in Burma (Chiangmai, Thailand: Images Asia, 1997), 7–8; Elliott P. Skinner, "Child Soldiers in Africa: A Disaster for Future Families," *International Journal on World Peace* 16 (June 1999), 10.

17. Eisen, *Children and Play in the Holocaust*, 122; Fraser, *Children in Conflict*, 105; Rosenblatt, *Children of War*, 40, 41, 44.

18. The most useful account of American children during World War II is Tuttle, *"Daddy's Gone to War."* For a look at the effect of the war on children's literature, see M. Paul Holsinger, "World War II Combat in American Juvenile and Paperback Series Books," *Primary Sources & Original Works* 4:1/2 (1996), 147–162. A brief general account of children's experiences in World War II Britain is Brown, *A Child's War.* An affecting collection of reminiscences of British children can be found in Robert Westall, comp., *Children of the Blitz: Memories of Wartime Childhood* (New York: Viking Penguin, 1985). For the responses of American children to the Civil War, see Marten, *The Children's Civil War.*

19. Inglis, *The Children's War*; Halls, *The Youth of Vichy France*; Davey, *A Generation Divided*; Marc Richards, "The Cold War According to *My Weekly Reader,*" *Monthly Review* 50 (October 1998), 33–46.

20. *Dear Unknown Friend, Children's Letters from Sarajevo* (New York: Open Society Fund, 1994), 35; Walter Lowenfels, *Walt Whitman's Civil War* (New York: Knopf, 1960), 12.

# Memory and Meaning

In the summer of 1876, Lt. Col. George Armstrong Custer and his men swooped down on a massive encampment of Sioux and Cheyennes along the Little Big Horn River—called the "Greasy Grass" by Native Americans. The battle became one of the worst defeats in American military history, with perhaps 2,500 or so warriors overwhelming the 500 men of the Seventh Cavalry, wiping out the 210 men in Custer's detachment, and pinning down the rest of the regiment in a brief, desperate siege. For many years, the story of the "Last Stand" was told only from the point of view of the white soldiers who survived. Saloons around the country displayed prints of "Custer's Last Fight," a heroic painting of the disaster commissioned by the Anheuser Busch Brewing Company; Native American veterans of the battle—which, of course, turned out to be only a temporary setback for U.S. forces attempting to force Plains Indians onto reservations—kept their silence, fearing reprisals from their white conquerors.

A lifetime later, in 1931, John G. Neihardt interviewed a number of Indians who had participated in the battle, including a Hunkpapa Sioux named Iron Hawk, who had been fourteen years old in 1876. The old man's story first appeared in Neihardt's famous book, *Black Elk Speaks*, which was originally published in 1932. Although clearly a child by "civilized" standards, Iron Hawk had been in the middle of the fighting. His account provides a glimpse of how Native Americans processed the knowledge of their own conquest, how they hung on to notions of courage and honor, and how they defined themselves as men.

The attack came as Iron Hawk sat down for his first meal of the day. The battle raged in the distance, on the bluffs overlooking the village. When soldiers appeared on his end of the encampment—many on foot, curiously, apparently trying to escape—Iron Hawk and other young warriors joined the fighting. "We all yelled 'Hoka hey!' and charged toward them, riding all around them." He soon "met a soldier on horseback, and I let him have it," shooting an arrow through his body, knocking him off his horse, and then beating him to death with his bow. "I kept on beating him awhile after he was dead," Iron Hawk recalled, "and every time I hit him I said 'Hownh!' I was mad, because I was thinking of the women and little children running down there, all scared and out of breath." Later, Iron Hawk took part in the frustrating skirmishing on "Reno Hill," at one point helping to kill soldiers who had sneaked down to the river to fill their canteens. "Some boys were down there," he remembered, "and they came out of the brush and threw mud and rocks in the soldiers' faces and chased them into the river." The older boys and men took over at that point: "I guess they got enough to drink, for they are drinking yet. We killed them in the water."

Iron Hawk's memory of his role in the battle suggests a number of meanings. Although barely a teenager, he obviously considered himself a man, declaring his intention to protect the children back in the encampment and his anger at the whites who threatened them. He ridicules the attackers. The first soldiers he sees "were so scared that they didn't know what they were doing. They were making their arms go as though they were running very fast, but they were only walking"; some shot their guns helplessly into the air. Later, while the women were combing the battlefield, stripping the bodies of the fallen soldiers, Iron Hawk was amused when one of the men, playing dead, leaped to his feet and, after a short struggle, was killed by one of the knife-wielding women. "It was funny," laughed Iron Hawk, "to see the naked Wasichu fighting with the fat women." The troopers under the command of Capt. Reno, Iron Hawk reported derisively, "had been digging to hide themselves." Although this rather logical tactic made them difficult to attack, to Iron Hawk it seemed less than honorable.

Iron Hawk's version of the Custer fight and of his role in the events that unfolded on that bright and dusty battlefield suggests the power of memory for the children of war. On this day, at least, he and his fellow Sioux were more than a match for the arrogant whites. "These Wasichus wanted it, and they came to get it, and we gave it to them." His defiance and pride, his sense of accomplishment and manhood, overcame, at least while he was telling his tale, years of dreary reservation life, of economic distress, and of cultural genocide.

War carries many meanings and can be remembered in many different ways. The essays in this section explore the ways that children have processed war—not only wars that they lived through, but also wars that their nations fought in the past. Not all of the meanings taken from wars are conscious ones; not all of the memories are accurate. The trauma of war can affect children in insidious and psychologically violent ways; memories can be blurred by age or manipulated by governments and individuals. Yet these impressions form an important part of the way children experience war.

# Chapter One

# Childhood, Memory, and the American Revolution

## *Elizabeth McKee Williams*

During the era of the American Revolution, the United States was both a young nation and a nation of young people. In 1790, according to the first national census, almost half the U.S. population was under age sixteen.[1] A large percentage of Americans who lived through the Revolutionary War (1775–1783) were children. Although writing an autobiography was a very rare undertaking for that era, over seventy people wrote memoirs in which they discussed their youthful experiences of the war. These memoirists include men and women, black and white, from all of the original thirteen states. They wrote memoirs for a variety of reasons, sometimes as part of a religious autobiography, sometimes to record details of military service, sometimes at the request of descendants. Some wrote each word themselves, others narrated their tale, not always to a sympathetic editor. This essay explores those memoirs in an attempt to understand the nature and range of childhood experiences of the Revolutionary War.[2]

These memoirs describe childhood experience but were written decades after the events they describe. Memoirs written retrospectively create problems for historians using them as a source of facts, which may be remembered inaccurately or intentionally reshaped. But precisely because the texts were written retrospectively, they reflect what the authors remembered and chose to include in their stories, and thus they reveal much about the attitudes and values and the meanings the authors assigned to their youthful experiences. So, while these stories may provide only equivocal evidence to the historian of "what really happened," they do offer a marvelous resource for exploring how men and women of this generation understood their childhood experiences of war, and how they thought the Revolutionary War affected the course of their lives.

Many memoirs mention fathers leaving their families for the war. Brothers, uncles, grandfathers, and other relatives often left as well. Children remembered missing the absent men and fearing for their safety, and recalled the difficulties of survival without the men. Their narratives described a series of family adjustments to the missing men, but tended not to discuss the further adjustments when the soldiers returned.

In the father's absence, families were sometimes dispersed, and not all such families were reunited after the war. And, of course, some fathers did not return. Arial Bragg of Massachusetts wrote about his father joining the army and leaving the family to the mercy of Tories, whom he called "blood thirsty cannibals that surrounded the poor soldier's wife and five small children." Unable to support her children, Bragg's mother applied to the town selectmen for aid. They bound out the four older children, sending Arial to masters who he claimed deprived him of food, clothing, and education. Bragg gives graphic descriptions of deprivation, of "small clothes" too tight to move in, and of being forced to steal bread to get enough to eat. Bragg's father later died of smallpox at West Point, and the rest of the family was never reunited. Bragg filled his narrative with bitter complaints, an attitude shown by only a few of the memoirists. In his memoir Bragg neither blamed his father for leaving the family nor for re-enlisting after poverty had scattered the children. Instead, he romanticized his father's sacrifice, and blamed authorities named and unnamed for his plight.[3]

Many narratives describe families leaving their homes because of the fighting. The Morton family fled New York, spending the seven years of the war in New Jersey. Loyalist Elizabeth Lichtenstein Johnston described the 1779 siege of Savannah: "Soon almost every family was removed from the town to an island opposite, where they made use of barns, and taking their bedding and some furniture divided it by portions. In the barn where I was there were fifty-eight women and children, all intimate friends, and who had each one or more near relatives in the lines." And Benjamin Van Cleve remembered hiding in the New Jersey pine swamps at age five while his father and uncles participated in the battle of Monmouth. They returned to find their home burned. "My father had neither a shelter for his family, nor bread for them, nor clothes to cover them save what we had on. He saved a bed and looking glass only which we carried with us—a yearling heifer had escaped the enemy and a sow whose back was broken with a sword lived and his anvil I believe remained among the rubbish and ruins of the shop." His neighbors, in similar straits, were unable to help.[4]

Some children endured enemy soldiers quartered in their homes. Enemy soldiers were, of course, frightening, and some memoirs describe youthful fears. Yet others tell stories of defiance. James Jenkins's story contained elements of both. He described hiding up a tree while Tories raided his South Carolina home and, after a later raid, his mother defying a British officer who had taken over their house. When asked how many sons she had among the rebels, she said, "'None, sir: the king has rebelled against us, and not we against the king.' 'Well, madam, how many have you with Marion?' 'I have three, sir; and I only wish they were three thousand.'" Jenkins probably recreated his mother's words as grand prose, a bold story to balance his earlier tale of hiding from the enemy.[5]

Not just enemy soldiers were quartered with families. Mary Palmer Tyler remembered seeing many French officers come to her house. One wounded French officer spent "many weeks" convalescing in her family's Massachusetts home. "When he discovered that my father and mother instructed us, he volunteered to teach us writing. He wrote beautifully as far as wonderful flourishes went, and Joseph profited by his instructions, but we girls were too young or too stupid to do so. He used to play the flute and sing with my father."[6]

About half the memoirs discuss family finances and, in every case, they tell a story of financial difficulties caused by the war. Some describe direct damage caused by fighting, or by armies passing through; others tell of goods being taken by the soldiers on either side, or of property being lost as the family fled. Still others, like Mary Palmer Tyler, remembered their family fortunes being ruined by rapid depreciation of wartime paper money.

Some families saw their homes confiscated or destroyed; others managed to salvage their property. Elizabeth Lichtenstein Johnston wrote that after her Loyalist father fled, "my grandfather had a petition drawn up which he made me take, accompanied by a lady (sorely against my will, for I felt so indignant at their treatment of my father), to the [rebel] Board of Commissioners, which set forth the orphan condition I was left in, and petitioned that my father's property might be given to me." She was twelve, and her property was not sold. A few writers, like Arial Bragg, wrote of financial hardship with great bitterness. But most minimized their complaints, often telling instead of triumph over adversity or of virtuous endurance of hardships. Edward Hicks, who confessed to Loyalist grandparents, claimed that virtue came from those hardships. "But the tremendous turnings and over-turnings that took place in the time of the Revolution, produced a great change in my mother's family, and the success of the American patriots, in laying the foundation of the present excellent government, deprived the royal aristocrats of their lucrative offices, reducing our family to comparative poverty" and, according to Hicks, changing their hearts.[7]

Fear played a large part in some children's experience. Dan Huntington described a state of constant fear, starting when his father led the militia to fight the British at New London, Connecticut:

> while he was absent, we saw at home the smoke of the conflagration, not knowing but he and they were among the wounded and dying . . . I was born in the midst of [the country's] bloodshed and battles; and I know not if I thought it would ever be otherwise. Carnage and slaughter made the common news of the day. The first questions among neighbors, as they met in the streets and in each others' houses, were, "What news from head-quarters? Has there been fighting of late? How many were killed? Who were they? On which side was the victory?" Such was the dreadful routine from day to day, from month to month, and from year to year.[8]

Fifteen-year-old John Greenwood promptly enlisted as a fifer when the war started. He said he was very frightened before the war started by "superstitious accounts" of a terrible conflict that would bring on the day of judgment and set the world afire. He was 150 miles from his family at the time of the battle of Lexington, and set out alone to try to see his family "who, I was afraid, would all be killed by the British, for, as I observed before, nothing was talked of but murder and war." His fears lessened after he joined the army, when a wounded black soldier reassured and comforted him.[9]

Children's fears were complicated by their lack of understanding. Jeremiah Mason was seven when his father left to fight at Lexington in 1775, leaving his frightened family in "an agony of tears." Mason feared that his father would die. "After two days of extreme distress, news came that the British had retreated into Boston. . . . We were consoled by the knowledge that our dear father was safe, and also by the belief that the war was over." Of course it was not over; Mason's father commanded a Connecticut militia regiment until after the war ended.[10]

Children were often frightened by enemy soldiers, whether they saw any or not. Adults sometimes encouraged or took advantage of those fears.

Mary Palmer Tyler described her aunt using threats of the Regulars "to frighten us children after we were in bed, if we were noisy."[11]

The noise and the shooting which frightened some children was exciting to others. Nathaniel Goddard was a small boy in Brookline, Massachusetts when the war started. His narrative does not mention fear, but includes excited lists of the weapons he saw used. At age ten he ran over fifteen miles with his brothers to see the American soldiers marching captured Hessian troops past town. They watched them pass and then "we followed them, passing through the lines and then waiting again for them to come up." They repeated this process several times, until the troops and prisoners reached the barracks. Goddard remembered that "Here was the greatest sight we had ever witnessed."[12]

Some memoirists mention fearing death, but more simply refer to specific deaths. During the late eighteenth century, death was a part of life in a way that Americans are spared today. Infant and child mortality rates were high in America, although generally lower than in Europe. Most children watched at least a few siblings and friends die. Another difference in the colonial approach to death was that death and the rituals surrounding it took place in the home, not removed to external institutions like hospitals and funeral homes. Children expected to see death, but the war made death more frequent and more violent, and made the fear of death more pervasive.

Over half of the memoirists studied describe childhood experiences of death. Not every death was caused by the war, but many were. A father's death could derail a child's life; the violent death of another child might make little practical difference, but could transform attitudes. John Greenwood wrote:

> I remember what is called the "Boston Massacre," when the British troops fired upon the inhabitants and killed seven of them, one of whom was my father's apprentice, a lad eighteen years of age, named Samuel Maverick. I was his bedfellow, and after his death I used to go to bed in the dark on purpose to see his spirit, for I was so fond of him and he of me that I was sure it would not hurt me. The people of New England at that time pretty generally believed in hobgoblins and spirits, that is the children at least did.

Greenwood claimed not to fear Maverick's spirit but says he spent the years after Maverick died obsessed with fear of violent death.[13]

Thus far, only the experiences of civilian children have been discussed: boys and girls who experienced the war without intending to participate. But some boys enlisted in the army or served at sea. Both before and during the American Revolution, the minimum age for military service was sixteen. Yet some boys served at much younger ages, often as fifers or drummers. Some boys served as waiters for fathers or uncles who were officers. And others lied about their ages, adding a few months or even years. Early in the war, soldiers would typically enlist for a relatively short time, for a specific campaign or until the year's end. An individual might re-enlist several times during the war, and many served first as boys and later as adults. Military service at ages younger than sixteen would have been considered childhood service in the Revolutionary War.

Young boys entered military service alongside their fathers, in place of their fathers, or in spite of their fathers. Levi Hutchins was not quite fourteen when his father was commissioned a captain in 1775, and he went along as a fifer. Hezekiah Packard also enlisted as a fifer at age thirteen, inspired by the victory at Bunker Hill. "The captain of the militia lived near my father's, and as he knew the family were high whigs, and that I had some skill with the fife, he appointed me a fifer in the company under his command. Soon after this he enlisted, or was drafted for five months, and solicited me to go with him as a fifer, promising that he would treat me as a son." His narrative says that promise was kept. Other relatives also filled a father's place for some young combatants. Thirteen-year-old Andrew Sherburne went to sea with "my two half uncles."[14]

Some boys served as substitutes for fathers or other relatives who had been drafted into the army; others served despite, and perhaps to spite, fathers or guardians. Some boys ran away to the army, and their fathers found out afterward. Others, like Joseph Plumb Martin, argued until they were allowed to enlist. And some apprentices, boys legally bound for a term of service, served in place of masters who had been drafted. Sometimes boys said they were made to go; others bargained with their masters, perhaps gaining a promise to be released from indenture. An apprentice might enlist with the consent of his master but not of his parents, as did William and Jesse Earl.[15]

Occasionally a boy enlisted in an attempt to get out of trouble. John Hudson tells such a story. He reports that he enlisted in 1781 at age twelve in a militia levy for short-term duty (he does not say why he joined the militia at such a young age), but was soon after induced to enlist in the Continental Army to avoid harsh punishment. He writes that, after returning from guard duty:

I had gone into our quarters and was sitting on the ground with my gun between my knees, when it went off accidentally and apparently without cause, the ball passing out of the hovel, but injuring no one. However, it was an offence punishable with one hundred lashes and the corporal of the quarter guard immediately came in with a file of men and took me to the guard house. Here a conversation took place between the sergeant major and quartermaster sergeant, and one of them remarked with an oath, that it was a shame to give a boy like this an hundred lashes for what was notoriously an accident. This was said, purposely loud enough for me to hear. Then turning to me he added—"Come, my lad, the best way for you to get out of this, will be to enlist—come along with us." I jumped up immediately and had my name entered on the muster roll of the company.[16]

Hudson was in real trouble for shooting a gun within camp, but almost certainly would not have been so severely flogged. The officers took advantage of a young boy's fear of punishment to increase their enlistments, something Hudson appears to have realized in retrospect.[17]

Recruiters often sought very young soldiers to meet their quotas. Andrew Sherburne claimed that ship captains also sought young boys, encouraging "this spirit of enterprise" that would lead youths to run away to sea, and to war. David Low Dodge, a small child at the time, remembered that his half brothers enlisted with the consent of their masters but not of their mother, persuaded by "a neighbor, who was to receive a captain's commission if he would enlist forty recruits to serve during the war, – which he effected by enticing the youth, a majority of whom would not average sixteen years of age." Both brothers died in the army. Dodge grew up to become a prominent pacifist, and left a memoir filled with stories of the harmful effects of war.[18]

Sometimes young boys had different duties from adults (although adults also filled "noncombatant" jobs such as waiters). Most of the youngest soldiers in this study do not recall firing weapons at the enemy, at least not in their first term of duty. Hezekiah Packard, who enlisted as a fifer at age thirteen, recorded little about his specific military duties but did note that his regiment marched from Boston to Bunker Hill to New London to New York, and described "balls and bombs" falling into his camp "killing some and wounding some." He saw the casualties, but recorded few feelings about them, other than his disapproval of men taking needless risks. "A soldier, soon after the balls and bombs began to fly into our camp," he wrote, "walking proudly upon the parapet, boastfully proclaimed, that the ball was not yet made that was to kill him. Not many minutes after this wanton proclamation a ball came and almost cut him asunder, thus warning others not to expose life needlessly, lest they also should die 'as the fool dieth.'"[19]

Some boys served in adult capacities as armed guards over prisoners, for example, and on occasion boys were imprisoned with adults. Andrew Sherburne, who first went to sea in the Continental service at age thirteen, was fifteen when the privateer to which he was assigned was captured and he was sent to the infamous Old Mill Prison. His captors locked him up with the adults, which may suggest that they took no notice of his youth. His shipmates recognized his youthfulness by arranging for him to be taught to write and to "enumerate three figures." Actually, officers of the ship which captured Sherburne did recognize his youth, and attempted to get him to serve His Majesty as a cabin boy. Sherburne claimed in his memoir that he fought to be treated as a prisoner of war.[20]

Like older soldiers, boys often enlisted for a specific campaign or a set term of service. A boy leaving early might do as Levi Hutchins, who received an honorable discharge at age fifteen when his father found "a young man to supply my place." Boys, like adult soldiers, were often expected to find their own way home when their service ended. Hezekiah Packard became ill and was in the "extremely filthy" hospital when his term of service ended on December 31. Two hundred miles from home, he left the hospital alone and on foot. En route home he was overtaken by an older friend with a horse, who allowed him to ride.[21]

Boys joined the army and served at sea and some boys, like their older counterparts, found themselves employed by the army in civilian capacities. Starting at about age ten, John Becker served with his father as a wagoner for the Continental Army. He recorded detailed and at times funny stories of his trips, mostly within New York, although he did go once to Montreal. His memoir presented his wartime experience primarily as an adventure, a catalog of places visited and events witnessed. Writing for his descendants just before the Civil War, Becker chose not to dwell on war's violence.[22]

Boys and girls were equally likely to include the Revolutionary War in their memoirs, but differed somewhat in the type of war story they constructed. Girls, obviously, did not report combat experiences, and their stories tend to describe less adventure and to focus more on the extended family. Girls seemed no more likely than boys to admit to fear in their memoirs. The women who wrote for religious reasons, focusing their narratives on personal religious experience, said virtually nothing about the war. In contrast, men writing for religious reasons often spoke at length about the war, sometimes but not always stressing the moral threats which accompanied wartime violence.

Gender differences also appear in how play was presented in the memoirs. A number of boys remembered martial play. Andrew Sherburne recalled that "Lads from seven years old and upwards were formed into companies and being properly officered, armed with wooden guns and adorned with plumes, they would go through the manual exercise with as much regularity as the men." Ashbel Green recollected companies of boys aged ten to fifteen, "training, drilling and marching . . . encouraged and cheered on by our parents." Green did not consider this drill as play, but as preparation for joining the militia at age sixteen. Others, like Billy Hibbard, later a Methodist minister, remembered youthful drills with disapproval and did not admit to having had any fun. Hibbard described the soldiers swearing and "saying it was right for them to swear because it was war time." He saw younger boys emulate the soldiers' profanity. "I remember, one day at a training, a boy swore wickedly, and another boy reproved him—he stared open his eyes and exclaimed, 'why, it's training day.'" Boys frequently remembered martial play, whether or not they admitted to participating; girls, not surprisingly, described play that was totally separate from the war.[23]

While girls were as likely as boys to include the Revolutionary War in their life stories, the same was not true for members of eighteenth-century minority groups. Black memoirists were far less likely than white ones to discuss the war in their texts. Only two of those studied for this project make any mention of the war. Richard Allen devoted exactly one sentence to the war, mentioning only his adult service "drawing salt from Rehobar, Sussex county, in Delaware." Isaac Jefferson was interviewed, and his experiences recorded, precisely because he had been a slave at Monticello. He was asked questions pertaining to Thomas Jefferson, life at Monticello, and the British invasion of the plantation, but was allowed little space to discuss or consider his own life.[24]

And the one memoir in this study written by a German-speaking American never mentions the war.[25] The American Revolution was a war for national independence, but was less relevant to the lives of minority Americans, who were less likely to think the war changed their lives. When they crafted the stories of their own lives, they tended not to think the Revolution merited a place in those stories.

The Revolutionary War lasted for seven years, and was second only to the Civil War both in the percentage of the total population who were of combatants and in percentage of men who were killed in the war.[26] For many Americans, like Dan Huntington, born in 1774, their earliest memories were of war. People born a few years earlier could remember and portray an idyllic childhood shattered by the disruptions of war. To the modern eye, almost all of these narratives report childhood experience without reflecting on childhood as a formative period, and tend to downplay the violence of the Revolutionary War.

Early nineteenth century Americans agreed that the Revolution was a good thing, and celebrated it with increasing ceremony. This consensus of the Revolution's great worth to the nation may have made it difficult for individuals to depict the war publicly as harmful to themselves, and very few did. Memoirists considered their wartime experiences special, to be preserved for posterity, and their youthfulness during the war was of interest primarily because it meant they were still alive decades later to tell about it. They would have agreed with John Becker: "Many persons at the present day would be pleased to know, and, if possible, to realize the feelings and reflections of even ordinary individuals during our revolution. . . . how we bore our share of the troubles of the times, how they affected our comfort, or disturbed our repose."[27] This was why they wrote.

## NOTES

I want to thank Jane Quigley and John Shy for commenting on earlier versions of this essay.

1. U.S. Census Bureau, *Historical Statistics*, 10.

2. This essay is drawn from the author's dissertation, which studies over 120 memoirs and discusses issues of selection, methodology, and statistics.

3. Arial Bragg, *Memoirs of Col. Arial Bragg* (Milford, G. W. Stacy, 1846), 14–26.

4. Eliza Susan Morton Quincy, *Memoir of the Life of Eliza S. M. Quincy* (Boston: J. Wilson and Son, 1861); Elizabeth Lichtenstein Johnston, *Recollections of a Georgia Loyalist* (New York and London, 1901), 58; Benjamin Van Cleve, "Memoirs of Benjamin Van Cleve," *Quarterly Publication of the Historical and Philosophical Society of Ohio* 17 (1922): 9–10.

5. James Jenkins, *Experience, Labors and Sufferings of Rev. James Jenkins* (n.p., 1842), 26.

6. Mary Palmer Tyler, *Grandmother Tyler's Book: the Recollections of Mary Palmer Tyler, 1775–1866* (New York and London: G.P. Putnam's Sons, 1925), 58–59.

7. Johnston, *Recollections*, 46–47; Edward Hicks, *Memoirs of the Life and Reli-*

*gious Labors of Edward Hicks* (Philadelphia: Merrihew and Thompson, 1851), 18–21.

8. Dan Huntington, *Memoirs, Counsels and Reflections by an Octagenary* (Cambridge, 1857), 5–6.

9. John Greenwood, *A Young Patriot in the American Revolution, 1775–1783* ([Tyrone, PA]: Westvaco, 1981), 39–49.

10. Jeremiah Mason, *Memoir, Autobiography and Correspondence of Jeremiah Mason* (Kansas City, MO: Lawyers International Publishing Company, 1917), 3–5.

11. Tyler, *Grandmother Tyler's Book*, 58.

12. Nathaniel Goddard, *Nathaniel Goddard: A Boston Merchant 1767–1853* (Riverside Press, 1906), 62–64.

13. Greenwood, *Young Patriot*, 40.

14. Levi Hutchins, *The Autobiography of Levi Hutchins* (Cambridge, 1865), 23–27; Hezekiah Packard, *Memoir of Rev. Hezekiah Packard, D.D.* (Brunswick, 1850), 7; Andrew Sherburne, *Memoirs of Andrew Sherburne: A Pensioner of the Navy of the Revolution* (Utica: William Williams, 1828), 19.

15. Joseph Plumb Martin, *Private Yankee Doodle* (Boston: Little, Brown, 1962); David Low Dodge, "Autobiography" in *Memorial of Mr. David L. Dodge* (Boston, 1854), 19.

16. John Hudson, "Such had been the flow of blood . . ." *Cist's Advertiser* (1846), reprinted in *American History Illustrated* 16:6 (1981): 18.

17. Thanks to John Shy for confirming my interpretation of this episode.

18. Sherburne, *Memoirs*, 19; Dodge, "Autobiography," 20 and *passim*.

19. Packard, *Memoir*, 9.

20. Sherburne, *Memoirs*, 68–81.

21. Hutchins, *Autobiography*, 31; Packard, *Memoir*, 11–12.

22. John P. Becker, *Sexagenary: or, Reminiscences of the American Revolution* (Albany: n.p., 1866).

23. Sherburne, *Memoirs*, 17. Ashbel Green, *The Life of Ashbel Green, V.D.M.* (New York: Robert Carter and Brothers, 1849), 55–56; Billy Hibbard, *Memoirs of the life and travels of B. Hibbard, Minister of the Gospel* (New York: n.p., 1843), 14–15.

24. Richard Allen, *Life, Experience and Gospel Labors of the Rt. Rev. Richard Allen* (Philadelphia: AME Book Company, 1887), 8; [Isaac Jefferson], *Memoirs of a Monticello Slave* (Charlottesville: University of Virginia Press, 1955).

25. Henry Boehm, Reminiscences, *Historical and Biographical, of Sixty Four Years in the Ministry* (New York, 1866).

26. Howard H. Peckham, ed., *Toll of Independence: Engagements and Battle Casualties of the American Revolution* (Chicago: University of Chicago Press, 1974), 132–133.

27. Becker, *Sexagenary*, 8–9; Tyler, *Grandmother Tyler's Book*, 326.

# Chapter Two

# "After the War I Am Going to Put Myself a Sailor"

## Geography, Writing, and Race in the Letters of Free Children of Color in Civil War New Orleans

## *Molly Mitchell*

In the fall of 1861, Etienne Pérault wrote a letter to his cousin, "J. Jeansème," in Paris. Etienne, a free boy of color some thirteen years of age, lived in New Orleans. At the time he was writing, however, the city of New Orleans, like other port cities in the Confederacy, was under blockade by the Union navy.[1] And yet Etienne wrote to Jeansème about a voyage he had taken in July to the islands of Saint Marc and Haiti. He explained that he had signed up to work for the captain of the ship *Laura* (a vessel that sailed between New Orleans and Haiti before the Civil War) for six months, earning twenty-five dollars a month. He also described the two islands as though he had an eye for settling there, remarking that "Saint Marc is more habitable than Hayti because at Saint Marc there are more fruits and the soil is fertile." When the boat started again for New Orleans, he wrote, "I was very angry that I could not stay longer."[2]

What was Etienne's fascination with islands in the Caribbean and why did he want to stay there rather than return to Louisiana? Indeed, how had he managed to sail through a blockade of Union ships? Etienne's voyage, it seems, was an imaginary one, given the wartime context in which it was written, and the fact that Etienne was still in school without the liberty to be a sailor for six months at a time. Etienne attended the *École catholique pour l'instruction des orphelins dans l'indigence*, or Catholic Institution, in New Orleans, a school for free children of color. His letter was a composition written for an English class and we have no evidence that it was ever sent.[3] Though Etienne's letter and those of his classmates (all boys) were written to fulfill an assignment, the boys made these letters their own, drawing on their imaginations and daily experience rather than an instructor's template.[4]

These compositions, like Etienne's description of his Caribbean journey, present an unfamiliar history of the sectional conflict in the United States. It is a narrative of the Civil War from the perspective of free children of color: a story about race and geography, childhood and war, writing and imagination. The students at the Catholic Institution placed the American Civil War on a map of their own drafting, one centered not on the United States, but on the wider Atlantic World. For them, the war was not just a hardship, a military conflict, or an unpredictable local event. Instead, it inspired them to a trans-Atlantic exploration of freedom, nation, and racial identity at a time when such ideas were the subject of violent debate in the United States.[5]

The students used letter writing to escape the bounds of the conflict, traversing battle lines, oceans, and national boundaries when the war, and the poverty that it brought, kept them in New Orleans.[6] And they most often charted their course toward countries that were home to communities of free people of color like themselves—most especially France, Haiti, and Mexico. Unlike the United States, these countries no longer harbored a system of slavery that denied full freedom to people of color, slave and free. By writing letters, the students crafted tales of freedom and power that contradicted their uncertain status in the wartime South. However, if the exercise of letter writing allowed them to navigate past the sharp realities of war, it did something else, too. Their focus on societies where people of color lived free from slavery gave the boys a view of the possible. Writing of travels to other, freer nations in the uncertain light of the Civil War, the students began to consider the prospect of freedom in their own country.[7]

The students at the Catholic Institution were part of a vibrant community of free people of color that had endured increasing repression in the decade before the war. This relatively large population of free people of color was somewhat exceptional in the antebellum South. Southern Louisiana was characterized by a three-tiered racial system closer to that of Haiti (from which much of New Orleans's *gens de couleur* had originated) than to the two-tiered (black/slave and free/white) system common to other southern states.[8] Since the colonial period under France and Spain, free people of color in New Orleans had dominated many of the skilled trades and secured the legal rights of *quasi*-citizens: the right to make contracts, for instance, or to testify against a white person in court. But since the 1850s, the limited freedoms of the *gens de couleur* had suffered at the hands of southern legislatures and even the U.S. Supreme Court; state laws and federal rulings in the late 1850s shored up the system of slavery and began to erase legal distinctions between slaves and free people of color. The most notorious of these was the Dred Scott decision in 1857, which determined that people of color, free or slave, could not be citizens of the United States.[9]

Given the precarious position of the *gens de couleur* in the South of the 1850s and 1860s, the leaders and teachers at the Catholic Institution believed they had a special duty to educate free children of color, both vocationally and politically. These leaders, who identified themselves as "Afro-Creoles," were accomplished thinkers, writers, and poets. They were ardent in their desire to see slavery abolished, and deeply influenced by the Romantic literary tradition and the radicalism of the French and Haitian Revolutions.[10] The kinds of letters Etienne and his classmates wrote reflect these intellectuals' concerns with instilling in free children of color a desire to be economically successful and politically connected to people of color around the Atlantic. The children wrote letters in the late 1850s, for instance, about the migration of free people of color from Louisiana to establish colonies in Mexico and Haiti. The migrants left in hopes of escaping and overcoming the harsh economic and political environment in the South.[11] The children's letters relayed news about the best crops to grow in Mexico and covered political events in Haiti, based on what they had heard and read. These writing exercises served to educate them about the possibility of establishing themselves and prospering outside the United States. Etienne's reflection on the fertility of the soil in Saint Marc and Haiti suggests that even after the start of the Civil War, the students were contemplating settling there. Yet as they would do with the letters they wrote during the war, the students also made their compositions about migration useful to their own understanding of the political uncertainties around them. Thinking about life in Mexico and Haiti, they exercised on the page the power and freedom that seemed further and further from their grasp at home.[12]

The arrival of the war meant even more uncertainty, as free people of color in New Orleans found themselves in a newly precarious position. Although most opposed the system of slavery, as "Creoles" (non-"American" people of African and/or French descent born in Louisiana) some felt a duty to defend their "native land" from northern invasion, particularly if Abraham Lincoln's army threatened to destroy the city of New Orleans.[13] When free people of color organized a Native Guard to fight for the Confederacy, however, they did so not only in the name of Louisiana, but also as a means to defend their community in the face of violent threats from local whites.[14] Other free blacks chose migration instead of military participation, and set sail for Haiti before Lincoln's blockade became fully operational.[15] For free people of color, then, the beginning of war did not promise freedom and equality. Indeed, it was not assured at the outset that the North would win or that slavery and its oppressive social system would collapse. Instead, it was a moment of uncertainty about the prospects for people of color in the South.

Haiti was the only black republic in the nineteenth-century Atlantic World, and it held up the promise of a life free of racial discrimination. After a successful slave revolt in 1791 and the establishment of black rule, Haiti became a beacon of hope for people of color around the Atlantic, free and slave.[16] Haiti clearly held a fascination for many of the students, too, since they had seen friends and acquaintances board ships in New Orleans bound for the island. John Bordenave, for instance, writing to a classmate (though choosing to address his letter to France) recorded the departure of his friend Joseph Lavigne on the ship *Laura* bound for Haiti just after the war began, in May of 1861. Young Bordenave was envious of his friend, reporting that he had gone to the docks "to make my last adieu to one of my friends named Joseph Lavigne who is going to leave us, and I believe he will be better than us for he will be in the country of our colour."[17] Indeed, Lavigne was going to a place where colored people were in control. Throughout the war, the students continued to address many of their letters to Haiti. Etienne's choice in his composition to become a sailor and visit Haiti perhaps was a means of following those who had migrated.

Etienne's letter, however, also reveals something of the importance of shipping to his experience of childhood in New Orleans. Living in the largest port in the South, the students were familiar with trading vessels and steamers and with the economic ties these ships signified between countries around the Atlantic. Boys like Etienne would have seen sailors arriving and departing on ships daily; perhaps they even knew some of them. Most important, the occupation of sailor gave a young man a transnational existence, along with the chance to be outside of the South. Yet with the blockade and the war, the flow of shipping commerce and overseas travelers into New Orleans was interrupted. The image of a once bustling port suddenly stilled makes the letters Etienne and his classmates wrote about imaginary voyages all the more interesting.

Some, like Etienne's, did not mention the war explicitly. But their fanciful nature suggests a rejection of the circumstances of war. Ysidro Bordenave, for instance, adopted for himself the persona of an adventurer. His letter described a voyage he took to Europe, when he sailed on a ship named the *Ceres*. On his arrival in Paris, he had "the fever which obliged me to keep [in] bed since six weeks." On his journey home, Ysidro wrote,

> I saw the Emperor of France and he was very well with me and he wanted me to be the General of his army which was at Rome, but I told him that the weather was not good for me and that I was going to set off for England to night he makes me a present of a fine horse and gave me $3,000 in present. When I was in England I saw the palace of Queen Victoria and the monuments of Edward the III and on returning at New Orleans I make the addition of time that I took I saw that it was of seven years and I spent $30,000.[18]

The details of Ysidro's letter involved large expenditures of money and clever relations with European royalty. But his underlying themes were mobility, political power, and great wealth—three things that were beyond the grasp of free boys of color in the Civil War South.

A few of the "voyage" letters did include the war in their narratives. But in these letters, the war appears as an obstacle to be navigated around rather than an event with which to engage. Henry Relf, for instance, took a tour as Ysidro did, but he focused on important architectural sites in the United States and Europe. He journeyed on a steamship, he wrote, "for the doctor told me that only a journey on the sea would cure me." He chose to visit Fort Sumter in Charleston (where the Civil War began), the Royal Exchange in London, the State Houses in Philadelphia and in New Haven, and the Capitol building in Washington. "In returning," he added, "I stopped at Richmond now the Capital of the Confederate States. I was at Manassas when the battle took place, and as I didn't want to fight, I came right back home."[19]

Henry also wrote another letter a few months later in which he imagined himself encountering the Union navy on his return from a trip to England. He told his friend that he had started for New Orleans before the blockade, and was returning by the steamship *Israel*. "When we were near Balize [*sic*] we saw three men of war of Lincoln who were coming to chase us," he explained, "and I was obliged to pass by New York, Pennsylvania, and the other States to come to my country."[20] John Bordenave wrote a similar letter, though he had just been to Portugal when he encountered the "the men of war of Black Lincoln" and had to pass by Maine and New Hampshire "to come to my native one."[21]

In the accounts of Henry Relf and John Bordenave, the war is less a sectional conflict than an impediment to be overcome on their travels. Indeed, despite their enthusiasm for watching soldiers "make their exercises" in New Orleans, the students rarely wrote about battles. Instead, they focused on the ways in which the war divided them from their correspondents (real and imagined) in other countries. Just as Bordenave and Relf sailed around Lincoln's blockade, so the students often wrote their way around the war, steering clear of the conflict (as Henry Relf did at Manassas) whenever possible.

When the boys did write about battlefields and casualties, their reports came with a certain ambiguity about what was at stake in the conflict, and what, exactly, had inspired it. John Blandin, for instance, complicated the notion of North versus South when he wrote about a battle at Hampton, Virginia, "in which six hundred of the Lincolnites were slain and only fifty of our brave Southerners were killed." He had heard that soldiers from Louisiana had been in the fight, too.

> Hurrah! for our brave Louisianans and may God bless them and the whole Southern Confederate Army, that they might lick the Northerners every time they have an engagement and make them see that we Southern men are not to be played with. . . . The best thing [the northerners] must do, is to acknowledge our rights, for we will give them the best licking they ever had since they know themselves.[22]

From these words, it seems that John Blandin, a free boy of color, was on the side of the Confederacy. This is not surprising considering that some of the *gens de couleur* of New Orleans were enlisted with the South in 1861. But John addressed his letter about battles and "rights" to "Port-au-Prince, Hayti," a nation born when slaves overthrew their masters and established a republic for people of color.

How, then, are we to interpret John Blandin's enthusiasm for the Confederates? A clue comes, perhaps, from the way that he signed his letter: "from the heart of a Creole . . . who is proud to be a Southern man." In addition to "Southern manhood," the importance of being "Creole"—that is, identifying himself according to the geography of his birth as well as his heritage—seems to have underpinned his notion of rights. If John Blandin viewed the Civil War as a war about the "rights" of Creole men to defend their native land (and by extension, the South as a whole), then perhaps it made sense to him to include Haiti in his thinking alongside Hampton, Virginia. Wasn't Haiti a country built from the demands of a people for their rights? The events of Haiti and the Confederacy were part of very different histories, to be sure. Indeed, one was created from the successful overthrow of slavery while the other was created for the sake of preserving it. But in Blandin's interpretation of the Civil War, these two very unlike events served a common purpose. His geography of the war, therefore, had Atlantic proportions. It was sketched according to Blandin's expansive notion of "rights" rather than simply by outlining the ground of military conflict in the United States. His interpretation of the war drew on both a deep history and a map much broader and more politically intricate than the battle lines at Hampton and Manassas would suggest.

This wider view of the war also appeared in the students' response to local conditions, most especially to the poverty that had descended upon the city after 1861. Local circumstances, too, had encouraged the boys to think about places outside of the South. In a letter he addressed to one of his classmates in Madrid, Spain, Henry Relf wrote that he had "learned that the State of Missouri fell into the Confederate States" for which he was glad since "when the United States will see that the South is of the same numbers as they, they will give up." Like most of the students, Relf wanted to see an end to the war that had put such a strain on life in New Orleans. "Here everybody is in great misery and every thing is out of price; the dearest of all is soap, we used to pay $5 for a box weighing 40 pounds, but now it is $19."[23] These dire circumstances led Henry Vasserot to think of escaping the states as soon as possible. "After the war I am going to put myself a sailor," he declared, "till I reach a good country for the misery is too hard every body is in tears there is no work to give the poor men and women nor bread enough to give the soldiers."[24] Like Etienne Pérault, Henry Vasserot saw becoming a sailor as an opportunity to find a new "country" in which to settle, one that would be more prosperous and stable than wartime New Orleans.

Once the Union army occupied New Orleans in 1862, however, the boys began writing a bit more optimistically about life in the city. In a letter addressed to New York City, Ernest Brunet wrote to his friend, "I tell you if the Yankees would not come here we would be starving to death. About two weeks before the Yankees came in, you could not get a loaf of bread without fighting for it, and after fighting for it you would pay $40 a loaf."[25] Much of the students' optimism was connected to a shift in military allegiance on the part of the *gens de couleur*. Soon after the Union army took the city of New Orleans in April 1862, the leaders of the Louisiana Native Guard (many of them also leaders of the Catholic Institution) presented themselves to Union officials, offering their services in the war against the Confederacy.[26]

The boys noted with great interest the large numbers of colored troops amassing in the city to fight for the Union that year. Etienne Pérault, in a letter to a friend addressed to Haiti, remarked: "dear friend, I had forgotten to tell you that there are about three or four thousand colored soldiers here. They had one regiment that has already been to the camp and that is at the camp now."[27] Pérault's letter was a counter-narrative to the migration of free people of color to Haiti before the war. Where once his friends and relatives had fled the racially repressive South for the Black Republic, now there were thousands of armed black men in the city of New Orleans aiming to bring an end to the southern slave power. Lest we forget, armed black men had overthrown slavery in Haiti and at the time Etienne was writing, governed the country. Troops of black soldiers, therefore, signaled for the students the arrival of a new order within southern society. One student reported that when a colored regiment left town, "some amongst them were singing, some that were saying that they would bring the four limbs of old Jeff Davis and some [of] the other ones the head of Beauregard."[28]

If large regiments of colored soldiers were an indication of the changes brought by the war, so were the actions of enslaved people on nearby plantations. After noting that anyone who sang the "Bonnie Blue Flag" in the city was "severely punished" by Union officials, Ernest Brunet reported that he also knew of "a great many Negroes who are running away from their masters and go away with the Yankees."[29] The students almost never referred to slavery in their letters, but they did take note of the political implications of emancipation for enslaved people as well as for free people of color. They understood the arrival of freedom within the context not only of their own country, however, but also in relation to other slave societies. Lucien Lamanière, for instance, noted the relationship between free people of color and the system of slavery, and was aware, too, of emancipation in the South as a transnational event. He wrote:

> I am very glad since the Federals are here, they are telling that Gen. Butler is going to make the colored men of this city who were born free vote, if he do that the colored men will be very glad to see equality reign here and if he is ever to be elected President of the United States I am sure that he will be President because the colored men will vote for him, and I must tell you another thing. The [white slaveholding] Creoles of this city will die when they will see the Negroes vote as well as them, those Negroes whom they were always whipping in the plantations [will] take their tickets and put it in the box, I do not think that [the Creoles] will stay here, they are all going to Havana, and there, they are dieing like flies with the country's disease, a letter

which we received from a friend told us that [the Creoles] are very bad there, the Negroes of that country are cursing them when they pass by them.[30]

The end of slavery in the South, like the war itself, was a political event that could not be contained within the boundaries of the United States. Rather, as Lucien noted, it affected other slave societies like Cuba, thus throwing into question the longevity of slavery throughout the Americas.[31]

The Civil War, in Lucien's interpretation, turned these slaveholding societies on their heads: giving political power to free men of color and "Negroes" in the United States and causing slaveholders to die "like flies" in Cuba. Etienne Pérault, too, had an impression of the southern social order turned upside down by the war. He wrote a letter within a letter, using the voice of a Confederate soldier writing to his sister. Etienne may have written this himself or he might have copied it from another source, perhaps a newspaper printing letters from the battlefront. Nonetheless, he chose to include this particular story, a story that speaks to the revolution taking place as he wrote. The soldier declared that he would rather "endure all the privations and perils of the service than to die the thousand deaths of the cowardly miscreants of Louisiana of French extraction." Deriding the (white) Confederate soldiers of Louisiana (in words that ring more with Etienne's playfulness, perhaps, than the thoughts of a Confederate), the soldier hoped that Union General Benjamin Butler "will conscript them, and work them in cleaning the streets, with collars on their necks."[32]

Writing about the war, then, was not just an imaginative exercise for the students; it was an exploration into the nature of, indeed the *possibility* of, power. In this upended society, the Union general fighting to end slavery—and to whose armies enslaved people were fleeing daily—would put in shackles white southerners who had fought in the name of slavery's preservation.[33] It is fascinating to consider, too, that Etienne addressed this particular letter to Haiti, the only example of slavery successfully deposed by enslaved people themselves, thus placing masters at the mercy of their former slaves.

The Civil War was never separate in the minds of the students from their thinking about other points in the Atlantic World. Just before writing about the Creoles going to Cuba, Lucien had penned another letter.[34] There would be nearly two more years of war, though Lucien could not know this. He recalled once visiting his aunt and cousin in Paris and told his friend: "I am going next year and I invite you to come. We will go to Paris together and before coming back to New Orleans, we will go and visit that fine country called Hayti and if you are not satisfied of those two countries, we will go and visit Mexico the finest country after Paris."[35]

Charged and bright as his plans were, they were dimmed somewhat by the words he had written at the foot of his letter. "Since the blockade," Lucien wrote in his postscript, "I have not heard any news from you. . . ." Captive in his own land, Lucien wrote of (dreamed of) finding a country where the system of slavery no longer held people like himself to a status neither slave nor free. Despite a civil war, he planned an ocean voyage. Yet if we consider Lucien's two letters side-by-side, his plans do not seem so fantastic. It was his belief in the existence of "fine countries" like Paris, Mexico, and Haiti, perhaps, that encouraged his faith in the rapidly changing society in which he lived. His love of these places gave him cause to believe that after the war in the United States "free colored men" and "Negroes" would be able to vote—to "take their tickets and put it in the box"—and that his own country might one day be as "fine" as the rest.[36]

## Notes

1. See James M. McPherson, *Battle Cry of Freedom: The Civil War Era* (New York: Oxford University Press, 1988), chap. 12.

2. E. Pérault to J. Jeansème, Jr., Esq., Paris, France, October 2, 1861, Catholic Institution English Composition Copybook II (hereafter Copybook II), Archives of the Archdiocese of New Orleans (hereafter AANO).

3. Etienne's letter and those of his classmates have survived because they were copied, by hand, into a large bound book by one of the students. The letters are housed in the Archives of the Archdiocese of New Orleans. The author plans to publish them as an edited collection.

4. The letter writers were all boys between twelve and seventeen years of age. I determined the ages of as many of the boys as possible using census rolls and the records of the school's board of directors. Etienne Pérault's age, of which I have found no record, is estimated here according to the ages of his classmates. Girls also attended the Catholic Institution, but they were instructed separately from the boys and none of their work has survived. See Mitchell, "Raising Freedom's Child," chap. 1.

5. On the usefulness of different histories and the recognition of "silences" in historical narratives, see Michel-Rolph Trouillot, *Silencing the Past: Power and the Production of History* (Boston: Beacon Press, 1995).

6. On the varied experiences of American children during the war, see Marten, *The Children's Civil War*.

7. My thinking about what writing allows children to do is drawn from Steedman, *Tidy House*.

8. On the imaginative aspects of nationalism, see Benedict Anderson, *Imagined Communities: Reflections on the Origin and Spread of Nationalism* (New York: Verso, 1983).

9. See Arnold Hirsch and Joseph P. Logsdon, eds., *Creole New Orleans: Race and Americanization* (Baton Rouge: Louisiana State University Press, 1992); Kimberly S. Hanger, *Bounded Lives, Bounded Places: Free Black Society in Colonial New Orleans, 1769–1803* (Durham, NC: Duke University Press, 1997).

10. *Dred Scott v. Sanford*, 60 (U.S.) 393 (1857). See John Hope Franklin, *From Slavery to Freedom: A History of Negro Americans*, 3rd ed. (New York: Vintage Books, 1969), 267–268. On free people of color in antebellum New Orleans, see H. E. Sterxx, *The Free Negro in Antebellum Louisiana* (Rutherford, NJ: Fairleigh Dickinson University Press, 1972), chap. 4; Judith Kelleher Schafer, *Slavery, the Civil Law, and the Supreme Court of Louisiana* (Baton Rouge: Louisiana State University Press, 1994), 20–21; Robert C. Reinders, "The Decline of the New Orleans Free Negro in the Decade Before the Civil War," *Journal of Mississippi History* 24 (April 1962): 90. See also Ira Berlin, *Slaves without Masters: The Free Negro in the Antebellum South* (New York: The New Press, 1974).

11. The Catholic Institution was founded in 1842 for the education of orphans and non-orphans of the *gens de couleur*. On the Catholic Institution, see Rodolphe Lucien Desdunes, *Our People, Our History*, Sister Dorothea Olga McCants, trans. (Baton Rouge: Louisiana State University Press, 1973); Mitchell, "Raising Freedom's Child," chap. 1; on the Afro-Creoles, see Caryn Cossé Bell, *Revolution, Romanticism and the Afro-Creole Protest Tradition in Louisiana 1718–1868* (Baton Rouge: Louisiana State University Press, 1997).

12. See Floyd J. Miller, *The Search for Black Nationality: Black Emigration and Colonization 1787–1863* (Urbana: University of Illinois Press, 1975).

13. Mitchell, "Raising Freedom's Child," chap. 1.

14. For a definition of "Creole" see Gwendolyn Midlo Hall, *Africans in Colonial Louisiana: The Development of Afro-Creole Culture in the Eighteenth Century* (Baton Rouge: Louisiana State University Press, 1992), 157–159.

15. Cossé Bell, *Revolution*, 229.

16. David Nicholls, *From Dessalines to Duvalier: Race, Colour, and National Independence in Haiti* (Cambridge: Cambridge University Press, 1979), 5; João José Reis, *Slave Rebellion in Brazil: The Muslim Uprising of 1835 in Bahia*, Arthur Brakel, trans. (Baltimore: Johns Hopkins University Press, 1993), 48; Alfred N. Hunt, *Haiti's Influence on Antebellum America: Slumbering Volcano in the Caribbean* (Baton Rouge: Louisiana State University Press, 1988).

17. J. Bordenave to A. Frilot, Esq., Metz, France, May 22, 1861, Copybook II, AANO.

18. Ysidro Bordenave to A. Cloud, Esq., Louisville, KY, October 2, 1861, Copybook II, AANO.

19. H. Relf to A. Cloud, Paris, France, October 2, 1861, Copybook II, AANO.

20. H. Relf to J. Bordenave, Esq., Bonfouca, LA, December 4, 1861, Copybook II, AANO.

21. J. Bordenave to R. Pavageau, Esq., Lavolle, Nand, December 11, 1861, Copybook II, AANO.

22. John Blandin to H. Vasserot, Esq., Port-au-Prince, Hayti, May 29, 1861, Copybook II, AANO.

23. H. Relf to T. Bordenave, Esq., Madrid, Spain, November 6, 1861, Copybook II, AANO.

24. H. J. Vasserot to A. Perroux, Esq., Mobile, AL, February 26, 1862, Copybook II, AANO.

25. Ernest Brunet to L. Mension, Esq., New York, NY, September 24, 1862, Copybook II, AANO.

26. Cossé Bell, *Revolution*, 229–231; Joseph T. Glatthaar, *Forged in Battle: The Civil War Alliance of Black Soldiers and White Officers* (New York: The Free Press, 1990), 7–10; Mary Frances Berry, "Negro Troops in Blue and Gray: The Louisiana Native Guards, 1861–1863," *Louisiana History*, 8 (Spring 1967): 167–169.

27. E. Pérault to A. Salonich, Esq., Port au Prince, Hayti, October 16, 1862, Copybook II, AANO.

28. Unknown to R. Duallim, Esq., Dubuque, IA, October 29, 1862, Copybook II, AANO.

29. E. Brunet to O. Percy, Esq., Port-au-Prince, Hayti, June 10, 1862, Copybook II, AANO.

30. L. Lamanière to E. Brunet, Esq., Dubuque, IA, November 26, 1862, Copybook II, AANO.

31. Slave emancipation in Cuba was gradual, beginning in 1870, only five years after the end of the American Civil War. See Rebecca J. Scott, *Slave Emancipation in Cuba: The Transition to Free Labor, 1860–1899* (Princeton: Princeton University Press, 1985).

32. E. Pérault to A. Nicolas, Esq., Port-au-Prince, Hayti, September 24, 1862, Copybook II, AANO.

33. On the demands of Louisiana's enslaved for their freedom after the start of the war, see Ira Berlin, Barbara J. Fields, Thavolia Glymph, Joseph P. Reidy, and Leslie Rowland, eds., *Freedom: A Documentary History of Emancipation 1861–1867*, series I, vol. I, *The Destruction of Slavery* (Cambridge: Cambridge University Press, 1985), chap. 4.

34. Both of Lucien's letters appear near the end of the surviving letters from the Catholic Institution. The last was written in the fall of 1863.

35. L. Lamanière to J. H. Sauvage, Esq., Tampico, Mexico, November 14, 1862, Copybook II, AANO.

36. Ibid.

# Chapter Three

# Flowers of Evil

## *Mass Media, Child Psychology, and the Struggle for Russia's Future during the First World War*

### *Aaron J. Cohen*

How does media violence affect children? This question is as difficult to answer now as it was during the First World War, when Russian pedagogues, teachers, and journalists first began to grapple with the problem. For them, the Great War loomed as a watershed event in human history, an event with the power to remake nations, peoples, and individuals. Today historians have little doubt that World War I introduced a new level of brutality into the European experience, but the precise relationship between the war and the subsequent violence of the twentieth century remains unclear. Was the First World War a product of long-term developments in the politics, economics, and culture of modern life? Or did it enable and legitimize the use of mass political violence on a qualitatively new scale? Educators and public figures in wartime Russia could not imagine the violent future that awaited Europe in the 1930s and 1940s, but between 1914 and 1917 they did seek to discover how imaginary violence might shape the future. Ironically, they found not the answer to the question but the question itself.

Scientific investigation into the effects of media violence on children seems to have begun in earnest during World War I. There was some scattered interest in the subject of war and children before 1914, but formal studies were rare, if they existed at all.[1] After the war began, however, scientific and popular interest in the topic increased dramatically.[2] Europeans suddenly faced warfare on an unimaginably large geographic, economic, and military scale, and they felt a strong need to understand this new war experience. Moreover, modern psychology was still evolving as a scientific discipline in the early twentieth century, and the institutions, practices, and theories of child psychology, like many of the social and human sciences, were not as well defined as they are today.[3] The issue of children and media violence, for example, was not yet institutionalized as a field of research, and investigative techniques were crude compared to present-day practices.[4] In 1914, the appearance of a specific type of war at a specific stage in the development of scientific culture helped create a new area for psychological study: children and media violence.

The war's almost immediate mesmerizing effect on children helped spur this new line of inquiry in Russia. To adults, Russian children appeared overwhelmed by the intense public patriotism that became pervasive in 1914 and early 1915. "Everyone who has had contact with children in this troubled year has probably observed the reflection of war fire and the echo of war thunder in children's lives," noted the pedagogue V. Voronov in late 1915. "Conversation, drawing, play, letters, questions, day-dreams—they all shine with the fire of war."[5] This overwhelming enthusiasm for war among children was to some extent a media invention, for it helped demonstrate both the war's popularity among the Russian people and the supposedly deep-rooted Russian national characteristics of hardiness, selflessness, and courage that would ensure victory.[6] Academic studies suggested, however, that children's interest in the war was real. Voronov found in December 1914 that 69.4 percent (107 out of 154) of pupils at one urban school answered the question "What do you want to be when you grow up?" with occupations that showed the "clear imprint of the war" (such as soldier, pilot, or doctor).[7] Late in the war, 24 percent of girls in one eighth-grade class still wanted to be doctors, a marked increase over prewar numbers.[8] In the experience of adult observers, the war remained important in the lives of children long after patriotic culture weakened in 1915.

Teachers, educational theorists, and social commentators wanted to know what to do about the fascination that many children had for the war. These specialists claimed, after all, to be the professional guardians of the child's psychological health. "How great and wonderful is the role of the pedagogue in guarding the child's soul from the poisonous 'flowers of evil' that grow so easily in difficult times," wrote one, "but how terrifying and critical is that role at the same time!"[9] Young Russians, they knew, learned about the war from family members, but they also learned from the general public culture, usually behind the backs of parents and teachers. Russian experts wanted to examine how the war shaped children's imaginations, and as professionals they hoped to learn to control and direct that influence.

An important focus of their attention was the mass media, especially after a wave of illustrated journals, postcards, and popular posters [*lubki*] flooded media space with witty and often violent propaganda images in the first months of the war.[10] Several writers presented anecdotal evidence that children were especially drawn to media representations. One girl who was curious about the war, for example, "enthusiastically" sought information about it in illustrated journals, despite her parents' prohibition.[11] The pedagogue V. V. Zen'kovskii, who later became a noted figure in the Russian emigration, provided quantitative data to show that media illustrations were an important part of the child's environment. He found that some 30 percent of children had seen the war in the movies and 76 percent had seen it in pictures. The older the child, the greater the exposure to illustrations: 81 percent of those older than ten years had seen the war in pictures.[12] Likewise, when another investigator asked schoolchildren about their wartime reading preferences, they mentioned a number of tabloid weeklies, cartoon digests, and satirical journals, as well as several mainstream newspapers.[13] "Children, almost never interested in the newspaper, now invariably display interest in it," noted M. M. Rubinshtein, one of Russia's leading psychologists.[14]

Contemporary findings suggested that media exposure to war images did influence children's imaginations. Zen'kovskii found in 1914 that most children had no real knowledge of the geography, political consequences, or reasons behind the war that one would gain by reading newspapers or studying history. Others, however, soon observed an increase in children's knowledge and curiosity. "Even small children with no previous interest in geography and politics," wrote Rubinshtein, "now display specific familiarity with great cities and the opposing sides and their composition."[15] Almost every commentator, whether specialist or popular, had anecdotes about children's desire to read about the war and to act it out through play. One boy described how news of the war captured his imagination and altered his behavior: "I got bored in school when the war with the Germans started. I began to read all the books [*knizhki*] and newspapers—and everything was about the war. I skipped anything that wasn't about the war. And I decided to run away to the front."[16]

One popular technique that pedagogues and teachers used to study the effects of the war on children was to analyze children's drawings, which were widely said to be full of war imagery. In 1914, for example, two teachers reported that their students drew war pictures during free sketch time, and at a 1916 exhibition of children's drawings there was still a "great number" of war images among the entries.[17] One observer noted that children's wartime images dealt with all aspects of the war, and his description betrays the detailed nature of that imagination:

> Soldiers besiege and bombard great fortresses with toothed walls, sink cruisers, shoot down and ram zeppelins, lie in trenches, capture a great elephant-like gun, run, walk, crawl, shoot, and slash, draw cannons, cross bridges, charge with bayonets, and so on. All the facts of complex war operations have found their expression at the child's hand in peaceful rooms far from the noise of battle . . . All the horrors of modern war, cruel and destructive, are depicted by children's colored pencils and inexpensive paint.[18]

Children's pictures, another writer stated simply, were a kind of "war reporting."[19]

The correspondence between children's drawings and popular war imagery in the illustrated press suggests that the Russian mass media mapped cognitive schemata and stereotypical images to its viewers. Today many researchers support the notion that most children learn violence through observation, where they form "a conception of how the behavior is performed, and on later occasions, the symbolic representation can serve as a guide for action."[20] Cognitive psychologists believe that symbolic representations and other information are organized into cognitive schemata, hierarchical patterns that structure individual reactions to the outside world.[21] Similarly, many observers in Russia during the First World War noticed that children's pictures often looked like war illustrations. The child who drew a picture of a military hospital with I. D. Sytin's newspaper *The Russian Word* [*Russkoe slovo*] lying on a table, for example, was clearly imitating a common image in the (often self-promoting) Sytin press.[22] P. Nesterov suggested that the war images of Russia's illustrated journals were being "impressed firmly into children's memories" and estimated that, of the thirty-seven drawings he investigated, two-thirds reflected general war themes "without determined direction" and one-third seemed to be "crude caricatures borrowed from all sorts of journals and newspapers." He was convinced that the popular press had great influence on children, yet he also recognized that the extent of such influence was difficult to judge: "it is hard to determine where in these works the borrowing ends and independent creation begins." In the end he concluded that media influence was nonetheless pervasive.[23]

Russian educators who investigated the correspondence between media war imagery and children's drawings did not like what they saw, for popular reading threatened their professional control over children's emotional and moral development. One psychologist lamented in 1914, for example, that schoolchildren learned about the war "from highly suspect sources (boulevard papers)" behind the teacher's back, and he called for teachers and parents to protect children from such "poison."[24] Almost all expert commentators criticized children's access to popular visual imagery, especially in tabloids and popular illustrated weeklies like *The Flame* [*Ogonek*], *World-Wide Panorama* [*Vsemirnaia panorama*], and *The Twentieth Century* [*Dvatsatyi vek*]. The boulevard press and its "yellow" journalism were dangerous because they presented children with corrupted, and therefore harmful, views of the war. "The influence of this literature darkens children's perceptions of world events," wrote Nesterov. "Where God is passing judgment over the multitudes, this press finds material for the clowning of buffoonish Petrushka, and children find dirty cursing in response to high, pure-spirited enthusiasm."[25] As Rubinshtein lamented, children were vulnerable to this alternative source of authority because "a picture is more powerful than the words of parents and educators."[26]

Professionals and popular writers feared the war images of the popular press, believing they corrupted children's morals. Teachers, parents, and pedagogues, it was argued, had a duty to protect children from the violence and trivialization of war that appeared in the popular press and patriotic culture. "We should not allow children's attention to fixate on the horrors of war," wrote V. V. Brusianin. "We must fight against the coarsening of morals that is molded by acclimation to atrocities, against all types of popular images [*lubochnago izobrazheniia*] of the war, against the vulgarization of current events, and against the degradation of the enemy."[27] This concern was stated over and over whenever issues of media violence and children came up. "The 'popular patriotic' press [*'narodnaia patrioticheskaia lubochaia' pressa*] has already lost any sense of measure and humanity and bets on the lowest instincts of the mob,"[28] wrote Nesterov, who concluded that "reading newspapers and journals has produced in schoolchildren a special mood of spite and superficial mockery, a mood undoubtedly undesirable and destructive for the normal development of the child's soul."[29] Others echoed sentiments that are still common today. One writer, for example, wondered why children at the front were valorized if "we would never allow them to see pictures of war on the cinema screen."[30] As a newspaper commentator argued in 1914, the popular culture "without a doubt" was awakening the "bloodthirsty, base, and cruel instincts in these children . . . as if there is not enough cruelty and savagery in our lives without it."[31]

Did exposure to media imagery of the First World War really damage the psychological makeup of Russian children? Many experts doubted that the war was truly harmful, especially early in the war. In late 1914, Zen'kovskii suggested that "the war has not brought a coarsening of morals in children's souls." Russian children, he asserted, had passed this "moral test" splendidly and showed their true "hearts of gold."[32] Most other commentators remained cautious, ready to pose the problem of "war and children" rather than draw concrete conclusions. Many suggested that exposure to war imagery was significant only for emotionally and physically sensitive children. Rubinshtein, for example, argued in 1915 that a successful (or at least "not unsuccessful") war would have few adverse effects on "normal" children, since children were attracted to the heroic side of war. Most children, in his view, could recognize legitimate war violence and separate it from their daily lives under such circumstances.[33]

Expert voices and the liberal press became more pessimistic and critical as the war continued. One writer argued in 1917 that subsequent data belied Zen'kovskii's initial conclusions that society need have no special concern about the moral protection of youth and the war. "Even the unusually diverse material in the journal *Russian School*," he attested, "gives us the basis to treat these conclusions with caution."[34] Sergei Levitin, who studied the problem of children and war in a series of wartime articles (later published in a book), concluded that the war had strong negative effects on children. His analysis of a 1915 questionnaire [*anketa*] circulated among schoolteachers suggested that the war had caused a significant change "in the content, coloration, and direction" of children's thoughts, feelings, and ethical conceptions. The new ethical criteria brought by war, Levitin believed, were so dehumanizing that "even a three-year-old lad" knew killing was forbidden, yet the child could in the same breath argue that "you can kill Germans, not people."[35] Levitin was not willing to admit that some children were immune from the war's effects. "Most horrible of all," he wrote in 1915, "is that *not only the most impressionable but also the most sensitive, mild-mannered, and good-natured children are infected with the spirit of misanthropy and cruelty.*"[36] The war, in this view, was a psychological and moral catastrophe for millions of children who never got close to the actual zone of combat.

A strong note of fear thus entered the work of Russian pedagogues as the war continued: fear for a future generation brought up in total war, indifferent to its moral consequences and imitating its violence. Anecdotal evidence about children's behavior, in particular their play, supported this pessimistic view for those inclined to believe it. One newspaper editorialist, for example, gave a dark description of the war's effects on Russian children: "little beasts are awakening inside kids, and there are no words to describe the hatred that they violently [burno] express against the Germans."[37] One child even threatened to murder the Kaiser personally: "If I had Wilhelm I'd do him with a knife."[38] As a teacher observed in 1916: "children's 'war games' don't always end well. Often one side, the strongest, cruelly slaughters the weaker. Not seldom there are bloody noses and bruises, providing 'wounded' for the children in their games."[39] Understandably, few children wanted to take on the role of Germans, and the animal abuse that came from the enlistment of local cats or dogs to be the enemy unsettled everyone.

The professionals who worried about these phenomena were projecting children's violent behavior from the site of combat to the home front (and vice versa). As Zen'kovskii asked, "if childhood and playing war are closely connected, what will happen in the child's soul when real war begins!"[40] Many believed that grown-ups were better able to handle psychological stress than children. "Cruelty, coarseness, and callousness," wrote I. E. Potemkin in 1915, "these are the eternal companions of war. This is as yet not having an effect on us adults. It is affecting our children [and] young people, who are being brought up in an atmosphere of war."[41] Alarming reports from the front intimated that children were more violent than adults in combat. "Too early they have learned not to value human life, too early they are participants in bloodshed," wrote a commentator about children at the front. "In combat the acclimation to atrocities, the lowered appreciation for human life, ... and other characteristics of battle cause the coarsening of morals."[42] Front-line soldiers, according to an article not published until after the tsarist regime fell in early 1917, feared a time when young "volunteers" would re-enter civilian society. "It's awful," said one captain, "After the war they will be criminals, the cutthroats. God knows what kind."[43]

The data and observations gathered by early Russian child psychologists show that large numbers of Russian children were interested in war, that war influenced their behavior, and that media images helped structure their perceptions of war and violence. The cultural climate of total war that began in 1914, when enemies merited death, heroes celebration, and the homeland protection, continued in the Soviet Union for decades after the guns on the Eastern Front fell silent. Yet it remains speculative to link the media violence of the First World War with violence of the subsequent Civil War, Stalinist collectivization drive, and Great Terror. Modern psychologists have used several research strategies to demonstrate convincingly that an increase in aggression and violence does occur after the viewing of violent images, but their findings suggest that the increase, the so-called "effect size," is small as a percentage of overall behavior.[44] The vast majority of Russians who viewed war images during World War I, after all, did not become killers, and without a study that tracks Russian children through World War, Civil War, and the Stalinist period, we have no specific cases to prove that the fears of Russian educators for the future were realized.

The greater significance of this interest in the effect of media on children is perhaps that the Russian pedagogical establishment was interested in the question at all. Their counterparts in other European countries showed much less interest in the negative effects of the media war on the child's psyche. In France, professional pedagogical interest in the topic of children and war focused, for the most part, on devising effective propaganda lessons for the classroom. Children were a force to be mobilized for war, not people who needed protection from its effects, and French pedagogues seem to have expressed few doubts about the desirability of inculcating martial values and hatred among French schoolchildren.[45] When German psychologists discussed the impact of the war on children in one extensive study, the negative effects of media violence were mentioned only on a few pages. Even there the author urged that children's hatred for the enemy be channeled into "service for the strengthening of the fatherland" so as not to "eat the souls" of German children.[46]

Why were Russian child development specialists more inclined to explore the negative consequences of media violence and children's exposure to the war? For one, Russian educational theory already focused heavily on moral development before the war.[47] Moreover, most intellectuals had long considered the mass commercial culture of late Imperial Russia, with its cheap novels, tabloid journalism, and popular entertainment, to be morally suspect.[48] What linked these concerns to specific fears about violent media imagery was the political context in Russia, where great changes in political life were widely expected to take place after the war. Russian teachers generally had a reputation for political opposition before 1914, and on the national level "pedagogical activism and political liberalism were strongly correlated."[49] Liberal educators felt their mission was to educate children in the spirit of human compassion, moral responsibility, and true citizenship [*grazhdanstvennost'*],[50] the values necessary for a younger generation, who, in the words of one writer, represented the "hopes of a future great Russia."[51] French educational leaders wanted to mobilize youth to strengthen the existing political institutions and culture of the Third Republic during the war.[52] Their Russian counterparts, in contrast, expected their work in education to transform the tsarist order, not support it, in a quest to build a new nation.

Russian educators feared that children's exposure to war and war imagery would undermine the values that they hoped would form the basis for a future, democratic Russia. They therefore welcomed the feelings of "civic animation [*grazhdanskago odushevleniia*] and civic solidarity and unity" that appeared among children during the war.[53] Negative effects of war, however, had to be understood and controlled, for these might persist into the postwar period. "For this reason, present events demand a special obligation," wrote Potemkin, "to raise the young generation so that coarseness, callousness, and cruelty do not slink into the child's soul." Children needed protection from media violence and the popular press to prevent a potential catastrophe. "We must refuse to follow the call of the yellow press," wrote Rubinshtein, "on account of our children and future society."[54] These Russian educators distrusted children's exposure to war because they believed it would educate the citizens of a future Russia to accept violence, hatred, and antagonism toward others, not the more desirable values of democracy, empathy for humanity, and mutual cooperation.

The war thus had real effects on the culture of Russian educational theorists even if we cannot gauge its impact on children. They probably would have found no way to protect children from media violence even if the political, economic, and social chaos that swept Russia after 1917 had not cut their investigations short. These discussions did open up, however, a field of research that continued after the war. V. V. Zen'kovskii continued his work in Czechoslovakia, where he investigated the effects of war, civil war, and emigration on Russian émigré children. In contrast to 1914, when he argued that children would not be affected by war, he observed in 1924 that émigré children would "grow up and become mature, independent people, but all those wounds that life brought to them in childhood will not heal by themselves."[55] Russian pedagogues, teachers, and psychologists in 1914 thus could not imagine the Soviet Union as it eventually took shape, but they could imagine a future where mass violence and war would be a part of daily life of Russian people. They did not find conclusive answers to their questions about the relationship between media violence and children, but they did begin to define a problem that has, alas, occupied psychologists, teachers, and parents ever since.

Notes

1. I found no articles about children and media violence in Russia's two major pedagogical journals, *Vestnik vospitaniia* and *Russkaia shkola,* during the Russo-Japanese war of 1904 and 1905.

2. For an extensive discussion, see Stéphane Audoin-Rouzeau, *La guerre des enfants 1914–1918* (Paris: Armand Colin, 1993).

3. A. A. Nikol'skaia, *Vozrastnaia i pedagogicheskaia psikhologiia v dorevoliutsionnoi Rossii* (Dubna: Feniks, 1995), 8–11.

4. Investigations were, for example, usually conducted by pedagogues (educational theorists) and interested laypeople, usually teachers. Because of the ill-defined nature of this emerging discipline, I use *pedagogue, child psychologist, child development specialist,* and *educational theorist* as synonyms in this essay, although all but the first are anachronistic.

5. *Vestnik vospitaniia* 26 (November 1915): Section I, 133.

6. See, for example, Stephen Graham, *Russia and the World* (London: Cassell, 1915), 88.

7. *Vestnik vospitaniia* 26 (November 1915): Section I, 146.

8. *Psikhologiia i deti* (March–June 1917): 61.

9. *Deti i voina* (Kiev: Izdanie Kievskogo frebelevskogo obshchestva, 1915), 39.

10. For numerous examples, see Jahn, *Patriotic Culture in Russia during World War I.*

11. *Russkaia shkola* (May 1915): Section I, 88.

12. *Deti i voina,* 50.

13. *Russkaia shkola* 26 (February 1915): Section I, 40.

14. *Vestnik vospitaniia* 26 (February 1915): Section I, 12.

15. Ibid., 18–19.

16. A. Kaiskii, *Deti na voine* (Petrograd: Novoe vremia, 1915), 44–45. A summary of children's reactions (based on a reading of pedagogical journals) is in Dimitry Odinetz and Paul Novgorotsev, *Russian Schools and Universities in the World War* (New Haven: Yale University Press, 1929), 57–62.

17. *Deti i voina,* 97; *Iskusstvo i zhizn',* no. 5 (1916): 12

18. *Vestnik vospitaniia* 26 (February 1915): Section I, 49.

19. *Russkaia illiustratsiia* 3 (22 February 1915): 23.

20. A. Bandura, quoted in Robert Baron and Deborah Richardson, ed., *Human Aggression* (New York: Plenum, 1994), 34. See also L. Rowell Huesmann and Laurie Miller, "Long-term Effects of Repeated Exposure to Media Violence in Childhood"

in L. Rowell Huesmann, ed., *Aggressive Behavior: Current Perspectives* (New York: Plenum, 1994), 153–186.

21. On schemata and stereotypes in the American mass media, see Doris Graber, *Processing the News: How People Tame the Information Tide* (New York: Longman, 1988).

22. *Vestnik vospitaniia* 26 (February 1915): Section I, 47.

23. *Russkaia shkola* 26 (February 1915): Section I, 41–43.

24. Quoted in *Sovremennoe slovo*, 30 October 1914, p. 1.

25. *Russkaia shkola* 26 (January 1915): Section I, 47.

26. *Vestnik vospitaniia* 26 (February 1915): Section I, 17.

27. V. V. Brusianin, *Voina, zhenshchiny i deti* (Moscow: Mlechnyi put', 1917), 122.

28. *Russkaia shkola* 26 (February 1915): Section I, 41.

29. Ibid., 43.

30. *Russkaia shkola* 28 (May–August 1917): Section I, 6.

31. *Sovremennoe slovo*, 28 October 1914, p. 2.

32. *Deti i voina*, 63.

33. *Vestnik vospitaniia* 26 (February 1915): Section I, 11–12.

34. *Psikhologiia i deti* (March–June 1917): 85

35. *Russkaia shkola* (May 1915): Section I, 83.

36. *Russkaia shkola* (September–October 1915): Section I, 85. Italics in original.

37. *Sovremennoe slovo*, 19 September 1914, p. 1.

38. Quoted in *Russkaia shkola* (September–October 1915): Section I, 87.

39. *Russkaia shkola* (December 1916): Section I, 60.

40. *Deti i voina*, 3.

41. *Vestnik vospitaniia* 26 (November 1915): Section I, 207.

42. *Probuzhdenie* (1 July 1915): 447.

43. Quoted in *Russkaia shkola* 28 (May–August 1917): Section I, 2.

44. Linda Heath, Linda Bresolin, and Robert Rinaldi, "Effects of Media Violence on Children: A Review of the Literature," *Archives of General Psychiatry* 46 (April 1989): 378.

45. Audoin-Rouzeau, 91, 105, 157.

46. William Stern, ed., "Jugendliches Seelenleben und Krieg: Materialien und Berichte," *Beihefte zur Zeitschrift für angewandte Psychologie und psychologische Sammelforschung* IV Folge, no. 12 (Leipzig 1916): 116–117.

47. Nikol'skaia, 7.

48. Jeffrey Brooks, *When Russia Learned to Read: Literacy and Popular Literature, 1861–1917* (Princeton: Princeton University Press, 1985), 296.

49. Ben Eklof, *Russian Peasant Schools: Officialdom, Village Culture, and Popular Pedagogy, 1861–1914* (Berkeley: University of California Press: 1986), 244–245.

50. *Deti i voina*, 69.

51. *Vestnik vospitaniia* 26 (February 1915): Section I, 79.

52. Jean-Jacques Becker, *The Great War and the French People* (Leamington Spa: Berg, 1985), 154–160.

53. *Vestnik vospitaniia* 25 (October 1914): 70.

54. *Vestnik vospitaniia* 26 (February 1915): Section I, 32.

55. *Vospominaniia 500 russkikh detei* (Prague, 1924), 4.

# Chapter Four

# Imagining Anzac
## *Children's Memories of the Killing Fields of the Great War*

## *Bruce C. Scates*

On Armistice Day 1921, a grim crowd of returned soldiers and widowed mothers huddled on the balcony of Sydney's Soldiers' Club. As 11 A.M. approached, the great city around them fell suddenly silent, the bells of the post office clanged to a solemn close, and traffic spluttered to a standstill. The company on the balcony bowed their heads in prayer. All seemed perfect reverence. "The silence," one wrote, "was as of a Sunday":

> Th[en came the] sound [of] laughter and giggling from the girls leaning out of the windows [next door]. A soldier, an old scarred man said, "Those girls, it cut me like a knife—I was at the Cenotaph in London last year!"

The moment the ceremony was over, Dr. Mary Booth went down to "interview" the young culprits. One of the girls was brought back "and sent . . . to the old soldier." Then came the father: cowered with remorse he apologized on behalf of his children. By late that afternoon, even the old scarred soldier had regained his composure. The memory of Australia's war dead had been honored and the thoughtless youth of the city called to order.[1]

The disruption of Sydney's Armistice Day by children careless of its meaning suggests the major themes of this article. It highlights what cultural historians have called the selective and contested nature of collective memory. To those old scarred men who went to fight, and the women who waited for them, the Great War was a defining experience. Australia's war dead numbered 60,000, a crippling loss to a nation of just under 3 million people. They were buried far from the homes of those who loved them, on the killing fields of the Western Front, Gallipoli and Palestine. For veterans and bereaved alike, this was a sacrifice that could not be forgotten; the memory of Anzac (acronym of the Australian New Zealand Army Corps) was to be cherished, honored, venerated. The "giggling girls" belonged to a very different generation. For them, the memory of Anzac was less a sacred trust than a tiresome burden: the stuff of school speeches, sermons, and slightly ridiculous ceremonies. Their laughter signaled much more than casual irreverence: It actively renounced a dark memory many would sooner have forgotten.[2]

Dr. Booth's determination to bring these children to task prefigured a wider movement in the culture of commemoration. Long before the war was over, Booth and her "Fellowship" had taken on themselves the duties of remembrance. From 1916 on, they had held commemorative services on Sydney's wharves, strewing flowers and prayers at the place their men sailed away from them. They raised the funds for the city's war memorial and marked the graves of returned soldiers with wreaths of wattle and rosemary. But by the early 1920s it was clear that commemorative services could no longer be centered on just the men who returned or their immediate families.[3] There was "a danger," Booth warned, of "Time obliterating the memory of Anzac," of a new generation growing up with "no personal experience of war . . . [or] what our soldiers had achieved," and that even Anzac Day itself (the much feted anniversary of Australia's first major battle at Gallipoli) would become just another public holiday. The search was on for what Booth called "some more enduring form of remembrance."[4]

The task which faced the Anzac Fellowship of Women, and of the commemorative bodies that succeeded it, was "to capture the interest of youth." From the 1930s to the 1950s, Booth presided over the Anzac Festival, a series of competitions incorporating song, essay writing, art work, and dramatic performances. In the 1990s (as the wounds of Vietnam slowly healed), the tradition was revived. Working in close association with the Department of Veterans' Affairs, the History Teachers Association of Australia fielded the Simpson Prize, an essay-writing competition in honor of Australia's best-known war hero. The records of both these bodies (along with interviews and questionnaires) offer a rare opportunity to reconstruct children's memory of war. They present what historians of childhood have called a child-centered view of history.[5]

## The Anzac Festival

Established in 1931, the Anzac Festival Committee involved a radical departure in the accepted practice of commemoration. Since the end of the war, and the return of Australia's soldiers, Anzac Day in particular had become a reunion of veterans. Each year men marched the streets in military formation, often drowning "the solemn task of remembrance" in the boozy camaraderie of bars and gambling halls. The Festival, on the other hand, sought "to express the traditions of Anzac through drama, music and poetry," creative activities as far from brazen military display as one could imagine. And far from being a concern of men, the festival was very much a celebration of children.[6]

At first it was thought that the Festival's aims "would best be accomplished through music." Clubs, schools, and societies were invited to form their junior choirs and to sing for the honor of an Anzac Shield. The proposal was well received from any society that equated music with self-improvement, Mrs. Blain (of the Girl Guides) believing "an Anzac Song would inculcate in the minds of children something [truly] beautiful."[7] The problem was that whilst children might perform in a musical competition, few could actually compose the material they presented.[8] By 1934, the Festival had extended its creative scope—the program now included an Anzac Day Anthem and music for the same, choir singing for senior and junior divisions, choral verse speaking, and play writing and poster competitions. The Literature Section soon proved the most popular.[9]

In its thirty-year history, the Festival attracted literally thousands of entries. Usually only the winning plays and poems were preserved or published, but a folder of unsuccessful essays from the 1950s (the authors' real names still safely sealed in attached envelopes) has survived.[10] All these entries are from New South Wales and most were from private or selective schools in the Sydney area.

Unlike the children of the 1920s, the generation who wrote for the Anzac Festival of 1952 had no immediate memory of the Gallipoli Landing. The "battle [had ended] twenty years before I was born," one contestant noted, all that remained were "coldly printed history books."[11] But the memory of Gallipoli could also assume a vicarious quality. It could be relived, reimagined through the stories passed down from one generation to another. At fifteen years of age, Graham recalled the Anzac Day his uncle came to visit. Seated "in the lounge room after the evening meal," the old digger revisited "the barren and rugged beaches," "the sheer cliffs" and "fierce battle" that faced him on the Day of the Landing. Graham's essay retold the story with care and reverence, citing line after line that a young boy had committed to memory. One can almost hear the shaking voice of the old soldier, mourning mates "dead and wounded" as the evening closed in on them.[12]

Others grew up in the shadow of men killed a lifetime ago. From the time she was "a little child" Mary Anne had "known" Uncle Bert: "I had never met him, as he was a soldier [lost in] World War One but I had heard many stories of jolly Uncle Bert who had never returned."[13]

Every day, Mary Anne made her way to the local Cenotaph carrying a "modest bunch of Rosemary" for a man who would never come home to them. For others, most more remote from the experience of loss, the service on Anzac Day ritualized remembrance. "C" was too young to know the men who died, and knew the sharpest grief fell to "friends and relatives who [could] never forget." At first the "stamp of thousands of feet and the stirring notes of the brass band" filled her with pride. But then "a hush . . . settled on the crowd" as "cars loaded with maimed victims" drove slowly past the Cenotaph. Though "C" had been spared the "hardship" of war, she could see its cost all around her:

> Looking around the silent grim faced crowd I saw a stout old lady quickly brush a tear from her eye. Was she thinking of a husband or son whose grave was marked by a path of lawn and neat white cross in some foreign country? The grey headed old man staring fixedly ahead perhaps remembering the last time he had seen his fine, manly son wave good bye. Then there was a young girl tearfully watching the gallant procession, with her secret thought of sorrow. Yet all these people were proud too as they watched. What was the pride, what could we be proud of? It was the fact that they were all one—everyone of us—Australians.[14]

The ambivalent emotions felt by "C," pride in her countrymen's valor and grief for their loss, was shared, to greater and lesser degrees, by all of the contestants. So too was that closing sense of "Australianness." In the parlance of the day, Gallipoli had been the nation's "baptism of fire." Before the landing, as one contestant noted, Australia had been just another colony of the British empire, "untried in war," its recent origins as penal colony of England compromised any claim to nationhood. On April 25, 1915, "men who had been farmers, stockmen and businessmen" proved themselves the worthy sons of Empire"; though barely fourteen Enid knew the day "had made our southern land famous . . . blazing through the world the gallantry

of our yet young nation." Her essay involved a significant shift in emphasis—the "solemn task of remembrance" was all but lost in a jingoistic nationalism.

> The troops landed in complete silence in the darkness which heralds the
> dawning of the day. . . . It was a trying moment, but the Australian volunteers
> rose to the occasion; they waited neither for orders nor for boats to reach the
> beach, but, springing out into the sea they waded ashore, and, forming some
> sort of rough line, rushed straight on the flashes of the enemy's rifles; in
> some cases the magazines were not even charged. The enemy was securely
> fixed in the surrounding hills and it looked as if it would be impossible to
> oust them . . . but the Anzacs . . . went to their work . . . determined to win,
> to conquer.[15]

Amidst this enthusiastic chauvinism, the failure of the attack was sometimes forgotten. Boys and girls alike went to considerable lengths to reinvent
a military failure as a triumph of "matchless courage" and "superhuman effort." And when it was acknowledged that the Australians had been "pushed
back" (failing to secure the high ground that commanded the Gallipoli
peninsula), the inference was that the Turks had somehow cheated. Hidden
"in the scrubby upland hills and gullies . . . ten resolute men could withstand
attack from a hundred," even if they were Australians. The Turks were "cunning," "cruel" and worst of all "helped by the Germans."[16] And demonizing
the enemy meant denying his humanity. Rose may have got the dates wrong
and she had at best a shaky sense of geography, but there was no doubt in
her mind that "our men [were] martyrs who suffered a sinful death" at the
hands of "savages."

> It was the morning of April 25th in the year 1914. It was spring and the air
> was fresh and clean and the sea all around them was crystal clear. . . . As their
> ship glided past the Dardenelles in the Agean Sea they gazed ahead tense and
> anxious wondering what was going to happen. [Then] . . . [t]he Turks rode up
> unexpectedly over the hills and butchered our men leaving their poor bodies
> to decay upon the beach. . . . We shall never know the agony and torture of
> those brave hearts—never to return from an unknown land far from home.[17]

Though some essays were more nationalistic than others, the vast majority
saw Gallipoli as more a triumph of British virtues rather than a redefinition
of what it meant to be Australian. England was addressed as "home"; their
flag was the Union Jack, their anthem "God Save the King." In short, for
these young Australians (many of whom attended elite private schools in

Sydney or Melbourne), Gallipoli "meant . . . the right to go where I liked and when and to say 'I am British.'"[18]

Those British values were unmistakably conservative. In an era of cold war politics, the Anzac Festival functioned as part of the cultural repertoire of the Menzies government, a government committed to breaking union power, banning the Communist party, and strengthening Australia's alliance with the "free world." The story of Anzac became a metaphor for yet another world struggle: "the menace of the Turk" was conveniently replaced with "the insidious influence of communism." Essayists complained of "the slackening of the nation's moral fibre," a host of evils ranging from industrial unrest to sexual promiscuity. Amidst what Margaret Christie called "a welter of contending ideologies," the "values of Anzac: courage, comradeship, loyalty, unselfishness and self sacrifice" stood "like pillars of granite." And one after another these young writers likened themselves to the soldiers that went before them:

> They died for freedom—a freedom which we must perpetuate. They have given their lives, we must give our hearts. Let not these dead voices cry out in reproach from their cold, grey graves! . . . let us [not] fail those men, those thousands of men who laid down their lives for our freedom. . . . [We must] keep our country pure and beautiful.[19]

## The Simpson Prize

The search for those defining Anzac values continued well into the twentieth century. On the eve of remembrance day 1999, the Federal Minister for Education announced the establishment of the Simpson Prize. The scheme owed much to its predecessor. Like the Anzac Festival, the Simpson Prize was to see that "legacy of the Anzac spirit" was passed on to a new generation. It too was directed at year nine students, inviting essays on a topic designed to further understanding of the "Anzac Heritage."[20] And much to the relief of a conservative government, the meaning of that heritage appeared (at first) to have altered very little. Like their predecessors of the 1950s, the children of the new millennium evoked a familiar litany of Anzac values. The Landing at Gallipoli was still an act of "unparalleled valour": staggering ashore, Australian soldiers carried the heavy virtues of "courage, endurance and fierce determination." But a closer reading of these essays reveals a number of important departures: far from being solid, monolithic, and unchanging, the Anzac Legend, that "pillar of granite," had become a site of fierce contestation.[21]

To the old values were added others. Devotion to duty was the virtue most commonly celebrated by the schoolchildren of the 1950s; citing passages from Kipling, they praised men who followed orders, however impossible. By the end of the twentieth century, essayists were more inclined to emphasize the diggers' resourcefulness, initiative, and ingenuity.[22] Mateship, a word rarely used in the 1950s, became the essential Australian quality: "disrespectful of authority, an egalitarian, a brilliant fighter, and above all, loyal towards his mates . . . the Australians . . . had something that set them apart from the soldiers of other nations."[23]

Here there was scope for questioning and irreverence. Indeed, the most admired digger is something of a larrikin distinguished by his ragged appearance, indifference to rank, "carefree manner," and a blunt Australian idiom.[24] For Jason Morrison, the Anzac's "high spirited way" was captured by a single incident on the Peninsula:

> Mustafa Kemal [the Turkish commander] . . . and two Australian generals were meeting in a dug out at ANZAC Cove to discuss a truce in order to bury the dead. . . . An Australian soldier walked in on the negotiations and enquired, "have you bastards got my kettle[?]"[25]

And usually, in these essays, the generals are British. In the 1950s, the Australian digger was seen as a loyal soldier of the empire; by the 1990s, he is more likely to be depicted as its victim. The "tactical blunders" of a "tragic and inept campaign" are attributed to failings of British rather than Australian intelligence.[26] Even more important, there is a sneaking suspicion that we should not have been at Gallipoli in the first place. For Rachel Jennings, the lesson of the Great War was that the interests of "the mother country" and Australia were altogether different. Her great-grandfather had been "sent" to fight "some other bugger's war," "eight months of machine fire falling like rain—eight months of pointless waste of life" awaited him on the Peninsula.[27]

Pointless was not a word one encountered in the 1950s, nor was the nationalism of that era inclusive in terms of ethnicity or gender. Essayists of the 1990s are at pains to incorporate women into the experience of Gallipoli. On the home front, women "provided economic support" for families men left behind them; at war, they nurse men broken by battle, their diaries and letters an eloquent condemnation of the carnage.[28] These are active roles, "to wait and to weep" no longer sets the boundaries of women's experience. By the same token, the gender identity of men is subtly questioned. The narrative of the 1950s is dominated by the warrior; by the 1990s the character of John Simpson Kirkpatrick is far more attractive.[29] A medic rather than a soldier, "Simpson" was killed rescuing the wounded on Gallipoli. For all these young essayists, he embodies the "feminine" quality of nurture and compassion, a Christ-like figure leading his donkey laden with wounded across the unforgiving landscape of the Peninsula. Finally, if the heroes had changed, so too has the enemy. In none of these accounts do the Turks appear as cruel, treacherous, or "other." To the contrary, Turkish and Australian soldiers bravely endure the hardships and indecencies of war, their common suffering a vindication of their common humanity.[30]

## Journeys

To write about Gallipoli is one thing; to visit is quite another. The winning entries to the Simpson competition (one chosen from each state and territory of the Commonwealth) join an Australian War Memorial Tour to Turkey and attend the Anzac Day Dawn Service on the Peninsula. They are not the only children present. In recent years, a number of state and private schools have organized "pilgrimages" to both the Western Front and Gallipoli.[31]

These excursions, as one boy put it, are "journeys into history." Invariably an extension of the school curricula, the young were well prepared for their visit. A party of twenty year-ten students from Mackay in rural Queensland researched the unit histories of ninety-eight men killed from the district; they interviewed their aging relatives, collected memorabilia, and even carried messages from loved ones. In some cases, the men killed were their own family members: great uncles, distant cousins, men remembered only through fading photographs and letters and lost to their loved ones a lifetime ago.[32] When Paula visited the Western Front, she felt she laid to rest a man she could only imagine.

> While I wandered along row after row reading the inscriptions it made me feel sad when you thought that every one of these men killed there [had] family and friends left behind at home. When I visited the grave of my relative I in no way expected to be so emotional. I had never known him as a person but . . . I felt like I did and to see his grave was an overwhelming experience.[33]

And all without exception were overwhelmed by the enormity of human sacrifice, none prepared for what one girl called "the high amount of grieving."

> We had done so much research leading up to the trip, we'd seen casualty rates, death rates. But I still don't think I had a proper appreciation for the extent of these numbers. Somehow, whether it be standing at the Menin Gate [and] looking up at all the names, or standing in a cemetery [and] looking out at the sea of graves, they just seemed to go on forever, and you stop and look at those graves as men. Not even men but many still boys. I found this to be a highly overwhelming experience.[34]

The surveys these young travelers completed are a sensitive reconstruction of the lost landscapes of war. As they trudged along subsided trench lines or stood on the stark beaches of Gallipoli, these haunted places "spoke" with unexpected meanings. Placing poppies on Simpson's grave, they saw dolphins playing in the sea off Ari Burnu; several recorded the passage of clouds across the sky or noted "the awful hush" that settled on the ridges and gullies of the Peninsula.[35] Barely sixteen, Christine could still shudder at the silence: "The Lone Pine . . . grave site is the one that still stands out in my mind. It was so quiet up there. Not a bird seemed to sing. Nothing moved. On the Memorial it said, 'Their Name Liveth Forever More.'"[36]

This was a journey to a sacred place; like every such pilgrimage it involved a sense of "quest," a journey "out of the normal parameters of life [and] entry into a different other world." Returning home, these young travelers were themselves somehow altered, as if they had left something of themselves behind them.

> Even now, as we watch video clips of the . . . wreath laying, and listen to the Last Post we all become emotional and feel as if we were back there—on the shores of ANZAC Cove, amidst the rows of headstones. . . . It was an experience I will never forget.[37]

At its most extreme, the "experience" of pilgrimage led to a crisis in personal identity. Standing on that "eerie" beach at Gallipoli, where the graves of young men tumble down to the sea, several Simpson prize winners confessed their essays concealed a great human tragedy.

> [Now I see] we had no idea of what it was about. We comprehended but we did not understand. You know I wrote all this stuff really sucking up to the judges and I'm really ashamed of it now because I don't believe any of it any more. [I said that the Anzacs] . . . were so determined, they sacrificed so much

and all in the name of their country. And then you see the graves. It's not like that. They shouldn't have died. . . . [But the judges] want to hear the good stuff, [the patriotic stuff] they don't want to hear the bad stuff. . . . Like, we omitted stuff, I omitted stuff.[38]

Confronting the massed graves of her countrymen was hard enough; harder still meeting their "enemy." "Sarah" told me she felt ashamed to be Australian, ashamed to have invaded a country on the other side of the world, ashamed to visit grief on a people who had now befriended them.[39] And as if to make amends for all those "omissions," three angry, disappointed girls wrote a new poem, not just to Simpson's memory, but to all who died with him.

> In our ignorance
> We betrayed a sacred memory
> For all the men and women who fought and died
> In any war
> And in every country
> And the generations that should have been
> BLESSED BE.[40]

## Conclusion

There was no one childhood response to the Killing Fields of the Great War. Even in the 1950s, when the Anzac Festival was at its most prescriptive, the quality and substance of essays varied considerably. Some were commemorative, others jingoistic; some emphasized imperial loyalties, others believed an unquestioning faith in Britain died with Australia's youth on the bloody beaches of Gallipoli. With the approach of the new millennium, the meaning of the Anzac heritage broadened considerably. To some extent it was completely reinvented, modernized to accommodate a multicultural society, and re-imagined in ways that incorporated women's experience. Even so it remained a powerful wellspring of Australian nationalism, interpreting the Great War as a defining moment in a "new" nation's history. What this essay also suggests is that children's view of war was by no means an ideological given.[41] As they journeyed across the cemeteries of Gallipoli, France, and Belgium, they encountered a range of quite conflicting emotions, shame and pride, pity and anger, reverence and confusion. For the greater part of a century, children have been exhorted to remember war in a way which bolstered conservative values and promotes a simplistic sense of nationhood. The quest for a more inclusive form of remembrance is the surest sign of their maturity.

NOTES

1. Minute Book of the Soldier's Club, November 11, 1921, Anzac Fellowship of Women Papers (henceforth AFW papers), ms 2864, box 1, Australian National Library.

2. Smith and Hamilton, *Memory and History in Twentieth Century Australia*, introduction. The literature on war and commemoration is extensive and the bibliography of Jay Winter's recent study a useful introduction. See Jay Winter, *Sites of Memory, Sites of Mourning*. For Australian scholarship, see Scates and Frances, *Women and the Great War*, ch. 5, and Inglis, *Sacred Places*.

3. Bruce Scates, "The Forgotten Sock Knitter: voluntary work, emotional labour, bereavement and the great war," *Labour History* 81 (November 2001); Anzac Fellowship of Women, Monthly Report, April 8–May 13, 1924, AFW papers, box 1; "Out of Fellowship," *Daily Telegraph*, April 26, 1957.

4. Anzac Festival of Song Competition, Committee Minutes, October 6, 1931; Anzac Festival, Committee Minutes, November 7, 1932, AFW papers, box 21.

5. Ibid., November 7, 1932; discussion with Michael Rowland and Beatriz Cartlidge of the History Teacher's Association of Victoria and the History Council of New South Wales, respectively.

6. Anzac Festival, Committee Minutes, October 6 and 24, 1932; Scates and Frances, *Women and the Great War*, ch. 5.

7. Anzac Festival, Committee Minutes, October 24, 1932; Anzac Festival Committee, *Anzac Eve Festival at the Conservatorium*, Sydney 1937, AFW papers, box 5, folder 2.

8. See, for example, Dora Wilcox and Alfred Hill, *Anzac Day*, Sydney 1938.

9. Anzac Festival, Committee Minutes, May 8, 1933, July 7, 1936; *Anzac Festival Committee, Anzac Festival Competition, 1937–8*, Sydney 1938, AFW papers, box 6, folder 9.

10. See, for example, Kitty Winter, "*The Toast is Anzac, Gentlemen*" (Sydney, n.p., n.d.); W. L. Williams, *The Rising Sun* (Sydney, n.p., n.d.), AFW papers, box 5, folder 2.

11. Essay by Vivien Inder, Greenwich, AFW papers, box 13, folder 8.

12. Essay by Graham Goodsire, no school/suburb listed, ibid.

13. Essay by Mary Anne Campbell, North Sydney Girls High, ibid.

14. Essay by "C"; see also essays by Nancy Smith, North Sydney Girls High, and Ann Holden, Concord, ibid.

15. Essays by Mary Anne Campbell, North Sydney Girls High; Enid Buckley, Forbes, ibid.

16. Essays by Patricia Holder, Fort Street High; Ann Holder, Concord; Jennifer Fleur Crocker, no school/suburb listed, ibid.

17. Essay by Rose Ann Fuller, Randwick, ibid.

18. Essays by Doreen Fansley, Gosford; Judith Campbell, Fort Street, Vivien Inder, Greenwich, ibid.

19. Essays by Shelley Benson, Chatswood; Margaret Christie, North Sydney Girls High School, essay by anonymous author; ibid; anonymous, undated and untitled essay, box 6, folder 5.

20. A background to the prize is provided by the History Teachers' Association of Australia Website, http.//www.pa.ash.org.au.

21. Essays by Dan Vo, Parade College, Victoria; Anna Verney, Canberra girls Grammer, Australian Capital Territory. All the Simpson essays are provided by the courtesy of the History Teacher's Association of Australia. I have cited both winning essays and the "runners up."

22. Essay by Rachel Jennings, Marrana Christian School, Northern Territory.

23. Essay by Jane Geraghty, St. John's College, NSW.

24. Essays by Sarah Crawley, Walford Anglican School for Girls, South Australia; Yvette Tan, St. Mary's Anglican School, Western Australia; Lachlan Foy, Shore School New South Wales.

25. Essay by Jason Morrison, Malanda State High School, Queensland.

26. Essays by Christine Hopkins, Montague Bay, Tasmania; Sarah Crowley, Walford Anglican School for Girls, South Australia; Anna Verney, Canberra Girls High School, Australian Capital Territory.

27. Essay by Rachel Jenning, Marrana Christian School, Northern Territory.

28. Essays by Catlin Hurley, Canberra Church of England Girls School, Australian Capital Territory; Laura Gumley, Gosford High School, New South Wales; Birra-li Riethmuller, Harristown State High, Queensland.

29. Only one essay, and that by a boy, mentioned Simpson in the 1950s. For early efforts to promote Simpson as a symbol of men's vulnerability in war, see Cochrane, *Simpson and the Donkey.*

30. Note the essay by Katherine Anderson reflecting on the plight of her German ancestors, Trinity College, South Australia.

31. I am indebted to Ashley Ekin, Graham Beveridge, and Ian Kelly of the Australian War Memorial for assisting my own pilgrimage to Gallipoli and introducing me to the Simpson Prize winners. See also my earlier work, Scates, "'From a Brown Land Far Away,'" 6–13.

32. Interview with Will S.F., Sydney, NSW; Questionnaires completed by Michael G., Paula L., Corrine C., Katrina T., North Mackay, Queensland; note the essay pinned to the last questionnaire. For the experience of other school groups, I

draw on discussions with David Cooper, Baker College, Sydney; Brian Mackenzie, McKillop College, Swan Hill.

33. Questionnaire completed by Paul L., Mackay, Queensland.

34. Questionnaire completed by Katrina T., Mackay, Queensland.

35. Questionnaires completed by Leonie B., Mackay, Queensland, Alex S.F. Sydney NSW.

36. Questionnaire completed by Christine H., Montague Bay, Tasmania.

37. Ian Reader, "Introduction," in Reader and Walter, *Pilgrimage in Popular Culture*, 8; Victor and Edith Turner, *Image and Pilgrimage in Christian Culture*; questionnaire completed by Rachel B., Mackay, Queensland.

38. Interview with "Myra," Gallipoli, April 23, 2000. (Name changed at her request.)

39. Interview with "Sarah," Gallipoli, April 23, 2000. (Name changed at her request.)

40. Interview with Simpson Prize winners, Gallipoli, April 23, 2000.

41. For a sensitive reconstruction of the way children negotiate national identity see Coles, *The Political Life of Children*, esp. ch. 2 and 7.

# Chapter Five

# Rescue and Trauma
## Jewish Children and the Kindertransports during the Holocaust

## Eric J. Sterling

Although the Nazis wished to liquidate all Jews, they especially targeted the children, who represented the future and the potential of Judaism. The Nazis considered the children special threats because unlike the middle-aged and the elderly, Jewish children had many years ahead of them in which to produce more offspring and renew the ethnic group, thus hindering the Nazi "Final Solution." But the Nazi war against Jewish children was more than physical extermination; it also involved emotional and spiritual attacks against both children and parents. James E. Young observes that because "the greatest test for Abraham's faith had been his aborted sacrifice of Isaac, the least bearable kind of suffering in Jewish tradition seems always to have been that of children."[1] Elie Wiesel adds that Jewish history "continues with Jewish children being massacred by Pharaoh, Nebuchadnezzar and Titus, Haman and Hitler—all our enemies saw our children as the primary target."[2] According to Jewish law, bearing children was a blessing, a responsibility, and a gift to God. In Genesis 1:28, God told Adam and Eve to be fruitful and multiply. Psalms 127:3 reads, "Lo, children are an heritage of the Lord: and the fruit of the womb is His reward." Therefore, by destroying Jewish children, the Nazis attempted to break a spiritual bond between Jews and God while devastating the parents psychologically.

Despite the refusal of the United States and other countries to provide refuge within their borders for Jewish children, England arranged for 10,000 Jewish children to emigrate from Nazi Germany and Austria via train—the *Kindertransports*—from November 1938 through September 1939. Although 10,000 Jewish children were saved, the onset of World War II prevented more trains from carrying children to safety in England, which was unfortunate considering the dire circumstances that Jews endured. As anti-Semitism prevailed in Germany and Austria during the 1930s, Jewish children watched in horror as their parents were beaten up in the streets, harassed, murdered, or sent off to die in concentration camps. These children also became embittered as their Aryan friends shunned or taunted them, and as they were expelled from schools because of their religion and ethnicity. Although many people living in 1938 could not have foreseen the slaughter of 6 million European Jews, the horrors of *Kristallnacht* (November 9–10, 1938) manifested the need to save Jews from the growing anti-Semitism in Nazi Germany and Austria. When an appeal by the Movement for the Care of Children from Germany in November 1938 requested urgently that at least the Jewish children should be saved, most countries steadfastly maintained closed borders, refusing to allow Jewish children to enter their nations in order to survive. However, on November 21, 1938, England's House of Commons agreed to save 10,000 Jewish children. Germany consequently permitted England to rescue Jewish children under the following conditions: the Germans would receive fifty pounds sterling ($250) per child; the children, called *Kinder*, would be under eighteen and possess a health certificate and a photograph for identification; the move to England would be temporary; and the refugees would travel without their parents.

From 1938 to 1939, Jewish parents shipped 10,000 children to England, even though they were not allowed to accompany them and suspected that perhaps they would never see their children again. Their fears were justified, for 80 percent of the parents, in fact, never saw their children again. An eleven-year-old *Kind*, who left with several hundred other children in December 1938, remembers the devastation his mother (the Nazis only allowed one parent to see the children off) felt at the train station: "My mother insisted on kissing me over and over again, and I got impatient with her demonstrativeness, not realizing of course that this was to be the final parting. I have often wondered since what she must have felt as the result of my impatience."[3] Another *Kind*, Peter Morgan, remarks: "imagine my parents' predicament, as well as that of thousands of other parents. Mine had to choose between putting two young children, ages eight and ten, onto a train, knowing only that they were going to England and might never be seen by them again, or keeping the children with them, thus hindering their own chances of escape. The other possibility was for all to be deported to a concentration camp."[4]

These Jewish children, traveling in sealed and guarded trains, voyaged to England, where they started new lives. Employing survivor testimonies, sociological and psychological criticism, as well as Diane Samuels's powerful 1993 drama *Kindertransport*, this essay will demonstrate that although many children attempted to preserve their Jewish and German heritage, some proved unable to do so because of their need to suppress the hardships they encountered in Germany and because of the favorable treatment they received from their English surrogate parents. One might assume that all of the youngsters would appreciate their parents' altruistic gestures because the parents sacrificed their families in order to save their children's lives; but some children felt no gratitude toward their parents and even expressed anger that their parents had deserted them, saving their lives at the expense of the cohesive family unit. Some of the children adjusted well to life without their parents in a foreign country, but this was not always the case. Although many parents considered it their responsibility to save their children's lives, no matter what the cost, they failed to comprehend fully the extent of the trauma that the children would experience during and after the *Kindertransports*; as Samuels demonstrates, some children never forgave their parents for "abandoning" them and would rather have stayed—and even died—with their parents in Germany than be transported to another country and live with strangers who often failed to understand their language, customs, religion, and pain.

Samuels's play concerns Eva, a nine-year-old *Kind* who arrives in England and is cared for by foster mother Lil Miller. Eva is a composite of several actual children interviewed by the playwright. As the years progress, the emotional distance between Eva and her parents naturally widens, proportionate to the strengthening attachment between her and Lil. She feels obligated to Lil for taking good care of her and does not wish to appear ungrateful by pining for her mother, Helga. Lil bonds with Eva and transforms into Eva's mother, while Helga, incarcerated in a concentration camp, becomes "the other," a fading memory. But perhaps more importantly, Eva suffers from what Sander Gilman refers to as "Jewish self-hatred." Gilman says that the "translation of what had been abstract patterns of anti-Semitism into a program for action based on the Western stereotype of the Jew meant that all 'Jews' could be at risk."[5] Knowing that many people hate her and even wish her dead because she is Jewish, Eva wonders whether she deserves to be punished, whether she is in fact inadequate because of her ethnicity, as Nazi propaganda affirms. She therefore wishes to dissolve her bonds with her Jewish parents and heritage.

Part of Eva's trauma derives from her confused identity and the problems that ensue from it. She wonders, for instance, if she is German or Jewish. Although Eva was born and has lived her first nine years in Germany, millions of her compatriots hate and want to destroy her because they do not consider her one of them; instead, the Nazis consider her an alien, "the other," an *Untermensch* (subhuman). She is a German Jew, but the government considers this term an oxymoron because the Reich Citizenship Law of September 1935 declared that Jews are not German citizens.

When Eva, one year after her arrival in England, excitedly awaits the arrival of her parents at the railway station (they do not come because they receive their visas a fortnight after the war begins), she encounters an English station guard. The guard acts benevolently and pleasantly toward Eva until he discovers that she has emigrated from Germany; he then becomes suspicious of her and acts in a xenophobic and hostile manner toward her. He demands to know from where she emigrated and then attempts to arrest her merely because of her German birth. When he learns that Eva's parents have remained in Germany, the English station guard implies that the child is a spy and asks Lil, "What's she doing here then? She should be in Germany with them. . . . If they put one foot into this country, they'll be interned straight off. Got to protect ourselves."[6] The callous man, despite his comprehension of the reprehensible persecution of innocent people in Germany, would like for Eva and her parents to remain there.

The British guard's animosity and disdain affect Eva's self-esteem, making her feel unwanted and inferior. The Nazi clearly distinguishes between Germans and Jews, considering them two distinct groups. In contrast, the English guard fails to distinguish between the two, considering them both aliens and unwanted foreigners. Although the views may be diametrically opposite, both employ their views to justify their prejudice against innocent Jews such as Eva. Eva responds immediately to the English guard's verbal abuse by removing her jewelry and her Star of David, valuable mementos given to her by Helga just before she boarded the *Kindertransport*. Eva's removal of the keepsakes, as well as her subsequent decision to sell them, symbolizes unquestionably her desire to dissociate herself from her Jewish and German heritage. Eva's need to distance herself from her identity is typical of some actual *Kinder*, such as Karen Gershon. In her book, Gershon confesses that she "chose to marry a non-Jewish Englishman to declare myself

(I now see) on the side of life."[7] Eva, like Gershon, feels ashamed and thus wishes to transform herself because of the anti-Semitism that she has encountered.

But Eva's removal of the jewelry, upon learning one year after her arrival that her parents cannot join her because of the war, also symbolically distances herself from her mother, who has provided her with these keepsakes. After taking off the jewelry, Eva asks Lil how long she can stay in England with her, implying that she now considers Lil, not Helga, her mother. Because of anti-Semitism and xenophobia, Eva considers Lil, an Aryan Englishwoman, more socially acceptable than Helga, a German Jew; this scene prepares the audience for Eva's subsequent rejection of her mother after the conclusion of World War II. In her effort to assimilate and feel socially acceptable, Eva disowns her mother and even changes her name from Eva to the more Anglicized Evelyn; she also switches her birthday on her naturalization papers to the day she arrived in England—her rebirth as an English Christian. That is why Samuels sandwiches the scene involving Eva and the guard in between two scenes in which Evelyn (the grown up Eva) tears up almost all the papers that identify her as Eva and that connect her to the scared nine-year-old German Jew who escaped to England. When Evelyn shreds these papers, she effectively kills her former self, her life as a German Jewish child.

But Eva cannot totally hide from her past, as Samuels demonstrates by portraying her during several stages of her life—her arrival as a nine-year-old refugee, a year later when she discovers that her parents cannot join her, her encounter with Helga after the war, and her daughter's (Faith's) discovery two decades later of the few remaining papers that reveal Eva's identity as a *Kind*. When Faith finds the remaining documents, she confronts her mother. This encounter leads to Eva's flashbacks, such as when she reminisces about the incident two decades before when Helga came to reclaim her after the war. The audience also discerns that the past has remained with Eva because of her manifold idiosyncrasies. For instance, she is an obsessive compulsive cleaner, suggesting that she feels unclean; her cleaning neurosis might derive from her feelings of inferiority because she was born Jewish during the Holocaust (in her attempt to assimilate into English culture, she has been baptized) and may relate to the postman's remark about the smell of Jews and Germans. Yet her need to clean might also derive from a feeling that she has sullied herself by rejecting a reunion with her mother who has survived Auschwitz. Eva's obsession with cleaning possibly originates in her shame for having sacrificed her identity, faith, and heritage in exchange for safety and social acceptability. Her refusal to throw away documents, despite being compulsively neat, suggests that unconsciously she realizes that she can never completely dissociate herself from her Jewish past.

The protagonist's feelings reflect those of other *Kinder*. One *Kind* tells of his ambivalence:

> my attitude towards Germany was complex, tortured and muddled. From within I had dissociated from everything German. I no longer regarded myself as German and I strongly resented that others should still do so. I cursed my accent which prevented me from hiding my German origin. Nothing enraged me more than to be told, "once a German, always a German."[8]

Furthermore, the friction between Evelyn and Faith indicates that the past still haunts the *Kind*. Evelyn tries diligently to persuade her daughter to leave the house and achieve independence, even though Faith does not feel ready to move away. When Faith changes her mind about leaving home after initially agreeing to do so, Evelyn responds adamantly, "I think that if you say you're going, you should go," and she proceeds to give Faith glasses, silverware, and other items.[9] Evelyn's behavior indicates that she is more like her birth mother than she cares to admit. Evelyn's desire for Faith to leave might constitute an unconscious need to separate the parent from the child, a need that originated decades before, during the Holocaust, when Helga puts her on a *Kindertransport*, saving her life. Karen Gershon muses, "When I left my parents I was fifteen years old and I have always believed—or behaved as if I did—that once they reached that age, my children no longer needed me; I am astonished and inadequate when they do."[10] And before Eva leaves Germany, Helga gives her some prized family possessions, the aforementioned jewelry, just as Evelyn provides family valuables as she attempts to convince Faith to leave home; unconsciously, Evelyn repeats the past. The difference is, however, that in both cases it is the *Kind* who creates the separation (she sells her mother's heirlooms and persuades Faith to move away). This fact, along with the absence of a husband, suggests that the trauma of the *Kindertransport*, with the abrupt breach with her parents, has caused her to have truncated and fragmented relationships with people. Gershon admits, "I still cannot have much of a relationship with anyone; I still need to struggle against the feeling that people don't really matter."[11]

Eva never forgives her mother for sending her away on a *Kindertransport*. Helga tells Eva that Carla and Heinrich (Eva's friends) cannot go on a

*Kindertransport* because of the high demand, there are no available spaces, that Eva is lucky: "Of course they [Carla's and Heinrich's parents] would send them away if they had places. Any good parent would do that."[12] Helga realizes that by sending her beloved daughter away, she will save Eva's life. This belief represents historical fact. The *Kindertransports* clearly saved the lives of these children, especially when one considers that 1.5 million European Jewish children—the vast majority of those alive in 1940—died during the Holocaust. Nechama Tec reports, "In Nazi-occupied Europe the prewar Jewish child population came to about 1.6 million. During the war an estimated 1.5 million Jewish children were killed, leaving only 6 to 7 percent of them alive at the end of the war."[13]

Jewish parents sent their children on the *Kindertransports* to save the lives of the youngsters, knowing full well that they would miss their offspring and worry about them greatly; they considered their actions to be sacrifices in the best interest of their children. The parents invariably promised their children that they would join them in England, but in many cases, the parents died. They did not consider that even though they were saving the lives of their children, the youngsters would resent it, believing that their parents abandoned them and destroyed the family. *Kindertransport* child Fred Barschak describes:

> the trauma of reestablishing some infrastructure of normality in a strange land, with new families, however sympathetic and kind, with the child enjoying a dubious status, neither a temporary guest, nor adopted, a sort of twilight world of not knowing where he or she belonged, which was a state of being that was to last, for some, all their lives.[14]

Although many children, particularly the teenagers, understood their parents' sacrifice, others resented it and never forgave their parents for sending them to live with strangers in a foreign country where they did not speak the language or even know anyone. In one of Eva's flashbacks, Helga, having survived Auschwitz, travels to England to enjoy her greatly anticipated reunion with Eva (now Evelyn), but the daughter shocks her mother by expressing anger:

> You should have hung on to me and never let me go. Why did you send me away when you were in danger? No one made you. You chose to do it. Didn't it ever occur to you that I might have wanted to die with you? Because I did. I never wanted to live without you and you made me! What is more cruel than that? Except for coming back from the dead and punishing me for surviving on my own.[15]

Eva's desire to die with her mother is not unusual; Felicja Karay documents numerous cases of females (albeit older than nine) in concentration camps who willingly died with their mothers rather than being abandoned. Felicja Karay implies that gender plays a role, that females handle separation from their mothers differently than do males and are perhaps more willing to die with their mothers.[16] Perhaps that is one reason why Eva believes that her mother has comported herself irresponsibly by abandoning her. Eva might also wish to shun her mother, as well as her Jewish culture, because she experiences survivor guilt; people who survived the Holocaust often suffered pangs of guilt because they lived while others perished or endured atrocious ordeals. Every time she sees Helga, she is painfully reminded of how fortunate she has been compared to her parents and other children who could not acquire a place aboard a *Kindertransport*. Her anger toward her mother projects her guilt. Judith S. Kestenberg asserts:

> The greater the guilt feelings [of the survivor], the greater the anger at not having been treated fairly and the greater the need to blame others—not the Nazis, who created havoc in these children's lives, but surviving parents or caretakers instead. The greater the guilt feeling, the more anxiety it generates. In the final analysis, shame and hiding from people of whom they are ashamed reveal a low self-esteem, stemming from pregenital sources and reinforced by the depreciation suffered at the hands of the Germans. [Jewish] [c]hildren who grew up in German culture are especially prone to thinking that they can never become as good as the Germans and that they are destined to be inferior. This, in turn, engenders a fear of being abandoned, left alone because of their badness.[17]

As a young child, Eva loves her mother dearly and thus feels betrayed by her mother's insistence that she travel on a *Kindertransport* to England. Although the daughter's accusations may appear illogical, the audience must remember that she was a young girl when she initially blamed her parents for not joining her in England (their visas became worthless when the war started); emotions rather than reason rule the mind of young Eva, and now, as Evelyn, she believes that her mother acted shamefully because she seems unable to consider the situation from her mother's perspective.

The daughter blames Helga for saving her life by sending her away, indicating that she would have preferred death to rescue. Yet Evelyn also blames her mother for surviving Auschwitz and interprets Helga's desire to reunite with her daughter as a punishment. If the daughter actually wishes that she were dead, why is she so angry that her mother has returned to take her away from her life in England? This contradiction suggests the ambivalence created by her confused identity. Judith S. Kestenberg and Janet Kestenberg Amighi note that with child survivors of the Holocaust "who were taken in by foster families, there is often a confusion concerning identity and concerning modes of forming and breaking off relationships with others. . . . Problems of identity affect making relationships and dealing with separations."[18] Evelyn's identity confusion and inability to maintain relationships, problems created by the trauma she has experienced, explains in part her refusal to reunite with her mother. Evelyn's reluctance to relinquish her way of life in England and her love for Lil indicate clearly that despite her guilt, she is happy that she has survived and that Helga has made the correct decision in sending her daughter on a *Kindertransport*.

Helga has not behaved cruelly but rather has acted in a socially responsible manner. Evelyn only interprets Helga's appearance in England as cruel because she wants no one to interrupt the normal life she now leads; thus, she considers her mother's return not as a happy occasion, but as a threat to her assimilation into English culture (her mother insists upon calling her Eva, not Evelyn, and speaks with a German accent). Evelyn's refusal to reunite with her mother resembles historical truth: Kestenberg claims that some child survivors "are still upset because they were taken away from loving and beloved foster parents, by their own estranged parents."[19] Helga is no longer the mother but rather a stranger, the *Ratcatcher* (a threatening creature in Eva's children's book who stalks youngsters and destroys their happiness). Some children such as Eva rode to freedom on the *Kindertransports* at such a young age that when the war ended six years later, they barely remembered their parents and chose therefore to remain with foster parents who raised them.

Furthermore, if Eva agrees to leave England and the Millers when Helga arrives after the war to claim her, she would feel that she would be deserting Lil, just as her mother had abandoned her, and she would consider herself ungrateful to the woman who took her into her home, raised her, and assimilated her. With Lil's help, Eva has successfully transformed herself into Evelyn (Faith does not even realize that her own mother was born in Germany). The fact that she changes her name is telling because Eva is the name of her great-grandmother and thus part of her heritage—a heritage that she clearly wishes to disown. Evelyn learns English and British customs, and she starts smoking cigarettes like Lil, despite the fact that she initially finds smoking repulsive because her natural parents have told her that it is a dirty habit. By smoking (she becomes a chain smoker, no less), Evelyn manifests that she embraces the ways of her English adoptive mother rather than her German parents, selecting the Millers as her parents.

Although Eva initially clings to her German language, she now disowns it, linking it with Nazism. Gilman says that "German is damaged, and the damage has come from the banalization of the language of Goethe, Heine, and Nietzsche ([George] Steiner's triad) through the Nazis. Descriptions of language as 'barbaric,' as mere 'noise,' as 'creat[ing] no sense of communion' recycle the Nazi charges against the language of the Jews. The German now speaks the corrupted and corrupting language ascribed to the Jew. Indeed, following the war there appeared a spate of books about the irreversible decay of the language of German culture through the Nazis."[20] David Hackel, a *Kindertransport* survivor, says that when he first arrived in Harwich, England, Jewish refugees taught him and some of the other children German songs that were banned by the Nazis in order to give them some pride in their Jewish culture and to help them retain their German language. However, English citizens in Harwich complained, not wanting to hear German songs in the streets. But a week later, the boys felt much better about being in England because "the Mayor of Harwich paid us an official visit and bid us welcome. What none of us realized at the time was that this incident was the beginning of our '*Entdeutschung*.'"[21] The favorable treatment the *Kindertransport* boys received in Harwich made them willing to relinquish their language (that of their oppressors) for the language of their rescuers, and this alteration enhanced their assimilation into English culture.

Evelyn believes that she has a responsibility to herself to be safe, to be English rather than "the other," and so she achieves a new life. But such a transformation involves a cost. When Helga realizes that Eva does not love her anymore and chooses her adoptive parents over her, she angrily remarks to her daughter:

> I lost your father. He was sick and they put him in line for the showers. I saw it. You know what I say to you. I lost him. But I did not lose myself. Nearly a million times over, right on the edge of life, but I held on with my bones rattling inside me. Why have you lost yourself, Eva? . . . I am going to start again. I want my daughter Eva with me. If you find her, Evelyn, by any chance, send her over to find me.[22]

Helga believes that she is strong, but her daughter is weak. Despite all the hardships that Helga encountered in Auschwitz, she maintained her faith and her identity; she would let no one strip her of her self. Helga manages to survive and now feels compelled to cling to the last vestige of her former life—her daughter, Eva. She has been strong emotionally and thus assumes that her child has been the same way. Perhaps she fails to realize that while time seems to have stood still for her in Auschwitz, it has proceeded at its normal rate for her child, who has had several years to forget her past. Eva, affected by her separation from her parents and by the anti-Semitism that had surrounded her in Germany, has chosen assimilation and Christianity. Stung by her daughter's refusal to join her in New York, Helga realizes that her daughter Eva is indeed dead to her, replaced by an older girl named Evelyn who does not know her.

Diane Samuels's *Kindertransport* dramatizes one way in which anti-Semitism traumatized the lives of young children and their parents. Although the *Kindertransports* saved 10,000 lives, some of those lives were shattered anyway. Some children never forgave their parents, and most parents never saw their children again. During precarious times, people must make desperate decisions. Parents such as Helga made socially responsible but difficult decisions, attempting to save their children's lives by sending them friendless and impoverished (the Nazis confiscated all the money they could find on their victims, whom they searched thoroughly before allowing them to leave the country) into a foreign land where strangers raised them. Eva's resentment, like that of some historical *Kindertransport* children, might seem illogical and even perverse, but it is normal because the youngsters often felt betrayed and homesick. But the *Shoah* was a very unique era in history, when parents sacrificed to benefit their children and generations to come.

N O T E S

1. James E. Young, *Writing and Rewriting the Holocaust: Narrative and the Consequences of Interpretation* (Bloomington: Indiana University Press, 1988), 139.

2. Elie Wiesel, "Keynote Address, Plenary Session of the First International Conference of Children of Holocaust Survivors," New York, May 28, 1984.

3. Karen Gershon, ed., *We Came As Children: A Collective Autobiography* (London: Papermac, 1989), 19.

4. Dorit Bader Whiteman, *The Uprooted, A Hitler Legacy: Voices of Those Who Escaped Before "The Final Solution"* (New York: Insight Books, 1993), 142.

5. Gilman, *Jewish Self-Hatred*, 319.

6. Diane Samuels, *Kindertransport* (New York: Plume, 1995), 72–73. All quotations from the play derive from this edition.

7. Gershon, *We Came As Children*, 9.

8. Ibid., 131.

9. Samuels, *Kindertransport*, 5.

10. Gershon, *We Came As Children*, 9.

11. Ibid., 9.

12. Samuels, *Kindertransport*, 7.

13. Nechama Tec, "A Historical Perspective: Tracing the History of the Hidden-Child Experience," in Jane Marks, *The Hidden Children: The Secret Survivors of the Holocaust* (New York: Fawcett, 1993), 276.

14. Fred Barschak, "Personal Accounts of the Kindertransport," quoted in Samuels, *Kindertransport*, xix.

15. Samuels, *Kindertransport*, 96.

16. Felicja Karay, "Women in the Forced-Labor Camps," in Ofer and Weitzman, eds., *Women in the Holocaust*, 304.

17. Judith S. Kestenberg, "Overview of the Effect of Psychological Research Interviews on Child Survivors," in Kestenberg and Fogelman, eds., *Children During the Nazi Reign*, 13–14.

18. Judith S. Kestenberg and Janet Kestenberg Amighi, "Children in Concentration Camps," in Kestenberg and Brenner, eds., *The Last Witness*, 23, 25.

19. Judith S. Kestenberg, "Children Under the Nazi Yoke," in ibid., 196.

20. Gilman, *Jewish Self-Hatred*, 319–320.

21. Bertha Leverton and Shmuel Lowensohn, eds., *I Came Alone: The Stories of the Kindertransports* (Sussex: The Book Guild, 1990), 136–137.

22. Samuels, *Kindertransport*, 95.

*Chapter Six*

# Mama, Are We Going to Die?

*America's Children Confront the Cuban Missile Crisis*

## Chris O'Brien

Monday, October 22, 1962 dawned warm and sunny in Allentown, Pennsylvania. Eleven-year-old Deborah spent the day in the pleasures of the moment. Within twenty-four hours, her world would spiral into chaos. As she recalled:

> You can imagine what I thought when my normally reassuring mother went up to the corner market, Raders, and came home, and right in front of me, proceeded to unload box after box of canned goods for the basement. It was the Cuban Missile Crisis. I took some solace in the fact that our 100 year old home had a one foot thick foundation and was deeply buried into the ground, but not that much solace, you know? I honestly believed, with no denial present, that the end was, quite possibly near. I was a nervous wreck. I usually rode my bike from one end of Allentown to the other, day in and day out, pretending and practicing—I thought—driving a car. That week I went only up the block and to the corner and came back. . . . I remember every chunk of sidewalk on my side of Union Street between 24th and 25th St. I wanted to be able to hear my mother yell if the "button" got pushed. Come to think of it, my Dad didn't go to the office during that time. They were both around, which was a novelty. God, I was scared.[1]

In the history of children, as in the history of all other Americans, this much is known—the Cold War infiltrated every aspect of American life for nearly fifty years. Historians have delved into the myriad ways that Atomic Age consciousness permeated films, television, school instruction, and popular culture. The best of their works capture the split reality that came to typify the American mind-set by the early 1960s: the perpetual tension between the security that nuclear weapons seemed to provide and the gnawing knowledge that this powerful deterrent might mean the end of life itself. In the crystallizing moment of the Cuban Missile Crisis, this uneasy mental truce was challenged—and for none so dramatically as children. This essay explores that unhappy week in American history as it was seen by young citizens and argues that the Missile Crisis stands out as a critical flash point in the consciousness of American youth; the abstract threat that had so dominated their lives became frighteningly real. In October 1962, the Cold War came to Allentown and to every other town where small children turned to their parents and teachers for guidance and found it lacking. Deborah was not alone in being scared.

When discussing children, the most famous image of the Atomic Age is popularly reduced to disturbing footage of children diving under desks. Now eerily laughable, this image does, in fact, make sense. Americans of an age might, with a little prompting, sing along as Bert the Turtle retreats into his shell to the tune "Duck and Cover." Others remember the Cold War for bomb shelters, or recall the 1955 television footage of a small house shredded in a military test that was supposed to determine the effects of a nuclear explosion on a typical family and their home. The results were not pretty.

There was also a world beyond bomb tests and civil defense drills where nearly every child was certain Soviet nuclear planners had targeted their hometown. Whether living in a major population center like New York or Los Angeles, or in cities near military installations like San Antonio or Topeka, or alongside vital industrial centers like Cleveland or Detroit, American children felt threatened. Whether an actual target or not, home was so important to children that it *must* have been important to America's enemies.

In the Atomic Age, as in so many other times, the issues of family, home, and security dominated most young lives. In the last decade, historians have authored a small wave of literature on children in the Cold War. Studies of those who grew up in Los Alamos, of civil defense in schools and community organizations, and of teenage culture in the Atomic Age have artfully laid the groundwork for a more comprehensive understanding of the era.[2] Few of these studies, however, incorporate one of the richest resources available—the memories of adults. This chapter builds on a small collection of adult memories drawn from letters to the author as well as reactions to a popular television documentary. Some nine hundred responses in various forms have been gathered, a substantial portion of which deal with the Cuban Missile Crisis.

Memories of the Atomic Age are inevitably intertwined with the Cold War that emerged from the ashes of World War II. As Paul Boyer, Allan Winkler, Stephen Whitfield, Laura McEnaney, and others have demonstrated, American politics, art, film, comic books, church sermons, and nearly every other imaginable public mode of expression was profoundly influenced each time international tensions in the Cold War flared.[3] Spencer Weart's examination of the rapidity with which this occurred provides a useful model for understanding the manner in which new information is incorporated into a society and then retained in forms that are familiar. Ideas that atomic energy held the keys to future abundance or to ultimate destruction played on archetypes already present in American life and thus were brought to the surface each time a crisis emerged.[4] Unlike Weart, who explores both hopes and fears, it is not the glorious vision of a world with energy "too cheap to meter" that concerns us here, but rather, the darker angels of atomic power.

The initial euphoria of VJ Day was accompanied by a nearly contemporaneous sense of dread. The fear that atomic weapons presaged a new and ultimately dangerous future can be seen in Norman Cousins' "Modern Man is Obsolete," which appeared in the *Saturday Review of Literature* a scant two weeks after Hiroshima.[5] Or it might be seen in the spate of films, radio dramas, comic books, and other media ephemera that found a ready audience in 1945 and 1946. *The Beginning or the End?*—one of the first films to present the case for using the atomic bomb in Japan—is symptomatic of the time.[6] Even though it was a pseudo-documentary meant to justify the bombing and was screened by the Pentagon before release, the ambivalence the title implies is evident. Crises in Germany, Iran, Poland, and Eastern Europe from 1946 to 1949 only heightened the tensions at home. The second Red Scare, which swept the country from 1947 until the early 1950s, saw actors, teachers, ministers, and others removed from positions of power and influence, often on the most dubious of charges. Frequently, the effect of all this on children was immediate. For example, historian Ellen Schrecker remembers wondering what became of a beloved elementary school teacher who was quietly ousted due to his leftist leanings.[7] That America was frightened of the "communist menace" seems a remarkable understatement.

And yet, sated by the enormous prosperity that emerged in the 1950s, many ignored the more troubling aspects of the era. Newfound wealth propelled a burgeoning of the middle class. An explosion of suburbs, coupled with the advent of nuclear families surrounded by the latest conveniences, lulled many into a quiet complacency. While this was certainly not the case for all Americans, or arguably for most of them, the popular image of prosperity was fueled by smiling families in television advertisements which provided a powerful inducement to conformity. Korea caused consternation and the U-2 affair and Sputnik brought renewed concern to many, but looking directly into the maw of worldwide annihilation became the province of fewer and fewer activists. While the nation seemed to look away from the abyss, however, America's children, huddled under their desks, were often reminded of the tenuous nature of their own existence.

The election of John F. Kennedy to the White House brought renewed urgency to the Cold War. From his campaign pledge to close the "missile gap," to the early blunder at the Bay of Pigs, to the construction of the Berlin Wall by the East Germans, his brief tenure in office was undoubtedly a time of heightened international tension. Never would this be more apparent than on the night of October 22, 1962. On that fateful Monday, a somber JFK took to the nation's airwaves to announce that the ongoing Soviet military buildup in Cuba included missiles "capable of striking Washington, D.C., the Panama Canal, Cape Canaveral, Mexico City, or any other city in the Southeastern part of the United States, in Central America, or in the Caribbean area."[8]

The normally graceful president was collected but clearly concerned—as well he should have been. He began by denouncing the "secret, swift and extraordinary build-up of Communist missiles" as "a deliberately provocative and unjustified change in the status quo which cannot be accepted by this country." The United States could not stand idly by while this occurred. The nation must act, Kennedy intoned, "if our courage and our commitments are ever again to be trusted by either friend or foe." While the action that he proposed was limited to a "quarantine" of Cuba, the stakes of the game were clear as Kennedy laid out in the most frightening phrase of the speech:

> It shall be the policy of this Nation to regard any nuclear missile launched from Cuba against any nation in the Western Hemisphere as an attack by the Soviet Union on the United States, requiring a full retaliatory response upon the Soviet Union. [9]

For the next seven terrifying days, the world teetered on the brink of nuclear war.

Newspapers reported runs on grocery stores Tuesday, October 23. Clearly, the time to prepare was at hand. Young Deborah, riding her bike up and down one block of Allentown, was frightened—an emotion shared by many other children. Born in 1955, James Kenna was a mere boy when the

Crisis struck but, in some ways, he was prepared for it as well as any American. As he recalled:

> In elementary school, we regularly practiced civil defense training. The teachers would talk to us generally about what to expect; mostly we practiced quickly hiding under desks and in corners. We had to kneel on the floor, put our heads between our knees, and our hands over our heads. The teacher would yell at us if we even looked up. We were told to keep our eyes closed too. This scared us.[10]

Nonetheless, James felt a certain sense of pride at "how quickly first and second graders could move to their positions and take proper cover" and "stay there without moving until the all-clear signal was given."[11] But even this rigorous training left him unprepared for the enormous tension created by the Cuban Quarantine; it was not at school that this realization hit home most clearly but at church. As James explained:

> The Sunday before the end to the Missile Crisis our church was packed. My dad was an usher and I got to help him sometimes, so I know the count was over 1,000 that Sunday, we usually had less that 400. They put folding chairs in the aisles, there was not room to sit, many stood. I had to sit in the balcony that day. Most were sad, many were crying, the fear could almost be felt. I think that past Friday the Crisis had escalated greatly. I remember going to bed thinking it was all over. We were kinda shocked Saturday came. That Sunday I think most of the adults realized how serious it had gotten. The Crisis de-escalated that next week; the following Sunday we had maybe 600 in church. Two weeks later, we were back to 400 or less. I remember thinking how fickle men were.[12]

Church also proved an important setting for young Jack Passetto in this moment of turmoil. He remembered one of the crucial days of the Cuban Missile Crisis when he was in a religious instruction class after school in the basement of his Catholic church. Jack was in seventh grade and remembered "the priests telling us to pray for our President and the country as the President was going to speak that evening. They also said that this could mean nuclear war between the United States and the Soviet Union." Most troubling was the response among his classmates. Jack recalled "the pall that descended in that class as we usually were a raucous class." But that day, they prayed and then prayed some more.[13]

That adults would join together in prayer seems eminently logical— where better to turn, one might ask. That they included children served another purpose beyond the appeal to the Divine: It gave some sense of stability in what was a very dark moment. In some cases, however, actions taken to calm young fears backfired.

Curt Fettinger was in second grade in Orange County, California during the Cuban Missile Crisis. As he recalled:

> the school had regular duck-and-cover drills, but during the week of the crisis we had a duck-and-cover drill almost every day. One day, apparently our teacher had not been notified of that day's drill. When the school klaxon suddenly started the one long, two shorts duck-and-cover signal, our teacher screamed "GET UNDER THE DESKS NOW!" and dove under hers, which she had never done before. I remember being crouched under the desk, my face buried in my arm and just shaking, too scared to cry. After what seemed forever, the one long all clear sounded. I don't think I have ever been so frightened in my life.[14]

Fear was not the only response, of course. Wanda Schubmehl worried about the others in her community and the moral dilemmas the crisis posed. She was nine years old at the time, and could:

> clearly recall going down to our basement, curling up on an old red couch, and waiting in terror for the bomb to drop and end the world. I also spent a lot of time trying to sort out the ethics of refusing people entry to one's bomb shelter (although we didn't have one, I worried about the conflict between saving someone's life and saving my own).[15]

Other children clung to hope that their town would be spared or their parents would protect them or simply that the Crisis would end peacefully. Some dug for solace like Michael Bertsch, who worked with friends on a fallout shelter. He recalled, "Sean's dad had the plans and we kids were the labor. After ten days we had a complete shelter dug into an ivy bank."[16] Sean's father may have been doing what he could to protect his family and friends or, perhaps, he was just keeping a worried group of boys busy. Undoubtedly, the two tasks seemed very similar.

Other parents were less successful in easing the fears of their children. During the Missile Crisis, ten-year-old Bob McCown took a nuclear survival course with his parents and brother. When they got home, they "equipped our basement with food and water storage—we lived in a rural area about 30 miles east of Cincinnati, Ohio at the time, in a huge old brick and stone house." Most troubling was the memory of his mother:

> telling me that I could pick up a can using a piece of paper or aluminum foil to keep from touching fallout, and turn it over to open it from the clean bot-

tom. I dreamed of nuclear fallout several nights a month until the Berlin Wall fell.[17]

This concern with safety occasionally took a bizarre turn in the mind of a child. For example, Joanne Wendelin recalled:

> mother talking about storing gallons of water and saltine crackers in the basement for our bomb shelter. I even remember her showing us a crawl space where we should go in the event of an atomic bomb. A girlfriend's parents had a newer home with a very nice basement under it. And off of the basement, there was a really nice bomb shelter—a small room with lighting and shelves with canned food.

In the midst of the Crisis, she was horrified by:

> my mother setting a bottle of Wishbone brand Russian salad dressing on the supper table. I thought, "Why is my mother doing this? Why would we want to eat this?! The Russians have probably put poison in it!!"

Her fears grew as the crisis intensified. She was sure that she would see:

> legions of Russian soldiers (with their tall black boots, rifles with bayonets on the end, black Cossack hats on their heads) marching 8 or 10 abreast down the country road! I hoped my father could defend us![18]

Joanne emerged from the crisis unscathed but nonetheless harbors no warm feelings for the moment.

For others, the memory has grown less frightening with the passage of time. Joyce Decker reminisced that her family had stored provisions and:

> we all had jobs to due [sic] in case we heard the air raid siren. Mine (I was 9 years old) was to get our pet dog and my pet white rat and head for the shelter. My brother was to collect all the pillows from the beds.

In 1995, more than three decades after the Missile Crisis, Joyce and her brother happened to be visiting their mother on the last Friday of the month. It was the day that the emergency sirens were tested. Times had changed for the siblings, as "neither my brother nor I live in places where sirens are still tested, so it was weird to hear it after so long of a time." Joyce quickly figured out that it was a test, but as:

> my mom and I were talking, generally ignoring the sirens, my 44 year old brother came running in carrying every pillow in the house, announcing loudly "I got the pillows; where's the damn rat?!" We all laughed hysterically, but I remembered how scared I was in 1962."[19]

For most, it was a frightening time. Many recalled watching the Soviet tankers slowly steam toward the quarantine line and wondering if the world would survive. Not all shared such a dire outlook, of course. A few hardy souls remembered that "no one was scared," "we were ready," or even "we would be fine: we were Texans!" It would be comforting to think that the memories of most children of the Missile Crisis would now reflect this sunnier outlook. After all, a resolution was reached and the world did survive. But even now, separated some forty years from the event, the memories still provoke dread, softened somewhat by time perhaps, but still very much alive. It was possible to ride a bike during the Cuban Missile Crisis—but only near home.

A perpetual question in the study of children is how their experiences affected them as adults. The answer is more complicated than many historians have let on. The oldest children in this cohort might have served at the tail end of the Vietnam War or opposed it. In a perfect narrative, these children, angered by the complacency of the 1950s, frightened by the Missile Crisis, and scarred by the Kennedy assassination, would have become a generation of rebels. Some did. Most did not. The vast majority went on to buy homes, build families and, as their parents had before them, seek prosperity and stability. The youth of the Cuban Missile Crisis now hold much of the political power in the country and a substantial portion of the wealth. We have not seen them turn away from nuclear weapons, or from war, or even from tilting with Cuba. So what lessons did they draw?

Wanda Schubmehl, who curled up on her red couch and worried about the neighbors, is still troubled by the events of October 1962. It was, she says, "a lot for a child to try to deal with." But in some ways, the moment has passed. Wanda has perceptively noted:

> Even though my own children have had to grow up in a nuclear age, with the threat of nuclear annihilation every day, I don't think it has had the same intensity of my childhood's fear during that time—and as we now know, my fear was justified, as the world came very close to exchanging nuclear attacks.[20]

Fear passed even more quickly for Michael Bertsch. In the years after the Crisis, the fallout shelter he had helped dig in a neighbor's yard "became the make-out zone." Nonetheless, Michael saw the moment as one of frightening personal realization. "The most striking thing about the Cold War for me," he wrote, "was my acceptance that at any moment we would all be vaporized by a Russian atomic bomb." But for Michael that time has passed.

He is "glad my son has no personal knowledge of that feeling."[21] While Michael does not acknowledge it in his letter, this comfort, of course, is cold. The weapons have not been dismantled and the threat of nuclear annihilation has not been removed. That his son does not feel the threat is a very good thing. But there is little reason he ought not.

In fact, not all would agree that the world has grown better for young people. Deborah Twiss, who rode her bike on Union Street, was more disillusioned by the Crisis and its aftermath. Terrified during the Crisis, Deborah hoped that a saner world would emerge, but fears that it has not. As she explains: "At least kids of today haven't been bamboozled into some false sense of security about the world in which they live." Indeed, Deborah believes that American society spun out of control in recent years and that we have "created a monster we are not going to be able to feed forever." Americans consume "alcohol and drugs to numb our fear and pain," are plagued by "gangs, crime, gruesome inhumane acts committed one human to another," she argues and, rather than cherish the next generation, even suffer the horrors of "kids abused" and "neglected." But strikingly, all is not lost, according to Deborah, for "we have opportunity and a beautiful planet on which to dwell—in short, wonder." While Deborah stops short of blaming the Cuban Missile Crisis for all the ailments of modern society, certainly, that fateful week in October did much to shatter her youthful innocence.

Michael, Deborah, and others who were children at the time find some comfort in something simple that their own parents would have appreciated: a deep-seated desire to make the world more secure. Most do that on the home front by trying to raise their own children without the fear that they themselves knew so well. Duck-and-cover drills have disappeared and the Soviet Union is gone, but the issue has grown more complicated rather than easier. More nations than ever have nuclear weapons technology: the United States, Russia, China, France, Great Britain, India, Pakistan, Israel, and South Africa, to name but a few. Others, like Iraq and North Korea, seem hell-bent on developing missiles and atom bombs.

So what did the nation, and particularly her youngest citizens, learn from those harried days? A possible answer lies in the fact that two distinct ways of viewing the meaning of the Missile Crisis have emerged in the years since. The first might be likened to the children's game of "Stare-down" in which the object is to stare into the eyes of your opponent until someone blinks. He who blinks loses. For most Americans, this remains the popular understanding of what happened in those fateful days of October 1962: Kennedy and Kruschev sat eyeball to eyeball until the Russian dictator blinked. The lesson is straightforward; one should not back down from a threat. Not everyone, however, saw the Missile Crisis in this fashion. Historian Arthur Schlesinger, Jr., wrote that Jack Kennedy took a decidedly different lesson away from the Cuban Missile Crisis. "His feelings," Schlesinger explained:

> underwent a qualitative change after Cuba: A world in which nations threatened each other with nuclear weapons now seemed to him not just an irrational but an intolerable and impossible world. Cuba thus made vivid the sense that all humanity had a common interest in the prevention of nuclear war—an interest far above those national and ideological interests which had once seemed ultimate.[22]

This is a decidedly different lesson: that to prevent catastrophe, cooperation must prevail. A generation of arms control treaties, test bans, and increased international cooperation attest to the potency of this interpretation.

But at best, the lessons of the Cuban Missile Crisis have been mixed. For those children who lived through it, the fear that they felt has not led them on a single path to ending the nuclear threat, since they can reach no real consensus on how best to achieve that aim. Some call for greater international control through the United Nations or other alliances. Others envision a cache of bombs so staggering that none would dare attack the United States. Even the current debate over the magical missile shield may very well be an outgrowth of this quest for security; a giant desk in the sky we all can crouch beneath. But one thing is clear: For those who were young in the days of the Cuban Missile Crisis, there is no desire to go back to those less than halcyon days of youth. Those tense days were, to quote Deborah Twiss, "rotten, in retrospect."

NOTES

I want to thank William M. Tuttle, Jr., and Jasonne Grabher O'Brien for their insightful comments and criticisms to several drafts of this essay.

1. Deborah J. Twiss, letter to author, December 31, 1996.

2. Oakes, *The Imaginary War*, 105–144; Michael J. Carey, "Psychological Fallout," *Bulletin of the Atomic Scientists* 38:1 (1982), 20–24; Robert K. Musil, "Growing Up Nuclear," *Bulletin of the Atomic Scientists* 38:1 (1982), 19; Michael J. Carey, "The Schools and Civil Defense: The Fifties Revisited," *Teacher's College Record* 84:1 (1982), 115–127; Skolnick, *Embattled Paradise*, 49–74; Brown, "A is for Atom, B is for Bomb," 68–90; Elaine Tyler May, "Explosive Issues: Sex, Women and the Bomb,"

in Lary May, *Recasting America: Culture and Politics in the Age of Cold War* (Chicago: University of Chicago Press, 1989), 154–170. One historian who has used adult memories of childhood extensively is William M. Tuttle, Jr. See particularly his *Daddy's Gone to War*; and "America's Children in an Era of War, Hot and Cold: The Holocaust, the Bomb, and Child Rearing in the 1940s," in Peter J. Kuznik and James Gilbert, *Rethinking Cold War Culture* (Washington: Smithsonian Institution Press, 2001).

3. Boyer, *By the Bomb's Early Light*; Winkler, *Life Under a Cloud*; Tom Engelhardt, *The End of Victory Culture: Cold War America and the Disillusioning of a Generation* (New York: Basic Books, 1995); Whitfield, *The Culture of the Cold War*; McEnaney, *Civil Defense Begins at Home*.

4. Spencer Weart, *Nuclear Fear: A History of Images* (Cambridge, MA: Harvard University Press, 1988), 421–426. For a similar explanation of how Americans first reacted to the Bomb, see Boyer, *By the Bomb's Early Light*, 15.

5. Norman Cousins, "Modern Man is Obsolete," *Saturday Review of Literature* (August 18, 1945).

6. *The Beginning or the End?*, MGM, 1946. See Mick Broderick, *Nuclear Movies: A Critical Analysis and Filmography of International Feature Length Films Dealing with Experimentation, Aliens, Terrorism, Holocaust and Other Disaster Scenarios, 1914–1989* (Jefferson NC: McFarland and Company, 1991), 6, 49, 60. See also Nora Sayre, *Running Time: The Films of the Cold War* (New York: Dial Press, 1982); Margot Hendrickson, *Dr. Strangelove's America: Society and Culture in the Atomic Age* (Berkeley: University of California Press, 1997).

7. Ellen Schrecker, *Many Are the Crimes: McCarthyism in America* (Boston: Little Brown, 1998), ix.

8. Laurence Chang and Peter Kornbluth, eds., *The Cuban Missile Crisis, 1962: A National Security Archive Document Reader* (New York: The New Press, 1998), 160.

9. Chang and Kornbluth, *Cuban Missile Crisis*, 162–163.

10. James Kenna, letter to author, May 31, 1997.

11. Ibid.

12. Ibid.

13. Jack Passetto, November 16, 1998, <http://www.cnn.com/SPECIALS/cold.war/episodes>, ET, #117 of 768. The interactive CNN message board that housed these messages is no longer accessible. Copies of the messages are in the author's possession.

14. Curt Fettinger, November 23, 1998, ibid., #138.

15. Wanda Schubmehl, February 21, 1999, ibid., #578.

16. Michael Bertsch, December 30, 1998, ibid., #324.

17. Bob McCown, February 3, 1999, ibid., #498.

18. Joanne Wendelin, letter to author, February 28, 1997.

19. Joyce Decker, February 5, 1999, ibid., #521.

20. Wanda Schubmehl, February 21, 1999, ibid., #578.

21. Bertsch, #324.

22. Arthur Schlesinger, Jr., *A Thousand Days: John F. Kennedy in the White House* (Boston: Houghton-Mifflin, 1965), 893.

# Chapter Seven

# Bereavement in a War Zone
## *Liberia in the 1990s*

## *Cynthia B. Eriksson and Elizabeth A. Rupp*

Ella[1] was thirteen years old at the beginning of the civil conflict in Liberia. Her father was a fisherman working on the lush coastline of the capital city, Monrovia. Two years later, Ella was living in an orphanage. Her parents had been killed during the early fighting. A Liberian counselor asked Ella to talk about the most difficult experience she had had during the war. Ella explained that soldiers had killed her father right in front of her. He was forced to tell his children "goodbye" before he was shot. From now on, when Ella remembers her last moments with her father, it will be in the context of torture and violence.

At a very simple level, grieving is learning to "remember well": to have memories of the lost loved one that can bring joy, as well as sadness, to mind. Living must continue, and grieving allows these memories to become part of the new journey and the new relationships that are formed. A healthy adult brings life experience, cultural beliefs, established support relationships, and emotional resources to the task. A child is in the midst of developing those resources; navigating the world depends upon the love, support, and education provided by parents and caregivers. Understanding death and forming good memories of lost parents requires consistent care from other adults.

In the best of circumstances, bereavement can be painful, time-consuming, distracting, and bleak. In a war zone, memories are filled with horror, deprivation, and fear, as well as loss. Violence and trauma can sabotage the journey of grief for adults and children. After a trauma, it is often difficult to move forward, to keep living in the world that holds such pain and violence. Remembering the painful event is something that one tries to avoid, but reminders can catch one off guard and create a renewed sense of fear. For a child like Ella, remembering her father brings images of brutality and blood. Her fear for her own life and horror at this act of violence are intricately woven with the loss of her father. If remembering is so painful for her, how can grieving happen?

In a time when wars continue to rage around the world and civilians and children are more often the targets of violence, it is critical to consider the experience of those children left to grow and grieve without parents. One example of this growing humanitarian need is the orphans of the civil conflict in Liberia. The civil war in Liberia raged for most of the 1990s, with periods of uncertain stability and times of horrific massacres. A group of sixty-three children were living in an urban orphanage during the early 1990s. All of the children had been separated from family members; however, there were striking differences in how their losses occurred. Some children actually witnessed the murder of their parents in atrocious ways. Others lost their parents to illness and starvation. Another group of children did not know what had happened to their parents. The mother and father may have left to find food, but never returned.

These children's stories offer a glimpse into one facet of the tragedy of war. This essay will use their experiences to highlight issues of bereavement in a war zone: the emotional consequences of loss and trauma, the added horror of witnessing death, the uncertainty of a parent that is missing, and the spiritual/cultural connection to lost family.

## The Civil War in Liberia: The Context of Loss

In December 1989, Charles Taylor recruited soldiers and civilians from the Gio and Mano tribes and launched a rebellion against the government of Liberian president, Samual K. Doe. Doe was of the Krahn tribe, and his methods of retaliation against Taylor's National Patriotic Front of Liberia (NPFL) included killing and torture of civilians who were of the Gio and Mano ethnicities. Doe's forces perpetrated one of the worst atrocities of the civil conflict on July 29, 1990 at the St. Peter's Lutheran Church in Monrovia; one estimate is that 600 civilian men, women, and children died and 150 were injured during that massacre.[2]

The Economic Community of West African States (ECOWAS) joined the conflict and sent a peacekeeping force. On September 9, 1990, Doe was captured, tortured, and killed by another rebel leader, Prince Johnson. Doe's death, however, did not end the conflict. Johnson named himself leader of Liberia; Taylor remained in control of the majority of the country; and ECOWAS established an interim government.[3] In January 1991, Charles Taylor and his NPFL forces established a separate seat of government in Gbanga; he continued to recruit civilians for his rebel forces, including a large number of children.

In the summer of 1992, the country remained divided. The peacekeeping forces kept control of the capital city Monrovia, and interim President Amos Sawyer was recognized as the leader of Liberia by the international community. However, Charles Taylor, who refused to recognize Sawyer's leadership, controlled 95 percent of the country.[4] During this time of "stand-off" the international relief community continued to bring needed food, medical care, and psychosocial relief. It was during this period that the sixty-three children living in a Monrovia orphanage were interviewed.

## The Psychosocial Interview: Remembering Their Stories

The children often came to live in the Monrovia orphanage after trying to escape with family or village members from areas in the interior part of the country that were troubled by conflict and lack of resources. One nine-year-old boy told his interviewer, "While we were traveling my mother was arrested by fighters and killed and I had to go on my own—with other people. I later learned of my father, but he joined the fighters. He was shot on the war front and later died of bullet wounds." His story was not unusual. Eighteen percent of the children did not know if their parents had actually been killed; many of these had been separated because the parents had gone to look for food. Another 21 percent of the children living in the orphanage had actually witnessed the brutal deaths of their mother, father, or both parents. Without the orphanage care, most of these children would have been living on the street due to their parents' death or abandonment. Life at the orphanage allowed the children reasonable levels of security. One older woman was the "Mother" of the orphanage, and she was the administrator and advocate for the needs of the children.

In 1992, a psychosocial relief team organized by a Swiss relief agency, MEDAIR, partnered with area orphanages and civic organizations to offer training and support in caring for child victims of the civil conflict. Five Liberian mental health workers were employed by MEDAIR as a core group of professionals to establish an ongoing program of psychosocial service. Visiting Western mental health professionals trained and collaborated with the Liberian counselors.

The five Liberian counselors interviewed all of the children between the ages of five and twenty-two living at one Monrovia orphanage (27 girls, and 36 boys). The children represented a wide range of ethnic groups and former socioeconomic status. The counselors used a structured interview developed by the Center for the Study of Human Rights at Columbia University that included the following surveys: *The Childhood War Trauma Questionnaire* (CWTQ);[5] the *Child Behavior Inventory* (CBI);[6] and the *Post-Traumatic Stress Reaction Checklist for Children* (PTSRC).[7] The interview had been pilot-tested by a consultant to UNICEF, and questions were adapted to fit the Liberian Civil War context.[8] Information from the interviews was used to identify children in particular need and to create grief intervention groups that the Liberian counselors would facilitate.

## Trauma and Remembering: Bereavement in a War Zone

Most published literature examining a child's experience of parental loss considers the child's task of remembering in a situation of peace and resource. The children have a surviving parent and a stable societal and cultural environment. A child grieving during a time of peace has the familiar routine of school, activities with friends, and caring adults as a buffer to the waves of yearning for the lost parent. Children need the opportunity to talk about the lost loved one and the circumstances of the death with adults who have the emotional resources necessary to listen patiently and communicate openly.[9] The child needs to know that he or she is safe, and needs to have an adult confront any of the child's confused ideas about their own responsibility for the loss.[10]

Western literature has also identified the importance of a child's ability to create a healthy set of memories and ideas about the lost parent. The goal of healthy grieving is not forgetting the parent; instead, it is a type of ongoing remembering.[11] As the child ages, new information can be incorporated into this "picture" or image of the parent. The child's ongoing "relationship" with the lost parent actually aids in adjustment. It was previously popular to assume that the child would need to "let go" of the dead parent, in order to attach to a new parent figure. This has proven to be a false assumption.[12]

For the children in the Monrovia orphanage, creating a set of healthy memories and ideas about the lost parents was a complicated matter. Their lives were torn apart by violence, illness, lack of food and shelter, loss of family members, and loss of security. Losing parents happened in the midst of ongoing exposure to violence and threat of violence. Remembering became interwoven with images of destruction.

The war also destroyed the natural social support structure that would ordinarily have provided respite for the orphaned children. They had limited contact with people who knew their parents and could help them remember and establish that internal relationship with the lost parents. Only 16 percent of the children stated that they had any siblings or extended family with them in the orphanage. Also, the adults that they were living with carried their own pain and loss. This limited support created a difficult challenge for the children to effectively remember.

### Violence and Loss: Remembering the War

The Liberian children have endured trauma and loss staggering in its scale and severity. What do they remember from the early years of the war? Table 7.1 outlines the high percentages of violence and deprivation that the children described in response to the *Childhood War Trauma Questionnaire*. Research in a variety of cultural settings with children traumatized by war has shown symptoms consistent with the psychiatric diagnosis of

TABLE 7.1
*Report of Exposure to War-Related Trauma*

| Category of Experience | Yes (%) |
|---|---|
| Displacement (forced to change residence and/or school) | 98.4 |
| Deprivation (going without food, water, and/or shelter) | 98.4 |
| Bereavement (the death of family members during the war) | 95.0 |
| Separation (separated from both parents during the war) | 85.5 |
| Witnessing violent acts (seeing someone hurt or killed) | 84.1 |
| Exposure to armed combat (gunfire, shelling, explosions) | 87.1 |
| Victim of violent acts (personal experience of violence) | 55.6 |
| Immigration (forced to leave Liberia during the war) | 11.1 |
| Physical injuries (personal injuries due to conflict) | 9.8 |
| Military activities (involvement in fighting with weapons) | 4.8 |
| Killed or injured someone (violence against others) | 4.8 |

Posttraumatic Stress Disorder (PTSD).[13] These symptoms include: intrusive thoughts, memories about the traumatic events, and physiological hyper-arousal. Research in some ethnocultural settings has also revealed avoidance of reminders of the event.[14] As is evident from these symptoms, remembering is a central part of the pain of PTSD. Remembering the horror when one does not want to, remembering in dreams, or avoiding things or people that one knows will be reminders of the experience are all hallmarks of this disorder.

The Posttraumatic Stress Reaction Checklist used in the interview includes questions phrased for children that explore these symptoms of re-experiencing the event, hyper-arousal, and avoidance. Table 7.2 lists the striking percentages of these posttrauma symptoms in the Liberian children. Research examining loss of loved ones in Western nations has already identified the similarities of symptoms between PTSD and difficult bereavement:

> Symptoms of separation distress (e.g., yearning, searching for the deceased, excessive loneliness resulting from the loss) form a unidimensional cluster with symptoms of traumatic distress (e.g., intrusive thoughts about the deceased, feelings of numbness, disbelief about the loss, being stunned and dazed, [and] a fragmented sense of security and trust).[15]

TABLE 7.2
*Report of Posttraumatic Stress Reactions to the Child's "Most Upsetting Event"*

| Reaction | Currently Experiencing (%) |
| --- | --- |
| Thinking about the event now | 82.5 |
| Trying not to think about the event | 77.8 |
| Getting scared or upset when thinking about the event | 73.0 |
| Going over the event in one's mind; images or sounds | 71.4 |
| Avoiding situations or activities that are reminders of the event | 61.9 |
| Being more easily startled; feeling jumpy | 61.9 |
| Dreaming often about the event | 57.1 |
| Feeling isolated, not understood | 52.4 |
| Having difficulties falling or staying asleep | 46.8 |
| Having difficulties concentrating or paying attention | 44.4 |
| Feeling like the event is happening all over again | 44.4 |
| Having difficulties with memory | 42.9 |
| Experiencing less enjoyment of previously pleasurable activities | 41.9 |
| Foreshortened future; worrying that one might not live to adulthood | 38.1 |

In a complicated bereavement, remembering can lead to loneliness, isolation, distraction, and loss of trust. It is not surprising that depression and anxiety would be a result.[16] The Liberian children who were interviewed demonstrated a high level of depression. More than three-quarters of the children indicated that they: cried easily, felt sad, worried about many things, were afraid of losing other family members, and felt tired. Over half of the children stated that they felt lonely and helpless. The orphans also reported a significant number of anxiety symptoms. Almost all of the children stated that they needed to be around an older person to feel safe. About two-thirds of the children interviewed indicated that they were scared that something bad would happen to them, or felt scared of things that did not scare them before. It is interesting to note that the children's report of PTSD symptoms, anxiety, and depression were all significantly related to each other. Children with high levels of PTSD also had high levels of depression and anxiety.

## *Witnessing Death and Atrocities: Remembering Horror*

There are certain factors in war-related deaths that increase the pain and confusion of memories. One of the most horrific is when a child is the witness to the murder of her own mother or father.

Research in war zones has identified that children who witness the death of a family member experience more severe and chronic emotional distress.[17] Many of the Liberian children witnessed atrocities against their parents. For example, one eleven-year-old girl lost both parents to violence during the conflict. She was a survivor of the horrible St. Peter's Lutheran Church massacre. She told the interviewer, "My mother was shot and killed at the Lutheran St. Peter's Church while she was trying to escape through a window." Later in the interview, this child was asked about her enjoyment of fun activities, and she responded that she could enjoy playing with friends, "when I am not thinking about her [mother]."

How does human perpetration and witnessing a violent death affect remembering? There are critical questions for bereavement in a war zone. The Liberian children are in a particularly difficult position, as 20 percent of them lost one parent and 43 percent of them lost both parents to a human-perpetrated act of violence. Spencer Eth and Robert Pynoos write, "human accountability only adds to the child's anguish and difficulty achieving trauma mastery."[18] Research on child witnesses to parental murder in Western cultures has shown that witnessing the death creates a painful disruption in the grieving process. Children struggle with intrusive images and thoughts about the death. In fact, the child may focus specifically on the moment of death: the screams for help that end in silence, the fatal gunshot, the blood pooling around a parent's body. Remembering mother or father becomes a frightening thing. It is critical to provide psychosocial support to resolve the trauma, in order to free the child to be able to remember warm, positive memories of the parent.[19]

A statistical analysis of the interview responses from the Liberian orphans did not indicate a significant difference in emotional distress between those who witnessed the deaths of their parents and those who did not. It is reasonable to believe that differences between subgroups of the orphans may be confounded by the extraordinarily high rate of war-related violence and atrocity the children experienced. For example, a seventeen-year-old boy lost his mother to cholera during the war and his sister disappeared. However, during the interview he also described the following situation: "a man was arrested by soldiers and demanded to dig his own grave and stood in there and his head was amputated and put in a bag and carried away. This is no joke I am always thin[king] on this situation. It bothers me when I think about it." Yet when asked about his worst experience he stated, "the death of my mother. My appetite suppresses sometimes when I think on the event." This boy acknowledges both the horror of seeing a beheading, as well as the painful loss of his mother. Either experience in itself is an overwhelming event for a child, and it is impossible to separate certain symptoms as associated with certain events.

## Family Members Missing: Incomplete Memories

How does a child grieve for a parent who is missing? Memories of the time of separation bring questions and uncertainty. Sam[20] was ten years old and living with his parents in Monrovia when the conflict began. One day, he left his parents to go look for food. When he returned, his parents were gone. He told the interviewer that he asked his neighbors what had happened, but they refused to tell him. Sam has not seen or heard from his parents since that day. Other families were separated for the sake of survival or due to arrests. A seventeen-year-old boy told the interviewer that his parents suggested that he try to escape during the conflict. He left them at age fifteen, and tried to find a safer area in which to live. Two years later, he told the interviewer that the worst thing that happened to him was "I left my parents suffering." He does not know if they are dead or alive.

One sixteen-year-old boy described to the interviewer the last time he saw his mother and father. They were arrested by soldiers. His father was "tarbayed"—tied up with his arms contorted behind his back and tortured—in front of him, and his mother was taken away. That was the last time he saw them. The boy explained to the interviewer that he knew the soldier planned to kill his father and take his mother as wife. However, when asked if there were other difficult things that happened that they had not talked about, the boy answered, "I don't know, but please find my parents."

As the stories suggest, the child may understand at a certain level that his parents are dead. However, the fact that there is no information or knowledge of the death leads to a painful wish and hope for reunion. For a few, the reunion may take place. For others, the grief remains uncertain and mixed with hope. Research with children in Central America, where people would vanish at the hands of government and guerrilla soldiers, suggests that the child has a terrible choice. If the child decides to believe that the family member is dead, she may struggle with the feeling that she herself has "symbolically" killed the loved one.[21]

## The Cultural/Spiritual Context of Remembering

It has been noted in Western research that bereaved children have fears about seeing their parents' ghosts or spirits. It is not uncommon in adults and children for the grieving to "see" their loved one in a crowd, out of the corner of their eye, in dreams, etc. Children may become quite anxious about "seeing" a parent because the child might believe that the parent is still alive somewhere, or that the parent is going to come back to discipline a child's bad behavior.[22]

Two brothers, ages six and seven years old, came to the orphanage with their sister. Their father had been part of the security personnel for the Executive Mansion, and their mother had a small market business. Their mother traveled with the children to another town, where she became ill. The six-year-old described to the interviewer that his mother became sick and needed to be put in a wheelbarrow to be taken to the hospital. She died in the hospital. The children do not know what has happened to their father, and they lived on the street until coming to the orphanage. During the interview, both young boys described being frightened by seeing their dead mother dressed in white appear to them.

Two other orphans expressed concerns about their parents' spirits. A twelve-year-old boy stated that he had difficulties falling or staying asleep, "because of my father's presence."

A teenage girl told the interviewer that she is afraid that her mother may appear to her "in spirit form." She stated that she thinks about dying when she thinks of her lost family. She said, "I want bad sickness to catch me so I can die." Here was intense sadness, a fear of spiritual visitation, and a wish to be reunited with her dead family.

In many cultures, beliefs about ancestors and spirits play an important part in the grieving process. The burial ritual is often vitally important in the culture's beliefs about the spirit's ultimate resting. In the war zone, special rituals or actions against a perpetrator may be impossible. The child who knows that a parent was not buried, or whose death was not revenged, may feel guilty or anxious that the parent will remain in pain, or not be able to move to the supernatural realm.[23]

## *Grieving in an Orphanage: Remembering Together*

Research in Western settings consistently emphasizes the importance of a secure relationship and open communication with a surviving parent, after the death of one parent.[24] This raises critical issues regarding the consequences of losing both parents and living in an orphanage setting. In the war zone caretakers do not have a pre-existing relationship with the child, staff are busy with daily survival tasks, and the community is still in the midst of the threat of conflict. However, the results of a large research project in Rwanda suggest that in a war zone a center for unaccompanied children can provide stability and psychosocial support. The centers offer a parentless child a place of connection with children in similar circumstances, basic daily care, resources for education and play, and psychosocial and medical attention.[25] The international community can offer assistance in creating both family reunification programs and centers for unaccompanied children that create the best environment for continued material and psychosocial support.

## Conclusion

Children are vulnerable, by nature of their limited cognitive development and their dependence on others.[26] Adults have the capacity to feed, clothe, and protect themselves, and they have had years of experience with which to process and structure the chaos in the world around them. Children may have little framework for processing traumatic experiences or understanding their loss. The United Nations concurs:

> War violates every right of a child—the right to life, the right to be with family and community, the right to health, the right to the development of personality, and the right to be nurtured and protected.[27]

We would add, the right to "remember well." The children of war need the safety of peace and the care of knowledgeable adults, in order to support the memories of their parents as whole and loving, to dream good dreams, and to face a future with a strong connection to their ancestors.

### Notes

1. Not her real name.
2. Joseph K. Tellewoyan, *The Liberian Tragedy*, online at http://pages.prodigy .net/jtell/Civilwar.html.
3. "In Death as in Life," *Africa Events* (October 1990): 16.
4. Tellewoyan, *The Liberian Tragedy*.
5. Mona Macksoud, "Assessing War Trauma in Children: A Case Study of Lebanese Children," *Journal of Refugee Studies* 5 (January 1992): 1–15.
6. Mona Macksoud, Atle Dyregrov, and Magne Raundalen, "Traumatic War Experiences and Their Effects on Children," *International Handbook of Traumatic Stress Syndromes*, ed. John Wilson and Beverly Raphael (New York: Plenum Press, 1990), 625–633.
7. Ibid.
8. A local Liberian psychologist was available to respond to critical issues with the children that were identified during the interview process.
9. Victoria H. Raveis, Karolynn Siegel, and Daniel Karus, "Children's Psychological Distress Following the Death of a Parent," *Journal of Youth and Adolescence* 28 (April 1999): 165–180.
10. John Bowlby, *Loss: Sadness and Depression*, vol. 3 of *Attachment and Loss Trilogy* (New York: Basic Books, 1980), 274–275, 285–287.
11. Ibid., 285.
12. Phyllis R. Silverman, Steven Nickman, and William Worden, "Detachment

Revisited: The Child's Reconstruction of a Dead Parent," *American Journal of Orthopsychiatry* 62 (October 1992): 494–503.

13. American Psychiatric Association, *Diagnostic and Statistical Manual of Mental Disorders, 4th ed.* (Washington, D.C.: American Psychiatric Association, 1994).

14. Atle Dyregrov, Leila Gupta, Rolf Gjestad, Eugenie Mukanoheli, "Trauma Exposure and Psychological Reactions to Genocide Among Rwandan Children," *Journal of Traumatic Stress* 13 (January 2000): 3–21.

15. Selby Jacobs, Carolyn Mazure, and Holly Prigerson, "Diagnostic Criteria for Traumatic Grief," *Death Studies* 24 (April–May 2000): 187.

16. Dora Black, "Childhood Bereavement," *British Medical Journal* 312 (June 1996): 1496.

17. Richard D. Goldstein, Nina S. Wampler, and Paul H. Wise, "War Experiences and Distress Symptoms of Bosnian Children," *Pediatrics* 100 (November 1997): 873–878; Mona Macksoud, J. Lawrence Aber, and Ilene Cohn, "Assessing the Impact of War on Children," in Apfel and Simon, eds., *Minefields in Their Hearts*, 218–230.

18. Eth and Pynoos, *Post-traumatic Stress Disorder in Children*, 29.

19. Ibid.

20. Not his real name.

21. Anitha Ronstrom, "Children in Central America: Victims of War," *Child Welfare* 68 (March–April 1989): 145–153.

22. Dora Black, "Bereavement in Childhood," *British Medical Journal* 316 (March 1998): 931–933.

23. Cynthia Blomquist, "Comfort for the Grieving Child," in Kilbourn, ed., *Healing the Children of War*, 51–65.

24. Raveis, Siegel, and Karus, "Children's Psychological Distress," 165–180.

25. Dyregrov, Gupta, Gjestad, and Mukanoheli, "Traumatic War Experiences and Their Effects on Children," 16.

26. Spencer Eth and Robert S. Pynoos, "Developmental Perspective on Psychic Trauma in Childhood," in *Trauma and Its Wake*, vol. 1, Charles R. Figley, ed. (New York: Brunner/Mazel, 1985), 36–52.

27. United Nations, *Promotion and Protection of the Rights of Children*, paragraph 30.

# Lessons and Literature

Anyone who doubts that the writing of history books for schoolchildren—or for any audience, for that matter—is subjective, messy, and highly politicized should observe the Texas State Board of Education's textbook review process, "an exercise," according to a wry account of a recent round of hearings, "in the short-sighted leading the stone-blind bravely into the pitch-darkness." The most contentious category is normally the social sciences; the public hearings, the committee's own comments, and the media coverage surrounding the Board's approval of the books that every school district in the state must choose from demonstrates that history, far from being a dead topic, is alive with meanings and values that can change from generation to generation. Special interest groups and amateur historians enter the fray, as do editorial writers, opportunistic politicians, and publishers desperate to tap into the potentially huge profits of the Texas textbook market. A text that finally emerges from this chaos, according to Michael King's 1996 article in the left-leaning newsmagazine, *The Texas Observer*:

> has less in common with, say, a real book of history, than it does with a ritualized, patriotic public relations pageant. Whatever else it includes, a social studies textbook is certain to be full of bright colors, uplifting noises, and ponderous hot-air balloons, like a hard-cover Thanksgiving Day Parade.

Although factual errors or perceived factual errors, reading levels, and other relatively objective points do enter the debate, most of the sparks fly over such issues as race—the extent to which slavery had a positive influence on its victims, for instance, or how to handle violence committed in the name of civil rights; foreign policy—the Cold War, especially in the long shadow of the Vietnam War and the arms race, tends to be a hot topic; and religion—whether or not the founding fathers were Christians and whether or not the United States is a "Christian nation." Groups like the Daughters of the American Revolution, veterans' organizations, and fundamentalist

Christian groups are often the most vocal critics, but everyone has his or her say about the appropriate content and emphases of the textbooks.

The end result of this process is less important than the tumult it inspires and what it reveals about the ways that countries and cultures try to influence the learning of history. The books they read in and out of school can be among the greatest influences on the formation of children's values and interests. Since the nineteenth century, with the rise of universal education and the creation of a vibrant children's book publishing industry in most developed and developing nations, schools and literature have been potent agents of socialization and politicization of the next generation. As a result, changing interpretations of historical events are yanked out of abstract academic circles and into the hot seat of public policy. It is important what we teach our children, and how we teach our children, and what meanings those children take away from their studies.

Nowhere does the potential for bitter controversy over the content of textbooks lurk as close to the surface as in Japan, where debates over how to explain the country's motivations and conduct during the Second World War hinge on subtle choices of words, cultural assumptions, and attitudes toward Japan's relationships with former enemies and current allies. For instance, a 1982 report—later determined to be mistaken—that the Education Ministry had required that history textbooks change the wording in passages related to Japanese expansion into other parts of Asia prior to the Second World War from "invasion" to "advance" inspired both China and South Korea to lodge official diplomatic protests. The Tokyo government responded by adding a new requirement to future textbooks that they "show the necessary consideration for international understanding and international harmony in their treatment of the events of modern and contemporary history." The normally internal debate over content of schoolbooks had suddenly been immersed in foreign policy. Similar controversies have arisen over coverage of the Korean "comfort women" forced to act as prostitutes for Japanese soldiers fighting in Japan.

A backlash has recently appeared against what critics call the "masochistic" version of Japanese history that has prevailed in schoolbooks ever since 1945 and was confirmed in the apology issued by a government official in 1993 regarding the use of "comfort women": "we hereby reiterate our firm determination never to repeat the same mistake by forever engraving such issues in our memories through the study and teaching of history." Comprised of academics, teachers, and journalists who believe that present-day textbooks ignore the conditions and realities of the past, organizations like the Society to Make New History Textbooks called for a more balanced and less condemnatory presentation of the past. They complain that modern texts present everything Japan did prior to the Second World War as aggression against the rest of Asia, and that, according to a spokesperson, the books are "full of hatred against our own country."

Obviously, the stakes in explaining history to young people are very high. How will past actions of any country be presented to the boys and girls who will one day become voters and leaders? Laura Hein and Mark Selden are the editors of *Censoring History*, a recent anthology examining the textbook writing and review processes in Japan, Germany, and the United States; they argue that "Schools and textbooks are important vehicles through which contemporary societies transmit ideas of citizenship and both the idealized past and the promised future of the community." Properly conceived, "they provide authoritative narratives of the nation, delimit proper behavior of citizens, and sketch the parameters of the national imagination."

This section deals with schoolbooks, but also with children's magazines and artistic representations of war and articles from parenting journals; the intended audiences are not necessarily children. Yet they all wrestle with similar questions: How should war and conflict be presented to children? What lessons can be learned from victory and defeat? How does the history of past wars relate to the present and the future? What lessons do the experiences of children in wartime hold for adults?

*Chapter Eight*

# Representations of War and Martial Heroes in English Elementary School Reading and Rituals, 1885–1914

## *Stephen Heathorn*

> It is a characteristic of a healthy child's nature to delight in action. Stirring events, such as battles at sea and on land, and adventures of all kinds, have a strong attraction for boys. Nor need we hesitate to indulge this natural taste, so long as we keep within reasonable bounds. Whatever may be thought of "drum and trumpet" history, as it is termed, its influence in giving a liking for the subject is important, and should be kept in view in school teaching.

So wrote John Landon in his teachers' manual of 1894.[1] Landon, while clearly addressing objections to this position, was certainly not alone in his views. In English elementary schools in the period 1885–1914, working- and lower-middle-class students, particularly but not exclusively the boys, were explicitly instructed in the importance of martial values. Representations of warfare and warrior heroes literally surrounded schoolchildren from a very early age: War was a central theme in the books that taught them to read; classroom decorations were often prints of famous battles, of soldiers and sailors in uniform, or of historic battleships; war games structured schoolyard play; military drill was the preferred means of physical education; and the memorializing of great wartime victories was the rationale for special celebration days and rituals in the school calendar. This short essay

can only hint at the myriad ways in which a glamorous image of war saturated the reading and rituals of the English working-class elementary school
at the turn of the century.[2] Yet, even a cursory inspection reveals that the
omnipresence of martial values in these schools was both a form of social
prescription and a symptom of what John Gillis and Geoffrey Best have
called the cultural militarization of British society in the three decades before World War I.[3]

## Citizenship, Patriotism, and the Glory of the Battlefield

Although education remained class-stratified in nineteenth-century England, elementary schooling had become both compulsory and subsidized
by local taxes by the 1880s.[4] However, the rise of a more democratic polity
caused by the Third Reform (1884) and Redistribution Acts (1885) gener-
ated concern that teaching the "three Rs" (reading, writing, and arithmetic)
was insufficient education for the increasingly enfranchised masses. Classroom instruction in "good citizenship" was now advocated as a means to inculcate working-class boys into the dictates of social respectability, national
responsibility, and imperial duty. Meanwhile, instruction in domestic duties
and "racial motherhood" was advocated for working-class girls.[5] The advocates of using elementary schools as workshops of civic training came from
all political positions and parties. Both liberals and conservatives approved
of educating students in their "imperial duties," although what this meant
was debated between the liberal advocates of "national efficiency" and the
more conservative proponents of aggressively advancing the empire or en-
acting peace-time conscription.[6] Some liberals and socialists objected to the
"flag-waving imperialism" and "war-mongering" in the later 1890s, and especially during and after the Boer War. However, most of the objections
raised about the content of the elementary curriculum tended to focus on
denominational religious issues rather than on implicit nationalism. Moreover, the objections raised by pacifist and socialist groups tended to be po-
litely received by local school officials at public hearings, only to be totally
ignored when it came to educational practice.[7]

For boys especially, martial values and corporatist ideals were prescribed
as central to the aim of imparting these ideas of good citizenship in the elementary school.[8] Fear of falling behind continental neighbors, the military
security of the empire, and the possibility of the collapse of Britain's com-

mercial world-leadership, were all connected to the need to reform schools.[9] Curriculum reform couched in militarist rhetoric was increasingly mirrored in classroom culture, which came to depict war and martial values as romantic and chivalrous in order to reinforce youthful nationalism. Although present throughout the period 1885–1914, this militarism in the classroom was especially marked in the years after the Boer War (1899–1902).

A whole spate of teachers' instructional manuals propounded the importance of the teaching of citizenship and patriotism in the elementary classroom in the later 1880s and 1890s. The use of history, either in directed lessons, or more commonly in reading books with historical content, was advocated by educationalists as the most appropriate way to develop a civic and patriotic understanding among the young. David Salmon's *The Art of Teaching* (1898) noted simply, "History fosters patriotism." His reasoning was typical of the educational establishment's view of the merits of history instruction: "It fills the student with admiration for his forefathers' wisdom, heroism, and devotion to duty, which have made the nation what it is; with longings for a chance of emulating their glorious deeds; and failing that, with a firm resolve to do nothing that shall tarnish the fair fame of their common country, and to pay the debt which he owes his ancestors, by transmitting down entire those sacred rights to which he himself was born."[10] This view of the need to instill reverence for the glorious deeds of the child's forefathers also became government-recommended policy. In 1905, the national Board of Education suggested that classroom reading be tailored to what children could readily understand: "personal character and prowess, adventure, discovery, invention, war." Consequently, the most appropriate topics of history instruction were "the Crusades, the Civil War, the reign of Elizabeth, the great wars for Colonial Supremacy, and the war of American Independence."[11] Moreover, in order to strengthen patriotism, the Board thought it desirable that history be made into a stirring and enjoyable subject. The mid-Victorian style of teaching—lessons in which the names of monarchs, generals, and events were simply memorized—ought to be replaced with reading lively stories and biographies, and historical romances.

Textbook writers and publishers were actually ahead of the government in revamping the types of books produced for classroom reading. Most of the "readers" authored and produced in the period 1885–1914 were designed—with commercial considerations foremost—to make reading as engaging as possible.[12] Regardless of their supposed subject (English, history, geography, civics, domestic economy), they often employed narratives of war and martial adventure. For instance, John Finnemore's series *Famous Englishmen* (1901), a two-volume set of readers widely used to develop reading skills, was actually a catalogue of military adventures, which valorized the warrior exploits of heroes of the battlefield. The type of deeds that made someone a "famous Englishman" is made clear in the following excerpt from Finnemore's treatment of the Saxon king Harold and his last stand at the Battle of Hastings: "The bravest and the boldest of the Normans charged fiercely to capture the Dragon Standard, but charged in vain. Harold, at the head of his men, fought like a hero. Before the sweeping stroke of his tremendous axe down went horse and rider crushed at a single blow. . . ."[13] Similarly, the following passage about the naval battle of Cape Vincent could easily be mistaken for a G. A. Henty juvenile novel, yet it is from a volume of the *Raleigh History Readers*: "Our ships threw the Spanish fleet into confusion, and the men of Nelson's ship jumped on board an enemy's ship, which was closely locked with his and captured it. . . . Nelson, inspiring his men by the words, 'Victory, or Westminster Abbey!' leaped on [to a second ship], and soon the Union Jack replaced the Spanish flag at the mast-head of this second prize."[14]

The romance and glory of the battlefield were ubiquitous themes in the new elementary school readers. Both victories and defeats were glamorized. Finnemore's account of the Battle of Waterloo was again typical. No explanation of why the battle was fought was provided; rather, the description starts with a conversation about how the famous Englishman, in this case the Duke of Wellington, was to win the battle: "My plan," Wellington was reported to have said, "consists in dying here to the last man." It was then reported how, during the battle, Wellington had given his soldiers encouragement, to which his troops replied, "Never fear, sir, we know our duty." The result of fulfilling this duty was then made plain:

> Man by man, file by file, rank by rank, they had fallen, preserving in death the iron order in which discipline and their own stout hearts called upon them to die. Seen through the battle smoke, the regular rows of the slain, who had given up their lives rather than the ground upon which they stood, looked like a living square. That is how Waterloo was won.[15]

The glamour of this sacrifice was also evident in the disastrous defeats and blunders that also found their way into readers of all types. "Heroic" defeats were given the romanticized gloss common to regimental histories. The infamous destruction of the Light Brigade during the Crimean War, for example, received generous attention in many history readers. A reader published in 1904 conveys the typical treatment of this episode:

> By some mistake a wrong order was given. The six hundred men of the Light Brigade were told to attack the whole Russian army.
>
> The men felt the order was wrong, yet no one hesitated. They dashed grandly on through the thousands of Russians, cutting their way as they went. Then they turned back but "not the six hundred." Only one hundred and ninety came back. The rest were dead, or wounded, or left as prisoners in the hands of the Russians. It was a glorious deed, and inspired Tennyson to write a great poem about it.[16]

Death in battle in these accounts is depicted as glorious and worthy of poetry. Indeed, Tennyson's "war" poetry figured frequently in both English and history readers. Perhaps the most popular was his 1878 poetic rendering of the tale of Richard Grenville's ship *The Revenge*. The Elizabethan "sea dog" Grenville had allowed his ship to be destroyed rather than surrender to fifty-three Spanish vessels. School inspectors found that this story and Tennyson's poem were favorites in the elementary school classroom.[17] Many educators endorsed the use of such stories, although F. H. Hayward was critical of the lesson that was being conveyed:

> The teacher may ask . . . whether the sailors of any other country than England would have fought as bravely as Grenville's men. The class unanimously answers "no." . . . There is something unwholesome in the unanimity above referred to; it is so utterly foreign to the plainest facts of history and human nature.[18]

The liberal Hayward rebelled against the nationalist stereotype that he rightly believed was understood by the children reading these stories.

"Common" seamen and soldiers also received praise in school lessons and reading, both for loyalty to their superiors and for their own "plucky" actions:[19] "the common seamen were worthy of their commanders. They loved their country, and would have died for their commanders. They cheerfully put up with the bad and scanty food."[20] Officers and men were thus locked together in these stories: The officers were always brave and doing the *right* thing; the men were always brave and loyal to their superiors. Such accounts of battlefield heroics and loyalty were almost always accompanied by romantic illustrations, making use of new technology for inexpensive color pictures. The combined effect—further reinforced by the prints of battles or other military themes often hanging on the classroom walls and by ceremonial marching and saluting the flag on Queen Victoria's Birthday (the later) Empire Day and other special occasions—was to glamorize warfare, valorize physical sacrifice, and depict martial figures as the essence of English heroism.[21]

## Romancing the Military Hero

The figure of the soldier/sailor was cast as the individual around which elementary school boys, in particular, should model their own identity. In the romantic depictions of warfare and military adventure which formed the core of both historical and fictional reading, the whole of the narrative tended to be subordinated to the activities of martial hero. School books here mirrored literary romance, wherein the heroic deeds of the protagonist were part of a worthy quest. Readers usually identify the hero as a figure of desirable and virtuous masculinity. Glorified and depicted in romantically structured narratives, historical martial figures provided the role models for the sort of masculine patriotism that was held to be at the core of good citizenship.

Perhaps the epitome of the English military hero in this period was General "Chinese" Gordon, accounts of whom were featured in every history reader published after 1885 and in teachers' lesson plans as well.[22] Gordon's death at Khartoum in 1885 was depicted as more than simply heroic: It was seen as martyrdom for imperial English virtues and values. Gordon was represented as the exemplary Englishman; he was brave, steadfast, dignified, charitable, kind, and above all, dutiful.[23] But it was the death of this man, "beloved by all his countrymen," that was especially revered.[24] Gordon's death, "fighting for his queen and country" in a faraway place and supposedly without any thought for his own fame or legacy, demonstrated the classroom moral that "those who love their country best are content to serve it without the hope of immediate reward, or even the encouragement of praise."[25]

Another figure of immense symbolic stature was Admiral Lord Nelson. Logbooks and other school records attest that many elementary school teachers spent a disproportionate amount of time discussing his "deeds."[26] Nelson was depicted as one who overcame many personal difficulties through the strength of his character, eventually sacrificing his life for his nation in its time of need.[27] A volume of the *King Alfred Readers* (1900) proclaimed that students should never forget that Nelson's "strength was in his heart and in his will, not in his body."[28] Nelson was consistently pointed to as the kind of leader the young should emulate.[29]

The association of Nelson's greatness with his will rather than with his natural physical (dis)abilities—he had already lost an arm and an eye, among other wounds, by the time of his final battle in 1805—suggested that what made Nelson heroic and worthy of emulation was his attention to duty and willingness to sacrifice. Attention to duty was regarded as something uniquely English in some reading books. One reader reported that:

> English sailors were brave and skillful, and they had one admiral—Horatio Nelson—who was as great a commander by sea as Napoleon was by land, and was, beside, a much better man; for while Napoleon was always thinking of himself and his own glory, Nelson thought only how he might best do his duty to England.[30]

Glory and sacrifice on the battlefield, as the examples of Nelson and Gordon demonstrated, were motivated by this sense of duty: the nationalist purpose of celebrating warrior heroes was here quite explicit.

Duty, and its corollary, discipline, had multiple meanings in the classroom: obedience to teachers and other figures of authority was shrouded in martial symbolism.

The very specific social context of elementary education gave martial metaphors a socially specific function. For example, one civics reader ended a description of the British armed forces by suggesting:

> [w]hen boys and girls go out of school in order, one by one, class by class, they show that they have learnt the use of discipline. When they do their drill, moving their hands or feet together at the word of command, they show that they have learnt the use of discipline.[31]

The discipline of the military was thus projected into the classroom in an effort to create social deference. Another general reader was even more direct in making the analogy between school and the military. Under the heading, "little soldiers," the text suggested:

> Little boys like to play at soldiers. They make paper caps and wooden swords. Then they march together like little men. Some play on their toy trumpets.
>
> Now let us think we are soldiers in school. Here we are sitting all in a very straight row. Heads up! Eyes Straight!
>
> Who is the officer? Why, the teacher, of course. He calls, "Fold arms!" We must obey at once like the soldiers.

Then he says "Look at me!" Every eye is turned to our officer, just like the real soldiers in the street.

We are little soldiers. We have learnt to obey at once, and with happy smiling faces. This makes the school hours pass very pleasantly.[32]

Children learning to obey orders from their "teacher-officer" suggested that classroom discipline was as important, as necessary, and as enjoyable, as that of the lives of "real" soldiers, whom the children were clearly thought to admire. Social obedience to figures of authority was thus figured into the everyday practices of the classroom. But in passages like those above, the value that was placed on military virtues infused such exercises in classroom discipline with social prescription, all the while cloaking them in "national" indispensability.

## Drilling for Discipline

Martial discipline was also central to the main form of physical exercise instruction practiced in elementary schooling: drill. This was the performance of stylized physical movements in the playground. When first advocated, in the early decades of the nineteenth century, drill was an extension of the ethos of the mid-Victorian classroom in which all manner of tasks were done in step-by-step unison: forming lines before and after instruction; strict maintenance of correct posture; and regimented movements in the classroom. These activities were thought to help teach obedience and discipline, inculcate respect for law and order, and help to eradicate the pauperism caused by inbred and inherited moral shortcomings. Drill was thought to diminish the desire of the poorer child to commit crime, to create an aversion to personal sloth and idleness, and to reduce impatience and individual disobedience.[33] Clearly, drill had very little to do with physical fitness or well-being.

In the last decades of the century, the insistence on keeping drill in the curriculum retained many of these aims, but it also became associated with more overtly martial themes. To remove any possible doubt about the intentions of drilling students, the word "military" was inserted into its description in the Education Code of 1875.[34] Drill now became part of the process whereby working-class children were to be socialized in a properly regulated and military-like fashion. Organized drill in the 1870s and 1880s increasingly took the form of calisthenics and regularized periods of marching and parade-ground activities.[35] By the 1890s, local educational authorities, like the London School Board, were organizing huge drill competitions in which precision marching, club-tossing, and other exercises were all part of a great military-tattoo-like spectacle.[36]

This association of drill with military as opposed to physical educational purposes was contested. In the later 1880s and 1890s, social reformers tried repeatedly to have drill replaced with other, less militarized forms of physical exercise, including organized games and swimming. Innovative physical education was advocated by reformers as desirable in the "full healthy development" of each child, and as the means by which the lives of the working class as a whole might be improved.[37] Yet despite the growing interest in progressive schools for fitness systems like Ling's Swedish Gymnastics, drill remained the national Board of Education's favored and heavily promoted form of physical education throughout the period 1885–1914.[38]

The continuing relevance of military drill was in fact given a major boost during the Anglo-Boer War (1899–1902), when a full-scale debate on the place of drill within elementary schools erupted in the House of Commons and in the popular press. The poor physical condition of British volunteers in the early days of the war caused numerous politicians to argue that education in general, and physical education in particular, were not serving the "best interests of the nation."[39] Drill was advocated as a means to improve the physique of working-class boys, and many commentators called for drill that was more directly related to military considerations, including the use of dummy rifles. It was argued that these measures were necessary in order "to lay the foundations of a military spirit in the nation."[40] In 1902, at the end of the Boer War, the War Office, in consultation with the Board of Education, issued instructions to all General Officers Commanding Districts (the regional commanders of the British army) that they should assist schools in the promotion and teaching of drill whenever possible.[41] While some school authorities, like the London School Board, resisted this development, throughout the period physical training was typically urged as a "national concern, involving issues that permanently affected the character of the race."[42] Commentators right up to 1914 ominously warned that the "neglect of physical training has caused empire after empire to dwindle, crumble and finally fall to pieces."[43] Consequently, in most elementary schools, drill remained a core part of the curriculum.

## Conclusion

It is quite remarkable that since the impetus behind the calls for teaching good citizenship was the expansion of the franchise, very little effort seems to have been expended in teaching children about the nature of voting or the workings of parliamentary institutions.[44] Instead, martial themes in elementary school reading and rituals amalgamated ideas about English nationality with appropriate social and gender roles in a way that was suggestive of what "citizenship" actually entailed. The upholding of a masculine identity based on martial duty and discipline was presented as integral to citizenship and national identity. True citizens were those who emulated the great Englishmen of the past, and did "their duty" just as unhesitatingly as had Nelson or Gordon. And while it was not expected that all working-class boys (and certainly no girls) would become soldiers—although that was clearly an overt duty of citizenship in times of national crisis—all ought to emulate their forebears' example in daily life, primarily through deference to authority and willingness to sacrifice when called on by the nation.

Martial values have long been associated with the elite private educational institutions of Britain—the public schools—where members of the upper classes were trained for their imperial leadership duties. And much of the reforming rhetoric at the end of the nineteenth century was directed at reinforcing this educational effort as well. But elementary schools, long the preserve of the working- and lower-middle classes were, until the 1880s, mostly concerned with basic literacy, promoting moral virtues, and inculcating social deference. It was only from the 1880s on that martial and overtly nationalist values were added to the socializing project of elementary schooling, precisely at the moment when most of the male working class was granted real political power. And clearly, for the elementary student these martial values were those of the lowly soldier who was to follow orders, not of the elite officer who was to lead. The glorification of martial values, and the romantic projection of war in the classroom, thus seems to have been connected with the reinforcing of established social boundaries. However, the ease with which the liberal state in Britain called on millions of working-class volunteers between 1914 and 1918, and quickly and readily transformed their society into one geared for total war, suggests that elementary education also had its part to play in the process of cultural militarization that allowed this remarkable feat to occur.

Notes

I wish to thank Kevin Cramer for his assistance in preparing this essay.

1. John Landon, *The Principles and Practice of Teaching and Class Management* (London: Alfred Holden, 1894), 395.

2. Typicality, authorship, and readership issues regarding the school books cited are fully discussed in my monograph, *For Home, Country and Race.*

3. John Gillis, "Introduction" in Gillis, ed., *The Militarization of the Western World*, 1–10.

4. Hurt, *Elementary Schooling and the Working Classes.*

5. Heathorn, *For Home, Country and Race*, 24–55.

6. Ibid., 4–7, 27–38.

7. Ibid., 207–211.

8. See, for example, J. G. Fitch, *Lectures on Teaching* (London: W. B. Clive, 1906), 97–98; James Welton, *Principles and Methods of Teaching* (London: W. B. Clive, 1906), 227; W. F. Trotter, *The Citizen and His Duties* (London: T. C. and E. C. Jack, 1907), 7–8.

9. Heathorn, *For Home, Country and Race*, 24–55, 141–176.

10. David Salmon, *The Art of Teaching* (New York: Longmans, Green, 1898), 213.

11. *Suggestions for the Consideration of Teachers and Others concerned in the work of the Public Elementary Schools*, Cd. 2638, Vol. LX (1905), 61–64. All quotations are from the history section, which was reprinted as Board of Education Circular No. 599, *The Teaching of History* (1908), 1–7.

12. Stephen Heathorn, "English Elementary Education and the Construction of National Identity, 1880–1914" (Ph.D. dissertation, University of Toronto, 1996), 78–120 and appendices.

13. John Finnemore, *Famous Englishmen I* (London: Adam and Charles Black, 1901), 8–9.

14. *Raleigh History Readers* V (London: Blackie, 1896), 166.

15. Finnemore, *Famous Englishmen* I, 127–128.

16. *King Edward History Readers* II (London: Pitman, 1904), 169.

17. Public Record Office [hereafter PRO], Ed. 14/95, *Report on the Teaching of English in London Elementary Schools* (Aug. 1908), Appendices; Ed. 14/96, *Report on the Supply and Use of Books in London Elementary Schools* (Nov. 1912), 2.

18. Landon, *Principles and Practice*, 406; F. H. Hayward, *The Primary Curriculum* (London: Ralph, Holland, 1909), 28.

19. *The Warwick History Readers* II (London: Blackie, 1895), 68.

20. *Raleigh History Readers* IV, 193.

21. Mackenzie, *Propaganda and Empire*, 183; Pamela Horn, "English Elementary Education and the Growth of the Imperial Ideal, 1880–1914," in Mangan, ed.,

*Benefits Bestowed?*, 44–45; Anne Bloomfield, "Drill and Dance as Symbols of Imperialism," in Mangan, ed., *Making Imperial Mentalities*, 75–76.

22. Bristol Record Office [hereafter BRO], Eastville Board School, *Log Book* (1892), 78; Greater London Record Office [hereafter GLRO], Cobold Rd. Board School, *Log Book* (1900), 45.

23. *Longman's New Historical Readers* IV (London: Longman, 1888), 193.

24. *Chambers's Alternative History Readers* IV (London: Chambers, 1898), 160.

25. H. O. Arnold-Forster, *Citizen Reader* (London: Cassell, 1887), 26.

26. BRO, "Syllabus and notes on curriculum," St. Philip's National School, *Log Book* (1904), 16. GLRO, "Notes on lessons," Drayton Park Board School, *Log Book* (1894), 1.

27. *Tower History Readers* VI (London: Pitman, 1911), 101.

28. *The King Alfred Readers* III (London: Edward Arnold, 1900), 43.

29. *Raleigh History Readers* V, 166; *Chambers's Alternative History Readers* V, 145.

30. *Simple Outline of English History* (London: Cassell, 1884), 168.

31. Arnold-Forster, *Citizen Reader*, 102.

32. *The King Alfred Readers* I, 15–16.

33. J. S. Hurt, "Drill, Discipline and the Elementary School Ethos," in McCann, ed., *Popular Education and Socialization in the Nineteenth Century*, 169–170.

34. See the *Report of the Committee of Council on Education, 1869–70*, C. 165, Vol. XXII.1 (1870), cxxxvi; *Minute Modifying Provisions of New Code*, C. 1192, Vol. LVIII.73 (1875); and also *Parliamentary Debates*, 3rd Series, Vol. 223, Col. 1203–4.

35. F. M. Normon, *The Schoolmasters' Drill Assistant: A Manual of Drill for Elementary Schools* (London: Cassell, 1871), 3; Penn, *Targetting Schools*.

36. Hugh Philpott, *London at School: The Story of the School Board, 1870–1904* (London: T. Fisher Unwin, 1904), 116–118.

37. P. C. McIntosh, *Physical Education in England Since 1800* (London: Edward Arnold, 1952), 146–148.

38. PRO Ed. 22/3B, *Model Course of Physical Training* (1901); Board of Education, *Syllabus of Physical Exercises for Use in Public Elementary Schools* (1909), vii.

39. *Parliamentary Debates* 4th Series, Vol. 79, Col. 410, and Vol. 81. Col. 831.

40. The 1902 Code specified the use of the manual *Infantry Drill, 1902*. See McIntosh, *Physical Education in England*, 139–140. For the use of dummy rifles, see Norman Lockyer, *Education and National Progress: Essays and Addresses, 1870–1905* (London: Longmans, Green, 1906), 241.

41. Letter from Adjutant General, July 1902, PRO Ed. 22/36.

42. C. Dukes, "Health and Physical Culture," in P. A. Barnett, ed., *Teaching and Organisation* (London: Longmans, Green, 1903), 362.

43. G. M. Campbell, "Physical Training" in J. Adams, ed., *The New Teaching*

(London: Hodder and Stoughton, 1918), 357. For other similar statements see John Gorst, *The Children of the Nation* (London: Methuen, 1906), 1; C. Jackson, *Outlines of Education in England* (London: Mowbray, 1913), 86–89.

44. Stephen Heathorn, "'For Home, Country and Race': The Gendered Ideals of Citizenship in English Elementary and Evening Continuation Schools, 1885–1914," *Journal of the Canadian Historical Association* 7 (1996): 105–124.

# Chapter Nine

# The Child in the Flying Machine
## *Childhood and Aviation in the First World War*

### *Guillaume de Syon*

In September 1914, a postcard entitled *"le taube"* circulated in France. *"Le taube"* was a Gallicism of the German word for "dove," and the "dove" shown was actually a German airplane similar to the one that had flown over Paris on a reconnaissance mission that month. The picture of a courageous mother shielding her child framed the inscription, "Your birds do not scare us." In its depiction of a mother and child in war, *"le taube"* exemplified the representation in popular culture and propaganda of several features of total war, including the increased involvement of civilians and the application of new technologies. In particular, *"le taube"* captured one aspect of Europeans' relationship to the machinery of war—the new prominence of aviation—while negotiating another modernism: the widespread involvement of children in war.

By exploring the intersection of childhood and flight as represented during World War I, this essay will argue that the adult world made use of the idealized constructs of youth and aviation to come to terms with total war; in so doing, it reinforced what one historian has identified as the trivialization of warfare.[1] As the conflict dragged on and transformed the home front, the intersection of childhood and flight took on multiple meanings: Children were portrayed as victims but also as future warriors, while flight was infantilized to help adults accept technology's new destructiveness. At base, the line between adulthood and childhood, drawn across the nineteenth century, became blurred.

3 Septembre 1914       L. MADRASSI, Sc

"Le Taube" (dove). This depiction of a mother protecting her child in the early weeks of the war appeared in direct response to German overflights of Paris. The somewhat naïve comment, "Your birds do not scare us," reflects the lack of danger awareness that pervaded the first months of World War I. When Zeppelin bombings began in 1915, such attitudes shifted. *Author's Collection.*

## The Romanticization of Flight and Childhood

Both inventions of nineteenth-century Europe, childhood and aviation were hallmarks of the modern era. With the rise of bourgeois Europe, childhood developed into a sacred sphere, where Rousseauian ideals emphasized the innocence of the child who was to be cherished and taught away from the adult world.[2] Although a reality only in 1903, flight was also romanticized in countless works of nineteenth-century fiction. Rarely seen as a means to either commercial or military ends, aviation entranced adults and children alike with its promise of a magic-filled future.[3] The fundamental challenge World War I posed to these dual ideals can be traced through popular culture, another form of modernism. Penny literature, postcards, mass-produced toys, bibelot, board games, books, and the tabloid media reflected the impact of industrialization on young and old Europeans; with the outbreak of hostilities, they also quickly reflected the impact of total war.

With the development of a new home front culture, the adult world spawned popular culture and propaganda, including books, toys, and school lessons, in order to ensure a moral and intellectual mobilization of children.[4] With the home front geared toward supporting the war effort, gender roles changed, but so, too, did the social standing of children; with fathers leaving for the front and mothers for the workplace, children assumed more adult responsibilities at home.[5] In the wake of this confrontation with violence, popular culture articulated new themes while simultaneously rearticulating older ideas. Most strikingly, although constructed as a safe haven, youth culture had idealized notions of fighting from the late nineteenth century onward, placing a heavy premium on visual evidence to romanticize war.[6] This tendency became increasingly pronounced under the pressure of total war, as was evident in the images of childhood and aviation in many forms of popular culture.

## The Early Airplane as Toy and Inspiration

In 1914, the flying machine was barely a decade old, and for half its lifetime had served largely as a tool of entertainment and prestige. An expression of modernist culture, the plane's acceptance was slow; most Europeans deemed it only for the foolhardy. Indeed, few armies foresaw the potential of the airplane beyond reconnaissance missions: The machine was unstable, fragile, and subject to the vagaries of the weather.[7] When Marshall Foch suggested dismissively before the war that airplanes were useless militarily but promising as toys, his assessment echoed the sentiments of many Europeans. Manufacturers could attest to the popular fascination with early flight as they capitalized on parents' eagerness to please their sons with airplane replicas. At playparks, children might pull the traditional wheeled

Gondry *éditeur* , *Paris*
727. Aérodrome Parisien, Chemin, Propriétaire

A Parisian merry-go-round. Mr. Chemin's idea to depict French dirigibles in lieu of traditional horses was such a success that it became the subject of a postcard sold in the area where the machine was set up. Ca. 1905. *Author's Collection.*

horse or sail a boat on the pond, but they could also test rubber band-driven toy planes and ride on merry-go-rounds in airships and airplanes.[8] The novelty of industrial warfare offered new avenues of entertainment to adults as well as children. So-called "anticipation novels" such as those by H. G. Wells suggested the dirigible would soon supplant naval dreadnoughts, and children often read adventures about imaginary airplanes racing each other on treasure quests.[9]

Flying machines in the prewar years were not, however, simply objects of innocent fun. By 1908, popular fascination with the flying machine also played into nationalist agendas, whereby the mastery of new technologies would demonstrate the superiority of a nation over its competitors. Pilots, initially viewed with a mix of disdain and begrudging admiration, gained in status, as was evident in children's games: French children admired Blériot, who had crossed the Channel in 1909, while their German counterparts lionized Count Zeppelin.[10] By the time war broke out, the public understood the importance of aviation as a nationalist symbol and a potential weapon, to the point where state-sponsored fund drives and parliamentary initiatives raised sufficient funds to begin building several air forces in Europe.

Reality differed considerably from serialized fiction, however, as air combat tactics barely existed, and no one could forecast accurately how fighters and bombers might affect the popular imagination. It was only the actual start of hostilities that fostered real widespread awareness of the airplane's potential destructive power and danger to civilians.[11] In grappling with the new violence of flight, Europeans produced numerous forms of representation; commonly, they invoked children as symbols of the unprecedented pressures of total war.

## Children as Victims

Not surprisingly in a war that erased the safe boundary between front and home front, children figured prominently as victims in wartime representations. The haphazard nature of air strikes (precision bombing did not exist) produced thousands of civilian victims of the flying machine, including children. Newspapers covering these losses detailed the family members who had died. In such cases, columnists found that simply citing the ages of the deceased children stirred their readership and focused popular anger on the faceless foe. At the most basic level, such incidents jolted readers into a new awareness of aviation's dangers, prompting a multitude of different reactions.[12]

## Infantilizing Flight's Deadly Potential

The *Taube's* flight over Paris and the ensuing postcard was but one of several attempts to come to terms with aviation as a weapon. Oftentimes, the adult world faced such novelty by adopting the gaze of a child, for the flying machine still represented a fascinating mystery that inspired as well as terrified. Intellectuals such as Marcel Proust likened a German bombing raid to a group of angry Walkyries, and the street, too, used metaphors to refer to the new technologies of death. Just as the heavy Krupp cannons that hit Paris became known as "Big Berthas" to adults and children alike, flying machines were familiarized, as a child would identify a common object. Early in the war, any plane over Paris became a *"Taube,"* with other nicknames to emerge later. In France, Britain, and Germany, all dirigibles and blimps were dubbed Zeppelins, the object of admiration on the German side (and the occasion of cheering and chanting for children) and disdain on the part of the British and French. In all of these cases, Europeans attempted to render dangerous technology more familiar or even childlike and consequently less frightening. Transforming the machine into a living thing, akin to a bird, also suggested purpose for what had become anonymous carnage.[13] By infantilizing the flying machine, adults sought to come to terms with a new technology that turned dreams of flight into bombing nightmares; in the process, they helped to dissolve the perceived divide between adulthood and childhood.

## Bombers Peppering—Real Pepper

One very prominent means of rendering war less threatening was through a process of trivialization of its means and effects. As masterfully explored by George Mosse, an explosion of kitsch after 1914 throughout Europe served to glorify war while aiding in the acceptance of its horrors. Tin soldiers, for example, rendered war both realistic and fanciful, as they provided boys and adults hours of fun at their war games.[14] In the realm of flight, manufacturers who had capitalized on flight enthusiasm before the war developed a whole range of diverse offerings once the conflict began. In France, manufacturer F. Martin transformed a French Wright Flier by attaching it to a metal mobile balanced by a German "*Taube*," while another company affixed a cannon to a previously "civil" Voisin aircraft model. In Germany, Christmas ornaments came to include airships and biplanes alongside other imperial symbols. Board games also involved aerial combat; the English journal *Hobbies Weekly* suggested a woodcut design for teenagers that represented the downing of an airship.[15]

War conditions were unlikely to facilitate the purchase of entertainment items for children, and what sometimes appeared to be a toy may actually have been intended for an adult, as was the case with collectible salt and pepper shakers made of crest china. Although such items reflected an adult interest in the air world, they also tapped into the fascination and fear grown-ups felt when facing the war. When adults eager to catch sight of airships forsook safety measures such as blackouts and running to the basement, their irresponsibility testified to the complexity of adult responses to flight's deadly potential.[16] The need to demystify death contributed to the popularity of childlike toys; these may have reflected nostalgia for distant childhood or a simple desire for escapism. In all of these ways, the infantilization and trivialization of war as well as adult behavior served to destabilize the porous boundary between European adult and child.

## Learning about the War

As adults joined children in infantilizing flying machines to render them less threatening, popular culture and propaganda deployed other means of rendering war flight more palatable, including an intensified romanticization of the flying man. Most strikingly, the "birds" drew life from a new breed of soldiers: pilot heroes who dared the ultimate challenge.[17] By 1914, the foolish daredevil had become the stuff of myth, while increasingly new pilots who joined the military were depicted as epic knights. The dehumanization of trench warfare, where death struck anonymously, helps explain the popular fascination with newly minted "aces" (men who had achieved at least five aerial victories); such images contrasted markedly with the anonymity of infantry and artillery, suggesting that the new hero was not merely a fighter pilot, but someone who had mastery of the machine and deserved personal recognition for his lone actions.[18]

The idealization of the ace salved the horrors of war not only for adults, but for children as well. The marketing of these flight heroes to boys, targeted as future soldiers, represented a blurring of adulthood and childhood in both propaganda and popular culture. Arguably the most prominent example of this phenomenon was the propaganda surrounding French ace Georges Guynemer. Shot down in 1917 at age twenty-three, Guynemer was immediately cast as a figure for youth to emulate. In Paris, the publisher Larousse (known to generations of schoolchildren for its textbooks and dictionaries) published a biography of Guynemer within months of his death in its "*série rose*" designed for youth aged seven to thirteen, while special directives from the French Ministry of Education to French teachers stressed how schools should use the pilot's martyrdom to inculcate pupils with a stronger sense of civic duty and sacrifice. By equating Guynemer with earlier heroes of the French Revolution, the adult world modernized Republican myths in order to inspire younger generations.[19] In this way, the adult rendering of aviation's destructive potential was extended to children with little regard for the "safe haven" of childhood. Pre-adolescent boys were future fighters, and were addressed as such.

If boys were to be enthralled with the victories of their combatants in the sky, then nationalism was hardly to be eschewed in materials directed at them. This was clearly evident in German children's relationship to the airship.

Although all sides involved in the conflict used dirigibles, Germany was most committed to this kind of machinery based in part on Count Zeppelin's importance as a popular figure before the war.[20] Children's songs, repeated in schools and in games, stressed the inventor's "uniquely" German traits of duty, endeavor, and sacrifice. One children's poem proclaimed, "They do not have him and never will!"[21] In the world of youth culture, Count Zeppelin's exemplary courage would foil attempts at destroying Germany as the Zeppelin airship dropped bombs over cities such as London and Paris.

Attempts to inculcate German children with nationalism were hardly limited to Zeppelin representations. "War Books for the Youth," inexpensive booklets with two-color cover illustrations, reflected the defensive nationalism that sprang from the German fear of encirclement before the war. Often rendered with violent imagery, airplane attacks in the "War Books" were ends in themselves that proved Germanic superiority while demonstrating the utter barbarity of the enemy.[22] When depicting the air war, the books positioned the pilot as a lonely hero, one for whom sacrifice was the stuff of everyday life. Zeppelins attacked cities, for example, for the purpose of breaking a stalemate, akin to medieval knights laying siege to a castle. The parallel ended there, however. Designed to inculcate a profound dislike of the enemy, these youth fiction pieces brushed aside notions of the enemy as honorable, rendering him either faceless (a victim of bombings) or cunning (the enemy who bombed the home front). True, the episodes of air chivalry that occurred during the war, such as not firing on a pilot whose guns had jammed or throwing a wreath over the departure point of a downed enemy, were recorded in a manner that suggested medieval knights had simply traded their horses for airplanes.[23] While the official war record on both sides acknowledged this state of relative "fair play," however, in popular youth accounts, such gentlemanly behavior was mostly one-sided. The child reading such literature was to be manipulated into hatred, a hatred to be channeled into a utilitarian nationalism that would make any youth eager to reach his eighteenth birthday so he, too, could engage in the fighting.

Cherubs in love. This drawing of a little boy and his "girlfriend" typically reflects adult ideas depicted in childlike style. The female figure is a passenger, while the boy controls the plane. This French picture carried three comments, in each of the languages of the members of the Triple Entente: France, England, and Russia. *Author's Collection.*

## The Child as Hero and Warrior

In targeting boys as future soldiers, it is perhaps not surprising that war propaganda went one step further to the actual depiction of the child as warrior or hero. While there were instances of actual child soldiers in the Great War, such isolated cases were greatly exaggerated by rumor and propaganda. The notion of the child hero became a mainstay of war culture, often mimicking heroic David and Goliath exploits of previous wars. Only the means of destruction differed, as cherubs were depicted boarding planes and attacking large targets. By placing children in this context and portraying them as pre–grown-ups braving danger, adults articulated fantasies of wrath against the enemy while enjoying cheap entertainment.[24] They also clearly weakened the "safe sphere" of European childhood.

At the same time they created images of children at war, adults enhanced the fantasy of children as heroes by indulging in occasional images of gender equality. Despite episodic reports of "maiden heroism," notions of the child warrior traditionally emphasized the boy as the future defender of nation. The girl hero, when she did appear, generally did so as a supporting cast member (mimicking nurses, girlfriends, or mothers). But in infrequent episodes of imagination, girls assumed actual warrior status. In a play at Châtelet Theater in Paris in 1915, for example, a young French girl played the pilot attacking a Zeppelin.[25] While this Joan of Arc moment was rare, it highlighted the importance of gender to depictions of children in wartime propaganda and popular culture, and reminds us that, for most Europeans, child as a wartime construct equaled boy.

## The Intersection of Childhood and Aviation in Postcards

Of the numerous sources of propaganda and popular culture in War World I, perhaps the most illustrative of the varying images of childhood during the war was the postcard. A relatively recent invention at the time, the medium's golden age (1890–1914) had been characterized by thousands of designs, themes, and illustrations: any photograph of anyone or thing could, potentially, end up with a stamp and a message. Consequently, what was public and traveled openly also entered and influenced the private sphere of the home. Under conditions of war, censorship and the need for cheerful missives recast the industry into an engine for boosting the nationalist spirit and trivializing the war experience. Indeed, popular histories of the Great War assert that the conflict was in some ways fought with postcards.[26] The childhood motif was essential to this process on both sides of the trenches.

Postcards reproduced widely the range of themes evident in other representations of the child in propaganda and popular culture, including that of

"Horrible crimes of the Boches pirates." This photograph, one of a series approved by the French censorship board to increase hatred of the enemy, depicts two children, or possibly two sisters, in their bombed-out apartment after a Zeppelin raid. *Author's Collection.*

children as victims of the war. A typical example, a French postcard produced in 1916 in response to a Zeppelin bombing of Paris, pictured a mother and her child in front of their destroyed apartment. The title of the card, "Horrible crimes of the Boches pirates," requires no elaboration: A sacred space protecting childhood had been invaded and destroyed, with the horror of war evident for all to see.

While most cards were produced by free-standing photographers, established painters and designers were sometimes solicited by the media to produce cards that would involve children in a variety of settings. One of them, Poulbot, a cartoonist for the Parisian newspaper *Le Journal*, was arguably the most successful in defining the conditions of childhood in wartime Paris. The adult reception of such images varied, yet was positive enough to ensure that many of Poulbot's designs were reprinted in a book collection and as postcards.[27] In subtle and sentimental ways, Poulbot's postcards often underscored the position of children as innocents in an age of adult war. Children mimicked airplanes by jumping from small hills, or simulated aerial attacks on each other. Several designs involved children's reactions to Zeppelin attacks. Two boys, eyeing a public balloon merchant's merchandise, asked a *gendarme*, "Would you punish us if we burst his Zeppelins?"

In another drawing, published on the occasion of an airship crashing in the sea, a child suggested, "Now the fish get to see Zeppelins, too." Finally, two children of Montmartre, a working-class area of Paris, were depicted on a postcard standing on a roof, declaring longingly, "If we don't get to see Christmas [Santa], perhaps we'll see a Zeppelin."

As postcards revealed the theme of child as victim, they also represented the child warrior or hero. In a German postcard entitled, "The Little Airshipman," a toddler held a balloon with the admonition, "He must always

Cartoonist Poulbot's depiction of French children doing their bit for the war effort: "Would we be in trouble if we burst his Zeppelins?" one asks the puzzled gendarme. *Author's Collection.*

"The little airshipman." This German depiction suggests the child will strive to achieve greater heights, and presumably, greater success in the war. *Author's Collection.*

rise to greater heights." Another German postcard depicted a caricatured child in uniform asking a Zeppelin on a night flight where it was headed. In both cases, the child emulated his absent father and related to a symbolized airship as an authority figure. In a French postcard, a young boy in sailor's uniform dared the ugly airship to scare him, while another card in the same series pictured the sailor child complaining to his mother about the Zeppelin: "It farts." Responding here to the need to minimize danger by making it child's play—the enemy was not only evil, but it smelled—this card combined the illusion of the child warrior (the boy in uniform) with the infantilization of war technology; in so doing, it captured competing themes of the war's reception within one image.

As postcards offered a range of images of childhood and aviation during the First World War, they also revealed the degree to which those images were gendered. In contrast to boys, girls rarely appeared in relation to an airplane on postcards; when females were depicted, they appeared as mothers or as girlfriends. The positioning of females as mothers was part of the larger and powerful current of pro-natalism evident throughout Western

"It farts." This postcard was one of a series depicting a child in sailor suit holding daddy's pipe and standing tall to the rumbling Zeppelin. The childlike comment was both humorous and intended to diminish the psychological impact Zeppelin raids had on the population. *Author's Collection.*

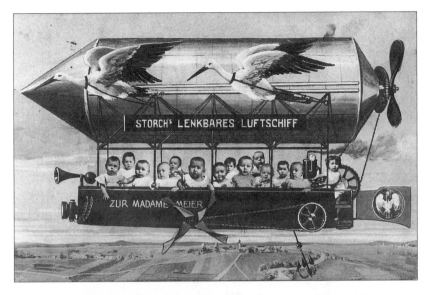

"Stork dirigible airship." This German depiction of an express baby service was one of many popular visions of childhood started before the war, yet carried on during the conflict. Such cards circulated on both sides of the trenches and served either to send quick notes of affection, or simply announce the new arrival to lonely fathers at the front. *Author's Collection.*

Europe, but particularly in France, where declining demographics had been a central state concern for decades.[28] In postcards, the proverbial stork announcing the arrival of a child (an Alsatian tradition) was transformed into an airplane or an airship delivering the male baby trophy. It was also not uncommon for new parents to send postcards that announced, "Here comes the new conscript."[29]

## *Influence of Popular Culture and Propaganda*

That war became a central part of the school curriculum, as seen earlier, comes as little surprise in light of the duration and the devastation of the hostilities.[30] Determining how youth reacted to representations of aviation during the war is difficult for obvious reasons. Despite its newly revealed deadly potential, aviation clearly continued to fascinate children, in no small part due to the romanticization of in-flight combat. In Germany, teenagers reportedly lied about their age to sign up after reading stories and witnessing an airship on its way to complete a mission.[31] In his journal of four years in a war zone, Yves Congar, later a French Cardinal, recorded his painful exposure to the war: his father being held hostage by the Germans, regular shellings, and his teacher's claims about impending victory. But the single airplane Congar drew in his 1915 schoolbook journal to record the plane's overflight was piloted by an adult and cast against a strangely serene landscape: romanticized flight remained a peaceful and distant endeavor, at least from the vantage point of this eleven-year-old who apparently did not experience a direct aerial bombing.[32]

## Conclusion

Writing about the automobile in World War I, poet Guillaume Appolinaire observed that:

> At the time they announced the mobilization [of the troops], my friend and I understood that the little car had brought us into a new era, and that although we were mature men, we had in fact just been born.[33]

A clear parallel can be drawn to the experience of the airplane, for the representation of children and flying machines in the popular and propaganda arts of the Great War reflected the unprecedented intersection of childhood and aviation in a time of total war. Not only was there government-approved use of childhood for indoctrination purposes, but civilians incorporated the child victim and child warrior into everyday life and its images. The success of the flight motif suggests not just an awe of aviation, but a desire to render it childlike and nonthreatening as well as to trivialize it. That this psychological need survived the war was evident in the continuing representation of flight as child's play: A 1920 Christmas postcard, for example, showed Santa Claus in an airplane "bombing" his targets with colorful packages, signaling that the flying machine's relationship to childhood had been fundamentally transformed. As an effect of total war and the deadliness of flight, the safe realm of the child had been destroyed and with it disappeared the clear boundary between adulthood and childhood in times of total war.

Santa's benign bombs. Earlier depictions of Santa usually showed him either walking to houses (in the tradition of St. Nicholas), or in his sled. The inclusion of the character aboard an airplane reflected a new awareness of modernity and of the machine's uses. This card was sent for new year 1920. *Author's Collection.*

NOTES

1. Mosse, *Fallen Soldiers*, chapter 7.

2. Hugh Cunningham, *Children and Childhood in Western Society* (London: Longman, 1995), chapter 4; Michelle Perrot, *A History of Private Life, Vol. IV* (Cambridge, MA: Harvard University Press, 1990), 204–223.

3. Joseph Corn, *The Winged Gospel* (New York: Oxford University Press, 1983), 30–33.

4. Stéphane Audoin-Rouzeau, *La guerre des enfants 1914–1918* (Paris: Armand

Colin, 1993), 24–65; Karl Hess, *Der I. Weltkrieg und die Schule* (Friedrichshafen: Schulmuseum, 1989).

5. Ingeborg Weber-Kellerman, "The German Family between Private Life and Politics," in Philippe Ariès and Georges Duby, eds., *A History of Private Life*, vol. 5 (Cambridge, MA: Harvard University Press, 1991), 511–512.

6. Mosse, *Fallen Soldiers*, 58–60.

7. Edmond Petit, *La vie quotidienne dans l'aviation en France au début du XXe siècle* (Paris: Hachette, 1977), 65–66.

8. Jacques Borgé and Nicolas Viasnoff, *Archives de l'aviation* (Paris: Trinckvel, 1996), 34–35; Frédéric Marchand, *Avions-jouets des origines à 1945* (Paris: Maeght, 1993), 12–38, 67–84.

9. Peter Fritzsche, *A Nation of Fliers: German Aviation and the Popular Imagination* (Cambridge, MA: Harvard University Press, 1992), 40–43; Robert Wohl, *A Passion for Wings: Aviation and the Western Imagination 1908–1918* (New Haven, CT: Yale University Press, 1994), chapter 3; Guillaume de Syon, *Zeppelin! Germany and the Airship 1900–1939* (Baltimore, MD: Johns Hopkins University Press, 2001), chapter 1.

10. Fritzsche, *Nation of Fliers*, chapter 1; Wohl, *Passion for Wings*, 53–66.

11. John H. Morrow, *The Great War in the Air: Military Aviation from 1909 to 1921* (Washington, DC: Smithsonian, 1993), chapters 1–2.

12. Jules Poirier, *Les bombardements de Paris* (1914–1918) *Avions-Gothas-Zeppelins-Berthas* (Paris: Payot, 1930), 198–201.

13. Mary R. Habeck, "Technology in War," in Jay Winter et al., eds., *The Great War and the Twentieth Century* (New Haven, CT: Yale University Press, 2000), 110–115.

14. Mosse, *Fallen Soldiers*, 139–142.

15. Marchand, *Avions-jouets des origines*, 135, 137; Jones and Howell, *Popular Arts of the First World War*, 89.

16. Jones and Howell, *Popular Arts of the First World War*, 96; de Syon, *Zeppelin!*, chapter 3.

17. Marie Luise Christadler, *Kriegserziehung im Jugendbuch* (Frankfurt am Main: Suhrkamp, 1978), 191–193.

18. Dominic Pisano, et al., *Legend, Memory and the Great War in the Air* (Seattle: University of Washington Press, 1992), 30–41; Fritzsche, *Nation of Fliers*, chapter 2.

19. Pascal Venesson, *Les chevaliers de l'air. Aviation et conflits au XXe siècle* (Paris: Sciences Po, 1997), 69–71; *Guynemer, un mythe, une histoire* (Paris: SHAA, 1997), 95.

20. De Syon, *Zeppelin!*, chapter 2; Fritzsche, *Nation of Fliers*, chapter 1.

21. Reinhold Braun, *Deutsche Kriegsbücher für die Schuljugend, 4. Band: Der Krieg in der Luft* (Langensalza: Julius Belss, n.d.), 7.

22. Audoin-Rouzeau, *La guerre des enfants*, 67–69, 80–83.

23. Venesson, *Les chevaliers de l'air*, 65–69; Mosse, *Fallen Soldiers*, 121.

24. Audoin-Rouzeau, *La guerre des enfants*, 110, 129–133; Mosse, *Fallen Soldiers*, 137.

25. Audoin-Rouzeau, *La guerre des enfants*, 129–133; Jones and Howell, *Popular Arts of the First World War*, 90, 96–98.

26. Marie Monique Huss, *Histoires de famille: cartes postales et culture de guerre* (Paris: Noesis, 2000), 40. Paul Vincent, *Cartes postales d'un soldat de 14–18* (Paris: Jean-Paul Gisserot, 1988), 5–10.

27. Huss, *Histoires*, 167; Poulbot, *Des gosses et des bonshommes* (Paris: n.p, n.d.), 1–5.

28. Marie Monique Huss, "Pro-Natalism and the Popular Ideology of the Child in Wartime France: The Evidence of the Postcard," in Wall and Winter, eds., *The Upheaval of War*, 329–367; Audoin-Rouzeau, *La guerre des enfants*, 124–129.

29. Mosse, *Fallen Soldiers*, 139; Audoin-Rouzeau, *La guerre des enfants*, 129–131; Huss, *Histoire*, 173–174.

30. Audoin-Rouzeau, *La guerre des enfants*, 104–105.

31. Fritzsche, *Nation of Fliers*, chapter 3; Morrow, "Knights of the Sky," in Franz Coetzee and Marilyn Shevin-Coetzee, eds., *Authority, Identity and the Social History of the Great War* (Providence: Berghahn, 1995), 315–317; Carl Heeg, "Ein Zeppelin über der Burg Olbrück im Jahre 1915," *Jahrbuch des Kreises Daun* (1977): 134–135.

32. Yves Congar, *Journal de la guerre 1914–1918*, ed. Stéphane Audoin-Rouzeau (Paris: Cerf, 1997), 99.

33. Guillaume Appolinaire, *Calligrames* (Paris: Gallimard, 1966).

# Chapter Ten

# World Friendship
## Children, Parents, and Peace Education in America between the Wars

### Diana Selig

"Will Our Children Outlaw War?" asked *Parents' Magazine* in 1933. "The answer to that question depends on what they are learning now in home and school." Psychologist and author Helen K. Champlin urged parents to instill "world-mindedness" in their offspring through readings, games, and activities in the home. The potential benefits were great. "Getting acquainted with children of other lands through travel and books can help build attitudes that will abolish war."[1]

Champlin's article was part of a widespread trend toward international education in the United States. Galvanized by the experience of the Great War and by the political isolationism and nativism that emerged in its aftermath, liberal educators looked for ways to realize the dream of a harmonious world order. Their efforts constituted one aspect of what historian Akira Iriye terms "cultural internationalism." The increasing interdependence of nations, and the perceived shrinking of the globe through new forms of communication and transportation, suggested that ordinary people needed to cooperate across national boundaries to prevent war. Internationalists experimented with new forms of mass culture, using film and radio to reach a wide audience along with exchanges of students and teachers, revisions of school textbooks, and the promotion of travel overseas.[2]

The image of the child played a particular role in the internationalist vision. The new science of the child, which gained prominence in the interwar years, sharpened the view of childhood as a distinct and malleable stage of life deserving of special protection. Peace advocates drew on this science to describe children as both vulnerable and impressionable, the most easily injured and the most likely to escape the ills of prejudice, violence, and war. As the youngest citizens, children offered the best hope for redemption and renewal. It seemed that children raised to cherish peace would bring a future of international goodwill.

The burgeoning parent education movement offered an effective means to reach children with the internationalist ideal. Parent education aimed to popularize scientific knowledge on child development to help parents rear their children. Its chief vehicle was *Parents' Magazine*. Founded in 1926 (and still published today), the magazine reached a wide audience of middle-class parents: 200,000 subscribers after five years, 400,000 by its tenth anniversary. Since subscribers shared issues with neighbors and friends, the actual readership was even higher, as the cover boasted: "Guides the rearing of more than a million children."[3] The magazine informed parents that they shaped children's outlook as they guided them through the impressionable early years. "What will come out of the home depends upon what the home-makers put into it," asserted publisher George Hecht in the introductory issue.[4] Every month for decades, the editorial page reproduced a quotation to remind readers what was at stake: "The future of the race marches forward on the feet of little children."

*Parents' Magazine* provided a consistent voice for international education. Its editor, Clara Savage Littledale, herself the mother of two children, lent impassioned attention to international cooperation, along with education for democracy and cultural pluralism. "How teach peace?" she asked. "Teach our children that the world is full of other children like themselves who can be their friends, whatever their race, color, or creed."[5] Littledale situated children and parents as key players in the movement for international understanding, suggesting that the very youngest members of society—and the adults who raised them—held the key to better world relations. Readers who turned to the magazine for childrearing advice regularly encountered such titles as "Mothers, Fathers and World Peace," "World Friendship Among Children," and "Will Our Children Outlaw War?" During three decades as editor, from the magazine's founding until her death in 1956, Littledale helped define a child-centered approach to international peace.

## Remembering the World War

Littledale's opposition to militarism emerged from her experience as a foreign correspondent in Europe during and immediately after the First World War, when she visited the front and saw the traumas of war first-hand.[6] Throughout her career, she aimed to abolish the "ghastly insanity" of war. She supported the League of Nations and promoted disarmament, both because military preparedness came at the expense of maternal and child welfare programs and because it deprived children of their right to live in a world at peace. "Can anyone who lived through the last war believe in war?" she wondered in a talk to a Quaker group. "Can the strong-arm method of preparing for peace still be accepted among nations?"[7] Years later, Littledale's obituary in the *New York Times* noted that in returning from war-torn Europe and beginning to write about family life, she "turned from international to domestic relations."[8] But to Littledale the two were linked. She tied public concern for peace with the private realm of parenting, underlining the political meanings of childhood. In her account, childrearing offered the best possibility for a future without war.

Littledale's writers declared that it was the duty of parents to tell children of the horrors of combat. "War as we have known it is a thing of starvation and death and sorrow," recalled Rachel Dunaway Cox, a contributor to the magazine. Memorials must "pass on to our children our own sense of regret, our grief that our race should have involved itself in such a gigantic blunder, and our own determination of 1918 that it shall never happen again." To teach children to build a different kind of world was the most urgent task.[9]

Disenchanted by the sentiments that had led to war, parent educators rejected events such as loyalty parades in favor of a "wider patriotism" that respected the aims and achievements of all peoples. Littledale frequently used the occasion of the Fourth of July to call for a new kind of patriotism. Although independence was won by war, she observed, children should understand that the world was now working toward peace. She encouraged readers to assess what messages children absorbed on the holiday. "Are they growing up to be the kind of people who must always boast of their country as the biggest and the best, the richest and most powerful?" she asked. "Are other peoples, other ways ridiculous or wrong to them?" She hoped that they would learn that liberty and justice were truly for all.[10]

To dispel romantic views of battle, parents should help children look beyond the flags and music to the barbarity and bloodshed. They should clarify the causes and results of war, suggest heroes who were scientists and statesmen rather than warriors, prove that times of peace offered opportunity for adventure and courage. Modern warfare was no game, for it brought disaster to both victor and vanquished. One reader from Minneapolis sent in an anecdote about the effects of such teaching. "Finding that her small boys were becoming greatly interested in the heroic aspects of war, a conscientious mother decided she should give them a picture of some of the less pleasant realities," related the reader. "The six-year-old listened with eyes growing bigger and bigger. Finally he burst out, 'I hope I'll never be invited to a war!'"[11] Such peaceful attitudes should be inculcated at the earliest age. Helen Champlin, the psychologist, suggested that parents use playroom disputes as an opportunity to instill world-mindedness. As toddlers shared toys, built blocks together, and waited their turn, she predicted, they would learn to cooperate and to play peaceably—thereby gaining the foundation for world citizenship.[12]

But while parents could teach peace, they could also instill wrong attitudes. Underneath the upbeat, optimistic tone of *Parents' Magazine* lay the suggestion that parents were at fault for their children's shortcomings. Just as there were many things for parents to do right, there were many ways they could go wrong. Children might absorb wrong attitudes from terms of derision or disparaging remarks, from scornful tones of voice or grimaces of superiority. Even inadvertent or unconscious expressions could instill narrow thinking. Poor parenting could bring dire consequences. Helen Champlin predicted a dark future for a four-year-old whose father encouraged him to fight for a toy train: "It is reasonable to expect that the man who Robert will become will be uncooperative, domineering, pugnacious," and in case of international conflicts, he would "rush unthinkingly to an inhuman recourse to arms." Champlin did not hesitate to assign responsibility for this terrible outcome. The training that parents gave to the smallest children at play would determine if the future would be "with the overmilitant Roberts or with personalities trained to understand one another."[13]

Indeed, if parents could end war, perhaps they were to blame if it continued. If expanding armies were "symptoms of political maladjustments that have their roots in the biased attitudes of children, grown to manhood and womanhood," as a minister explained, it was parents who had first shaped those attitudes.[14] The advent of peace, stated an editorial, depended on a "maturity among nations" in which cooperation would replace hate and guns, just as "maturer social intercourse replaces the fights of childhood."[15] The absence of peace could be linked to the failings of parents who had not dealt wisely with childhood disputes.

This undercurrent of blame assumed gendered dimensions. "Mothers Can Work for Peace" headlined one article, implying the contrary as well.[16] The magazine's frequent alternation of "parents" and "mothers" suggested a certain ambivalence over childrearing roles. Although men regularly contributed to the magazine, most of the writers implicitly addressed a female readership, understanding that mothers provided most of the child care. The majority of readers who sent in suggestions identified themselves as mothers—or as aunts or female neighbors. It was mothers, in other words, who deserved the credit—or the blame—for future international relations.

## Strategies for World-Thinking

"If we would spare our children the miseries of war, we must teach them to make friends around the world," proclaimed Rachel Dunaway Cox in *Parents' Magazine*. Readers encountered frequent suggestions on how to fulfill this duty. They could decorate their homes with art and handicrafts from other countries, introduce songs and dances from around the world, and organize costume pageants and plays. Posters, stamp collections, dolls, games, toys, and pen pals would inspire curiosity about life in other nations. A common suggestion was to have children find out the origins of the things that they wore, ate, or used in the home to illustrate the interdependence of countries. Readers sent in such suggestions. One mother decorated the playroom walls with maps to encourage a "world viewpoint." A reader from Missouri described scrapbooks in which her daughter collected pictures and stories of different places. "The towns and countries that to most children seem so far away are like friends to this child," the parent wrote. "She feels that through the postcards, newspapers, and magazine articles she has become acquainted with all states and peoples."[17]

At the same time, parents could support the myriad projects of schools, religious groups, and secular organizations to promote international goodwill. Readers learned of new trends in education: innovative geography instruction, revising textbooks to emphasize instances in which conflicts were settled peaceably, participation in student government and the model League of Nations, correspondence with children overseas, sending of dolls and treasure chests to children in other countries, and student and teacher exchanges. Some parent educators recognized that international goodwill depended on harmony among groups within the United States. Littledale's advocacy of international and interracial understanding, for instance, made few distinctions between brotherhood abroad and at home. But other authors advanced world-thinking without confronting the knotty problems of American race relations. They developed understanding of people far away, with whom children would likely have little contact, but did not address racial prejudices closer to home.

In *Parents' Magazine*, readers learned of the benefits of travel—to immigrant neighborhoods, to different regions of the United States, and to other countries. A visit to Canada would demonstrate international cooperation and help children understand that "a foreigner is a neighbor just over the way," while a family trip to Europe would foster an international point of view. Exchange programs, youth hostels, foreign study, and summer camps provided opportunities for young people to go abroad.[18] Reading offered another way for children to "visit" foreign lands, and a monthly column highlighted books that offered sympathetic portrayals of other countries. In a radio talk, Littledale told her listeners that:

> Children who know and love Heidi of the Alps, Hans Brinker, and Kees of Holland, Little Pear of China, Lucy Fitch Perkins' twins and all the other book-children of many lands will have a sound basis for international friendship and understanding.

When they grew up, Littledale implied, these children would be unlikely to wage war against the homelands of their favorite fictional characters. Eleanor Roosevelt recommended in another article that children read books from Europe as well as translations of Indian and Chinese poetry to "help them to that international point of view so important to the world today."[19]

Likewise, motion pictures could foster or inhibit feelings of international goodwill. Children easily identified with soldiers on the screen, surrounded by glamour, dressed in impressive uniforms, marching to music. The magazine criticized certain films for instilling wrong ideas: *The Cossacks* offered unpleasant portrayals of Russians, while a youngster watching *The Streets of Shanghai* "might easily draw the conclusion that all Chinese are the scum of the earth." *We Americans* was a "miseducational film" that encouraged "bigger and better wars, deeper and darker ignorance, and red-white-and-bluer patriots." According to the psychologist who reviewed the film, its "hodgepodge of stale war shots, moldy maxims and unmitigated mush" was dangerously sentimental, and "nothing is more injurious to a child than to link an error with an intense emotion." In contrast, movies that promoted tolerance, such as the series *Children of All Lands*, received high marks.[20]

To encourage parents to adopt these suggestions, the magazine published outlines for study in each issue and made copies available free of charge. A regular column on Books for Parents reviewed such recent publications as *Adventuring in Peace and Goodwill*, *Educating for Peace*, and *Why Wars Must Cease*. It is difficult to know how parents actually responded to articles, study guides, and reading lists. But there is evidence that parents did discuss this material: The magazine reported that hundreds of organizations—mothers' clubs, Parent-Teacher Associations, child study groups—requested copies of the study guides.[21] And while the magazine did not print letters to the editor, it did publish suggestions that parents submitted for how to foster international attitudes. At least some readers took these ideas to heart and implemented them in their own homes.

### *"The Boy-Gun Problem"*

The fighting of boys was a vexing problem for parents who wanted to instill pacifist values. Despite parental efforts, boys insisted on playing with toy soldiers and toy guns. According to Sidonie and Benjamin Gruenberg, leaders in the child-study movement, "a child playing soldier arouses the mother's apprehension, not because he might hurt himself with the toy gun, but because he might become militaristic; and she would hate that." A poet illustrated this fear as she imagined a dark future for her "little rugged soldier" who stalked the house and ravaged his block towers. She was struck with dread by the vision of her son marching "to bloodshed and to war."[22]

What was the best strategy for handling children's war play? Some parent educators argued against giving toy guns and soldiers. "Many soldiers have traced their war-craze to the influence of military toys," reported Mr. and Mrs. Robert E. Simon of the United Parents Association of New York City. When given tin soldiers, a child "may be thinking what these figures might or could do in real life," and the pleasurable associations of play would color his later attitude. After the experience of the world war, asked the Simons, "Is it not unwise and harmful to bring into the lives of young children, when their thinking is in a formative state, any toys which will leave upon them the impression that warfare is glorious?" They cited Eleanor Roosevelt's urging that toy-makers cease production of military toys and that parents stop purchasing them.[23]

Other parent educators suggested that it was best not to forbid fighting entirely. Littledale feared that prohibiting certain toys would enhance their allure and pointed out that boys would create weapons and soldiers out of whatever materials they had. Toy soldiers and guns, she suggested, might simply allow a boy to express his urge to make noise, to pretend to be fierce and strong; his actions were play, which neither the boy nor his parent need take seriously. She allowed her own son to "get all over it at an early age. Otherwise, I feel there is a possibility of the warlike urge backing up and bursting out later in life—with vastly more serious results."[24] Contributor Frances Frisbie O'Donnell presented her children with an alternative dramatic activity, hoping to convince them that fairy stories or historical incidents could be as exciting to act out as life in the trenches. A mother from Idaho submitted her solution to the problem of "everlasting gun-play": when she began to construct wooden cities from old crates, her boys became absorbed in the new activity and soon "guns were forgotten." Parents were encouraged to discuss this problem in child-study groups, responding to such questions as: "Do you believe that playing with soldiers develops a militaristic spirit and would you discourage their use for that reason?"[25]

That boys were more likely than girls to engage in play fighting was evident. Parent educators debated whether this behavior was innate. One asserted that since "fighting was a natural and normal instinct in every boy," parents should channel that instinct into self-defense rather than aggression.[26] In contrast, Margaret Stroh Hipps, who had lived in China, observed differences between American and Chinese boys that suggested that their behaviors were learned rather than instinctive. She watched American boys "digging trenches, arming themselves with wooden guns, and carrying on a tremendous mock war among themselves," while Chinese boys, who had been taught to respect the scholar above the soldier, did not approach war as a glorious game. The study guide that accompanied Hipps' account asked readers to consider the effects of allowing children to play with toy soldiers, guns, and knives.

> Do you believe that the impulses to fight, to be possessive, competitive and aggressive are inherent in human nature, or have such traits been cultivated

by the kind of civilization in which we live? If you hold the latter view, how can such traits be altered?[27]

One psychiatrist, in a rare article on sex discrimination, noted the influence of toys on children's development, pointing out that only boys were given tin soldiers or drums, and only girls were expected to play with dolls or toy kitchens. Such manifestations of sex prejudice, she warned, could cause inequalities in later life.[28]

Indeed, attempts to deal with play fighting were complicated by attitudes toward male gender roles. Modern parents wanted to raise boys who were peace-loving—but not overly passive; who opposed war—but could defend themselves when necessary. An occasional fair fight seemed to have its benefits: It cultivated strength and skill while teaching a boy to be a good loser. A mother from Ohio wrote in to explain her change of heart. She had taught her two sons never to fight, but when she found them losing out to more aggressive playmates, she gave them boxing gloves and instruction in "the manly art of self-defense." She reported that neighborhood boxing bouts developed sportsmanship and reduced incidents of actual fighting.[29]

The advisability of forbidding actual guns, like toy guns, seemed equally doubtful to many parent educators. O'Donnell told of two mothers who opposed firearms: the first, who prohibited guns, found that her tirades gave greater appeal to what was forbidden, while a second mother, who allowed gun ownership, was able to convince her children that the world should not use weapons to settle difficulties.[30] In a forum on "Should a Boy Have a Gun?" a writer from *Field and Stream* portrayed pacifist concerns in female terms. "Women as a rule instinctively fear and mistrust guns" as tools of war and destruction rather than as "implements of peace" that maintained law and order, he complained. The way to solve "the boy-gun problem" was to offer proper training and supervision in gun ownership to build character in boys and offer healthy sport.[31]

By the late 1930s, as the world moved closer to war, events in Europe made painfully clear that the internationalist vision had not yet been realized. Efforts to instill world-thinking seemed more important than ever. "The world is seething with racial hates and national fears and misunderstandings that threaten to lead us all into another world war," *Parents' Magazine* worried in 1938.[32] It reiterated strategies parents could adopt to save children from such destructive influence. "In troubled times," explained an article the next year, books can "help keep alive our children's honest sympathies for the people of other lands."[33] The magazine promoted travel to Latin America as war made Europe a troublesome destination and as the Good Neighbor policy focused attention on the Western Hemisphere. Families were urged to attend the World's Fair in New York or the Golden Gate International Exposition in San Francisco, both of which included exhibits on peace.[34]

Littledale recommended that parents discuss current events with children and talk with them about the war. She reminded readers that children were "alert intuitive and really thoughtful young human beings" whose ideas deserved respect. Parents should not laugh at children's attempts to discuss important affairs but should listen with interest and take their comments seriously.[35] The magazine reported on youth groups that pledged to work for peace, implying that young people could serve as models for their elders.

Despite their persistent pleas for world-thinking, however, Littledale and her writers recognized the limitations of their efforts. They had helped bring about greater awareness of the need for international understanding—yet war and violence had not disappeared. They grappled with the reality of continuing hostilities and their devastating consequences. On the eve of American entry into the war, it was clear that world-mindedness would be far more difficult to achieve than parent educators had optimistically predicted. A decade earlier, in a *Parents' Magazine* editorial, the chairman of the American Red Cross had recounted the comments of a German teacher whose pupils received friendship gifts from American schoolchildren:

> Boys and girls, this was done by children whose fathers were fighting against ours in the last war! You will grow up into men and women. Can you imagine that you will aim at those, kill *those* men who today have sent you their gifts?

The teacher exhorted his students to remember the bridges that linked countries. A letter from a school in Japan had expressed similar sentiments: "You are American and we Japanese. But, in the spirit of our organization, let us work together for the welfare of the world. Let us be friends forever."[36] Yet in fact these children would not be friends forever. In a sad and ironic outcome, the children the internationalists had raised to be world-friendly would be enlisted to fight in the next world war.

### Notes

1. Helen K. Champlin, "Will Our Children Outlaw War?" *Parents' Magazine* 8 (July 1933): 14.

2. Iriye, *Cultural Internationalism and World Order*.

3. Clara Savage Littledale, "Our First Ten Years," *Parents' Magazine* 11 (October 1936): 32.

4. George J. Hecht, "A Magazine for Parents," *Children, The Magazine for Parents* 1 (October 1926): 4. The name soon changed to *Parents' Magazine.*

5. Clara Savage Littledale, "How Teach Peace?" *Parents' Magazine* 1 (January 1937): 13.

6. Littledale to Marion Savage Sabin, December 2, 1918, Box 3, Folder 56, Clara Savage Littledale Papers, Schlesinger Library, Radcliffe College.

7. Clara Savage Littledale, "The 1935 Needs for Children," *Friends Intelligencer* (Fifth Month 4, 1935): 277. Also see Clara Savage Littledale, "Women and Children Last?" *Parents' Magazine* 13 (February 1938): 11, and "For the Sake of Our Children," *Parents' Magazine* 14 (February 1939): 13.

8. Obituary for Clara Savage Littledale, *New York Times,* January 10, 1956.

9. Rachel Dunaway Cox, "World Friendship Among Children," *Parents' Magazine* 5 (July 1930): 52.

10. Clara Savage Littledale, "How Safe Is the Fourth?" *Parents' Magazine* 7 (July 1932): 9; "We Celebrate Fourth of July," *Parents' Magazine* 12 (July 1937): 15.

11. E.R.C., no title, *Parents' Magazine* 9 (May 1934): 88.

12. Champlin, "Will Our Children Outlaw War?" 50–51.

13. Ibid.

14. Walter Van Kirk, "Will Our Sons Go To War?" *Parents' Magazine* 7 (January 1932): 9.

15. "With Malice Toward None," *Parents' Magazine* 14 (November 1939): 13.

16. Margaret Stroh Hipps, "Mothers Can Work for Peace," *Parents' Magazine* 13 (May 1938): 21.

17. Mrs. E. E. E., "A World Viewpoint," *Parents' Magazine* 5 (May 1930): 60–61; L.P.S., "Creating Geography Interest," *Parents' Magazine* 7 (April 1932): 44.

18. See, for example, Clara Savage Littledale, "Invitation to Travel," *Parents' Magazine* 13 (April 1938): 15; "Travel Together," *Parents' Magazine* 14 (April 1939): 17. Also see Littledale's talk "Give Your Child Happy Memories," September 30, 1932, Box 2, Folder 42, Littledale Papers.

19. Radio talk, no title, n.d., Box 3, Folder 39, Littledale Papers; Mrs. Franklin D. Roosevelt, "Books I Loved as a Child," *Children, the Magazine for Parents* 3 (December 1928): 15.

20. See, in *Children, the Magazine for Parents*: Walter B. Pitkin, "Motion Pictures for Children," 3 (May 1928): 30, 3:6 (June 1928): 32, and 3 (September 1928): 24; Beatrice Black, "Motion Pictures," 4 (June 1929): 40.

21. For example, see "Special Offers to Groups," *Parents' Magazine* 12 (June 1937): 105. On reader response to childrearing literature, see Jay E. Mechling, "Advice to Historians on Advice to Mothers," *Journal of Social History* 9 (Fall 1975): 44–63.

22. Sidonie Matsner Gruenberg and Benjamin C. Gruenberg, "Your Child's

Opportunity," *Parents' Magazine* 7 (March 1932): 47; Ruth E. Hopkins, "Mother Fear," *Parents' Magazine* 5 (March 1930): 69.

23. Mr. and Mrs. Robert E. Simon, "Should a Boy Have a Gun?" *Parents' Magazine* 9 (October 1934): 26.

24. Littledale, "How Teach Peace?" 13.

25. Frances Frisbie O'Donnell, "Educating for Peace," 6 (July 1931): 15; Mrs. C.C.R, "Parental Problems and Ways to Meet Them," *Parents' Magazine* 7 (March 1932): 40; "Program for Discussion at Your Next Meeting," *Parents' Magazine* 6 (June 1931): 80.

26. Ruth Leigh, "Must Boys Fight?" *Parents' Magazine* 6 (May 1931): 25.

27. Hipps, "Mothers Can Work for Peace," 21; Anna W. M. Wolf, "Study Course on the School-Age Child," *Parents' Magazine* 13 (May 1938): 89.

28. Olga Knopf, "Turning Children into Boys and Girls," *Parents' Magazine* 7 (December 1932): 46.

29. Leigh, "Must Boys Fight?" 25; Mrs. H.F.C., "Childhood Problems," *Parents' Magazine* 14 (July 1939): 26.

30. O'Donnell, "Educating for Peace," 60.

31. Bob Nichols, "Should a Boy Have a Gun?" *Parents' Magazine* 9 (October 1934): 26.

32. "Coming Soon," *Parents' Magazine* 13 (January 1938): 42.

33. Blanche Weber, "Books Around the World," *Parents' Magazine* 14 (November 1939): 27.

34. See, in *Parents' Magazine*: Heloise Brainerd, "Introducing Children to the Other Americas," 9 (May 1934): 15; Catherine Conrad Edwards, "Take Them to the Fair," *Parents' Magazine* 14 (April 1939): 26; Louise Bailey Burgess, "Family Vacation in Mexico," 14 (November 1939): 24; Elisabeth Shirley Enochs, "Getting Acquainted With The Other Americas," 16 (June 1941): 17.

35. Clara Savage Littledale, "Discovering Our Children," *Parents' Magazine* 14 (March 1939): 15.

36. "Young Citizens of the World," *Children, The Magazine for Parents* 2 (August 1927): 7.

# Chapter Eleven

# Ghosts and the Machine
## Teaching Emiliano Zapata and the Mexican Revolution since 1921

## *Stephen E. Lewis*

Since the time of Napoleon Bonaparte, "revolutionary" states emerging from civil wars have sought to consolidate and institutionalize their rule through ambitious federal education systems. In the Soviet Union and postrevolutionary China, federal schools strove mightily to carve nations of productive, nationalist citizens out of ethnically heterogeneous, traditional, and predominately illiterate populations. In Latin America, Cuba and Nicaragua consolidated their leftist nationalist revolutions through schools and highly publicized literacy campaigns. In all four settings, schools anchored state control, disseminated official ideology, and attempted to create a sense of national identity and unity. Meanwhile, the revolutionary regimes took credit for extending the gifts of literacy and schooling to the masses, and education became part of the official revolutionary nationalist ideology.

Mexico's federal Ministry of Public Education (SEP), created in 1921, intended to use schools to similar ends following the Mexican revolution. Although the outcome of the violence of 1910–1920 was hardly "revolutionary," the *process* was highly popular, and many participants believed they were indeed fighting for revolutionary ends.[1] After 1920, the rhetoric of revolution actually masked a regime bent on demobilizing the population and reestablishing capitalist patterns of economic growth. Charged with "modernizing" and "civilizing" Mexico, the SEP was also expected to introduce a national sentiment in unsettled, war-torn regions where armed locals demanded resolution of their long-standing grievances. Rather than attempt to suppress revolutionary populism, the SEP tried to harness and appropriate it to forge a state and nation. Over time, an excruciatingly divisive and bloody civil war became transformed into a unifying nationalist crucible for generations of Mexican schoolchildren and a founding myth for Mexico's ruling party of seventy-one years, the Party of the Institutional Revolution, or PRI.

## The Mexican Revolution: Promise and Predicaments

Before proceeding with our discussion of how the revolution was taught in the classroom and used to anchor state control, a brief sketch of the chaotic events between 1910 and 1920 is in order. The Mexican Revolution generally refers to the decade of violence triggered by the overthrow of Porfirio Díaz, who ruled as dictator from 1876 to 1911. Under Díaz, "order" in Mexico was finally achieved (often brutally) and material "progress" followed. Foreign-built railroads linked Mexican production sites to ports and U.S. markets and sparked a revival of the Mexican mining industry and export agriculture. By 1894, Mexico was running a budget surplus. But such economic growth came at a high social cost. Elections were routinely rigged, and opponents of the regime were either jailed or killed. Porfirian land policy came at the expense of Mexico's overwhelmingly rural population. Those who resisted this policy, like the Yaqui Indians of Sonora, were subjected to forced labor and genocidal campaigns. In cultural terms, the elite typically scorned things Mexican and aped foreign (especially French) culture.

In 1910, the eighty-year-old dictator rigged his reelection for yet another term. Soon after Díaz "won," his frustrated challenger Francisco I. Madero escaped jail and issued a manifesto declaring the results of the recent election "illegitimate" and calling for a national uprising. Gradually, armed resistance to Díaz materialized. Two extraordinary men of humble origin seconded Madero's call. In the north, Pancho Villa, a cattle-rustling journeyman from the state of Chihuahua, fought several pitched battles for Madero in spring 1911. Farther south, in the state of Morelos, Emiliano Zapata seconded the revolt as a means of recovering land that sugar planters had stolen from his community.

After Díaz agreed to go into exile in May 1911, Madero became president. Peace was short-lived, however, because Zapata and his followers refused to lay down their arms as a precondition to Madero's agrarian reform program. Less than two years later, Madero was betrayed and assassinated by his own army commander, Victoriano Huerta. Villa, who had remained loyal to Madero, joined fellow northerners Alvaro Obregón and Venustiano Carranza in forming a coalition against Huerta. Villa's army, the División del Norte, was probably the largest popular army that Latin America ever produced. Zapata never joined this coalition, but continued his crusade for local autonomy and land reform in the south. For the next three years, Mexico would become a swirl of turmoil and devastation. Peasants, Indians, industrial workers, teachers, women, children, students, lawyers, unemployed miners, bandits and others joined the fray. The civil war(s) took on a truly national dimension.

In late 1914, Villa broke with Obregón and Carranza and forged an alliance with Zapata. In December of that year, the armies of Villa and Zapata occupied Mexico City. This represents the first and only time that peasant-led, truly popular armies have occupied a national capital in the history of modern Latin America. Although the occupation was to last less than two months, the genuinely popular nature of the conflict would leave its mark on postrevolutionary cultural policy.

In early 1915, the Constitutionalist army staged its comeback and forced the popular armies out of Mexico City. Later the following year, with both Villa and Zapata largely de-fanged, Carranza called a constitutional convention, inviting only members from his coalition. Surprisingly, perhaps, so-called middle class "Jacobins" took over the convention, believing that some measure of reform was necessary if there was any hope for peace in Mexico. The end result was arguably the most progressive legal code for its time in the world. Article 3 established mandatory, secular education. Article 27 enshrined Zapata's call for land reform, claimed Mexico's subsoil (including oil reserves) for the nation, and set limits of foreign landholding. Article 123 established an extremely progressive labor code.

Although Villa and Zapata continued fighting Carranza from the north and south, respectively, both grew increasingly desperate as the Constitutionalists consolidated power. Zapata's urgent need for allies led him into a trap sprung by Carranza and one of his generals. In April 1919 he fell in a hail of bullets. Villa agreed to go into retirement after Obregón offered him a large hacienda and an armed entourage of five hundred men. Some historians believe that he was assassinated three years later because he threatened to come out of retirement and participate in a rebellion against the revolution's victors; others attribute his death to one of his many local enemies.[2]

Once the dust settled, the revolution's victors faced major challenges. Since they had come to power by force of arms, intrigue, and assassination, they suffered a profound crisis of legitimacy. How could they restore peace to a profoundly divided country with deep class, ethnic, linguistic, and regional differences and a recent legacy of violence? On another level, how could they meet the terms of the new Constitution without either enraging Mexican landowners, factory owners, businessmen and foreign investors, on the one hand, or well-armed Mexican peasants and workers, on the other? Education was the answer to both dilemmas. The SEP was to forge a sense of national identity that would ideally supersede other, more divisive identities. Conveniently, among the "big three" articles of the new Constitution, education was the one least likely to create opposition because it did not directly affect the class interests of domestic or foreign elites. Finally, as SEP director Narciso Bassols (1931–1934) flatly stated, since most adult Mexicans were too fanatical, backward, and illiterate for redemption, the nation's future depended on how well teachers shaped Mexican schoolchildren. In the end, the (former) ruling party's appropriation of the Zapata myth and the revolution in general is a study in how a truly popular movement ended up legitimizing an authoritarian state.

## Early SEP Ideology, Pedagogy, and Textbooks

Shortly after taking office in 1920, Obregón began remaking the image of Zapata, formerly known in Constitutionalist circles and the Mexico City press as "the Attila of the South." Soon the regime was offering lavish commemorations in lieu of substantive land reform. As Samuel Brunk writes, "Once cleansed of certain troublesome realities—like the fact that Zapata had fought for years against the Constitutionalist faction to which Obregón belonged—[Zapata's memory] promised to be helpful in retaining the support of the peasantry."[3] Zapata's comeback was also part of Obregón's attempt to distance himself from his former ally Carranza, who had ordered Zapata killed.[4] By April 1924, five years after Zapata's assassination, the new regime officially claimed Zapata as its own in an elaborate commemoration held at his gravesite in Cuautla, Morelos. In attendance was muralist Diego Rivera, whose didactic art taught illiterate Mexicans (still the majority in the 1920s) the importance of Zapata and his crusade for land. Pancho Villa, on the other hand, was excluded from official Mexican ideology, at least until 1934, largely because the revolution's victors had fought countless pitched battles against the División del Norte. To celebrate Villa's accomplishments might have raised doubts about the official narrative of the revolution.[5]

If President Obregón was willing to revive and remake Zapata and celebrate select elements of the revolution, the SEP's textbook writers in the
1920s were not as easily convinced. The limitations of textbook analysis are
well known: we can never be sure whether and/or how students assimilate
the information presented, nor can we be sure if the books are being used
and being used correctly.[6] However, as Dennis Gilbert wrote in his essay
about the 1992 textbook controversy in Mexico, "[w]hether or not school
texts possess the power over young hearts and minds attributed to them,
faith in their power is widespread among elites. It is this faith that makes
textbooks such revealing cultural artifacts."[7]

The SEP's early history texts suggest profound confusion in the Ministry
over how to tell the story of the revolution. Porfirian texts were reissued
with only minimal changes, and values that were wildly out of step with the
alleged new priorities of the postrevolutionary Mexican state—such as
adulation of French and North American culture and submission to au-
thoritarianism—were disseminated and propagated in classrooms just as
before. Three of the SEP's text writers had held important posts in the Porfirian educational bureaucracy. Not surprisingly, their texts still glorified
positivist "order and progress," celebrated private property, and eulogized
Díaz just as before, though with slight modifications. His dictatorship was
depicted as "a necessary evil," the excesses of which were blamed on his
cronies and underlings. None of the text writers celebrated Mexican nationalism; the standard-bearers of "civilization" remained the French and
Anglo-Saxons.[8]

On the subject of Mexico's recently concluded revolution, textbooks
were either silent or dismissive. Some text writers portrayed the revolution
as a purely political event. Others, like Rafael Aguirre Cinta in 1926, expressed contempt for the revolution's "so-called agrarista leaders" and dis-
missed Villa and Zapata as bothersome obstructers of order. In Lóngino Cadena's 1921 history text, North American workers still provided the model
for enterprise, punctuality, and prudence; as in Porfirian days, Mexican
workers were criticized for their alleged proclivity to laziness and political
disobedience.[9]

By the late 1920s, however, the SEP began to close ranks around a revolutionary nationalist narrative. In 1929, it published *Fermín*, its first textbook to celebrate the popular character of the revolution. Fermín was the
fictitious son of an hacienda peon who had fought with the Constitutionalists (Carranza's faction) during the revolution. Fermín embodied the
characteristics of the imagined "revolutionary" *ejidatario*—hardworking,

literate, patriotic, sober, and armed, in case reactionaries attempted to roll back the gains of the revolution.[10] Zapata, too, was enlisted in the middle 1930s, during the height of the federal agrarian program. Stripped of his drinking, his gambling, his penchant for fighting cocks, his womanizing, and his fatal opposition to Carranza, he was transformed into "the intransigent of the revolution, an immaculate symbol of the emancipation of the rural masses . . . humbl[y] clothed in sandals and the white cotton uniform of the Morelian peasantry. . . ."[11] In most texts Díaz appeared as a dictator who had cozied up to foreign capital at the expense of average Mexicans; the revolution was discussed for its social as well as political causes; and peasants and workers became protagonists in their own history. In the words of Mary Kay Vaughan, "[c]oncepts of rebellion, struggle, and the right to social justice were etched into the core of the Mexican cultural nation and legitimated as intrinsic to national identity."[12]

Just as SEP textbooks took a popular turn in the late 1920s and early 1930s, so too did SEP pedagogy. When Lázaro Cárdenas assumed the presidency in December 1934, the SEP adopted "socialist" education as its official operating philosophy. Socialist education used the Marxist rhetoric of class conflict to celebrate and mobilize Mexico's rural and urban masses. It also placed a new emphasis on the redistribution of resources like land and credit. In spite of its internationalist rhetoric, socialist education was a highly nationalist educational agenda. Teachers were literally asked to create the new "revolutionary" Mexican—rational, secular, modern, hygienic, and sober. They taught a popular, celebratory version of the revolution and led a dizzying number of civic celebrations commemorating important moments in national history. Future violence could be avoided, it was believed, if teachers taught "that the conglomerate of regions that form the country constitute a single fatherland (*patria*), linked during many centuries by common traditions and identical aspirations."[13] In the southern border state of Chiapas, for example, schools were to honor a total of forty state and national holidays per year, roughly one holiday per school week. This attempt to replace the cult of the saints with the cult of the state raised the hackles of many Catholics and conservatives, but the main tenets of revolutionary nationalism took hold and remain a potent unifying force in Mexico to this day.[14]

Although the Mexican government and the SEP became more conservative after 1940, popular revolutionary nationalism continued to flourish in the schools. In 1962, President Adolfo López Mateos introduced the Free

Text program. The SEP provided texts to all students free of charge, and required all schools in Mexico—whether federal, state, or private—to use them. López Mateos during his presidency attempted to revive the popular nationalism of the Cárdenas years, and this was reflected in the 1962 textbooks. Not surprisingly, Porfirio Díaz appeared as a dictator, and his achievements were dwarfed by reminders of the social costs of Porfirian growth. Foreign investment and Yankee imperialism were roundly condemned. Zapata received a more ambiguous treatment. The fourth-grade history texts insinuated that Zapata was too quick to rebel against Madero in 1911, and never explained Zapata's opposition to his eventual assassin, Carranza.[15] This ambiguity reflects the fact that the López Mateos regime was challenged by rural guerrillas and others demanding immediate, effective land reform. As we shall see, Zapata's provocative legacy would continue to give headaches to textbook writers and politicians.

## *Whose Side Are They On, Anyway?*

The summer of 1968 was a turbulent one in Mexico, as hundreds of thousands of high school and university students took to the streets to protest police brutality, the lack of political democracy, and the empty promises of the PRI. In their marches, students initially paraded images of Che Guevara and Mao Zedong, who had become international symbols of revolutionary utopianism. So effective was the SEP's appropriation of Mexico's popular heroes that one student remarked that:

> I never thought of Zapata as a student symbol, an emblem. Zapata ha[d] become part of the bourgeois ideology; the PRI ha[d] appropriated him! We never thought of Pancho Villa either. His name never even crossed our minds![16]

But once the government-controlled press attacked the students for being anti-Mexican, strike leaders made a conscious attempt to purge internationalist symbols and instead embrace national heroes. "From now on we're going to carry placards with the portraits of Hidalgo, Morelos, Zapata, to shut them up. They're our Heroes. ¡*Viva Zapata! ¡Viva!*" read new orders from the strike committee.[17] As Eric Zolov writes, this decision constituted a direct challenge to the PRI's monopoly on revolutionary symbolism. Government forces crushed the movement several weeks later, killing hundreds of students at Tlatelolco on the eve of the opening of the 1968 Summer Olympics. Symbolically the regime had lost the monopoly that it enjoyed over its revolutionary heroes; practically, its decidedly anti-revolutionary, authoritarian character had manifested itself in no uncertain terms.

The regime attempted to regain control of the Zapata and Villa legacies in subsequent years. In 1969, one year after the massacre and fifty years after the assassination of Zapata, the PRI's official peasant union organized more than 20,000 commemorations in honor of the "Martyr of Chinameca."[18] In the 1970s, a proposal to move Zapata's remains to Mexico City's Monument of the Revolution was blocked by independent peasant groups who argued that it was unacceptable for his body to rest next to that of his archenemy Carranza.[19] Villa's remains experienced a different fate. When they were reburied in 1976 alongside those of Madero, whom he had revered, and Carranza, whom he had hated, a federal deputy from Mexico's ruling party stated that it would help promote the unity of all Mexicans.[20]

In 1975, the second generation of Free Texts was issued during the presidency of Luis Echeverría, whose likely role in the Tlatelolco massacre has never been fully understood. While these texts were slightly more nuanced than those issued in 1962, they still marked a clear commitment to revolutionary nationalism. Porfirian society was depicted as deeply divided and unjust. On the revolution itself, the Echeverría texts called no attention to the deadly divisions in Mexico's "revolutionary family." Although considerable attention was paid to Zapata's notion of social justice, the fact that he was assassinated by Carranza is not mentioned.[21]

Zapata, in other words, remained a complex character for revolutionary mythmakers. In the 1980s, his image would be invoked in oppositional rallies as Mexico's economic and political system suffered under the weight of collapsing oil prices, spiraling debt payments, peso devaluations, hyperinflation, and official corruption. Zapata was becoming a liability. Once the Mexican government agreed to IMF austerity programs, one of the first casualties was revolutionary nationalism. In 1992, President Carlos Salinas announced the death of the Mexican revolution and abandoned those provisions in Article 27 that authorized agrarian reform and protected communal landholding. Critics remarked that Salinas had merely revived Porfirian economic and social policies. Clearly the official ideology had changed in Mexico. Would SEP textbooks follow suit?

### The 1992 Textbook Controversy and Beyond

"In order to avoid being accused of running counter to Mexican history, the government resolved to alter it through a vast operation of ideological revision," wrote Miguel Granados Chapa in *La Jornada*, Mexico's influential center-left daily.[22] In fall 1992, President Carlos Salinas and his Education Secretary, Ernesto Zedillo, introduced a third generation of texts for fourth, fifth, and sixth graders. The history texts' authors were Héctor Aguilar Camín and Enrique Florescano, well-respected historians with close ties to the administration. While critics claimed that the new textbooks intended to rewrite history, the authors claimed that they were replacing simplistic, binary narratives of heroes and villains with objective history based on modern scholarship.[23]

The 1992 texts represented an unmistakable departure from the two previous generations of free textbooks and provoked a firestorm of protest. As one critic wrote, the books presented a history of the Mexican state, not the Mexican people.[24] Since the neo-liberal, pro-NAFTA economic and social policies of the Salinas administration were similar to those of the Porfiriato, the Salinas-Zedillo texts took pains to reverse the decades-long tradition of Porfirian vilification. The new texts avoided class terminology, placed heavy emphasis on Porfirian "modernization," and celebrated the dictator's openness to foreign capital. The rural poor were stripped of their agency and, in fact, barely appeared at all. As Gilbert writes, "[s]tudents learn that 'commercial crops grew at the expense of the lands of [peasant] communities'— as if such crops sprouted spontaneously on peasant lands."[25] The Salinas-Zedillo texts also managed to divorce Zapata entirely from the issue of land reform. He is treated as a purely military leader who eventually created "instability" by fighting Carranza (the new texts' new champion) for unspecified reasons. His assassination is not explained either; as Gilbert concludes, "[t]he offhanded treatment of Zapata in the Salinas-Zedillo texts obscured the meaning of his career and the Revolution itself."[26]

Opposition to the 1992 texts came from precisely those sectors that had supported earlier texts, including leftist intellectuals, PRI-affiliated labor and peasant confederations, and the army. Dissident elements in the teachers' union refused to use the new texts in their classrooms. Those who supported the new texts included traditional critics such as the Catholic Church and the center-right Catholic party, the Party of National Action (PAN). Since the texts were a political liability, Zedillo withdrew them in late 1992 and announced a new competition in early 1993. After the winning manuscripts were chosen and prizes awarded, these texts were also withdrawn and a third set was published. These texts are still in use today.[27]

On January 1, 1994, PRI politicians and SEP pedagogues reaped what they had been sowing for three generations. In the impoverished southern border state of Chiapas, where federal schools had been raising the flag, honoring national heroes, and hosting patriotic and sporting festivals for decades, Maya insurgents calling themselves Zapatistas declared themselves in rebellion against the Mexican government and seized several towns. Demanding justice, democracy, bilingual bicultural schools, and a resumption of land reform, the Zapatistas were also skilled in the rhetoric of the Mexican nation. They appropriated the revolutionary nationalist language, ideas, and symbols first and most emphatically introduced by the SEP in the 1930s. They named themselves after the immortalized peasant hero Zapata, they called their base "Aguascalientes" after the city of the same name where Zapatista and Villista delegates drafted a radical Constitution in 1914, and they skillfully used the imagery of the Mexican flag. Never a separatist movement, the new Zapatismo claimed the rights of national citizenship for Mexico's most marginalized indigenous communities. These Mexicans would not allow the country's ruling class to abandon the populist and nationalist traditions so carefully constructed and appropriated in the 1930s. Mexico's federal schools, in conjunction with local communities, had constructed an imagined nation, and neo-liberal technocrats in the PRI paid the price for turning their backs on that nation's revolutionary nationalist past.[28]

## Conclusion and Epilogue

This chapter has shown how the postrevolutionary Mexican state reconciled its bloody and divisive genesis by appropriating the revolution and refashioning peasant heroes through the SEP. Cult heroes in life, Villa and Zapata became even larger in death. Ironically, their legacies were appropriated by the very regime that killed them. Revolutionary nationalism remains a potent legacy in modern Mexico, even as the PRI and the PAN have tried to distance themselves from this legacy in recent years. Mexican schoolchildren may have learned the lessons of revolutionary nationalism contained in SEP classrooms and textbooks, but the PRI had no control over how angry university students, peasants, schoolteachers, and insurgents would appropriate these lessons in later years.

Revolutionary nationalism, disseminated by the SEP and its teachers, helped Mexico's former ruling party remain in power for seventy-one consecutive years. Ironically, it was a guerrilla group using the symbols of revolutionary nationalism that posed the most potent challenge to the PRI in the 1990s. On July 2, 2000, Vicente Fox of the PAN defeated the PRI's candidate for president and broke the former ruling party's monopoly on political power. At the time this manuscript went to press, the full ramifications of this change were still being measured and many questions remained. How will the PAN change the way that the revolution is taught? As Mexico's political system becomes more plural, it becomes harder for the SEP to impose on Mexican schoolchildren a single, unifying version of Mexican history. And what will happen to the revolution's popular heroes? Agrarian reform is dead, and the pro-business PAN has little use for Villa and Zapata. The free textbook program may also be in serious jeopardy. The SEP, now directed by the PAN, is likely to favor the privatization and decentralization of school textbooks on ideological grounds. In many states other books are already used in lieu of the SEP's free textbooks; it is further estimated that more than half of Mexico's rural schools nationwide do not use the books. Finally, because revolutionary nationalism became so closely associated with the PRI, the "Party of the Institutional Revolution," the PAN may wish to let it fade in the collective conscience. The PAN, after all, claims to represent change and a break from the past. In all likelihood, the utopian attempt to impose a single, unifying version of Mexican history in the classroom—always a dubious and controversial enterprise—will likely succumb to SEP decentralization, the PAN's penchant for privatization, the growing plurality of Mexican society, and the fact that revolutionary nationalism is considered the anachronistic relic of the erstwhile "heir to the Revolution," the PRI.[29]

## Notes

I want to thank SEP employees and friends Verónica Arellano, Carlos Carrizales, and Angel Cabellos for their insights.

1. Adolfo Gilly, *La revolución interrumpida* (México: El Caballito, 1971); Alan Knight, *The Mexican Revolution* 2 vols. (Lincoln: University of Nebraska Press, 1986) and "Revolutionary Project, Recalcitrant People: Mexico, 1910–40," in Jaime E. Rodríguez O., ed., *The Revolutionary Process in Mexico: Essays on Political and*

*Social Change, 1880–1940* (Los Angeles: UCLA Latin American Center Publications, 1990).

2. On this controversy and on Villa generally, see Friedrich Katz's indispensable biography *The Life and Times of Pancho Villa* (Stanford: Stanford University Press, 1998), 761–794.

3. Samuel Brunk, "Remembering Emiliano Zapata," 464.

4. *El Maestro Rural*, Tomo 11, Núm. 9 (Sept. 1938): 13; and Ilene V. O'Malley, *The Myth of the Revolution: Hero Cults and the Institutionalization of the Mexican State, 1920–1940* (Westport, CT: Greenwood Press, 1986), 44–50.

5. Katz, *Life and Times of Pancho Villa*, 790; O'Malley, *Myth of the Revolution*, 98.

6. For a useful study of textbook usage, see Laura Giraudo, "Bibliotecas rurales, maestros indígenas y lectores campesinos. México, años '20 y '30 del siglo XX," paper presented at the International Standing Conference of the History of Education, Alcalá de Henares, Spain, September 2000.

7. Gilbert, "Rewriting History," 273.

8. Vaughan, *Cultural Politics in Revolution*, 37–38.

9. Rafael Aguirre Cinta, *Historia de México* 16th ed. (México: Sociedad de Ediciones y Librería Franco-Americana, S.A. 1926), 366, 374; and Lóngino Cadena, *Elementos de historia general y de historia patria* 3rd ed. 2 vols. (México: Herrero Hermanos, 1921), 72. Cited in Mary Kay Vaughan, "Cambio ideológico en la política educativa de la SEP: programas y libros de texto, 1921–1940" in Susana Quintanilla and Mary Kay Vaughan, *Escuela y sociedad en el periodo cardenista* (México: Fondo de Cultura Económica, 1997), 91–106.

10. Vaughan, *Cultural Politics in Revolution*, 38–42.

11. Samuel Brunk, *¡Emiliano Zapata! Revolution and Betrayal in Mexico* (Albuquerque: University of New Mexico Press, 1998 [1995]), xii–xiii.

12. Vaughan, *Cultural Politics in Revolution*, 40.

13. Eliseo Bandala, "El estudio de la historia es indispensable en las escuelas rurales," *El Maestro Rural*, 3:2 (June 15, 1933): 10.

14. Stephen E. Lewis, "Revolution and the Rural Schoolhouse: Forging State and Nation in Chiapas, Mexico, 1913–1946" (Ph.D. dissertation, University of California, San Diego, 1997), chapter four.

15. Gilbert, "Rewriting History," 275–279.

16. Eric Zolov, *Refried Elvis: the Rise of the Mexican Counterculture* (Berkeley: University of California Press, 1999), 127.

17. Ibid., 127.

18. Brunk, "Remembering Emiliano Zapata," 479.

19. Ibid., 479.

20. Katz, *Life and Times of Pancho Villa*, 789–790.

21. Gilbert, "Rewriting History," 279–280.

22. *La Jornada*, August 20, 1992, cited in Gilbert, "Rewriting History," 272.

23. Gilbert, "Rewriting History," 272–273; Arturo Cano, "¿Alguien está con-

tento?" *Hojas* No. 9 (October 1992). See also Carmen Cervera C., "¿Cómo evaluar los libros gratuitos de historia de México para primaria?" in *Proyecto: revista para la educación* 1(2) (October–December 1992): 8–12.

24. Paco Ignacio Taibo II, "Usaron blanqueador con las figuras negras de nuestro pasado," *Hojas* No. 9 (October 1992): 9.

25. Gilbert, "Rewriting History," 277. Also see Jesús Nieto López, "Porfirio Daz, a la galería de los hombres ilustres," *Hojas* No. 9 (October 1992): 15–18.

26. Gilbert, "Rewriting History," 281.

27. Ibid., 272, 289–291; various articles in *Hojas* No. 9 (October 1992).

28. Benjamin, "A Time of Reconquest," 446–448.

29. José Galán, "Terminar con el monopolio en libros de texto, 'recomienda' el Banco Mundial a México," *La Jornada* June 19, 2001, 43.

*Chapter Twelve*

# Japanese Children and the Culture of Death, January–August 1945

## *Owen Griffiths*

A year after Japan's defeat in the Pacific War, teacher Kayahara Kazan wrote to the *Mainichi* newspaper deploring the lack of a "scientific attitude of life" among his countryfolk. What was needed, he said, was a new moral spirit for the youth of Japan. Commenting bitterly on Japan's wartime culture of death, Kayahara made the inevitable comparison between Japan and the West. Naturally, Japan was found wanting. "If you want to learn how to live," he said, quoting an unnamed European source, "go back to Greece. If you want to learn how to die, go to Japan."[1]

Kayahara's comments resonated with many adult readers, all of whom had endured four years of unrelenting propaganda about victory through death and then one horrific year of near-death in incendiary bombing raids. To the very end, the government had exhorted the people—"the one hundred million"—to die for the nation as "a suicide squad," "a knife tearing into the belly of the enemy," and finally as "a shattered jewel."[2]

Like the civilian bombing campaigns which obliterated Japan's urban spaces, the propaganda of death touched every man, woman, and child. This story is now a familiar one. Numerous studies document its creation and deployment, as well as the attempts of some Japanese to undermine its power.[3] None, however, have examined the messages directed specifically at children through the Japanese print media, nor the ways in which they responded to these messages. This study analyzes the propaganda of death in the last months of the war by examining two of the most popular children's magazines of the day: *Boy's Club* (*Shônen kurabu*) and *Girl's Club* (*Shôjo kurabu*).[4] I will focus specifically on the ways in which myth and history were excavated, intertwined, and then pressed into the service of the state's larger propaganda machine. I will also examine the gendered nature of these messages and the degree to which history and myth reinforced traditional gender roles for boys and girls. That these messages centered on loyalty and sacrifice should surprise no reader familiar with the propaganda of national crisis. Nonetheless, the extent to which they created a seamless web of such completeness is truly overwhelming. Just as American incendiary bombing offered no escape for Japan's urban residents, so too were the pages of *Boy's Club* and *Girl's Club* similarly permeated with sacrificial death.

## Myth and History in Japan's Culture of Death

Media manipulation of Japan's martial traditions in wartime was nothing new to 1945, but dated back to all-out war with China in 1937. From late 1944 onward, these themes increased in intensity, reflecting a clear intent to place Japan's children directly in harm's way. Reflecting traditional gender roles of the martial male and the nurturing female, *Boy's Club* placed greater emphasis on the warrior heroes of the past than did *Girl's Club*. But this line became blurred as Japan's wartime culture of death steadily erased the distinctions between male and female and adult and child. Boys were instructed to die by engaging the enemy in combat: a gendered death. The horrific bloodbaths of Saipan and Okinawa notwithstanding, girls too were told to die, not in battle, but by their own hand—also a gendered death— to preserve the ideal of feminine purity and modesty.

An auspicious year historically, 1945 was the 2600th anniversary of the mythical founding of the Japanese empire by Jimmu Tennô and the fortieth anniversary of Japan's victory over Russia in 1905. Both magazines made every effort to link these events to the Greater East Asian War and continually urged their young readers to be resolute in this year of "certain victory."[5] Recalling the words of Kitabatake Chikafusa, *Boy's Club* contributing writer Fusauchi Yukinari emphasized Japan's unbroken imperial lineage, Hirohito's status as a living divinity, and Japan's unique place as a divine country.[6] He further urged children to follow the way of the old Mito Han scholars and the Meiji Restoration patriots known as "men of high purpose."[7] "Whenever our divine country was in danger," he said, "our loyal patriots, firm in the knowledge that theirs was the land of the gods, dispatched with valor the enemies of the Emperor. From the Manchurian Incident to the Greater East Asian War, the deaths of our officers and men for this eternally just cause is absolute proof that our country truly is the land of the gods." Fusauchi ended his piece by invoking the memory of the great Bakumatsu era patriot, Yoshida Shôin, who wrote on the eve of his death that he hoped to be reborn seven times to fight for the Emperor.[8]

On the opposite page, a small piece about the Mongol invasions ran under a picture of two brothers standing on the rocky shore of Imazu beach in Fukuoka. As the older, uniformed brother pointed to the ruins of an old fortress, he told his younger sibling, "Jirô, you and your friends must become like Kôno Michiari," a reference to a famous warrior who helped repel the first Mongol invasion in 1281.[9] *Girl's Club* echoed this theme by using a sampling of Prince Kameyama's calligraphy—*Overcome the Enemy*—to link the Mongol invasion with the Greater East Asian War. "You must do your utmost to uphold the imperial degree," the article instructed, and destroy "the ugly enemy American and British."[10] Frequent reference to the Mongol invasions underscored the growing desperation of Japan's leaders in the last year of the war. The Americans had not yet begun their civilian bombing campaigns, but military authorities had already begun preparing for an invasion of the home islands. The invasion never came but the ideological onslaught continued through the last wartime issues of both magazines.

In the last eight months of the war, young boys consumed a steady diet of martial valor. From the Christian-hating Devil-general Katô Kiyomasa, who led much of the fighting in Hideyoshi's ill-fated invasion of Korea, to Yoshida Shôin and the men of high purpose mentioned earlier, Japanese boys were constantly reminded that, despite their age, their duty and loyalty could be tested at anytime.[11] The May/June issue of *Boy's Club* confirmed this with a heart-wrenching story of a national school youth corps preparing for a bloody showdown with American marines on their beloved Akashima in the Okinawan island chain.[12]

"The teacher passed the grenades to the students . . . ," began writer Sakurai Chûon, who recalled how tears splashed onto the newspaper in his lap as he read these words only weeks before. He then went on to retell the story that had moved him so.

On the morning of March 31, members of the island's youth defense patrol noticed a gray, drumlike object washing up in the white surf. As one member poked it with his sword, an incoming artillery round from an enemy ship slammed into the sand nearby. Old men, women and children, braving the artillery barrage, came running but to no avail. The patrol members were dead. The invasion had begun. There the story shifted to the popular national school *Sensei* (teacher) and his final lesson. As students gathered round their beloved *Sensei*, he proclaimed emotionally, "How splendid! You've come to die with your teacher." He then reminded the boys that their mothers and fathers had already died on the beach. "A splendid end" he called it. "They became the Emperor's shield, laughing in death. Do you understand this?" *Sensei* asked. "Yes. We understand," the boys shouted in chorus. As if to further steel the boys to their fate, *Sensei* invoked a litany of names from Japan's martial past. He reminded them of the twelve- and thirteen-year-olds who fought against the Mongols centuries earlier, of ten-year-old Kusunoki Masatsura who vowed to defend the Emperor after his father's death, and of the beloved Minamoto Yoshitsune who began his legendary career at age thirteen.[13]

The time for talk was now over. *Sensei* and his troop approached a pile of wooden boxes. "What do you think are in these?" he asked. "Grenades," shouted the boys in unison. "That's right. Just as you were trained yesterday, throw them and kill the American soldiers. Now, let's open the box." With that, Sakurai described how the now-armed procession moved toward the beach, which was under sustained attack from enemy warships anchored offshore. "*Sensei's* sword gleamed in the sunlight as he and the boys charged the enemy." Here the story ended. Sakurai told his audience that he "simply could hold his pen no longer."[14]

## Children and the *Yamato Damashii*

Just as boys were regaled with tales of martial valor and sacrifice in preparation for their own direct participation in the war, so, too, were girls indoctrinated by messages of sacrifice unto death. In both cases, Japan's paragon of tragic heroism and epitome of imperial loyalty, Kusunoki Masashige (1294–1336), father of Masatsura, loomed larger than any other historical actor. From 1941 to the end of 1945, his exploits were serialized monthly in *Boy's Club's* "Historical Novel Series" but he also figured prominently in this genre of stories for girls. The New Year's 1945 issue of *Girl's Club*, for example, carried three songs written by Bakumatsu era (1853–1868) women, which honored Masashige's memory.

Because I was born a woman, I cannot use the bow and arrow or the sword. But in my next life I will be reborn a man and take up these weapons to serve my Emperor.

Even in this world, can there be anyone who does not know of the spirit that flows in the pure water of Minatogawa.

Just as the flowers bloom in spring, so too is it time for soldiers to fight bravely for the Emperor.[15]

In defining the limits of what was possible for girls, these songs still offered the promise of death in battle in the next life as men. Mention of the Minatogawa underscored this dream, for it was here that Masashige, suffering from some eleven wounds, committed suicide rather than face capture by the enemy. His actions exemplified the Yamato spirit (*Yamato damashii*), the most powerful attribute of wartime Japanese uniqueness and superiority. While boys were being prepared for death in battle or being regaled with tales of fathers, uncles, and older brothers who had died heroically, girls were offered their own role models for the Yamato spirit. Digging deep into the mythical past, one article in the July issue of *Girl's Club* maintained that the Yamato spirit was not simply founded on power, which girls did not have, but also on compassion, which they possessed in abundance.[16] Building on the words of Kamo Mabuchi, who was said to have been among the first to revise the Yamato spirit to include women, the article offered up Oto Tachibana Hime and Jingô Kôgô from the mists of Japanese legend as real-life exemplars of female *Yamato damashii*.

Oto Tachibana Hime was the wife of the mythical hero Yamato Takeru who gave her life so her husband might live to fulfill his mission for the Emperor. According to legend, Takeru angered the sea god while crossing the bay between Sagami and Kazusa en route to battling the Ebisu people. Enraged, the sea god called up a ferocious storm against him in revenge. To save her husband and his men for their mission, Oto Tachibana Hime leapt into the waves as a sacrificial offering. An equally mythical figure, Jingô Kôgô was the wife of the Chûai Emperor. Before he set out to quell a Kumaso revolt, the gods revealed to Jingô in a dream that he should first conquer Silla on the Korean Peninsula. Not heeding Jingô's advice, the Emperor died soon after his expedition against the Kumaso. To fulfil the gods' orders, Jingô, then pregnant, placed a rock in her sash (some say in her womb) to delay the birth of her child, rallied her loyal retainers and, together, they pacified Silla. Returning to Japan, Jingô gave birth to the future Emperor

Ojin. She ruled as regent behind Ojin for some seventy years and died at the age of one hundred.

Jingô's longevity notwithstanding, *Yamato damashii* more frequently illustrated life cut short by death. A short story in the February issue of *Girl's Club* illustrated this point starkly. It told of a young girl, Taiko, who lived near Wakamatsu Castle in Aizu, the last stronghold of anti-Restoration resistance at the beginning of the Meiji era.[17] With Imperial forces besieging the castle and the men away fighting, the women and children pledged to commit suicide rather than be killed by the enemy. "It is better the children die at the hands of their mothers," said one woman, "than to die at the hands of the enemy."[18] With that, the women killed their children and then themselves as the enemy stormed the castle. Taiko, however, remained alive, blood pouring from her self-inflicted wound as she slipped in and out of consciousness. As the enemy's guns roused her, Taiko heard a soldier approach:

> With a voice no louder than that of a mosquito, Taiko whispered, "Are you a friend or an enemy?" The enemy captain, already deeply moved at the sight of the dead women and children, felt hot tears fall from his eyes as he heard her voice. . . . He leaned over Taiko and said, "a friend." Filled with a compassion borne from the loyal acts of these women, the captain took out his sword and, to end Taiko's suffering, cut off her head. With his own head bowed and bloody sword hanging limply by his side, the captain was roused only by the cries of the women's friends who had come too late to defend them. Knowing he must move quickly to engage these new attackers, the captain nonetheless took a moment to place Taiko's head on the *tokonoma*.[19] He then bowed deeply from respect. "Just a woman," he mused, "but so strong."[20]

The significance of this story lay in the fact that the deaths of the women and children of Aizu validated their lives, despite the fact that they fought against the Emperor's army. At the same time, the captain's actions symbolized respect for a righteous enemy, an ideal that was supposed to define the Imperial army. Clearly, girls could embody the power of the Yamato spirit, just as boys could exhibit its compassion. They could also make the ultimate sacrifice. Females could not become soldiers but they could still serve the Emperor through their deaths.

To reinforce this point, *Girl's Club* again invoked Yoshida Shôin, paragon of male imperial loyalty, in its March/April issue as a model for both girls and boys: "To die in observance of Imperial orders," he said, " is really to live through death."[21] For Yoshida, one's death in the name of the Emperor was in fact an affirmation of life itself. The loyal subject's spirit, according to the laws of the gods, would live eternally through one's ancestors and through those who act similarly in the future. As Yoshida explained to a student almost one hundred years earlier:

> If one is loath to die at seventeen or eighteen, he will be equally reluctant at thirty. . . . Unless one performs some deed that brings a sense of gratification before dying, his soul will never rest in peace.[22]

Nowhere was the encouragement to gratify one's life through death more graphically illustrated to girls and boys than through the concept of *Yamato damashii*, and nowhere was this spirit more powerfully represented than by the selfless bravery of the Special Attack Corps (*shimpû*).[23] These young heroes paraded through every issue of *Boy's Club* and *Girl's Club* as shining examples to be honored and emulated. Created by General Onishi Takajirô in the wake of Japan's defeat at Leyte Gulf in 1944, the Special Attack Corps reflected the desperation of Japan's military leaders but, for children, they became examples of selfless devotion to the Imperial cause.

In the January 1945 issue of *Girl's Club*, Mishimi Takeya defined the unique character of the *shimpû* by describing the fundamental difference between Japanese and enemy soldiers. Unlike the enemy, said Mishimi, "Japanese soldiers went to war never hoping to come back alive."[24] Not only did this illustrate the superior Yamato spirit, it also gave power to the lie of "certain victory." To drive his point home further, Mishimi drew from a little-known eighteenth century record of martial training, *Hagakure* (Hidden Leaves), which proclaimed that "a true warrior still functions even though his head has been cut off."[25] This was then tied in with Kusunoki's famous words: "Seven times I am born to destroy the enemies of the Emperor." Mishimi closed by telling young girls that although they were still children and, as females, could never become *shimpû*, they could still contribute to the war effort by purging the selfishness from their spirit and allowing the flame of patriotism to burn fiercely. That girls could not aspire to sacrificial death did not stop the magazine from encouraging them to write letters to the pilots, to sew the famous one-thousand-stitch belts, or to make dolls for the men to wear on their final journey. Throughout 1945, numerous stories appeared reinforcing these themes, accompanied by the occasional picture of a young pilot preparing to enter the cockpit of his plane, proudly wearing in his belt a small doll made by a schoolgirl.

The February issue followed up with three letters from young female readers writing about their experiences of seeing off the young *shimpû* pilots. In the first, Takagi Toshie recognized the need for girls to "have the same heart as these brave [men]: affectionate, righteous, and strong to the end."[26] Following this, Otsu Riko and Umito Yurie described how they felt as they bade farewell to the men of the Special Attack Corps, flags held proudly aloft, eyes brimming with tears. "*Kamisama*," said Riko, referring to the pilots, "please make a direct hit. Destroy the evil Americans and British." "If I were a boy," sighed Yurie, "I too could join the youth air corps."[27]

Unlike little Yurie, boys could indeed aspire to become their heroes. Two letters in the February issue of *Boy's Club* illustrate dramatically their wish to die and live eternally in the spirit world.[28] The first, by junior high student Yamazaki Toyohiro, described the day he and his classmates bade farewell to the *Shimpû* pilots. "I stood in a row with my classmates, waving my flag as twelve brave young men paraded past us. I began to cry, thinking that they would soon become spirits." As the smiling young men filed past, saluting with one hand and holding a bouquet of flowers in the other, Toyohiro vowed that when he grew up he would "become a *shimpû* and ram [himself] into an aircraft carrier." Until then, he said, "I must make my body strong and study hard." The other letter, by high school sophomore Ishigami Kiyoyasu, told a similar tale. "We gathered in front of the school at seven in the morning. . . . As the young men passed in front of me, they smiled and bowed. My eyes filled with tears. In my heart I prayed silently that each would make a direct hit." Like Toyohiro, Kiyoyasu hoped to become *shimpû* when he grew up. "When I become a soldier and make this passage, I resolve to strike the evil Americans and British. Now, I am looking at living spirits." Like Yurie, Kiyoyasu proclaimed solemnly, "I will never forget this moment for as long as I live."

In Japan's wartime culture of death, boys and girls found no release from the litany of stories about heroic, tragic valor. Every article, letter, and picture concentrated on memorializing those who died, working hard for those who would die, and preparing for one's own death. The only escape from death, it seemed, was death itself. Yurie's comments, like those of Kiyoyasu, capture the naive trust of children, convinced absolutely in the messages they consumed from their elders.

## Conclusion: Back to Greece

Ultimately, it was defeat itself that provided the final escape from the culture of death. More importantly, it became the moment that no one would forget, forever enshrined in historical memory as the turning point. *Boy's Club* reflected this dramatic change in its first postwar issue, which carried a full reprint of the Imperial broadcast followed by the now-famous picture of dozens of Japanese prostrating themselves in remorse in front of the Imperial Palace, eyes burning with "bitter tears." "Even the trees wept," said one editorial.[29] The companion issue of *Girl's Club* did not carry this text but it did publish a smaller photograph of prostrate Japanese in front of the Imperial Palace. This was part of an article by Mishimi Takeya—the same writer who had regaled young girls with tales of *Yamato damashii* during the war—which explained the turning point and the Emperor's benevolence for saving the Japanese people and the world.[30]

It would be a mistake, however, to make too much of the turning point, at least as far as the messages to children were concerned. Men and women would no longer die fighting the enemy, "cherry blossoms" would no longer fall, carrying with them memories of Masashige and the Emperor, boys and girls would no longer be placed in harm's way, and incendiary bombs would no longer rain death on Japan's urban spaces. The culture of death may have died and been reborn as a culture of life through defeat and the Imperial broadcast, but underlying this dramatic change was the same message of selfless sacrifice and devotion. Indeed, the photograph and text of the Emperor's broadcast reflected this continuity because many of those prostrate figures were apologizing for not having sacrificed enough. Mishimi's article, too, expressed this continuity starkly by again invoking Masashige and his last stand at Minatogawa. Now, however, this image magically became a metaphor for life with Mishimi enjoining his young readers to study hard so they could build a new world culture and a righteous nation. In the Greece that would be the new Japan, everyone, including children, would be called on to sacrifice in the name of the Emperor to rebuild their nation.

For the remainder of 1945, and in the years that followed, the imperial institution remained the focus of sacrificial action. Hirohito retired to the wings, reincarnated as a "man of science," but his ancestors, especially the Meiji Emperor, emerged to remind children of their "great responsibility." In December 1945 the young protagonist of a short story, *A Chronicle of Idleness*, reflected on his wartime experience. "The war is over but our struggle continues," sighed Masasuke.[31] These words summed up the lives of Japanese children in the postwar as surely as they symbolized the propaganda of the "new Japan." The message to the children of this allegedly new nation was that selfless endurance conquers all. Tucked in one corner of Masasuke's story was a little box titled *Golden Sayings*: "He who perseveres wins, he who does not loses."[32] This reminded Japanese children that victory and defeat, however intertwined, were fleeting, like the cherry blossoms of spring. It was the manner in which one approached either that really mattered.

## Notes

1. Kayahara Kazan, *Mainichi Shimbun*, August 16, 1946, p. 2. All Japanese names here are rendered with the family name first, as is Japanese custom.

2. The one hundred million (*ichioku*) was a core phrase in the Japanese government's propaganda arsenal. A deliberate inflation of Japanese population of seventy million, it also included some thirty million decidedly unwilling Koreans, Chinese, and other Asian peoples trapped in the net of Japan's "Greater East Asian Co prosperity Sphere."

3. John Dower addresses Japan's wartime propaganda directly in *War Without Mercy* and more indirectly in *Embracing Defeat*. Thomas Havens' *Valley of Darkness* is also a good study of wartime domestic life. I have examined the gap between the rhetoric of propaganda and the reality of social action in "The Reconstruction of Self and Society in Early Postwar Japan, 1945–1948" (Ph.D. dissertation, University of British Columbia, 1999), and in a forthcoming *Journal of Social History* article entitled "Need, Greed, and Protest in Japan's Black Market, 1938–1949." Dower, too, gives an excellent account of wartime protest and subversion in "Sensational Rumors, Seditious Graffiti, and the Nightmares of the Thought Police," in Dower, ed., *Japan in War and Peace*, 101–154.

4. Both magazines were published by Kôdansha, one of Japan's oldest and most conservative publishers. For an internal history of Kôdansha's wartime role, see Noma Shôichi, General Editor, *Kôdansha no ayunda gojûnen* (Fifty Years of Kôdansha), vol. 2 (Tokyo: Shôwahen, Shashihensan Iinkai, 1959).

5. Most Japanese referred to war in the Pacific as the Greater East Asian War (*Daitôa sensô*).

6. Fusauchi Yukinari, "*Dai nihon wa shinkoku nari*" (Japan is the Land of the Gods), *Shônen kurabu*, January 1945, p. 2. Kitabatake (1293–1354) was a staunch supporter of Emperor Go-Daigo's southern court in the latter's ill-fated attempt to impose direct imperial rule. In wartime Japan, those who had supported Go-Daigo were regarded as patriots and exemplars of imperial loyalty. Conversely, those who supported the northern court of Emperor Kômyô, like Muromachi era founder Ashikaga Takeuji, were considered traitors.

7. The Mito Han was controlled by a collateral family of the Tokugawa shoguns and was known for producing many of early modern Japan's best neo-Confucian scholars. "Men of high purpose" is the translation of the Japanese word, *shishi*, and

refers to those men of the Bakumatsu era (1853–1868) who sought to expel the foreigners and support the imperial court, often through assassination.

8. Yoshida (1831–1859) was a lower ranking samurai from Chôshû (Hiroshima) who inspired many of the later Meiji leaders. He was arrested and executed for his part in an assassination attempt on a Tokugawa official.

9. *Gengô no bôrui ni tatsu*, ibid., p. 3.

10. *Shôjo kurabu*, January 1945, p. 1.

11. Katô (1562–1611) received his nickname (*kishôkan*) for the relentless pursuit of his enemies during the Korean campaign. His reputation as a Christian hater apparently came from his adherence to Nichiren Buddhism. He is honored in the temples of this sect under the name of *Seishôkan*.

12. Sakurai Chûon, "*Shônen wa teryûdan o tsukande: Akashima no kokumin gakkô seito no saiko*" (The Boy Clutches the Hand Grenade: The Death of the Students of the Akashima National School), *Shônen kurabu*, May/June 1945, pp. 4–7.

13. The pathos of Yoshitsune (1159–1189) is usually contrasted with his brother Yoritomo's more colorless, prosaic life, although there is scant historical evidence for depicting Yoritomo this way. For a good assessment of how the two are contrasted in Japanese mythistory, see Morris, *The Nobility of Failure*, pp. 67–105.

14. *Shônen kurabu*, May/June 1945, p. 7.

15. Kimata Osamu, "*Bakumatsu aikoku josei no uta: Minatogawa kiyoku nagareshi*" (Songs of Female Patriots of the Bakumatsu Era: The Minato River flows purely), *Shôjo kurabu*, January 1945, pp. 5–7.

16. Kamo Mabuchi, "*Yamato damashii wa omina mo nanka odoreru ya*" (Are There Ways in Which Women are Inferior Under Yamato Damashii?), *Shôjo kurabu*, July 1945, p. 3.

17. Sekimoto Tora, "*Kandô shôsetsu: Teki ka mikata ka*" (Motivational Novel: Friend or Enemy?), *Shôjo kurabu*, February 1945, pp. 54–63.

18. Ibid., p. 56.

19. A *tokonoma* is a small alcove in a traditional Japanese room normally used for arranged flowers, calligraphy, and paintings.

20. Sekimoto Tora, "Kandô shôsetsu," p. 63.

21. Yoshida Shôin, "Choku o hôjite shi su, shi su to mo nao ikeru ga gotoshi," *Shôjo kurabu*, March/April 1945, p. 9.

22. Quoted in Hirakawa Sukehiro, "Japan's Turn to the West" (trans. Bob Tadashi Wakabayashi), in Wakabayashi, ed., *Modern Japanese Thought* (New York: Cambridge University Press, 1998), p. 50.

23. These troops were originally named "*Oka*" or Cherry Blossoms but later became known as *Shimpû* (divine wind) after the miraculous storms that twice destroyed the bulk of the Mongol fleet centuries earlier. Although they are known as *Kamikaze* in English, the Japanese have preferred the Sino-Japanese rendering of the same character, *Shimpû*.

24. Mishimi Takeya, "*Honohoto moeyo* (Burn With Passion), *Shôjo kurabu*, January 1945, pp. 38–40.

25. Ibid., p. 40.

26. These three letters were published by Gotô Shôsa of the War Ministry's Information Bureau under the title "*Kamiwashi o miokuru*" (Bidding Farewell to the Divine Eagles), *Shôjo kurabu*, February 1945. pp. 19–21.

27. *Kami* best translates into English as "spirit." *Sama* is an honorific.

28. *Tokubetsu kôgekitai o omiokuri shite* ("Bidding Farewell to the Special Attack Forces"), *Shônen kurabu*, February 1945, pp. 24–25.

29. The rescript and the photograph can be found in *Shônen kurabu*, August/September 1945, pp. 2–3, 4–5 respectively. "Weeping trees" is from an *Asahi Shimbun* headline, August 16, 1945.

30. Mishimi Takeya, "The New Japan and Us" (*Shin nihon to watachitachi*), *Shôjo kurabu*, pp. 4–5.

31. Koide Shogo, "*Hyôryûki*," *Shônen kurabu*, November/December 1945, pp. 22–30.

32. Iwata Sankô, "*Kingen*," ibid., p. 24.

# Chapter Thirteen

# The Antifascist Narrative
## *Memory Lessons in the Schools of the Soviet Occupation Zone, 1945–1949*

### *Benita Blessing*

In May 1945, after twelve years of the National Socialist, or Nazi, dictatorship and six years of war, Germany surrendered unconditionally to the victorious forces of the United States, Great Britain, and the Soviet Union. The end to the fighting did not bring about immediate relief for many Germans, particularly for young people in the Soviet zone. The disappearance or death of family members during the war, long-absent fathers returning home from POW camps, and a new human landscape brought about by massive refugee movement (e.g., displaced persons) all contributed to a chaotic postwar situation. In the midst of these desperate conditions, young people had to be "denazified" and "democratized" through new school systems. In the three Western zones, which became the Federal Republic of Germany in 1949, this new curricular program carried the title of "reeducation."[1] In the Soviet zone, which became the German Democratic Republic in 1949, reformers referred more often to "antifascist democratic education." The Soviet zone school system, strongly influenced by German social democratic forces, was to educate young people in a new, antifascist, socialist-humanist, German national consciousness. Lessons about the war were taught through essays in history and German classes.

This essay examines how pupils in the Soviet zone learned to recount their memories of the war in a form that demonstrated a specific "antifascist democratic" understanding of these events. Children, no less than adults around them, struggled with issues such as trying to reconcile the new enemy status of Nazis—who were also possibly friends, neighbors, and family members—with the new liberator status of Soviets. Antifascist educational reformers, primarily a coalition of social democrats and communists, used a sort of "memory lesson" to teach young people how to remember their individual pasts and their collective (national) past. This was not an explicit program, but rather a function of the communication between school and society. In history and German classes, young people gradually learned to narrate their wartime experiences within an interpretative framework that encouraged them to remember certain elements, while suppressing or de-emphasizing others. This antifascist narrative helped pupils make sense of their recent wartime and postwar memories, a precondition for accepting the "new school's" and the new nation's legitimacy. In this manner, the close link between personal memory and public history construction becomes clear.[2] Pupils' essays in the context of curriculum guidelines from this four-year period illustrate how adults hoped to offer a new set of memories to children and how children carved out their own solutions to the dilemma of relearning their collective and private histories and memories. Just as their parents and teachers, young people sifted and weighed their memories against the new narrative structures they were offered. An analysis of these memory traces in the documents left behind by young people will shed new light on how children not only survived the war, but how they then went on to find strategies for mastering their present, making the transition from Nazis into antifascists.

The sources for this study include curriculum guidelines, educational policy directives, professional journals, educational conference minutes, newspaper articles, and approximately 1,300 pupils' essays. Almost all of these essays come from East Berlin, with a few dozen originating from other parts of the Soviet zone. Regional school administrators sometimes apparently suggested essay topics to schools, and then read them afterward to check on the state of young people.[3] Teachers could also find ideas for assignments in educational journals, or from supplemental teacher seminars.[4] Taken together, these materials comprise a dialogue between adults and young people, influenced by but also influencing the society around them, including family, peers, and religious and political organizations.

### Developing the Antifascist Narrative: From War History
### to War Memories

The actual decision of which new history should be taught and how this should ensue was not made by one single, homogenous administrative organization. Nor did standard curricula and centralized educational journals comprise the only area where administrators sought to influence how young Germans understood their nation's past. Nonetheless, clear broad pedagogical tendencies and philosophies can be identified, especially in educators' discussions of actual classroom instruction. Germans in East and West called upon history and German classes to imbue pupils with a positive sense of the nation, one that encouraged pride in Germany's accomplishments without belittling other nations' achievements.[5] Significantly, educational reformers repeatedly noted the need to connect history instruction to other subjects, particularly German.[6] But developing a new history curriculum is a time-consuming, delicate process. In the Soviet zone, both Soviet and German educational authorities decided to forbid history instruction for the first academic year until they could adequately train new history teachers and produce acceptable textbooks.[7]

Young people could not be prevented from remembering their pasts, though, anymore than teachers, parents, or politicians could avoid the topic in other contexts. Thus, as early as October 1945, the month in which schools reopened officially throughout the zone, the first examples of the classroom dialogue between adults and young people about interpreting their national and individual pasts can be found. Educational reformers encouraged this interactive approach to learning, as stated in a 1949 draft for the "Guidelines for the Didactics and Methodology of the German Democratic School": "*Lessons are a joint work of teacher and pupil.*"[8] The importance accorded classroom instruction drew on a larger tradition of believing that schools and their authority were the most important aspects in the formation of young people's world views.[9] But pupils were assigned, and took, an active part in the reframing of their memories and making sense of a new version of history. Much of this interaction took place during German classes, an important reminder that history lessons are not limited to history class.

Still, the driving force for the new national self-narrative came from outside the school building. In the Soviet zone, where the Social Democratic Party (SPD) and the Communist Party of Germany (KPD) joined forces in

1946 to become the majority Socialist Unity Party (SED), social reformers sketched out a "victim narrative" of national history that positioned their half of Germany as largely innocent of Nazi crimes. Since SPD and KPD members had actively fought against Nazism and fascism, often sacrificing careers and even lives, the SED-dominated government could claim that the two labor parties' only failure had been their inability to build a joint resistance against the National Socialists. The Nazis had been everyone else. The two other key parties initially admitted in the Soviet zone, referred to as the bourgeois (*bürgerliche*) parties, were the Christian Democrats (CDU) and the Liberal Democrats (LDP). Their smaller voices did not significantly contradict the SED narrative; nor did they question the emerging antifascist historical narrative that residency in the Soviet zone implied personal and national innocence. This interpretation of the Soviet zone as a rupture with the Nazi past proved to be the most significant aspect of teaching young people how to view their nation's history.

## Pupils Recount Their Memories

Young people quickly incorporated this version of history into their assignments when discussing historical events from other epochs. It was not difficult for them to accept new or rehabilitated distant figures in German history as part of their cultural heritage. When asked to express specific political viewpoints, they understood and accepted the new ideas being presented to them. A tenth-grader from the Saxony-Anhalt city Güsten, for instance, wrote a report for German class in 1948 on the minnesingers, referring to them as "Germany's glory," and a year later completed a critical essay on Bismarck's absolutist foreign policy.[10] A fifth-grader from Berlin dutifully listed the impressive accomplishments of favored sons such as Friedrich Schiller or Gottfried Lessing.[11]

But the essays took on a different, more emotional, and even questioning quality when pupils wrote about traumatic events that had touched their lives. When confronted with the task of narrating their own recent pasts and their relationship to the new German nation, young people clearly struggled to accept the official line of how to evaluate their national and personal histories. During the postwar years, young people learned to use the antifascist strategy of placing Soviet zone residents in the role of victim to denounce Germany's fascist past, without looking critically at their families' participation in the Nazi regime. This victim narrative, most striking when pupils recounted their own families' experiences and tried to make sense of their parents' roles during the war, was a sleight of hand that did not always come easily to them, especially not in the first months after the war. The contrast to pupils' more sober accounts of Nazi history highlights the difficulty that young people had in reconciling their personal histories and memories with the official collective consciousness proffered by the emerging antifascist, socialist state.

Two essays from the fifth-grader Otto Dieb vividly illustrate a young boy in the first postwar months who had not yet entirely accepted the antifascist narrative for framing the painful ruptures in his personal memory and national history. In December 1944, Otto wrote an essay for his German class entitled "My Friend," in which he proudly described a powerful, gray-eyed, blonde boy with his hair parted on the left and good skin color, a strong nose, good muscles, and a clear enunciation, who had earned a leadership position in the Hitler Youth.[12] There is then a silence of several months in the school notebook when, presumably, the final months of the Second World War kept Otto and his classmates at home. Then, in October, Otto completed the assignment "The Rebuilding of the Countryside and City."[13] Otto began with the standard judgment that the criminal deeds of the Nazis led to misery throughout the entire world. It becomes clear, however, that this essay lacked the earlier tone of self-confidence. This was due in part to Otto's misunderstanding that the Potsdam Accords intended for Germany to become an agrarian state. "Germany is to be placed into a central European standard of living, that is, such a life as is the case in the Balkan countries, thus living in huts." Otto believed that it would be hard for Germans to get used to life in this new Germany. He added that the reparation payments "demanded by those peoples that we attacked" led him and others to doubt the newspapers' rosy visions of quickly reconstructed cities. Shifting tone slightly, Otto then complained that the Nazis had lied to Germans, and only now was the truth about unjust property distribution emerging. In an optimistic conclusion, he closed by proclaiming that the future remained open for Germany.

Otto's specific situation demonstrates the limits on the school's ability to dictate a new understanding of his past to him. Other factors and institutions, including families, regional differences, and previous memories, contributed to young people's historical consciousness and thus affected their understanding of their national history. Otto lived in Oschersleben in Saxony-Anhalt, a region that switched hands from the Americans to the Soviets. The U.S. Morgenthau Plan, which had called for an agrarianization of Germany, was a topic of conversation in the West that would have reached Otto's ears. He could thus easily confuse it with the Potsdam Accords, which focused on the "4 Ds": demilitarization, denazification, decentralization, and democratization.[14] Perhaps Otto overheard outraged and even sarcastic discussions among his parents and their friends as they bemoaned Germany's plight, during which he won the impression that he might have to start living in a hut—an idea suggestive of persistent Nazi racist ideology about "primitive peoples." Yet he did not uncritically accept all that he heard. He was aware of optimistic reports in the newspapers, but these were not enough to convince him that everything would proceed smoothly in the rebuilding of his city. Yet even as young people like Otto established themselves as partial victims, they did not see themselves as helpless receptacles of knowledge or memories. He thus joined the ranks of determined Germans ready to write Germany a better future.

Essays from other pupils a year later demonstrate a clearer internalization of the new "memory lessons," which implicitly encouraged young people to use personal experience to explain the Soviet zone's collective history. The theme of the family's traumatic experiences during or after the war, for instance, served as the frame of reference in many pupils' essays. This tendency fits in with the specific outlines of the Soviet zone German curriculum for what types of writing pupils were to learn in the fifth through eighth grades. Educators considered three types of essays to be the most important types of written expression: narration, description, and reporting, with a particular emphasis on fantasy and reflection.[15] Thus, when thirteen-year-old Vera Müller wrote an essay on the last days of the war, she wrote about her family.[16] The personal memories and experiences of pupils lent an untouchable, authentic quality to the essays. On closer inspection, these accounts fit a clear style of antifascist narration that elicited this perception. This is evident in Vera's essay, in which she recounted a bombing during which she and her mother were attempting to run to their house: "I told my mommy that she should wait for a second so that we didn't all run across together, that might get noticed. Outside it was deathly quiet, only the dust of exploded grenades lay in the air. I ran as fast as I could, but too late. Just as I reached the sidewalk, I was hit by an exploding piece of grenade." Vera did not know at the time what had actually happened to her mother. "They told me everything but the truth. Only after I had been in the hospital for four weeks with no news from home did I find out that my parents had been victims of the Nazi regime."

There is a curious tension between the personal trauma recounted by Vera and the more distanced, formulaic description of her parents' status as "victims of the Nazi regime." In fact, it is unclear from her essay whether both parents died during this particular episode. It would seem that only the mother and she were present, although the "together" might indicate other persons. Another possibility is that Vera's father died in another context: in a concentration camp, perhaps, or as a soldier in combat. This interpretation would explain why Vera, after being hurt and brought into the air raid cellar, only asked about her mother. Pupils like Vera learned quite early to adjust the degree of subjectivity and emotion with which they related experiences depending on the function of the narrative. The essays portrayed the suffering and injustice felt by the authors, but within a clear interpretive framework. Thus, the retelling of even a painful memory about the war almost always further added an evaluative comment about the senselessness of the war, or the fault of the Nazis for disrupting everyday life.

It was not always easy for young people to remain within this framework. Trying to reconcile too many interpretations of the same situation, pupils found themselves caught in contradictory narrative strategies that clearly elicited discomfort in the young authors. Without commenting on its implications, Vera added the statement that she was the one who decided that she and her mother should cross the street separately. From the entire scene, this decision remained important enough in her memory to mention in a school essay. Rather than pose the heart-wrenching question of what might have happened had her mother run with her, Vera learned to give responsibility to the Nazis—the elusive others. And yet, her own role in this scene, which did not neatly fit into an analysis of Nazi responsibility for postwar sufferings, could not be forgotten, any less than the quiet protest that no one would tell her the truth about her mother.

In a time when schoolchildren struggled with the realization that the lessons taught to them during the war were lies, such small perceived injustices of being told "all sorts of stories" did not serve to smooth the transition into accepting the validity of the new system for pupils like Vera, even as she began to accept a new way of understanding Germany's, and with this her own, history. Vera's narrative draws its strength from the sense of a painful memory that, even though it is personal and individual, achieved a status of universality through its structure. Vera recounted the scene in such a way that invited contemporary readers to recognize the familiar sense of tragic fate that then segued into the moral of the story: "we were unfortunate victims." In fact, Vera's device of mentioning her suggestion to cross the street separately, without explicitly questioning how this decision affected her mother's death, allowed her and her readers to make this connection implicitly. Her audience and she were then led to immediately proclaim her innocence. In this manner, her readers could also exculpate themselves from their own similar, unarticulated fears of guilt, in private as well as public matters.

Memory lessons could also be used to help young people see the progress being made in the reconstruction of their nation since the war. The antifascist narrative, in this regard, turned the victim narrative of the war into an empowering one of overcoming difficulties. Typical of this strategy was the Berlin essay assignment "gas, water, and electricity services 1945 and 1946," in which pupils compared the state of basic services after the war and a year later. One of the more charming of these essays is by a group of seven girls from a Berlin-Prenzlauer Berg middle school. "Christel" and her friends wrote a short theater piece to illustrate the reconstruction progress made in Berlin.[17] The main figures are the girls themselves and one of the girl's families. In all the scenes, characters in the play struggle to retake up roles they had before the war. For instance, the "hundreds of people" standing in line for water right after the war are all "tired, [and] longing for quiet and a meal"; the new gas flame that finally burns again in Berlin-Neukölln, though weak, shows "its good intention." In the first scene, we learn that the father has returned home on the previous evening, presumably just after the last days of fighting. Exhausted and disoriented, his initial impressions upon arriving were too quick to notice the luxuries of electricity and the like. As he explains the next day, "I was just happy that it [our home] was still there!" This second day of his homecoming is described sentimentally, with the father surrounded by his proud family, who show off the return of running water. After a night's sleep, he is able to fully appreciate the successful reconstruction of his city. The play demonstrates the family's pride in winning the approval of the father, still a key reference point in young people's lives. The father is a physical marker of the past, both a reminder of where Germany had been and an indicator of how far it had come. Christel and her friends clearly valued the reunification of the family: Father was home again, and the family made room for him to take up his previous role. The assignment is perhaps the clearest example of educators' and pupils' attempts to make sense of wartime memories that were, literally, omnipresent, and to use them as markers of progress.

Not all homecomings proceeded so smoothly. In a 1947 letter to her friend, the young Brigitte Reimann, later a leading author of the GDR, described a different scene. She, too, wrote with enthusiasm of the return of her father from a Soviet prisoner-of-war camp to their home in Burg, a small city of 20,000 residents in Saxony-Anhalt. However, she and her three younger siblings had not been prepared for the figure that greeted them at the train station. Their scrawny, louse-covered, and now bearded father elicited shyness and fright in the children, particularly in the younger ones. Even his language had been distorted and rendered unfamiliar by the war experience, "so anxious, so sick and—I don't know, just so terribly strange!"[18] Worse, he had become "rather meticulous," so that the household had to be run under tighter control. None of this dampened Brigitte's determination to appreciate the once-again reunited family structure, and she reported that all of the family had grown used to having their father around.

The idealistic description by Christel and her classmates of the father's return might have been experienced by some of the girls already. Others, however, might still have been waiting for their fathers a year after the end of the war, or lost them. Many fathers returned home wounded and unable to perform previous tasks, or did not return at all.[19] In the Western zone city of Hamburg, to provide one example, three out of ten children did not have a father at home, due either to death or internment.[20] When fathers did return, they often experienced jealousy at the intimate relationships that had developed in their absences between their wives and children.[21] Very young children lacked memories of their fathers, in some cases putting both sides in the position of having to get to know a total stranger. Many families noted the insatiable hunger of the father upon his returning home, and this sometimes led to bitter fights over food in the family. The father who returned home sometimes seemed to be almost a different person.

## Conclusions

Young people in the immediate postwar period had directly experienced little else than war and its trying aftermath. In an instructional environment that encouraged them to learn from and work on their private memories, pupils learned to frame their memories in a way that helped them make sense of their past, present, and future. The framework that their schools' lessons offered them was a specific antifascist narrative, one that taught young people that they, their families, and their society were victims of the Nazi regime. The responsibility for the war rested on the shoulders of the unidentified "others," and the others were those who did not live in the Soviet zone. Although pupils occasionally expressed mistrust in the new political system during the first postwar years, they eventually successfully learned to manipulate the antifascist narrative to their benefit.

The cognitive nature of memory and remembering means it can be impossible in many instances to verify if pupils really experienced those events which they later recounted as memories.[22] In the process of being offered a new history, however, this distinction is not meaningful. Invented stories such as that of Christel and her classmates clearly had references in the girls' own experiences—or at least, in experiences they believed they should have had. Regardless of how the girls' home situations actually looked, they were able to use an antifascist narrative to recount therapeutic memories of how the war should have ended. In other examples, when pupils had the liberty to reflect on and compare their new and old memories, they showed an awareness of the work this entailed, and consistently employed a form of memory narration that coincided with larger social expectations of how to remember.

The school trained pupils to express their wartime memories within a certain antifascist framework that used real and imagined experiences as a means of establishing innocence. Pupils accepted this strategy and employed it to begin the work of mastering their private memories, establishing themselves as part of the antifascist collective in one half of Germany. Pupils were active participants in this process. They themselves learned to use their memories to create meaning for their present and their future, and to count themselves as part of their new nation.[23] Their wartime memories helped them break with the Nazi past and, expressing determined hope, accept the proffered role of reconstructing the nation according to an antifascist democratic vision of the future. By writing about the war in an antifascist mode, using both real and imagined memories, young people found a means of moving beyond their wartime traumas.

### Notes

1. JCS 1067, Directive from American Chief of Staff to Commander of U.S. Occupation Troops in Germany, approved by U.S. Congress, April 26, 1945 and by Truman May 10. 1945. In Rolf Steininger, *Deutsche Geschichte seit 1945*, vol. 1, 1945–1947 (Fischer: Frankfurt, 1996), 50.

2. Noa Gedi and Yigal Elam, "Collective Memory—What is it?" *History and Memory* 8, no. 1 (1996): 30–50; Susan A. Crane, "Writing the Individual Back into

Collective Memory," *American Historical Review* 102, no. 5 (December 1997): 1372–1385; Alon Confino, "Collective Memory and Cultural History: Problems of Method," *American Historical Review* 102, no. 5 (December 1997): 1386–1403; Ulrich Neisser, "Self-narratives: True and false," in *The Remembering Self: Construction and Accuracy in the Self-Narrative*, eds. Ulrich Neisser and Robyn Fivush (Cambridge: Cambridge University Press, 1994), 11; Niklas Luhmann, "Zeit und Gedächtnis," *Soziale Systeme* 2, no. 2 (1996): 307–330.

3. Annet Gröschner, *"ich schlug meiner Mutter die brennenden Funken ab:" Berliner Schulaufsätze aus dem Jahr 1946* (Berlin: Kontext, 1996), 9–10.

4. The first educational journal for teachers appeared in 1946: *die neue schule*, 1946 ff.

5. "Lehrplan für die Grund- und Oberschulen in der sowjetischen Besatzungszone Deutschlands, Deutsch, Entwurf der am 1. Juli 1946 veröffentlichten 2. Fassung," in Joachim S. Hohmann, *Deutschunterricht in SBZ und DDR 1945–1962* (Frankfurt a.M.: Lang, 1997), 114; "Die Forderung der Richtlinien der Alliierten Erziehungskommission," *Lehrplan für den Geschichtsunterricht an den Berliner Schulen* (Berlin [East]/Leipzig: Volk und Wissen, 1948), 3.

6. Karl Ellrich, "Die grundlegende Vorbereitung des Geschichtsunterrichts im deutsch-heimatkundlichen Unterricht der ersten vier Grundschuljahre," *die neue schule* 1 (1946: 12), 5.

7. P. Zolotuchin, Leiter der Abteilung für Volksbildung der SMA in Deutschland, to Paul Wandel, May 15, 1946, memorandum allowing history instruction in schools again, Bundesarchiv Berlin (BArchiv) DR 2/6269, no. 115.

8. Emphasis and double emphasis in original. Dorst, Muller-Krumbholz, Sothmann, "1. Entwurf: Richtlinien für die Didaktik und Methodik der deutschen-demokratischen Schule," Berlin, May 18, 1949, Deutsches Institut für Pädagogische Forschung, Bibliothek Bildungsforschung (DIPF/BBF/Archiv) NL Sothmann, fo. 20, no. 1.

9. "Protokoll über den Pädagogischen Landeskongreb im Maxim-Gorki-Haus," Schweren 25–26 May 25/26, 1948, BArch DR 2/1394, no. 80.

10. Dorothea Uebrig, Deutsch Kl. 10a, no title, Museum zu Kindheit und Jugend-Schulmuseum (SM) Do 88/555, 16 Feb. 1948, and Geschichte, Kl. 11a, "Absolutismus—Bismarcks Aubenpolitik," SM Do 88/550, fall 1949.

11. Ingrid Friede, fifth grade, SM/Do 87/107, July 1945–November 1945.

12. Otto Dieb, fifth grade, "Mein Freund (Hausaufsatz)," Oscheersleben, 15 December 1944, SM/Do 93/174.

13. Otto Dieb, fifth grade, "Wiederaufbau in Stadt und Land," Oscheersleben, October 1945, SM/Do 93/174.

14. Rolf Steininger, *Deutsche Geschichte seit 1945*, vol. 1, 41–45 and 85–101.

15. "Lehrplan für die Grund- und Oberschulen," 154.

16. Vera Müller, thirteen years old, "Angestellt bei Beschuss," [ca. 1946], Landesarchiv Berlin (LAB/STA) 134/13, 179, no. 20–21.1.

17. Christel Novak et al., "Wiederaufbau Prenzlauer Berg," girls' middle school, [May 1946], LAB/STA 134/13, 181/1, no. 103–117.

18. Brigitte Reimann, 10 October 1947, *Aber wir schaffen es, verlab Dich drauf! Briefe an eine Freundin im Westen* 2nd ed. (Berlin: Aufbau, 1999), 16.

19. Hilde Thurnwald, *Gegenwartsprobleme Berliner Familien: Eine Soziologische unterschung an 498 Familien* (Berlin, 1948), 96–97.

20. "Generation ohne Väter," in *Benjamin: Zeitschrift für junge Menschen* 1(vol. 1, 1 February 1947), 14.

21. Thurnwald, 191–192.

22. Kenneth S. Pope, "Memory, Abuse and Science: Questioning Claims about the False Memory Syndrome Epidemic," *American Psychologist* 51, no. 9 (September 1996): 957–974; Terry Castle's "Contagious Folly: An Adventure and its Skeptics," in *Questions of Evidence: Proof, Practice and Persuasion Across the Disciplines*, eds. James Chandler, Arnold I. Davidson, and Harry Harootunian (Chicago: University of Chicago Press, 1994), 10–42.

23. Jürgen Diederich and Heinz-Elmar Tenorth, *Theorie der Schule: Ein Studienbuch zu Geschichte, Funktionen und Gestaltung* (Berlin: Cornelsen, 1997), 235–240.

# Chapter Fourteen

# Humanitarian Sympathy for Children in Times of War and the History of Children's Rights, 1919–1959

## *Dominique Marshall*

The sympathy for child victims of war has been a major factor in the adoption of international declarations of children's rights. Since their formulation in the early 1920s, it has been a recurrent belief among governments and voluntary agencies that the notion of children's rights represented the surest way to channel the humanitarian movements of wartime toward international cooperation in peacetime. However, the interest in living in foreign countries tended to fade following times of reconstruction. This essay examines campaigns in favor of children's rights to show how they were influenced by the political culture of war. It identifies the sectors of society interested in the international promotion of child welfare and analyzes the terms of their understanding. Finally, it traces the legacy of features born in wartime for the history of children's rights in times of peace.

### *Herbert Hoover and the Relief of European Children*

The focus on children as an object of international cooperation originated in the feeding of the civilians of occupied Belgium during the First World War by philanthropist Herbert Hoover, mining engineer and future president of the United States. From September 1914 until the entry of the United States into the war in 1917, he chaired the Committee for Belgian Relief (CBR), a private charity. After 1917, he directed the American Relief

Administration (ARA), the public body devoted to the distribution of food to allied soldiers and civilians. From the armistice until the Versaille Treaty was signed in the summer of 1919, Hoover went back to Europe on behalf of the United States to feed civilians of countries devastated by the war, many of whom were still suffering from the victors' blockades. At the end of 1919, Hoover embarked on a solely private venture, the European Children Fund, which took over from the ARA. These agencies contributed to the feeding of more than 10 million children.[1]

Hoover and his colleagues insisted that their programs focus on children for medical reasons: They needed the special treatment owed to all immature and vulnerable beings. They were also struck by the psychological state of children affected by the conflict. Besides, the concentration on children met political concerns, as many donations could be attracted in their name. The CBR asked for support from the "public opinion of the world," in order to legitimate its claim of neutrality. The organization was so successful that it claimed to represent the main direct involvement of American citizens in the war until 1917. After the Americans entered the war, no other program of relief for allied civilians achieved the popularity of the efforts on behalf of children. Finally, during the years of reconstruction, focusing on the needs of children provided a way for Americans to retire from European relief without losing prestige.

The idea of children's vulnerability and the conviction that armed conflicts deprived them of a childhood inspired a sense of duty in adults. Hoover envisaged that this universal sense of responsibility could serve as the basis for larger humanitarian actions. Feeding children also helped to make the agency acceptable to the beneficiaries: "the troop of healthy cheerful chattering youngsters . . . " he wrote, was "a gladdening lift from the drab life of an imprisoned people." In this way, feeding children would lead to better American international relations.[2] The philanthropist was advancing a liberal conception of voluntary and peaceful economic competition between nations, without the typical restrictions established by national governments; moreover, feeding children would maintain the social and political order needed for international trade.

After the peace settlement, sympathy for children in time of war was redirected in two ways. In Europe, Hoover and the American Red Cross (ARC) transferred their remaining supplies to areas still devastated by the conflict, trusting that the people in those countries were "ready to accept a continuing responsibility in helping to create in Europe the conditions that would make democracy effective." But in the spring of 1921, Red

Cross officials, observing a postwar reluctance among donors to give money for European relief, were eager to pull their operations out of Central and Eastern Europe. Concerned that their absence would encourage the growth of Bolshevism, they decided instead to refocus their efforts primarily to children and opened 500 health centers.[3] The very nature of relief in wartime limited its ability to survive the armistice: American sympathies for European children decreased because it had become less easy to help countries that were recovering some institutional autonomy, in their defense and welfare budgets especially. Moreover, American citizens had never been unanimous "about the atrocity stories," according to relief agents, because of "the working man's . . . innate suspicion for 'propaganda' and [his fear] that someone would put something over him."[4]

Most Americans soon transferred their sympathies to children in their own country, as a journalist indicated in 1919: "we should not overlook the fact that many of our own children, judged by the same standards employed by the ARA . . . are in need of supplemental food."[5] Acknowledging Hoover's extraordinary success, the American Red Cross made child welfare a priority in its plan for peace. His list of principles explaining the philosophy of feeding children, a document informed both by his expert's predilection for systems and his constant efforts to convince individuals, inspired the list of social and economic children's rights he devised in the 1920s. In 1930, now President, he would ensure that a revised *Children's Charter* receive the approbation of the government.[6]

## *The Save the Children International Union and the Relief of Children of Former Enemies*

Two agencies based in Geneva took over some of the work started by the American Relief Agency in Europe: the Save the Children International Union (SCIU) and its patron, the International Committee of the Red Cross (ICRC). Eglantyne Jebb and her sister Dorothy Buxton had founded the Save the Children Fund (SCF) in London in 1919 and its umbrella association, the SCIU, a few months later in Geneva in order to rescue the starving children living in former war zones.[7] Members of the SCF were already used to seeking the support of the public at large. When Victoria de Bunsen had started her work two decades earlier with the British Balkan Committee, she had offered a perceptive justification of humanitarian appeals. The only way to push the government to take action on behalf of persecuted nationalities was to educate the British public. Visual and written accounts of atrocities were crucial in this political process, not only to give evidence of incredible problems but also because the process of "seeing" itself entailed a responsibility. Depictions of suffering children were prominent in their publications, as they could represent the endangered innocence of whole nations. Since the mid-nineteenth century, the Romantic movement had used the child as the symbol of the social problems resulting from social and economic change, and the general idea of children as "the emblem of a debased romanticism" rendered them apt to represent the calamities of war.[8] De Bunsen's assumption of a spiritual and psychological inability to act among victims, exemplified by children, represented a chief argument for the mobilization of benefactors.

The decision of the founders of the SCF to devote their movement solely to children represented a watershed, as they established the "fund-raising potential in starving children" to a previously unrealized level.[9] Jebb wanted to accomplish—with the general sympathy toward children—what, two generations earlier, the Red Cross had been able to realize with a new-found sympathy for wounded soldiers. "War which stops in front of wounded soldiers," she maintained, "must even more respect the innocent child."[10] The founding in 1864 of this oldest of humanitarian agencies had occurred in the context of significant political transformations: With the rising dependency of armies on democratic governments, the symbol of patriotism had shifted from the single soldier bound by personal and aristocratic duty to citizens fighting for their countries.[11]

Like Hoover, the SCF identified "a new feeling of international responsibility," on which peaceful international relations could be built. Childhood represented a "neutral ground . . . where all could the most easily meet."[12] In 1923, Jebb and her collaborators devised a "Declaration of the Rights of the Child," five articles which underlined the right of children for first assistance in case of conflict or catastrophe and underlined specific areas of children's vulnerability. The document was mostly a propaganda tool; indeed, much of the success of the SCF came from lessons learned by charities during the war. Among those who had been left behind the front of the warring countries of Europe, financing campaigns had constituted a major effort of patriotic mobilization. The public's attraction to graphic depictions of war, an early feature of the history of photography, had a paradoxical effect on political culture. On the one hand, they had occasioned more international solidarity by bringing home the vulnerability of the common soldier. Indeed, the foundation of the International Committee of the Red

Propaganda material of the British Save the Children Fund in the early 1920s. Archives de l'Union internationale de protection de l'enfance, Archives d'État de Genève, 12.1.2. Grande-Bretagne, Save the Children Fund, "Matériel de propagande, 1920–1940." *Reprinted with the permission of the Archives d'État.*

Cross coincided with the first armed conflict to be widely photographed, the Crimean War.[13]

On the other hand, the SCF and Hoover's agencies relied on a patriotic language which contained the very elements of moral superiority they sought to remedy. The propaganda of the home front had often invoked the innocence of children to vilify the enemy: Together with mothers and families, children embodied a serene and traditional society to be saved. The use of depictions of German atrocities by the Committee for Belgian Relief, for instance, could instill hatred for foreign authorities rather than a willingness for neutral collaboration with them.[14] In a milder manner, public answers to humanitarian appeals often mixed personal abnegation with national identity. Humanitarian fundraisers, for example, often praised the generosity of specific communities. In so doing, they often assumed the superiority of the benefactors: "On the British people, with their great heritage of achievement in humanitarian progress," wrote the editor-in-chief of the Save the Children Fund, "rests a special responsibility that the consummation [of the Declaration of Children's Rights] be not delayed."[15] The Save the Children movement used images of suffering children to narrow the personal distance between donors and beneficiaries. Pictures themselves seemed to offer a language immediately understood by all. Slogans such as

"Crushed in the Mill of International Dispute," *Mail and Empire*, 23 February 1924, National Archives of Canada, Canadian Branch of the Save the Children Fund, MG 28, I 42, vol. 7, file N.C. 1927.

"Every day you delay means a hideous death to a hungry little child" touched urgently one's sense of responsibility. Others triggered guilt, such as the words of the American Relief Administration: "And just as you say that you will not change your style of living, a starving baby dies in France."[16] Attracting the attention of individuals who were the most familiar with the situation of children in distress was one of the goals of humanitarian campaigns: "If I could only make it personal!" wrote the Canadian publicist of the SCF. "Supposing your child were one of the hungry ones?"[17] A British Columbian mother of four young boys expressed this sense of familiarity when she replied to the circular of the British aristocrat who served as president of the SCF. Her children had been moved by the description of the plight of children refugees in Greece. Aware of her own relative comfort, she identified with their mothers: "I have in the past known enough suffering to understand more closely than some the feelings of the European mothers of whom it is torture to think and whose children I shall never forget."[18]

Childhood seemed to offer an object especially suited to rallying the generosity of the poorer members of society. Associations of British workers were particularly responsive to the appeals of the SCF, and Canadian fundraisers commented that the "poor and middle classes" contributed more than the "rich classes."[19] The rights of children could bridge some distance between people of little means and fundraisers of a higher status, and the Canadian mother mentioned above took the circular from the Duke of Atholl as the mark of a new respect: "I shall keep and value your letter always as I keenly appreciate the honor of being so called upon to help."[20] In the eyes of such a donor, pictures had registered injustice in a way which enhanced the dignity of individuals under terrible circumstances.[21]

Humanitarian campaigners also believed that "[I]f a child was confronted with the choice between the horrors of war and the benefits of peace . . . the child's simple reasoning power would lead to a faith in the League of Nations as a means of promoting peaceful international relations."[22] The faith in the ability of children to be such "admirable propagandists" constituted the last of the five articles of the Declaration of Geneva and it informed the growing attention devoted by Red Cross Societies to their Junior Leagues.[23] However, this ability could easily apply to military patriotism: A poster of the American Relief Association, for example, showed the painting of a boy performing an army salute with the title "Little America do your bit."[24]

## The League of Nations, the Prevention of Wars, and the Consolidation of Children's Rights

In 1919, the signatories of the Treaty of Versailles pledged to protect the young and to "endeavor to secure and maintain fair and humane conditions of labor for men, women and children."[25] In September 1924, the Declaration of the Rights of the Child was approved by the General Assembly of the League of Nations (LON), which also created a Child Welfare Committee of which Eglantyne Jebb became a member. These developments came largely from concerns over the fate of children during the war. At its very first session in 1920, the Swiss delegation asked the Assembly to make the welfare of child victims of war a major concern and to appoint a high commissioner to coordinate the work of relief under way. By wounding, killing, or displacing adults, the conflict had deprived many children of the protection they had enjoyed in times of peace. To the Swiss, since the work of the League on behalf of prisoners was reaching completion, it was time to support child relief. Another benefit to the league would be an increase in prestige: "These millions of children rescued from death and deprivation will remember, when they become men, the debt they have contracted towards the League of Nations when it [was] just beginning, and they will work to cement this construction . . . of universal brotherhood."[26]

The General Assembly acknowledged the importance of the various efforts to provide food for millions of children, but it refused to accept direct responsibility, most still believing that work on typhus and prisoners should retain their attention. By 1924, however, several high officials trusted that "the saving of the children of Europe" represented one of the few "objects of a broad humanitarian nature, of general international interest, for dealing with which international co-operation is eminently desirable, in the interest of . . . humanity at large."[27]

The establishment of the Child Welfare Committee of the League also originated in the pressure brought by international associations of women. In Canada, for example, many members of the National Council of Women turned the energies they had invested in the war toward child welfare and humanitarian causes. Women provided the branches of the SCF and the League of Nations Societies with significant support. They believed in the power of the love of mothers to transform the abandonment of individual interest required by military engagement into the abandonment of the destructive features of patriotism: "[from] the interest of each mother in her own child must be built up an interest of the mother in the mother and child of all other countries, and in this way, we can join together to build up the welfare of the whole world."[28]

However, interest for international humanitarian causes paled in comparison to the attention churches and women's movements gave to domestic problems. The Canadian Council of Child Welfare (CCCW), for instance, was founded in 1919 to answer concerns about health issues facing the young raised by the war. In any case, the "new enthusiasm" for the promotion of social well-being during peacetime never matched the energy displayed in wartime.[29] However diminished, it was this concern for child welfare which resurfaced on the international scene. The CCCW Secretary, Charlotte Whitton, became a member of the Child Welfare Committee of the League. She believed that the promotion of children's rights was the most popular aspect of Canada's participation in the League.[30]

## The Invasion of Ethiopia and the Rights of Non-European Children

In the interwar years, only armed conflicts provoked enthusiasm for children's rights equivalent to the level reached during the Great War. At the end of the 1920s, the European activities of the Save the Children movement linked with reconstruction reached completion, and the charity turned its attention to Africa. The 1931 Conference on the African Child gathered some 200 participants in Geneva, but the Union failed to raise enough funds to act further until September 1935.[31] When Italy invaded Ethiopia, the SCIU launched newspaper campaigns in newspapers of Geneva, Zurich, and London. Aware of the number of organizations appealing for money for Ethiopia, the SCIU insisted on making children the first beneficiaries of foreign aid, quoting the Declaration of Geneva.

From January to April 1936, the SCIU sponsored a field worker in Addis Ababa, which was still under the control of the Emperor Haile Selassie, in what the historian of the African poor, John Illiffe, calls the first modern relief operation in Africa. Frédérique Small found that the city had sufficient quantities of food and that the care of the families on the front was in the hands of the Red Cross. Now that donors' sympathies had been awakened by the war in Ethiopia, she hoped to convert their support to the "normal and constructive" work which did not necessarily "strike the imagination," and she opened a child welfare center. In London, her colleagues still be-

Children of Ethiopian warriors examined at the dispensary of the Save the Children International Union, and wearing the new clothes distributed by the center of child welfare in Addis Ababa, in the winter of 1936. This material was used for propaganda. Archives de l'Union internationale de protection de l'enfance, Archives d'État de Genève, "Enveloppe de Madame Small." *Reprinted with the permission of the Archives d'État.*

lieved that only material related directly to the war would sustain public sympathy. "You can see for yourself that the children in the necessitous quarters of Addis Ababa with the addition of some rough social services [has] very little basis of appeal, and will not bring in large sums of money," wrote the president of the SCIU. "We can get money for bombed civilians, especially if we have lots of details, but we can't get money for endemic misery. Give us some really harrowing stories and the cure for the troubles and we will find the money.... Please let us have news and photographs."[32]

In Addis Ababa, war had also seen the rise of charitable work, as the local Ethiopian elite contributed funds for medical programs. The Ethiopian Red Cross, founded in August 1935 in direct anticipation of the war, served as the welcoming structure for Small. The Emperor insisted that children of soldiers be aided first. This relation to war determined the very nature of the action in the field, and the concentration of the efforts on the feeding of children was similar to the mass operations the SCF had pioneered in Europe during the Great War. Small's hopes of providing a basis for future

Frédérique Small, the field worker sent by the Save the Children International Union to Ethiopia in 1936, together with the member of the imperial family who was the patron of the center of child welfare. The main leaflet of the fund-raising campaign in Britain reprinted a similar picture. Archives de l'Union internationale de protection de l'enfance, Archives d'État de Genève, "Enveloppe de Madame Small." *Reprinted with the permission of the Archives d'État.*

work of child welfare proved impossible to fulfill. In April 1936, she left the center in the hands of local volunteers linked to the Red Cross. In keeping with the original agreement, she promised another four months of financial aid. Soon after her departure, the Italians entered the capital and closed the center. The SCF resorted to indirect help to Ethiopian refugees, sending funds rather than workers or supplies, and it remained in contact with the Emperor. But international interest for further child welfare work could not be sustained. Not until 1966 would the SCF work resume in Ethiopia.[33]

Another war provoked conditions of emergency which made fund raising popular. Just as the work in Africa had started when emergencies in Europe were less important, relief in Europe was taking precedence again. A few weeks after its withdrawal from Ethiopia, the Save the Children movement sent Frédérique Small to Spain. The suffragette and long campaigner against fascism, Sylvia Pankhurst, despaired of the general abandonment of the help toward Ethiopia, quoting the Archbishop of York: "It seems as though the springs of humanity are being dried up by continual pressure of horror upon horror, and we are in danger of becoming case-hardened."[34]

## The Second World War and Its Aftermath

During the Second World War, the Declaration of Geneva was often quoted as a standard against which to measure the fate of children in countries at war.[35] Such was the case, for instance, when the Canadian Charlotte Whitton toured the United States to lecture about war and social welfare.[36] Soon after the war, the SCIU held a conference on the right of children for protection in armed conflicts. One of the main humanitarian groups to call for a convention to protect civilians in wartime, it participated in the Geneva conventions of 1949. The organization succeeded in extending the sympathy toward children to the question of the rights of civilians of all generations in wartime.[37]

Between 1939 and 1945, expressions of urgency toward the relief of children echoed the demands of 1919, but the General Assembly of the United Nations answered them more readily than the League of Nations had done. With the help of an old collaborator of Hoover, Maurice Pate, and of the American Red Cross, the former director of the Health Organisation of the LON, Ludwick Rajchman, proposed to spend the residual relief fund of the UN on behalf of children exclusively. His reasons were by then familiar: Children were "the first victims of wars," as many had been orphaned or injured, others had lived for years without adequate food, and still others had witnessed untold horrors; the war had left them without stable social institutions in which to grow up; they represented an apolitical and safe target for international work; and, as adults, the beneficiaries of aid would help to work for a better world. The UN created the International Children's

Emergency Fund (UNICEF) in December 1946. Problems of isolationism similar to those of the early 1920s were still vivid. Canadian diplomats, for example, were reluctant to commit resources to newly independent countries of the South where the needs of children seemed endless. But the interest for UNICEF among Canadians was such that they helped to establish the Fund permanently.[38]

The Save the Children officials did not succeed in having the General Assembly of the UN confirm its support of the 1924 Declaration of Children's Rights. In the eyes of many, the Universal Declaration of Human Rights of 1948 made the specific declaration for children redundant. But the Cold War soon jeopardized further commitments and, at the turn of the 1950s, the theme of children's rights seemed to provide "a stopgap which was being used to give the impression that the Human Rights Commission was doing something."[39] As in all the events reviewed so far, the focus on children provided both an excuse to withdraw from securing universal rights for adults and a basis for international cooperation. To be sure, the possibility of a nuclear conflict added urgency to the negotiations. As an Indian delegate declared, "The achievements of science had made available unprecedented power for good and evil. If the leaders of the world were to use that power for good, their aim must be to ensure that man's moral evolution kept pace with the advance of science. In order to achieve that aim, a beginning must be made with the education of children."[40] The General Assembly adopted a new Declaration of the Rights of the Child in 1959, which included more social and economic rights than its predecessor and a stronger emphasis on public welfare.

## Conclusion

The fate of children in times of war has provoked spontaneous movements of sympathy for their rights, across borders and across enemy lines. This paper has shown that the strong association of children's rights with wars has often limited the possibilities of children's rights. An exclusive focus on children and the use of images of intense suffering to maintain public support have helped to remove avenues of international collaboration from engagements between equal, adult citizens. Moreover, they have perpetuated and even enhanced isolationist elements of nationalism. The opposition between the "abstract universalism" of the promoters of children's rights and this "narrow communitarianism" represents a recurrent theme in the history of compassion. At times such tension could be eased by the adoption of an "emergent universalism," informed both by local action and wider communication.[41] However, the rhetoric of children's rights has also helped to transform the patriotism of armed conflicts into humanitarian engagements for peace. On his way back from Geneva, in the fall of 1925, the Canadian delegate at the International Conference of the Child held by the Save the Children International Union reported that "the effect was to enlarge the boundaries of one's interest in child welfare as a whole, and this without detracting from interest in the needy home or national child, which indeed comes first. One became ashamed of a provincial point of view, and realized the universality of the child."[42]

## NOTES

1. Frank Macy Surface and Raymond L. Bland, *American Food in the World War and Reconstruction Period. Operations of the Organizations Under the Direction of Herbert Hoover 1914 to 1924* (Stanford: Stanford University Press, 1933); George I. Gay and H. H. Fisher, *Public Relations of the Commission for Relief in Belgium, Documents* (Stanford, Stanford University Press, 1929).

2. Herbert Hoover, *The Memoirs of Herbert Hoover, Vol. I, Years of Adventure. 1874–1920*, Vol. 2, *The Cabinet and the Presidency. 1920–1933* (London: Hollis and Carter, 1952), 159–171, 179, 321–322, and chapter 38; Suda Lorena Bane and Ralph Haswell Lutz, eds., *Organization of American Relief in Europe* (Stanford: Stanford University Press, 1943), 597.

3. Dulles, *The American Red Cross*, 196.

4. Quoted in Dickson, "The War Comes to All," 223, 225, 451–454.

5. Quoted in Richard Wagner, *Clemens Von Pirquet. His Life and Work* (Baltimore: John Hopkins University Press, 1968), 159.

6. Veerman, *The Rights of the Child*, 87–91, 231–237.

7. Murray Last, "Putting Children First," *Disasters* 18 (1994): 192–194; Buxton and Fuller, *The White Flame*.

8. Cunningham, "The Rights of the Child," 4, 9; Victoria de Bunsen and Noel Buxton, *Macedonian Massacres: Photos from Macedonia* (London: A.C. Fitfield, 1907).

9. Morehead, *Dunant's Dream*, 288.

10. UISE, *XXe Anniversaire* (Genève: UISE, 1940), 41, 38; Alice Salomon, *Eglantyne Jebb, 1876–1928* (Genève, 1936), 31; Hutchinson, *Champions of Charity*, 290–293.

11. Smith, *Between Mutiny and Obedience*.

12. "Memorandum concernant l'UISE," Genève, not dated, Archives de l'Union

Internationale de Protection de l'Enfance (AUIPE), Archives d'État de Genève, pp. 1, 18, my translation.

13. Laurent Gervereau, "La propagande par l'image en France 1914–1918. Thèmes et modes de représentation," in Laurent Gerverau and Christopher Prochasson, ed., *Images de 1917* (Paris, Musée d'histoire contemporaine et bibliothèque de documentation internationale contemporaine, Université de Paris: 1987), 136–137; Jonathan Marwil, "Photography at War," *History Today* (June 2000), 5; Heinz K. Henisch and Bridget Henisch, *The Photographic Experience 1839–1914, Images and Attitudes* (Philadelphia: Pennsylvania University Press, 1994); John Berger, "Photographs of Agony," in *Ways of Seeing* (London, Writers and Readers, 1980), 37–40.

14. Dickson, "War Comes to All," 216–219.

15. Edward Fuller, "The Development of Child Care Under British Rule," *The World's Children* (April 1924): 130–132.

16. Quoted in Dickson, "War Comes to All," 359; "Crushed in the Mill of International Dispute," *Mail and Empire*, February 23, 1924; Simon Fowler, "War Charity Begins at Home," *History Today* (September 1999), 18.

17. Frank Yeigh, *What I Saw in the Refugee Camps of Europe and the Neareast* (Toronto: SCF, n.d.).

18. Quoted in Frank Yeigh, "Saving the Child," *East and West* (August 2, 1924): 245.

19. *Bulletin de l'Union Internationale de secours aux Enfants* 3 (May 30, 1922): 226–227; Marshall, "The Formation of Childhood," 138.

20. B.vW. Allen, quoted in *The World's Children* (April 1924): 126.

21. Alan Trachenberg, *Reading American Photographs* (New York: Hill, 1989).

22. League of Nations Society, *Bulletin*, August 1927, quoted in Donald M. Page, "Canadians and the League of Nations before the Manchurian Crisis" (Ph.D. dissertation, University of Toronto, 1972), 317–318.

23. John F. Hutchinson, "The Junior Red Cross Goes to Healthland," *American Journal of Public Health* 87 (1997):1816–1823.

24. Dickson, "War Comes to All," 275–276, 298.

25. Covenant of the League of Nations, article 23; Marshall, "The Formation of Childhood."

26. Document 160 of the General Assembly of the League, A.20/48/160.[IV], December 2, 1920.

27. P. J. Baker, Note to the Secretary General, December 6, 1920, Archives of the League of Nations (ALON), 1919–1946, Section Files, Social, S152, 7.

28. Conference on the International Aspects of Child Welfare Work, summer 1921, sheet VI, ALON, 1919–1946, Section Files, Social, S152, 7, "Child Welfare etc., to June 30th 1924"; Carole Miller, "The Social Section and Advisory Committee on Social Questions of the League of Nations," in Paul Weindling, ed., *International*

*Health Organisations aand Movements 1918–1939* (Cambridge, Cambridge University Press, 1995): 154–175.

29. Veronica Strong Boag, *The Parliament of Women: The National Council of Women of Canada, 1893–1929* (Ottawa: National Museum of Man, 1976), 387–388; Page, "Canadians and the League of Nations," 164–165.

30. National Archives of Canada (NAC), Canadian Council on Social Development, MG 28, I 10, Vol. 15, 1927.

31. Frédérique Small, "Union internationale de secours aux enfants. Mission en Ethiopie," *Revue internationale de la Croix-Rouge* 18 (April 1936): 279–282, and 18 (May 1936): 376–392.

32. LGB to Small, February 4 and 19, 1936, AUIPE, "Suisse-Mme Frédérique Small—Lettres reçues (1935–1936)."

33. AUIPE, UISE, *Procès-verbaux Comité exécutif, 1934–1937* and "Ethiopie. Divers," in "Afrique. 1932–38"; John Iliffe, *The African Poor. A History* (Cambridge: Cambridge University Press, 1988).

34. Sylvia Pankhurst, *Italy's War Crimes in Ethiopia. Evidence for the War Crimes Commission* (Woodford Green: New Times and Ethiopia News, 1946).

35. This section summarizes my two articles "Reconstruction Politics" and "Canada and Children's Rights at the United Nations, 1945–1959."

36. "Problems of Childhood in Wartime Discussed Here," *Los Angeles Daily News*, September 29, 1942.

37. Françoise Krill, "The Protection of Children in Armed Conflicts," in Freeman and Veerman, eds., *The Ideologies of Children's Rights*, 347–348.

38. Maria Alexandra Balinska, "Ludwick W. Rajchman, 1881–1965: précurseur de la santé publique moderne" (Ph.D. thesis, Institut d'Études politiques de Paris, 1992); Black, *The Children and the Nations*; documents on UNICEF published in the volumes of *Documents on Canadian External Relations* pertaining to the period 1945–1959.

39. Humphrey, *Human Rights and the United Nations*, 231.

40. UN, HRC, E/CN.4/SR 636, April 6, 1959, 9.

41. Boltansky, *Distant Suffering*.

42. Frank Yeigh, "World Congress Recognizes Need of Caring for Children," *Toronto Star*, September 1925.

# Actors and Victims

After visitors to the Imperial War Museum in London examine the antique tanks and airplanes, explore the exhibits dedicated to Britain's major wars, wander a realistic trench from the First World War just as a squad of grimy tommies are about to go over the top, and survive the "Blitz Experience" in the blacked out bomb shelter—complete with explosions, dust, and trembling wooden bench—they can browse the gift shop. Among the magnets and postcards and propaganda posters and books and videos dedicated to military technology, Nazis, and Winston Churchill, they might find a packet blandly called "Children in War: Documents relating to the British home front, 1939–1945."

As their collective title suggests, the just over one dozen items in the collection provide snapshots of the lives of English children who lived through the Second World War. The letters, diary excerpts, government documents, posters, and other sources address nearly every way that children have been both actors and victims in the wars of the last two centuries.

They are refugees: A young evacuee from London describes his uninspiring wartime diet (lots of bread and jam), complains that his host took away his pen-knife "just because I cut myself," and urges his "mum and dad" to "let us come home."

They are the children of soldiers: A little girl crowds a carefully printed note to her father with a jumble of sentences:

> I hope you are alright and I hope you got my last letter. Mam has had some letters from you and thanks for your letter to me I have got a real school-girls hat made of felt with a rim that turns up. I hope it won't be long before you are home again with Mam and me. Bye-bye love from Love Pat XXXXXXXXXXX ....

On the envelope is stamped, "IT IS REGRETTED THAT THIS ITEM CANNOT BE DELIVERED BECAUSE THE ADDRESSEE IS RE-PORTED PRISONER OF WAR."

They are on the front lines, as targets of German bombs and torpedoes: A school essay describes the routine at a boarding school during an air raid, when the students rush to their gender-segregated shelters while the Head-master beats a drum, a Prefect rings a bell, and the boys dashing to their shelters "look like a herd of cattle kicking up a lot of dust." After the "all clear," the students march back to their classrooms and pick up their lessons where they left off. A telegram from "a northern port" to a Mr. Burton W. Mackay" reports the safe arrival of his child, one of scores of children being evacuated to Canada despite a U-boat attack that left the ship damaged "but all children well and happy."

They are chroniclers of the war: A diary excerpt shows the extent to which children immerse themselves in war news, statistics, and even strat-egy. During a fortnight in September 1940, during the height of the Blitz, Joan Thompson reports the exact times and lengths of air raid warnings; the number of British and German planes shot down each night; the dis-ruption of school and Girl Guide meetings; casualties and funerals among relatives and acquaintances; the nightly targets—Buckingham Palace, Ele-phant and Castle, the East End "bombed . . . to smithereens"; going out with friends to collect shrapnel. Along the way she speculates about the inten-tions of two boys—Eric and Will—and dreams of getting an Irish setter after the war.

They contribute to the British war effort: A certificate from the "Over-Seas League" presented to the Borrowash C. School on Empire Day, 1942, is illustrated with a parade of youngsters from all the ethnic groups living in the Empire, carrying packages and other items for the soldiers. The certifi-cate applauds the schools' contributions to providing "comfort and con-tentment to the soldiers, sailors and airmen of the British Commonwealth, who have rallied to the cause of safeguarding freedom, justice and security." A poster issued by the Board of Trade explains "Useful jobs that Girls can do—to help win the war"; "in these days when EVERYTHING must be made the most of," they consist of hints for household conservation, recy-cling, and repair. The equivalent poster for boys deals with repairing tools, cooking utensils, windows, furniture, and other household items. Another certificate, issued to thousands of English boys and girls over His Majesty's signature on June 8, 1946—a day formally set aside to celebrate victory—

declares that "you have shared in the hardships and dangers of a total war and you have shared no less in the triumph of the Allied Nations."

Obviously, the experiences of an American girl reading about the Civil War in the children's magazine *Our Young Folks* in 1865 differ from those of a working-class child living near the bombed out docks of London in 1940 or those of a late twentieth-century Ugandan boy enduring an endless, vicious civil war. Yet the hardships and attitudes and conditions described in these documents do address most of the categories—if not all of the variations—of children's experiences as actors and victims of war.

# Chapter Fifteen

# "These Unfortunate Children"

## Sons and Daughters of the Regiment in Revolutionary and Napoleonic France

## Thomas Cardoza

Children had long been a part of European armies when the French Revolution broke out in 1789. During the Thirty Years' War, the Spanish Army of Flanders was followed by "sutlers, lackeys, women, children, and a rabble which numbered far more than itself." A century and a half later, little had changed. A Hessian captain in 1812 wrote that "the army was also impeded by a vast clutter of sutler wagons, camp followers, *vivandières*, and their children." In neighboring Prussia, "boys receive pay only when they are old enough to bear arms. The sons of foreign soldiers are born soldiers and obliged to serve all their lives." The British army also had large numbers of wives and children following it. Meanwhile, in Austria, Maria Theresa set up special schools to educate soldiers' sons, removing them from regimental life and turning them into "some of the finest soldiers in the regiment."[1]

While virtually all armies included children in their train, their presence for the most part was unofficial and incidental to their parents' service. However, starting in 1786, the French army developed a unique system in which male children were officially incorporated into their parents' regiments as *enfants de troupe*. Female children remained an integral but unofficial part of the French regimental family, but boys could begin active service as young as two years old.

Like other European armies, the French army had long included children. However, by 1766 there was interest in regularizing these children's positions, with an eye toward improving the children's welfare as well as tapping a potentially valuable manpower pool. In essence:

> the idea of raising children for the army seemed like a panacea to certain people in France at the end of the 18th century, permitting the army to resolve all at once the problems posed by its needs, by the repugnance toward military service in certain provinces, and finally the problem of public assistance.

The monarchy took tentative steps in 1766, and again in 1786 and 1788, to provide army pay and rations for soldiers' sons as *"enfants de troupes."*[2] The Revolution of 1789, however, swept away the royal army, leaving *enfant de troupe* regulations in limbo.

The wars that France engaged in from 1792 to 1815, however, placed a heavy strain on French manpower, resulting in increased use of children, and their universal incorporation into the French military. There were two practical reasons for treating soldiers' sons as soldiers and providing them with pay, rations, and uniforms. The first was political. With battle losses mounting dramatically, and with the army's increasing importance as a political tool, the government needed to show its defenders that it appreciated and rewarded their efforts, and taking material care of their children or orphans was a good start. The second reason was military: *enfants de troupe* existed with their parents' regiments whether officially or not, and represented a manpower pool that could be trained and shaped almost from birth. Given the army's insatiable needs for musicians (drummers and buglers) and skilled craftsmen (farriers, gunsmiths, cobblers, etc.), these children represented a valuable resource. Living with the regiment, they could be fully trained and expert in their jobs before the age of sixteen. Minister of War Bartholomé Schérér summed up both motivations when he wrote that:

> we must come to the aid of these unfortunate children who, some through the loss of their fathers, some through their poverty, are dear to the government, and who, by its care and the examples of their fathers, will become virtuous citizens, [and] intrepid and generous soldiers.[3]

Schérér's ideas came to fruition with the law of 7 Thermidor, Year VIII (1800). It divided *enfants de troupe* into two classes: The first class received one-half a soldier's pay plus clothing and lodging. The second class received two-thirds pay, clothing, lodging, bread, and firewood. Each company was allowed two *enfants de troupe*, drawn from boys aged two or older who were the product of "the legitimate marriage of a woman attached to the unit as a *blanchisseuse* or *vivandière*, with a defender of the Nation currently in service or died of his wounds during wartime." Preference went to "those whose fathers and mothers have the most right to the thanks of the nation for their services."[4]

The law also fulfilled the army's second goal. Advancement to the second class (and therefore to better pay and benefits) went to "the *enfants* of the first class who have made the most progress in reading, writing, arithmetic, swimming, running, military and gymnastic exercises, and in a profession useful to the army." Each brigade commander chose one officer, two sergeants, and four corporals from "among the most educated and the most distinguished by their conduct and their morals" to act as teachers. The law also required that "all *maîtres ouvriers* attached to the unit must always have at least two *enfants de troupe* as apprentices."[5] This strong emphasis on providing skilled workers for the army gave the French "relative logistical independence" and led to the unprecedented strategic mobility that made Napoleon's great victories possible.[6] Those *enfants* not training as craftsmen usually became drummers and buglers, often going into battle long before the official age of sixteen. There was strong pressure for this, since drums and bugles provided the only means of signaling on the battlefield, and a Napoleonic army would no more go into battle without them than a modern army would go without radios.

These children were born into a harsh world, where death, maiming, and hunger were commonplace, and their births often occurred in unfavorable circumstances. The care given to their mothers in childbirth varied depending on circumstances, and reactions from the troops could range from callous indifference to tender solicitude. At Marengo in 1799, a *vivandière* gave birth on the battlefield, eliciting only a derisory, "Hey! Marie! You dropped something!" from a nearby soldier. A less fortunate son was born during the retreat from Moscow in 1812 to Madame Dubois, *vivandière* of the Imperial Guard. Though cared for by the regiment's colonel and surgeon, the child froze to death, and his mother found him "as stiff as a piece of wood." The parents were unable to spend time mourning. They "dug a hole in the snow, the father on his knees holding the child in his arms. When the grave was made, he kissed the baby, and placed it in its tomb. It was covered with snow, and all was at an end."[7]

Since their parents went where they were told, the children went, too. This could mean walking, riding in their mother's cart, or even crossing the Alps in baskets strapped to mules. In camp, small children fetched wood and water and helped wash clothes. But life was not all work and hardship.

When young, they had ample time for play, and the soldiers of the regiment adopted the children as their own. Although under harsh conditions soldiers could be callous, in good times they often showed familial affection for the regiment's children. One *vivandière* said, "There isn't one soldier in the regiment who doesn't act as father to my children, since they are used to seeing them, to caressing them, and playing with them during halts." Nor was family life lacking in garrison. *Enfant de troupe* Jean Chevillet recalled that after his parents retired, the Beaumont family acted as a surrogate home for him in the 8th Regiment of *Chasseurs à Cheval*, providing meals, companionship, and a family atmosphere.[8]

Eventually, military children began "adult" lives, usually around age fourteen to sixteen. Chevillet attended the cavalry bugler school at Saumur, then began active service with a cavalry regiment at age fourteen. Although officially the age to begin service was sixteen, Chevillet's case was fairly typical: The need for trained musicians in combat far outweighed any scruples about placing children in danger. Bugler Henri of the 20th Chasseurs à Cheval distinguished himself in combat at age 15, while an officer of the same regiment casually remarked on a twelve-year-old bugler named Saron in combat in 1807. Likewise, one officer saw a fifteen-year-old drummer lead a charge of the 4th Light Infantry Regiment in Spain in 1808, marching and playing under heavy fire.[9]

The sort of zeal these boys displayed justified the expectations of the army in training and paying them. Charles Parquin recalled his first sergeant-major, M. Lacour, in these terms: "it was said he was an *enfant de troupe*: a good and striking soldier, severe, but just." A sergeant at twenty-two, Lacour was a Lieutenant Colonel by 1815. Less illustrious but also impressive, Pierre-Laurent Paradis was one of the first "official" *enfants de troupe* in 1788, then rose to the rank of Captain by 1813. Relatively few *enfants de troupe* rose to high rank, but even among the most humble there was a striking devotion to duty. A group of officers came across a "young drummer" of the Imperial Guard after the Battle of Hanau in 1813. In the midst of a raging storm, he had managed to light a small fire. "He cooked a bit of flour [and water] and, seeing that we had no provisions, offered to share this sort of unseasoned porridge with us."[10] This type of selflessness was exactly what the French army required for its success, and boys raised with this trait from birth were valuable assets.

But armies on campaign were dangerous places, and many young soldiers paid a heavy price for their devotion. One *enfant de troupe* met his end crossing a flooded river in Italy in 1799. As General Boulart noted, "the current carried away several men before my eyes, and among others a father and his son who were drowned wrapped in each others' arms." Exposure to freezing temperatures was also a real hazard, especially to children with less body mass than adults. One army surgeon in Spain recalled:

> a young bugler of the 22nd Chasseurs who had his two legs gangrened along half their length due to frostbite. The tibias and the fibulas were skinned, and one of his feet was even entirely detached. Both legs were amputated.[11]

Many *enfants* also fell on the battlefield, where their duties often required them to be in the forefront. Four of the six Kintelburger children were blinded at Guntsburg in 1805 when an artillery caisson exploded. Their father was killed and they were captured along with their wounded mother. At Eylau in 1808, a sixteen-year-old drummer who followed his father into battle was reported killed, but was eventually found unharmed, buried alive under a file of soldiers killed by a cannon-ball. At Leipzig five years later, a soldier of the 150th Infantry Regiment watched his *cantinière's* son lose a leg to a cannon-ball. In the ensuing retreat, the mother had to abandon the dying boy. At Lutzen the same year, Captain Barrès watched as the young boys of the *Voltigeurs* of the Imperial Guard suffered horrible casualties. All of the regiment's drummers and trumpeters were killed or wounded.

> One of our buglers, a boy of sixteen, was of the number. He had a thigh carried away by a ball and died at the rear of the company. These poor children, when they were wounded but still able to walk, used to come to me to ask to leave the company to get their wounds dressed; it was a renunciation of life, a submission to their superiors, which touched one more than it astonished.[12]

Though campaigning certainly inured young boys to hardship and provided a practical military education, the War Ministry eventually forbade taking *enfants* on campaign, instead requiring them to remain with their regimental depots. This was partly to assure them of their proper education, but mainly to prevent corruption. As Inspector General J. G. Lacuée put it, keeping *enfants de troupe* with regimental depots "was the only means of preventing double payments of their salary," as well as of "assuring them of the education that [the law] wanted to give them."[13] Lacuée never mentioned the children's safety as a concern. Clearly it was in the interests of the state, both financially and in terms of future recruitment of skilled craftsmen, to exercise closer supervision of *enfants de troupe*.

Unfortunately, regimental depots were sometimes located in hostile, guerilla-infested areas of Italy or Spain, where the boys were in equal or greater danger. Captain François recalled a father, mother, and son who were hacked to pieces by Spanish guerillas, and such attacks were common.[14] Nor was this regulation extensively obeyed, for several reasons. Combat units needed drummers and buglers, and used *enfants de troupe* when available. Parents were also reluctant to leave their children behind, and as their interests coincided with those of their commanders, the regulation was rarely enforced. Several months after the publication of Lacuée's order, Cadet de Gassicourt spotted a *vivandière* on campaign near Vienna.

> She had a baby at her breast. Two others of a young age played close by her in the wagon. . . . "I brought him into the world at the field hospital. I have always stayed with the unit and these kids conceived in the bivouacs and baptized under our eagle will one day I hope be good grenadiers. . . . When we must align ourselves in front of the enemy, I stay with the rear-guard and I put our little family behind shelter. . . . If I die, the regiment will take care of my children, not let them out of sight, and they will never hear anything but good said of their mother." And saying these last words, she kissed her nursling and wiped away a tear that was ready to fall from her eye.[15]

Parents with such sentiments were unlikely to abandon their children in response to orders from Paris. Women also gave birth on campaign, with the result that newborns grew up in the field.

The most compelling evidence that children continued to follow the French army in large numbers, aside from the numerous *enfants de troupe* killed and wounded after March 1809, comes from eyewitness accounts of the retreat from Moscow in 1812. Few memoirs of the retreat fail to mention the suffering and death of the children accompanying their parents, showing that large numbers of children remained with the army even after a march of over 3,000 miles and a long and arduous campaign. One soldier fleeing the Russians in 1812 was caught in "a crowd of 10,000 men, women, and children all hurrying and thrusting past each other to get out first." Some soldiers tried to help the children. One regimental colonel found a number of *vivandières* from other units traveling with him.

> Many of these unfortunates dragged children along with them, and despite the egoism so universal otherwise, each one worked to help them. The drum major carried one child in his arms for a long time. The officers who still had a horse shared it among these poor people. For several days I had a woman and her child driven in a cart I still had.

However, a French civilian reported more brutal conditions.

I saw a superior officer have a stable guarded where his horses were and prevent anyone from demolishing it for firewood, even while . . . women were obliged to warm their children by covering them with their pelisses and crying tears of despair.[16]

The cold claimed many of these families. Sergeant Bourgogne saw an old veteran dying in the arms of his wife.

They had lost everything—carts, horses, baggage, besides two children who had died in the snow. . . . The poor creature, still a young woman, was sitting on the snow, holding her dying husband's head on her knees. . . . Behind her, leaning on her shoulder, was a beautiful young girl of thirteen or fourteen years, the only child remaining to her. The poor child was sobbing bitterly, her tears falling and freezing on her father's cold face.[17]

But though the rigors of the retreat were great, they reached a horrific climax at the crowded and chaotic crossing of the Beresina River. Discipline broke down as everyone strove to cross the flimsy temporary bridges under heavy Russian fire. "Men, horses, carts, canteen men with their wives and children, were all mingled in frightful disorder, crushed against each other." Among them, Bourgogne saw a soldier "carrying a child on his head. His wife was in front of him, crying bitterly." A staff officer, traversing the chaos, said "mothers called in vain with heart-rending voices for their husbands, their children who had in an instant been separated from them without return." Many children were crushed, and "this disordered crowd did not hear the cries of the victims it engulfed. The most fortunate gained the bridge, but by climbing over heaps of wounded, of women, of abandoned children."[18]

Others described more specific tragedies. One lieutentant saw that:

an unfortunate cantinière, in water up to her waist and wanting to climb back on the bridge, was pushed back by the soldiers. Despair filled her face and she held out her infant son to me; at the moment I went to take him, a crowd of soldiers lifted me up and carried me away.

General Rochechouart saw:

an unfortunate woman sitting, her legs hanging over the bridge, frozen in the ice. She held glued to her breast a child frozen for over twenty-four hours. She begged me to save this child, not realizing she was presenting me with a corpse.

De Ségur saw another family tragedy when a mother and her children attempted to avoid the bridge.

> A frail boat of birchwood, carrying a mother and her two children, foundered underneath the ice; an artilleryman . . . perceived them; all of a sudden he threw himself in, exerted himself, and finally he saved one of the three victims. It was the youngest of the two children; the unfortunate called his mother with cries of despair.

As the Russians closed in, the French burned the bridges, abandoning "an immense quantity of stragglers, of women, and of children" on the far bank.[19]

Though the retreat from Russia in general and the crossing of the Berezina in particular represent atypical events, the number of women and children traveling with the army was normal, perhaps even smaller than usual given the rigors of the campaign up to that time. The suffering and loss of these family members was unusual only in degree.

The question remains of contemporaries' attitudes toward children in war, and that of the children themselves. The French government saw no problem with using children in combat, and neither did most contemporaries. It was a normal, everyday practice that rarely elicited mention.

As for the government, the War Ministry clearly saw *enfants de troupe* as valuable resources, but not necessarily as "children." The 1800 law establishing *enfants de troupe* recognized no stages of child development. In theory, any child from two to sixteen was equally liable for service in uniform, and casualties came at all ages. Even the 1809 decree forbidding *enfants de troupe* from traveling on campaign was based on a desire to prevent embezzlement, not on keeping children out of danger. The decree's lack of enforcement again suggests that the War Ministry's need for child labor outweighed other considerations.

The responses of parents is more complex. Certainly, the devotion and anguish of mothers at the Berezina crossing suggest strong emotional bonds with their children, and a desire to protect them at almost any cost. Nor were they alone. When Auguste Beaumont, an *enfant de troupe* of the 8th Chasseurs, engaged in a duel with another boy, his mother soundly beat him for needlessly risking his life. Madame Beaumont favored fourteen-year-old Jean Chevillet because he reminded her of her son, a bugler killed in battle, and whom "she regretted still" years later. Even strangers sometimes felt "deeply moved" at the loss of a child, as General Boulart did upon witnessing the drowning of the father and son in Italy.[20]

On the other hand, parents could be callous. An *enfant de troupe's* pay and rations represented a very real economic advantage to a military family, and few parents were willing to give it up. Despite the loss of François Beaumont, his parents kept his younger brother in service. Devotion to duty often came before parental duties as well. When Drum-Major Sénot of the Imperial Guard was told his son had been killed, he replied, "'Too bad for him'" and went about his business.[21] Of course, none of these anecdotes can truly be representative, but they give an idea of the range of parental responses.

The children themselves are more problematical. Though in theory they all received instruction in reading and writing, this was not universal while on campaign, and in any case, many died before they could leave written memoirs. Nevertheless, there is strong evidence that many military children found life outside the army unthinkable. Jean Chevillet's father retired, but young Jean, wishing no career but a military one, promptly enlisted as a bugler. A more striking example came from Philippe Girault, whose friend married a wealthy woman and retired.

> An *enfant de troupe*, having always lived the life of the camps, he couldn't get used to the lazy and fortunate life. . . . His wife, who had a mansion and servants, could not remove his regrets at not being able to continue his military career.

The man eventually ran away and re-enlisted, resisting all pressure from his commander and his wife to return home. "He wouldn't listen, repeating incessantly that only the soldier's life suited him, that he could only be happy in the regiment."[22]

Clearly, the army in general and the regiment in particular formed a military family, to which many *enfants* felt fiercely devoted. This was often a reciprocal feeling. When parents were killed, officers felt an obligation to care for the orphans. When private Joseph Angot was killed at Wagram, the Colonel of the 67th Regiment wrote that he left "a wife and two young children *in the care of the unit*" (emphasis added). Likewise, young Pierre Boldevin came under the care of his parents' regiment after their deaths.[23] These examples correspond nicely with the sentiments of War Minister Schérer and Gassicourt's anonymous *vivandière*. For those who sacrificed all for the nation, the nation would reply by caring for their children, while taking care to turn them into "good grenadiers," and "intrepid and generous soldiers."

Ultimately, the presence of children in Napoleonic French armies was the response to the very real need for musicians and skilled craftsmen, as well as the equally pressing need to show gratitude to the nation's defenders. These pragmatic concerns of state had little to do with the children's well-being, although many parents were grateful for the added economic benefits, and the boys themselves served enthusiastically, even fanatically. Eventually, by 1845, the French military developed a theory of graduated stages of child development and instituted mandatory education. By 1885, *enfants de troupe* were removed from regimental life altogether and placed in state-sponsored military schools, ending a century-long tradition. The nineteenth century, then, marks a crucial transition in the way the French viewed childhood, when *enfants de troupe* went from being warriors to students. To what extent this represented a new benevolence and sensitivity toward childhood, or merely a lessening in the demand for "child labor" by the army, remains an intriguing question.

## Notes

1. Geoffrey Parker, *The Thirty Years' War* (London: Routledge and Keegan Paul, 1984), 199; Franz Roeder, *The Ordeal of Captain Roeder* (New York: St. Martin's, 1960), 17; Jules Finot, *Une mission militaire en Prusse en 1786* (Paris: Firmin-Didot, 1881), 283–284; F. Page, *Following the Drum: Women in Wellington's Wars* (London: André Deutsch, 1986); Christopher Duffy, *The Military Experience in the Age of Reason* (London: David and Charles, 1977), 128.

2. André Corvisier, "La société militaire et l'enfant," in L. Henry, ed., *Annales de démographie historique 1973* (Paris: Ecole Pratique des Hautes Etudes, 1973), 335–339; de Saugeon, *Collection des ordonnances militaires* (Paris: n.d.), 53, 66, 67.

3. "Lettre du Ministre de la Guerre aux Inspecteurs Généreaux, aux Commissionaires d'Ordonnances et aux Conseils d'Administration des Troupes de la République," 21 Thermidor An 6, 1W45, Service Historique de l'Armée de Terre, Vincennes (hereafter referred to as AT).

4. "Arrêté relatif aux enfans de troupe, et aux femmes à la suite de l'armée du 7 Thermidor, an 8," *Journal Militaire*, 2 semestre, An 8, 750.

5. Ibid., 751, 750.

6. Frederick Schneid, *Soldiers of Napoleon's Kingdom of Italy* (Boulder, CO: 1995), 80.

7. Louis Montigny, *Souvenirs anecdotiques d'un officier de la grande armée* (Paris: Goselin, 1833), 325–326; Adrien Bourgogne, *Mémoires du Sergent Bourgogne* (1812–1813) (Paris: Hachette, 1898), 72.

8. Louis-Vivant Lagneau, *Journal d'un chirurgien de la grande armée, 1803–1815* (Paris: Émile-Paul, 1913), 66; *Un camp de cavalerie*, lithograph, n.d.; Charles Cozette, *Vue du camp du Havre en 1756*, oil on canvas, Musée de l'armée, Paris; Charles

Louis Cadet de Gassicourt, *Voyage en Autriche, en Moravie et Bavière: fait a la suite de l'armee française, pendant la campagne de 1809* (Paris: L'Huillier, 1818), 76; Jean Chevillet, Ma vie militaire 1800–1810 (Paris: Hachette, 1906), 9.

9. Charles Parquin, *Souvenirs et campagnes d'un vieux soldat de l''Empire (1803–1914)* (Paris: Berges-Levrault, 1892), 5; Goriainov, Sergei, *Lettres interceptées par les Russes durant la campagne de 1812* (Paris: La Sabretache, 1913), 19; François Pils, *Journal de marche de grenadier Pils* (1804–1814) (Paris: Ollendorf, 1895), 217.

10. Parquin, 5; Léon Hennet, "Lettres interceptées par les Russes durant la campagne de 1812," *Carnet de la Sabretache* (1913): 19; Pils, *Journal de marche*, 217.

11. Jean François Boulart, *Mémoires militaires du général Baron Boulart sur les guerres de la république et de l'empire* (Paris: Librairie Illustrée, 1892), 52; Lagneau, 186–187.

12. Kintelburger au Ministre de Guerre, 6 février 1809, "Muller, née Kintelberger," Xs 12, AT; Jean-Roch Coignet, *Les Cahiers du Capitaine Coignet (1799–1815)* (Paris: Hachette, 1889), 476; Karl Röhrig, *Im Kampf um Freiheit und Vaterland 1806–1815* (Leipzig, 1912), 291; Jean-Baptiste Barrès, *Memoirs of a Napoleonic Officer* (London: Allen and Unwin, 1925), 162.

13. "Circulaire no. 163—Enfants de Troupe: Ils doivent être réunis au dépôt de leurs corps," 9 mars, 1809, Xs 195, AT.

14. Désiré-Joseph Lalo, *Cahiers inédits du Captiaine Lalo* (Paris: Belfond, 1888), 46–47; Charles François, *Journal du Capitaine François dit le dromedaire d'Égypte* (Paris: Tallandier, 1984), I: 664.

15. Cadet de Gassicourt, 74–77.

16. Bourgogne, 228; Raymond Montesquiou-Fézencas, *Souvenirs militaires de 1804 à 1814* (Paris: Dumaine, 1863), 269; G. Lacointe de Laveau, *Moscou avant et après l'incendie* (Paris: Giude, 1814), 144.

17. Bourgogne, 198.

18. Bourgogne, 203, 205; Philippe de Ségur, *Un aide de camp de Napoléon: mémoires du général Comte de Ségur* (Paris: Firmin-Didot, 1894–1895), II: 374.

19. Castellane, I: 196; Louis-Victor Leon, *Souvenirs sur la révolution, l'empire, et la restauration par le général Comte de Rochechouart* (Paris: Plon, 1889), 195; de Ségur, II: 376; Lagneau, 234.

20. Chevillet, 12, 9; Boulart, 52.

21. Coignet, 476.

22. Chevillet, 1–2; Philippe Girault, *Mes campagnes sous la république et l'empire 1791–1810* (La Rochelle: Siret, 1884), 77.

23. "Lettre au Ministre de la Guerre," 19 novembre 1810, "Angot," Xs 11 AT; "Lettre au Ministre de la Guerre," 2 Septembre 1807, "Boldevin, née Léger," Xs11, AT.

# Chapter Sixteen

# Children and the New Zealand Wars
## *An Exploration*

## *Jeanine Marie Graham*

The armed conflict which disrupted indigenous (Maori) and settler (Pakeha) relationships in several North Island regions of New Zealand during the 1860s was esssentially a war about government policy. Maori fought on both sides; colonists criticized Crown strategies; eminent Pakeha espoused the legitimacy of the Maori cause; military and political authorities quarreled openly over the nature of the campaign to be conducted.[1] For much of the country's immigrant population, resident in the South Island, the war touched child and adult lives lightly, if at all. Most Maori lived in the warmer North Island, where few tribes were unaffected. Communal lifestyles and a strong oral tradition ensured that successive generations heard, from an early age, the stories of conflict, confiscation, and land alienation. Only in the late twentieth century did awareness of the injustices of the 1860s and their repercussions begin to filter through into a wider New Zealand public consciousness.

Catalyzed by a disputed land purchase, fighting began at Waitara in North Taranaki 1860–61, spread to South Auckland and Waikato in 1863, extended to the Bay of Plenty by 1864, intensified in South Taranaki during 1865, and involved communities in Poverty Bay and Te Urewera from the mid-1860s onward. Pakeha children lost lives and livelihoods but their families were usually supported in some way by colonial authorities. The adverse impact of wartime destruction on Maori children was exacerbated by legislation which permitted the large-scale confiscation of tribal lands as a punitive measure and undermined the communal nature of Maori land ownership.[2] Yet demographic, geographic, cultural, and political factors enabled most colonial children, in and beyond the regions concerned, to grow up with minimal knowledge of the issues involved and without any comprehension of the consequences for the dispossessed. This was not an ethnic conflict, although racist rhetoric infused contemporary debate, but its repercussions caused major disparities between two societies that had co-existed with a high degree of mutual acceptance, friendship, and respect.

This essay explores the nature of children's involvement in the New Zealand Wars of the 1860s. It suggests that, despite clear differences in the severity of the impact, both Maori and Pakeha chidren were affected directly and indirectly, with consequences that were both short- and long-term. Whether Pakeha or Maori, those who developed formative impressions during these years and in the decades following were likely to have grown up with attitudes that would prove resistant to change. The legacies of Pakeha ignorance, Maori mistrust, and intertribal differences are still evident in contemporary political and social discourse.

Disruption, displacement, and destruction were the most common experiences of youngsters whose routines and surroundings were disturbed during the nine years of war which followed the declaration of martial law in Taranaki on February 22, 1860. Seasonal planting and harvesting routines were broken; the crops, stock, food stores, and homes of both communities were destroyed. As imperial and colonial forces grew in size and campaign strategies became more punitive, the scale of damage for Maori increased. The "scorched earth" and "bush-scouring" tactics used against tribal groups in South Taranaki (January 1866), Bay of Plenty (January 1867), and Te Urewera (May 1869) occurred at the height of the growing or harvesting seasons when supplies could not be replenished.[3] Infant and child mortality rates were already high, largely because Maori were only slowly building up immunity to introduced diseases: Food shortages further weakened children's resistance.[4] Settler children living in confined and over-crowded quarters during periods of "alarm" also had a much less nutritious diet than normal. Yet, as with the military forces who were paid and provisioned by official agencies, rations were supplied and compensation promised. Only in the aftermath of war, and in response to the pleas of local officials, was minimal assistance provided to some "widows and orphans" and Maori communities who were themselves impoverished as a consequence of trying to succour their displaced kin.[5]

Disturbances in one tribal domain influenced youth in another because of traditional loyalties. Within the Waikato, for example, the mission schools at Otawhao and Waipa lost older pupils as parties of Ngati Haua and Ngati Maniapoto traveled south to assist their Te Atiawa kin at Waitara. The girls, especially, would have helped with baking bread and cooking for the warriors. Class rolls continued to decline as Waikato Maori came to associate missionary with government interests: The schools at Kohanga, Otawhao, and Taupiri were all closed by the beginning of 1863. Government officials and long-serving missionaries and their families were expelled, and the Pakeha fathers of Maori children were faced with a choice of allegiance (most departed) in the months before troops invaded the Waikato in July.[6]

Trading and educational patterns built up over more than two decades of association were broken. A postwar generation of Waikato Maori did not possess the literacy levels or financial prosperity of their elders. Both during the war and subsequently, young people were also caught up in the tensions, between and within tribes, which resulted in part from the alignment of individuals and groups as kupapa, those who fought alongside government forces against other tribal groups (although often for reasons which Pakeha officials failed to appreciate).

The upheavals experienced by Pakeha children also varied in scale and intensity. During short-lived "emergencies" or "alarms," as in South Auckland and, later, the Bay of Plenty, outsettlers generally sought the protection of a blockhouse or redoubt during the military action. In the case of more prolonged campaigning, as in North Taranaki in 1860, where Maori quickly held the strategic advantage, a large-scale evacuation of New Plymouth's expanded civilian population became essential. With farming families having moved in from outlying areas in the weeks following the declaration of martial law, some 2,500 civilians were crowded into buildings that usually accommodated 800.[7] The pressure on shelter, food, water, public amenities, and personal tolerance was acute. Illness and epidemics soon developed; children were particularly susceptible to whooping cough, influenza, and typhoid. By the end of 1860, some 1,500 settlers, at least half of whom were children, had been evacuated to the South Island township of Nelson, where their subsequent experiences varied according to the children's ages and their families' social standing and income.

Most youngsters were without fathers (many of whom enrolled in the Taranaki militia); all were uprooted from familiar surroundings and routines. Some 200 evacuees in receipt of government rations were accommodated in the purpose-built Provincial Government Barracks. Rats were a problem as was the regimented access to food, but older children may have been more troubled by the social stigma of being so publicly the recipients of official aid. Yet for youngsters whose parents had the means to make independent arrangements, life was not necessarily easier. As house guests of the Anglican Bishop of Nelson, for instance, the six children of Reverend Henry Brown found their clothing, personal hygiene standards, and social relationships all critiqued by the Bishop's wife. Mary Hobhouse was generous in supporting the refugees, arranging a preschool facility for youngsters in her own home under the supervision of a thirteen-year-old "teacher," but the Brown children, made conscious of their "shabby badly made garments," would scarcely have felt comfortable in the presence of one who was so clearly their social superior.[8] And although some youth found employment as domestic servants or laborers, and younger siblings may have enjoyed developing new friendships, this was a period of transience and uncertainty that most evacuees were anxious to end.

By March 1863, only 36 of the 244 family groups who left their farms had been able to return to their devastated homes and properties; 113 families were lost to the province entirely.[9] Children and adults shared the emotional and financial strains of such upheaval, for compensation was some years in coming. Yet whether Pakeha families rebuilt their former homes or started again elsewhere, the children's memory and knowledge of a landscape was generally that of a first generation of settlers. They lost property and possessions but not access to a cultural heritage, perhaps the most destructive aspect of all for young Maori whose tribal lands were confiscated or sold through legislative processes that were far from just or fair.

Conventions of warfare for both societies upheld the separation of women and children from situations of armed combat, but this practice became increasingly difficult to observe as campaigning intensified and the safety of women, children, and the aged could not be guaranteed. The adoption of guerilla-style tactics by both sides put civilian lives at risk. Children and youth were among the victims. Colonists were outraged by a series of attacks in South Auckland late in 1863 which resulted in the deaths of three boys and severe injuries to two others, but the Maori actions aroused widespread fear in small and scattered Pakeha communities.[10] Few Pakeha realized that these incidents were reprisal raids by a subtribal group against whom imperial forces had leashed a dawn fusillade on September 18. One young woman who survived the "terrific volley" fired into the huts later described how she and her companions had retreated rapidly into the bush. "I carried my baby on my back."[11]

That imperial and colonial forces contravened prevailing notions of appropriate conduct concerning noncombatants was acknowledged but not well publicized at the time. Early in the morning of February 21, 1864, Imperial troops and Forest Rangers attacked and destroyed much of the unfortified Waikato settlement of Rangiaowhia, a village to which tribal leaders had sent women, children, and old people on the apparent understanding that this important economic base would be observed as a place of sanctuary.[12] At least twelve were killed; some died in burning *whare* (huts). Waikato chiefs left colonial authorities in no doubt about their bitterness over what they regarded as an act of treachery: "anything on our side you set down against us, and open your mouths wide to proclaim it. That deed of yours was a foul murder, and yet there is nobody to proclaim it."[13]

The Rangiaowhia incident was not an isolated one. In South Taranaki, the campaign by imperial and colonial forces, the latter including Maori, against the Ngati Ruahine leader Titokowaru, was hard fought. Children were among its victims, and two episodes were later the subject of official inquiries. The first concerned an unprovoked onslaught, by a force of 200 men, on the Tangahoe village of Pokaikai, a community that had already indicated its desire for peace to the commander of the attacking troops. Most occupants were asleep when soldiers burst into the settlement and began firing into the huts at one o'clock in the morning of August 2, 1866. One ten-year-old witnessed the deaths of her maternal grandparents, saw her mother's slashed ear and arm, and watched her village burn as she and a small group of prisoners were led away by the troops.[14] The children who lived through that night of terror and heard the stories retold in subsequent years might well have grown up to distrust government agents and oppose notions of reconciliation.

The sacking of Pokaikai remained relatively unknown, but an attack on a group of unarmed Maori boys at Handley's Woolshed in South Taranaki on November 27, 1868, was given greater prominence, both at the time and in a subsequent celebrated libel case. The incident involved a dozen Maori children, the eldest about ten and the youngest aged between six and eight, whose attempt to kill a large sow with pocket knives attracted the attention of a group of cavalry scouting in the area. Despite conflicting testimonies recorded two decades later, the men's pursuit of the children was ruthless, deliberate, and at close quarters. Two of the youngsters were killed by bullet and saber blows; at least five others received gunshot or sword wounds but lived to testify, with consistency and clarity, at the subsequent investigation. The episode was initially applauded in the local press as a "dashing affair" but later condemned when it became known that the victims were unarmed children. Such episodes did not accord well with notions of cultural superiority and civilized behavior, yet the survivors' translated evidence gave no sign that they held all Pakeha responsible for the actions of a few.[15]

For Pakeha youth, active engagement in the war was exceptional and more by circumstance than choice, as was the case with one fourteen-year-old caught with his father and grandfather when Maori launched a surprise attack against a small South Auckland stockade in September 1863.[16] As the military encounters moved farther away from enclaves of European settlement, the combination of imperial, colonial, and *kupapa* forces provided a large army that had no need of recruits below the minimum age of sixteen.

For Maori youngsters, though, the likelihood of their presence and participation in situations of armed conflict steadily increased as efforts to maintain a fighting force in the field became harder; the safety of noncombatants could not be guaranteed; and colonial and *kupapa* forces engaged in more relentless and determined pursuit of those deemed to be "resistance" or "rebel" leaders. Some older boys, aged fourteen or so, were present during the gunboat bombardment and physical assault at Rangiriri Pa on the Waikato River (November 1863), where at least one was killed and two others taken prisoner.[17] Another of similar age died during a hard-fought bush battle at Mangapiko the following February. His father was among those who came to the regimental camp, under a flag of truce, to collect the dead: He hugged his son's "lifeless form to his breast [and] cried bitterly."[18] For those warriors whose children or kin were slain at Rangiaowhia ten days later, there was little comparable opportunity to grieve. The presence of children and women inside the besieged *pa* at Orakau during the final pitched battle of the Waikato War (March 31 through April 2, 1864) was probably a direct consequence of that attack. Women and children were placed at the center of the body of surviving warriors when the decision was made by the defenders (who had been without water for two days) to break out of the *pa*. In the vigorous pursuit that followed, troops made no distinction on the grounds of gender or age.[19]

Te Kahipukoro of Ngati Ruahine was twelve when he took part in a determined attack against the Sentry Hill redoubt (April 30, 1864) as the second phase of the Taranaki War took on the dimensions of a religious crusade. Both his father and an uncle were killed; he was struck twice by bullets. "But I was so excited and so possessed by the fury of the battle that I did not feel it at first."[20] After a month of Maori medicinal care, he was able to travel back to a home village that was still intact. For other youngsters caught up in the latter phases of the conflicts, the situation was very different. Tribal groups constantly on the move, harried and pursued by colonial and *kupapa* forces, endeavored to take their women, children, and wounded with them if there were no kin or neutral communities with whom they might be left for safety. As government forces pursued Maori "rebels" through the dense bush and rugged terrain of inland South Taranaki or Te Urewera, children shared the privations and exertions of the adults.

On March 12, 1869, for example, colonial forces surprised Titokowaru at his South Taranaki camp on a foggy morning. Tents, baggage, tools of every description, clothing, blankets, fresh and potted meat, fruit, potatoes, and reserves of ammunition were all left behind in the group's desperate escape across the Patea River. The week-long pursuit was relentless. "We traveled for all we were worth half naked and foodless, tumbling over logs, scrambling in and out of creeks . . . just like the wild pigs before the hunter," one of the band later recalled. While some infants may have been left with neutral kin or deserting allies, many of the young Ngati Ruanui who fled may have died of exhaustion, hunger, or as victims of war. Two or three were captured on March 19 but, as James Belich has noted, contemporary documents were silent on their fate and "hasty smoke-curing might disguise both sex and age."[21]

There is an epic story of hardship and physical endurance to be told of the children whose lives became inextricably associated with the visions and exploits of Te Kooti Arikirangi Te Turuki, founder of the Ringatu faith. Initially many of these youngsters were among the women and children who were permitted to accompany their men folk when the government exiled East Coast Maori prisoners to the offshore Chatham Islands, 500 miles southwest of Napier. Over a ten-month period, March to December 1866, a total of 190 men, 69 women, and 45 children—four of whom were boys aged 12–14, were dispatched to this windswept place. Not all of the families made the journey. As a local official explained in a letter written from Napier in March 1866: "Ninety were brought here from Poverty Bay, but as some of these were women with young children, and several of the children [were] in a weak state of health, I offered those the option of remaining in this district, which they have done."[22] The rigors of war were already apparent amongst a once prosperous tribal people.

. . .

Conditions were often bleak on the Chathams.[23] By December 1867, fourteen of the exiles had died, including six children. Although official instructions stated that the accompanying families were not to be treated as prisoners, oral tradition refers to some children and women being required to yoke themselves to ploughs in lieu of animals. In July 1868, Te Kooti led the prisoners in a well-planned escape, commandeering a supply ship and its crew and sailing, with his compatriots, including seventy-one children (at least some of whom were infants) back to Poverty Bay. Over the next six months, those who remained with a leader whom colonial authorities regarded as a fugitive experienced privation, fear, and physical hardship. Rain and snow added to their discomfort. As they moved into the interior at Puketapu, back out toward the coast, and then inland to a defensive position at Nga Tapa, the nature of the armed pursuit changed, for in November 1869, Te Kooti and 100 warriors launched a devastating overnight attack on the Poverty Bay settlement of Matawhero. Some fifty children, women, and men, Maori and Pakeha, were killed. Five youngsters were amongst the Maori prisoners executed in daylight on Te Kooti's orders.

For Te Kooti it was "a war to reclaim his land"; for the kin of those killed, revenge was a matter of principle. Of the 130 men subsequently captured in January 1869 after the besieging of Te Kooti's defensive position at Nga Tapa, barely ten survived the *kupapa* retribution. Fifty women and sixteen children were taken prisoner. "They looked very thin and emaciated," one Pakeha recorded, "the children especially looked like so many skeletons."[24]

Te Kooti continued to elude his pursuers, even though colonial forces systematically destroyed the crops and villages of those who might give the group shelter and support. Yet children were still with Te Kooti during his final military engagement in September 1869, for some thirty women and children were captured. In the years following his official pardon (1883), Te Kooti devoted himself to developing the tenets of Ringatu belief. Possibly some of the young who shared in that first journey of faith lived to uphold and propound its doctrines. In the decades following the cessation of armed conflict, immigration continued to increase the demographic disparity between the two societies and settlement patterns made it harder for Pakeha and Maori children to associate. Even in those rural areas where they could interact, there was no encouragement for Pakeha to study Maori language and culture. The curriculum emphasized the civilizing mission of Empire: It was too soon to critique the consequences of colonialism.

In the South Island, where the dominant tribe had been parted from most of its land prior to the 1860s, the conflict had no meaning for Pakeha children, many of whose lives were disrupted instead by gold rushes, parental alcoholism, paternal desertion, maternal death. Only in Nelson might colonial youth have gained some awareness of the impact of the war in the North. In a few decades there would be war memorials and honor boards throughout the country, visible reminders of the trauma of community involvement in an external conflict. There was no comparable acknowledgment of the local one. Street and place names and administrative boundary lines drawn on colonial maps continued the process of indigenous displacement.

For many Pakeha who variously respected, admired, or tolerated a people whom they knew to be declining in numbers, the conflicts of the 1860s were an unfortunate but necessary episode in the march of progress, best put behind them. The role that children might play in forging a new relationship was symbolized in February 1872 when, after a self-imposed exile of twelve years, a grey-haired chief and some 400 of his kin walked through the streets of New Plymouth to a civic reception. Over the next five days, Wiremu Kingi of Te Atiawa, the man whose justifiable resistance to the sale of his tribal lands at Waitara had led to the outbreak of war, was a "centre of attraction." The local press noted that many of the old settlers brought their children to see him and Kingi responded warmly: "as each batch of children came in he laughed with delight as he took their tiny hands in his and kindly shook them."[25]

Yet the recollections of Taranaki-born children, raised in the decades of the 1870s through 1910s, reflect a mixture of attitudes, from matter-of-fact acceptance to curiosity to hostility mingled with fear. Neither those who grew up farming on confiscated land nor the families of military settlers positioned throughout the Waikato and Bay of Plenty learned of the circumstances which had led indigenous communities to be landless, itinerant, and dependent upon casual laboring as their primary means of earning a subsistence income.[26]

Two different cultural perspectives helped to shape children's attitudes toward the conflict of the 1860s. Pakeha sought to put the troubles behind them: Maori could not forget. Past and present were—and are—intertwined. All thought of the future was—and is—with reference to the past. Eventually there would be an apology from the Crown and some financial compensation, but in the decades immediately after the war, few young Maori could have grown up without a profound sense of injustice influencing their attitudes toward government authority. These youth would also have been aware of the consequences of military alignments during the 1860s. Kupapa were expelled from the King Country and families divided; tribal lands were occupied by rivals; Waikato tribes resisted conscription during the 1914–18 War while "loyal" tribes provided volunteers. Some of the tensions which developed in the Maori Pioneer Battalion in the First World War suggest that the legacies of the 1860s were well known to young soldiers fifty years later.[27] More than a century after the conflicts began, the work of the Waitangi Tribunal is at last ensuring that fewer young New Zealanders are growing up oblivious to the complexities of their country's colonial past.[28]

## Notes

1. Waitangi Tribunal, *The Taranaki Report: Kaupapa Tuatahi* (Wellington: GP Publications, 1996), 92.

2. New Zealand Settlements Act 1863 (plus amendments 1864, 1865, 1866); Native Land Act 1862 (amended 1865). Malcolm McKinnon, ed., *Bateman New Zealand Historical Atlas* (Auckland: David Bateman in association with Historical Branch, Department of Internal Affairs, 1997), Plate 39.

3. James Belich, *I Shall Not Die: Titokowaru's War, New Zealand 1868–1869* (Wellington: Allen and Unwin and Port Nicholson Press, 1989), 8; Evelyn Stokes, *A History of Tauranga County* (Palmerston North: Dunmore Press, 1980), 101–115; Waitangi Tribunal, *Taranaki Report*, 98.

4. Ian Pool, *Te Iwi Maori: A New Zealand Population Past, Present and Projected* (Auckland: Auckland University Press, 1991), Chapters 4 and 5, *passim*; Sally Maclean, "Nga Tamariki o Te Rohe o Waikato: Maori children's lives in the Waikato Region 1850–1900" (MA thesis, University of Waikato, 1990), 55–69.

5. Maclean, 44–45.

6. Ibid., 24.

7. Natasha Elliot-Hogg, "The Taranaki Refugees 1860" (MA thesis, University of Waikato, 1999), 14.

8. Ibid., 44–46, 55.

9. Ibid., Appendix I, "Lists Relating to the Relief Funds 20 March 1863," 86–95.

10. Graham, "Disrupted Lives," 9, 11.

11. James Cowan, *The New Zealand Wars: A History of the Campaigns and the Pioneering Period*, 2 vols., first published 1922–23 (Wellington: Government Printer, 1983 reprint with amendments), Vol. I, 290–291.

12. James Belich, *The New Zealand Wars and the Victorian Interpretation of Racial Conflict* (Auckland: Auckland University Press, 1986), 164–165.

13. Maclean, "Nga Tamariki," 36; Cowan, *NZ Wars*, I, 361–364.

14. *Appendix to the Journals of the House of Representatives (AJHR)*, 1868, A-3, "Report of the Pokaikai Commission," 3–27.

15. Belich, *Titokowaru*, 189–204; *Bryce vs. Rusden, 1886, In the High Court of Justice, Queen's Bench Division, Royal Courts of Justice (Thursday 14 March 1886), before Baron Huddleston and a Special Jury. Proceedings of libel suit by John Bryce against G. W. Rusden*, privately printed for John Bryce [available in the New Zealand Collection, University of Waikato Library], 517–638.

16. Cowan, *NZ Wars* I, 451–453, 273–282.

17. Ibid., pp. 291–292; Nona Morris, ed., *The Journal of William Morgan: Pioneer Settler and Maori War Correspondent* (Auckland: Auckland City Council Libraries Department, 1963), 84, 97–100.

18. John Featon, *The Waikato War*, first published 1879 (Christchurch: Capper Press reprint, 1971), 74.

19. Maclean, "Nga Tamariki," 33–34; Cowan, *NZ Wars*, I, 365–406.

20. *NZ Wars*, II, 23–26.

21. Belich, *Titokowaru*, 265–268.

22. *AJHR*, 1868, A-15E, "Papers Relative to Prisoners and Guard at Chatham Islands," 4, 10–11.

23. Details in the following three paragraphs are drawn from Judith Binney, *Redemption Songs: A Life of Te Kooti Arikirangi Te Turuki* (Auckland: Auckland University Press/Bridget Williams Books, 1995), Chapters 3–7; McKinnon, ed., *Historical Atlas*, Plate 40, for the tracing of Te Kooti's movements, 1868–1872.

24. Binney, *Te Kooti*, 146.

25. Sinclair, *Kinds of Peace*, 11–13.

26. Graham, "Childhood Experiences," 174–178.

27. Ian McGibbon, *Oxford Companion to New Zealand Military History* (Auckland, NZ: Oxford University Press, 2000), 296–299.

28. See the Waitangi Tribunal website for a list of published reports and details of claims in process. *<http://www.knowledge-basket.co.nz/waitangi/welcome.html>*

# Chapter Seventeen

# Stolen Generations and Vanishing Indians

## *The Removal of Indigenous Children as a Weapon of War in the United States and Australia, 1870–1940*

### *Victoria Haskins and Margaret D. Jacobs*

In 1906, a girl named Helen "awoke to find [her] camp surrounded by troops." A government official, she later recalled, "called the men together, ordering the women and children to remain in their separate family groups." "The government," he said:

> had reached the limit of its patience and that the children would have to go to school. . . . All children of school age were lined up to be registered and taken away to school. Eighty-two children . . . were taken to the schoolhouse . . . with military escort.[1]

In about 1915, the police came for a girl named Margaret. "They said they wanted to take my children away," Margaret's mother Theresa remembered. "I said 'My children are well cared for.'" A policeman took Margaret, her sister, and her cousin from their local school, in the face of the weeping entreaties of her mother. Margaret wrote that the policeman patted a holster at his belt while telling her resistant mother that he would "have to use this if you do not let us take these children now." Thinking that the policeman would shoot their mother, Margaret and her young relatives screamed, "We'll go with him Mum, we'll go."[2]

The similarity of these two stories is remarkable. In each case, government authorities forcibly removed children from their families for the stated purposes of educating them or improving their lives. Yet the incidents took place in almost opposite corners of the world. Helen was Helen Sekaquaptewa, a Hopi girl who lived in northeastern Arizona in the United

States. Margaret was Margaret Tucker, or Lilardia, an Ulupna/Wiradjuri Aboriginal girl from the southeastern corner of the Australian continent.[3] Despite being poles apart, Helen and Margaret, as well as their communities, shared a common experience at the hands of white governmental authorities.

As a central component of the assimilation agenda in the United States and of absorption plans in Australia, child removal became a systematic government policy toward indigenous peoples in both countries in the nineteenth and twentieth centuries. Using the rhetoric of protecting and saving indigenous children, reformers and government officials touted child removal as a means to "uplift" and "civilize" indigenous children. Modern-day historians, until very recently, have characterized child removal in similar ways: as a well-intentioned, though ultimately misguided, alternative to warfare and violence against indigenous peoples.

If we turn our attention to the perspectives of the indigenous peoples who confronted this policy, a different view emerges. While outright violence against indigenous peoples in both the United States and Australia did virtually end in the late nineteenth century, efforts by colonizers to pacify and control indigenous populations and to confiscate their lands continued with the removal of indigenous children. Such a policy was hardly a departure from military methods of subjugation; rather, the systematic and forcible removal of their younger generations represented an ongoing assault upon indigenous communities.

The removal of Indian children as a systematic state policy began in earnest in the United States in the 1880s. The idea to assimilate Indians through removing Indian children originated in 1875 with an "experiment" conducted upon Kiowa, Comanche, and Cheyenne prisoners of war incarcerated at Fort Marion in St. Augustine, Florida, under the command of Captain Richard Henry Pratt. Pratt decided to "rehabilitate" the prisoners by cutting their hair, replacing their native dress with military uniforms, and introducing military discipline and education to them. In 1879, with new authority from the government, Pratt opened Carlisle Institute, in Carlisle, Pennsylvania on twenty-seven acres of land, complete with stables, officer's quarters, and commodious barracks buildings, all donated by the U.S. War Department. As at Fort Marion, Pratt ran the school along military lines. He issued military uniforms to Indian boys, and required both boys and girls to form in companies, march, and drill each day before they carried out their assigned "details." Pratt deemed dormitories "quarters" and implemented a strict military regime.[4]

Thus even from their inception, Indian boarding schools were intimately connected with the U.S. military. The U.S. government adopted Pratt's plan for assimilating and remolding American Indian children. By 1902, they had established 154 boarding schools (including 25 off-reservation schools) and 154 day schools for about 21,500 Native Americans. There were also still a number of mission schools operated by various religious organizations. Commissioner of Indian Affairs Thomas Morgan claimed that through this new system:

> the Indians are not only becoming Americanized, but they are by this process of education gradually being absorbed, losing their identity as Indians, and becoming an indistinguishable part of the great body politic.[5]

While the federal government supposedly did not allow the removal of children without the consent of their parents, Indian agents resorted to force, withholding rations, or making bribes to fill boarding school quotas.[6] After World War II, the government revived assimilation policy under a new name—termination and relocation. Although many boarding schools remained in operation, Indian child removal now more often manifested itself in the form of social workers who removed Indian children from families they deemed unfit, to be raised in white foster homes.

In Australia, child removal policies were brought in under the banner of "Protection." Beginning with an 1871 regulation to the Victorian Aborigines Act (1869), and followed by the colony of Queensland in 1897, by 1911 all the newly formed states of federated Australia had their own raft of special legislation for the forcible removal, institutionalization, and indenturing of indigenous children. Child removal was aimed ostensibly at making Aboriginal children into "decent and useful members of the community" and couched in the language of benevolent welfare policy.[7] Thus, the New South Wales (NSW) Aborigines Protection Board had the power to secure custody and control of any Aboriginal child "if it is satisfied that such a course is in the interest of the moral or physical welfare of such child."[8] Powers enabling state governments to forcibly remove Aboriginal children at their own discretion, without parental consent or court hearings, were acquired piecemeal and by the 1930s were extensive around Australia. Child removal practices included the routine segregation of children from about age four in dormitories on large, regulated missions and reserves; the removal of very young children (especially of mixed descent) to distant institutions; and the forcing of children from about the age of fourteen into "training homes" and indentures. As in the United States, after World War

II the policies were renamed (ironically, as "Assimilation") and while the institutions remained, social workers increasingly removed Aboriginal children under general child welfare laws, for fostering and adoption.

Despite the lofty "saving the children" rhetoric, it became clear that government officials saw a more practical dimension to child removal. Authorities in the United States often remarked on the inverse connection between child removal to boarding schools and wars with the Indians. Thomas Morgan asserted, "It is cheaper to educate a man and to raise him to self-support than to raise another generation of savages and fight them." White officials also perceived that child removal had positive effects by making Indian parents more docile. John Miles, the Quaker agent to the Cheyennes and Arapahoes in Indian territory, wrote to his friend Pratt:

> There are so many points gained in placing Indian children in school. . . . The child being in school the parents are much easier managed; are loyal to the Government, to the Agent, and take an interest in the affairs of the Agency, and never dare, or desire, to commit a serious wrong. I am yet to know of the first individual Indian on this reservation who has joined in a raid, that has had his child in school.

Government officials made such policies explicit, as when the Commissioner of Indian Affairs expressly ordered Pratt to obtain children from two particularly resistant reservations, "saying that the children, if brought east, would become hostages for tribal good behavior."[9]

In Australia, government authorities also turned to child removal to control indigenous communities. As the NSW Aborigines Protection Board pointed out, white authorities "really had no control over the reserves and the residents could set authority at defiance" until such legislation enabled them to make "radical changes in the methods of dealing with the aboriginal population, more especially in the direction of training the young."[10] However, the overriding aim of most Australian authorities in targeting the children was to ensure the disappearance of the race. Discussion of child removal policies in the frontier regions of Australia, where sporadic conflicts and massacres continued, reflected anxieties over the vulnerability and impermanence of the settler population. Child removal would ensure that "the black population is speedily absorbed in the white," warned the Northern Territory (NT) Aboriginal Protector, "[otherwise] the white population will be absorbed into the black."[11]

In settled Australia where Aborigines were a clear minority and violent clashes a distant memory, such racial demographic concerns were still paramount. "These black children must be rescued from danger to themselves, and from being a danger to the whole of the white population," stated a NSW politician and Board member.

> They are an increasing danger, because although there are only a few full-blooded aborigines left, there are 6,000 of the mixed blood growing up. It is a danger to us to have a people like that among us looking upon our institutions with eyes different from ours.[12]

Since Aborigines were not "dying out" as expected, but instead had established themselves on rural land bases that were coveted by surrounding white settlers, authorities resorted to child removal. This, it was argued, would put "things into train on the lines that would eventually lead to the camps being depleted of their population, and finally the closing of the reserves and camps altogether."[13] In Australia, there was no Act designed to break up the reserves such as was legislated in the United States in the General Allotment Act of 1887, but child removal in the settled areas peaked in tandem with the revocation of reserved lands.[14]

Unlike assimilation policy in the United States, Australian child removal made no pretense of removing children for the sake of their education, it being held they were incapable of higher learning. Instead the stated intention of their removal was to "absorb" them into the "industrial classes" of white Australian society.[15] Officials considered the homes as "training" institutions for menial labor and as holding bays for workers prior to their indenturing to farm labor or domestic service. Furthermore, until the postwar era, girls and young women bore the brunt of the removal policy, as the authorities made their concerns about preventing Aboriginal "breeding" explicit.[16]

Upon close examination, it becomes clear that despite its more noble claims, the North American system also aimed at placing indigenous children into low-skilled, low-paid occupations at the margins of American society. Many boarding schools promoted a program of work for local employers in the afternoon, and also sought to place Indian children with white families during summers and other school holidays, "there to learn to work and to acquire civilized ways." Pratt and other reformers touted this plan, known as the outing system, as a means to break down Native American "superstition and savagery" and to more deeply inculcate in Indian children the values of white American society.[17] In reality, boarding schools became virtual labor recruiters for nearby families who sought cheap laborers. Thus, even as Australian and American policies diverged in semantics, they converged in practice.

Indigenous people rarely perceived the removal of their children as a benign alternative to war or as a humanitarian endeavor. Helen Sekaquaptewa remembered that:

> when we were five or six years of age, we, with our parents . . . became involved with the school officials, assisted by the Navajo policemen, in a serious and rather desperate game of hide-and-seek. . . . When September came there was no peace for us.

Hopi families often tried to hide their children in cupboards or baskets or took them outside the village to hide in cornfields or nearby ravines.[18]

Iris Burgoyne, a Mirning-Kokatha woman of South Australia (SA) described how adults warned the older children of the arrival of white officials on the mission, and these children then hid the younger children in the bush. Nuns would "go from house to house. The Sister would bark at the mothers, 'Where are your children?'" When unsuccessful with mothers, "this sister went to the old folks in search of the children. The old people never lied. . . . [t]hose children were ripped from their families, shoved into that car and driven away." Another girl from Western Australia (WA) in the 1930s recalled:

> During the raids on the camps [to collect children] it was not unusual for people to be shot—shot in the arm or the leg. You can understand the terror we lived in, the fright—not knowing when someone will come unawares and do whatever they were doing—either disrupting our family life, camp life, or shooting at us.[19]

In both Australia and the United States, growing up in such an atmosphere was akin to living in a war zone.

Once taken from their parents and tribal communities, indigenous children suffered enormously. Both American and Australian institutions set out to physically and mentally transform their inmates. Daklugie, a Chiricahua Apache, remembered that when he and several other Apache children were taken to Carlisle, "we were thrust into a vicious and hostile world that we both hated and feared. . . we had no choice but to submit." Once at Carlisle, Daklugie recalled, "the torture began. . . . The first thing they did was cut our hair." After a bath, "we were ordered to put on trousers. We'd lost our hair and we'd lost our clothes; with the two we'd lost our identity as Indians." Later Carlisle authorities "imposed meaningless new names on us." Daklugie always hated his new name, Asa; "it was forced on me as though I had been an animal."[20]

Indigenous children were prohibited from speaking their languages and subject to physical and psychological abuse aimed at ensuring their submission to control. Daisy Ruddick, placed in Kahlin Compound at Darwin aged six, talked of how total silence was maintained:

> if any of us made a noise. . . . You had a wooden post, and we had to stand in the hot boiling sun with our hands behind our back because we woke [the matron] up from her sleep. That was our punishment. You wouldn't believe it, would you? It sort of reminds me of a concentration camp. You'd stand in that hot boiling sun for . . . I don't know what . . . it seemed like a lifetime.[21]

Beatings administered with sticks and whips were also a feature of institutional life, while Aboriginal children in employment also commonly experienced physical violence (as well as psychological and sexual abuse).[22] Such tactics of enforcing submission also aimed at erasing indigenous identity. As Arrente man George Bray reflected on his experience, "We were taken away and brainwashed towards living the white society instead of living the old Aborigine way. We were brought in to forget that sort of thing."[23]

Many indigenous children found the whole experience of institutional life, particularly Christian proselytization, mystifying. After her first day at church, Kaibah, a Navajo (Diné) girl, asked Nancy, an older Navajo girl, "Who are God and Jesus? And why are they going to burn us all up?" Nancy concluded, "They are the white man's gods, who are coming very soon to burn people that don't live like they want them to live." For Jean Begg, Christian teachings at Bomaderry Children's Home gave her nightly terrors of the risen Christ inextricably intertwined with a fear of Aboriginal people, "knowing that they were evil, wicked and not understanding black, but only relating it to sin and drinking and cruelness."[24]

Such religious education taught indigenous children to deny, despise, and fear every aspect of their indigenous identity. The indigenous children of Australia and the United States were of a race and culture that had been singled out and targeted for control and, in the Australian case, eradication, and this purpose underlay all their experiences of removal and institutionalization.

As James Wilson points out, they "were thrown into a hostile universe in which everything that made them what they were was systematically ridiculed and condemned. Not surprisingly, many did not survive."[25] Indeed, the numbers of indigenous children who died after being removed to white institutions or homes is astounding and tragic. Aboriginal rights activist Roberta Sykes discovered a list made in 1938 of the names and "ages of death" of children removed by the NSW Aborigines Protection Board:

> I felt faint as I read through and found I had in my hand perhaps the earliest list of black deaths in custody . . . Girl taken, aged 13, died three years later, aged 16; girl taken, aged 8, died four years later, aged 12; girl taken aged 13, died aged 14; taken 13, died 18; taken 13, died 17; taken aged 7, died aged 12 . . . and so on.[26]

Some children were undoubtedly murdered, such as the child at Cootamundra Home in NSW in the 1920s who was "tied to the old bell post and belted continuously. She died that night, still tied to the post, no girl ever knew what happened to the body or where she was buried."[27] Others tried to kill themselves, either in the institutions or, more commonly it seems, after they left to go into domestic service.[28] Other deaths resulted from widespread disease.

Much of the illness that indigenous children suffered can be attributed to the miserable conditions in the institutions, which Thom Blake has labeled "passive violence" by the state.[29] Overcrowding, poor sanitation, a constant regime of physical work, and inadequate and poor-quality food were not conducive to good health. At the Bungalow, children supplemented their diet from the town dump; at Cootamundra and Kinchela Homes in NSW children picked grubs and weevils out of their food; while children in Kahlin Compound lived on a diet of peanuts during the Depression.[30] "It was very hard living," recalled one inmate of Cootamundra Home.[31] Very young children were most vulnerable to death from bronchial-related disease and gastroenteritis, while researcher Inara Walden found that the major cause of death listed for girls taken away in NSW was tuberculosis. Walden speculated that the children's "extreme social dislocation" could have made them susceptible to the disease.[32] Tuberculosis was also a killer of removed Native American children. In an 1889 War Department report, Lieutenant Guy Howard documented that of the 112 Apache children of POWs who had been sent to Carlisle, 30 had died, and another 12 had been returned to their parents because of poor health. Most of these sick children soon died, mostly from tuberculosis. Henrietta Stockel attributes such high rates of death to "the impact of a strange language, the unfamiliar situations, homesickness, the lack of sufficiently diversified exercise, and unusual food." The children had all experienced these factors along with their POW parents at Fort Marion, Florida, but as Stockel puts it, "the risk factors increased dramatically when the children were forcibly removed from their parents and families, . . . and put into yet another terrifying situation." Even a general in the U.S. military remarked that the children were more susceptible to disease because of separation from their parents. Pratt himself blamed the "deplorable and almost hopeless conditions surrounding them. . . . They have no home, no country, no future, and life has become hardly worth living." Yet Pratt failed to own up to his own role in the children's illnesses and deaths.[33]

If we regard indigenous children's experiences as living in a state of warfare, within which they were both targets and victims, we might also consider them as combatants, engaged in a struggle to maintain their identity as indigenous people. For those children who were taken, physical survival was hard enough, but they also had to struggle against all odds to retain any positive identification with their race and culture. Many indigenous children learned to cope by finding ways to keep their native ways alive, sometimes in new and surprising ways. Daklugie remembered:

> The thing that pulled me through was the athletic training at Carlisle. I enjoyed the sports and, although the conditioning didn't measure up to my father's and Geronimo's training routine, it kept me active and fit.

After football games, "to celebrate the victory, we had a party in the gym. Some of us did our native dances."[34] Aboriginal children placed in service in rural areas were able to maintain their knowledge of bush food and indigenous practices such as leaving cobwebs for birds to feed their young, knowledge which they passed on to the white children they looked after.[35]

Children in mission dormitories located near their own communities sometimes obtained bush food and brought "some meat back to the camp for the older people." Wadjularbinna at Doomadgee mission in Queensland recalled that the children there were "very fortunate" because older girls, who had learned from their parents:

> kept the culture alive in the dormitory. They told us stories, they kept us in the kinship system; they kept that alive. . . . Our culture was intact, but we had to do it really sneaky, don't let the missionaries know.[36]

Many children never adjusted and sought to escape. Such resistance could result in humiliating punishments. At a boarding school for the Navajos in Toadlena, Arizona, authorities punished four girls who ran away by subjecting them to a public ritual headshaving. Authorities knew that "to have one's hair cut short was a drastic break in Navajo tradition, but to have it all cut off, was a great disgrace."[37]

Aboriginal children also ran away from the institutions, and met with public shaming rituals and punishment on their return. A greater proportion escaped from their places of employment; when recaptured, most were dispatched to another employer, while others were drawn into the juvenile justice system, placed in reformatories, convents, or even mental asylums.

Ultimately, resistance for children removed under these policies was manifested most clearly by the enthusiasm of many of those same children as adults to find their cultural identity, to actively work toward cultural revitalization, and to assert their indigenous identity with pride. As Ngarrindjeri poet Margaret Brusnahan writes:

> Reared your way didn't make me white
> If only once you'd had the insight
> To know the day you set me free
> I'd return to my own The Ngarrindjeri.[38]

In the meantime, the effect of child removal on families and tribal communities proved profoundly devastating. Poignant letters from Apache POW parents at Fort Marion to their children at Carlisle provide testimony to the tragedy that befell native peoples when their children were removed. One mother, Chenlozite, wrote (through an interpreter):

My dear children,
Are you happy? You must be happy my two boys. I see well yet and I talk kind. When you went away from me I cried every day. I feel better now. We live very well here. I think we shall see each other again. You must not think about me. I don't think about myself.

While visiting the imprisoned Apaches at Fort Marion, famed nineteenth-century author Harriet Beecher Stowe witnessed Indian after Indian rise to speak at a prayer meeting, professing their adherence to white ways if only they be allowed to reunite with their families.[39] In some cases, holding children hostage and separating family members from one another did seem to produce the desired effect of the government to pacify and control Native Americans, at least temporarily. Many families submitted to the government's wishes in hopes of being reunited with their children as soon as possible. When Native American families did resist the removal of their children, they did so individually or in small groups, rather than through collective organization.

Yet just as the U.S. government found a new means to conquer and control Native Americans, so too did native people find new ways to resist absolute control over their lives. Ironically, boarding schools, by teaching Indians English and inadvertently cultivating a pan-Indian identity, furnished Indian students with tools to build a strong legal resistance to white control. The first major pan-Indian organization, the Society of American Indians, founded in 1911, included mostly Native Americans who had themselves been removed as children. The group was divided on the issue of boarding-school education and never took a stand against the practice of child removal. However, they began to agitate for greater American Indian sovereignty, a goal that future American Indian organizations would carry further through battles in court.[40]

For many Aboriginal Australians, maintaining their religious ceremonies and practices was made difficult if not untenable by the full-scale removal of children. In some areas, such as the south coast of NSW, carrying out important ceremonies such as initiations may have actually "been to offer cause for taking children away from their families."[41] Child removal ravaged whole communities and families. "I have nothing to work for, [my wife] is dead," wrote a North Queensland father in 1901.

> She died broken-hearted, killed on that unlucky day when [our daughter] was dragged by animal force from her family and home, and forced from the arms of her mother on a false charge of being neglected.

While numerous parents protested by anguished letters to the authorities, others took direct action; in WA, a number of men, on learning that their children had been removed while they had been away fighting in World War II, marched into the office of the Aboriginal authorities and, at gunpoint, demanded their children's return.[42]

Aboriginal people organized forcefully and collectively against the removal of their children. In 1927 Fred Maynard, president of the Australian Aborigines Progressive Association (AAPA), accused the authorities of removing Aboriginal girls "to exterminate the Noble and Ancient Race of sunny Australia." He wrote to the NSW premier demanding that children be left with their parents—the "family life of Aboriginal people shall be held sacred and free from invasion."[43] Four years earlier in SA, three Nunga men presented a memorial to the SA governor that likened the new South Australian Aborigines (Training of Children) Act to a state of warfare between the government and "mother's love." The Nunga men told the press that they did not "mind the Government taking [the children] and training them. We want them to get on and be useful. But we want to feel we have full rights over them and that they are our own children." The memorial itself, written by a Ngarrindjeri person, described the passing of the child removal legislation as an "ultimatum of one nation to another," and the refusal of the Aboriginal people to "comply with the demands" of this ultimatum, an "acceptance of a condition of warfare."[44]

Certainly, Aboriginal people experienced the removal of children as an act of warlike aggression, designed to intimidate them, to control them, and to ultimately destroy their communities. When we examine Aboriginal and American Indian perspectives on the removal of their children, rather than blindly accepting the national myths that have been constructed and reproduced over generations, it becomes clear that the hidden but real aims of the removal of children were not so different from the aims of violence and warfare against indigenous peoples. Warfare aimed at conquest and dispossession, at quelling indigenous resistance, and at transforming indigenous peoples from self-sufficient collective owners of their own land to impoverished and marginal members of society, who, in order to survive, had to work at menial labor for their conquerors. By the end of the nineteenth century, overt acts of violence against indigenous people may have become politically inexpedient, financially impracticable, or simply ineffective. Australian and American authorities continued to face the "problem" of a persistent indigenous population. Thus, officials turned to a new means of warfare, disguised as a humanitarian alternative. Child removal sought to accomplish the original aims of warfare against indigenous peoples, by the severance of tribal and land connections, the fragmentation of indigenous communities, and the training of indigenous children to serve their colonizers. The conquerors of Australian and North American indigenous peoples may have stopped the use of violence and outright warfare, but warfare against native peoples continued in a new but no less benign and damaging form.

## NOTES

1. Helen Sekaquaptewa, *Me and Mine: The Life Story of Helen Sekaquaptewa*, as told to Louise Udall (Tucson: University of Arizona Press, 1969), 91–92.

2. Theresa Clements, *From Old Maloga: The Memoirs of an Aboriginal Woman*, pamphlet, n.d. (Prahan: privately printed, 1948), in Anton Vroland papers, MS 3991, Series 5, Box 6, Manuscript Section, National Library of Australia, Canberra; Margaret Tucker, *If Everyone Cared* (London: Grosvenor Books, 1983), 93.

3. Where possible in this essay, we use the particular tribal or community affiliation that indigenous peoples prefer. Although there is much debate within in-

digenous and scholarly communities regarding proper terms for indigenous peoples in both countries, there is no consensus. Therefore, when we refer to indigenous peoples in the United States as a group, we use the words American Indians, Indians, and Native Americans interchangeably. In Australia, there are also a number of names by which Aboriginal people call themselves generically, such as Koori (southeastern Australia) and Nunga (South Australia), which we use where the name denoting the specific group affiliation is not known. When we refer to the indigenous peoples of Australia collectively, we use the terms Australian Aborigines, Aborigines, and Aboriginal people, these being currently acceptable terms.

4. Richard Henry Pratt, *Battlefield and Classroom: Four Decades with the American Indian, 1867–1904* (New Haven, CT: Yale University Press, 1964), 163, 233, and more generally, 104–166, 213–267; *The Redman* 1 (February 1909): back cover; Jason Betzinez with Wilbur Sturtevant Nye, *I Fought with Geronimo* (Lincoln: University of Nebraska Press, 1959), 150, 153.

5. Adams, *Education for Extinction*, 57, 58; T. J. Morgan, "Our Red Neighbors," *Baptist Home Mission Monthly* 16 (June 1894), 190.

6. For examples of how agents obtained Indian children, see *The Indian's Friend* 3, no. 10 (June 1891): 2; Mann, *Cheyenne-Arapaho Education*, 50, 59, 80, 89; Ball, *Indeh*, 219.

7. Individual colonies were responsible for their administration of Aboriginal affairs and after Federation, in 1901, this situation continued, the federal government being prevented by the constitution from legislating on Aboriginal matters until 1967. The federal government, however, administered Aboriginal affairs in the Northern Territory after 1911—prior to that the territory was administered by South Australia. Tasmania alone did not have special provisions for removing Aboriginal children—Aboriginal children were removed there under general child welfare laws.

8. *NSW Aborigines Protection Board Annual Report for 1910* (Sydney: Government Printer, 1911); Sec. 13(A), *Aborigines Protection (Amending) Act*, (NSW) Act No. 2, 1915.

9. Morgan quoted in *The Indian's Friend* 4 (Jan. 1892); Miles quoted in Pratt, *Battlefield and Classroom*, 242; Pratt, *Battlefield and Classroom*, 202.

10. *NSW Aborigines Protection Board Report for 1909* (Sydney: Government Printer, 1910).

11. Dr. Cecil Cook, Chief Protector of the Aborigines in the Northern Territory, in Commonwealth of Australia, *Aboriginal Welfare—Initial Conference of Commonwealth and State Aboriginal Authorities, held at Canberra, 21st to 23rd April, 1937* (Canberra: Commonwealth Government Printer, 1937), 13–14.

12. Second reading in NSW Legislative Assembly, Aborigines Protection Amending Bill, 27/1/15, *NSW Parliamentary Debates* Vol. 56 (Sydney: Government Printer, 1915), 1965.

13. F. Flowers, citing Donaldson's speech during the 1912 deputation, second reading in NSW Legislative Council, Aborigines Protection Amending Bill, 24 November 1914, *NSW Parliamentary Debates* Vol. 56 (Sydney: Government Printer, 1915), 1353.

14. Based on figures for child removal in *NSW Aborigines Protection Board Register of Wards* and unpublished research on reservation revocation NSW in John Maynard, "Fred Maynard and the Awakening of Aboriginal Political Consciousness and Activism in Twentieth Century Australia" (Ph.D. dissertation, Newcastle University, NSW, in progress).

15. See comment by E. Harkness in Commonwealth of Australia, *Aboriginal Welfare*, 21; Board official (unidentified) in a speech to the Australasian Catholic Congress, 1909, quoted in Coral Edwards and Peter Read, *The Lost Children* (Sydney: Doubleday, 1989), xiii–xiv.

16. It was not until "assimilation" replaced "protection" as official policy, and fostering superseded indenturing, that proportions of girls and boys removed became equal. See Heather Goodall, "Saving the Children," *Aboriginal Law Bulletin* 2 (June 1990): 9.

17. Quoted in *The Indian's Friend* 2 (November 1889): 1.

18. Sekaquaptewa, *Me and Mine*, 8–9, 31.

19. Iris Yumadoo Kochallalya Burgoyne, *The Mirning We Are the Whales* (Broome: Magabala Books, 2000), 65–66; confidential evidence 681, *Western Australia, Bringing Them Home Report*, Chapter 2, p.1.

20. Quoted in Ball, *Indeh*, 141, 142, 144.

21. Daisy Ruddick, "'Talking About Cruel Things': Girls' Life in the Kahlin Compound," as told to Kathy Mills and Tony Austin, *Hecate*, 15 (1989): 18.

22. See Polly Smith, quoted in Stuart Rintoul, *The Wailing* (Port Melbourne: William Heinemann Australia, 1993), 24–25; "Millicent," *Bringing Them Home Report*, Chapter 7, 12; Victoria Haskins, "My One Bright Spot: A personal insight into relationships between white women and Aboriginal women under the NSW Aborigines Protection Board Apprenticeship Policy 1920–1942" (Ph.D. dissertation, University of Sydney, 1998).

23. Quoted in Rowena MacDonald, *Between Two Worlds* (Alice Springs: IAD Press, 1995), 32.

24. Kay Bennett, *Kaibah: Recollection of a Navajo Girlhood* (Los Angeles: Westernlore Press, 1964), 220; Begg quoted in James Miller, *Koori: A Will to Win* (London: Angus & Robertson, 1985), 159, 162.

25. James Wilson, *The Earth Shall Weep: A History of Native America* (London: Picador, 1999), 313.

26. Sykes quoted in Inara Walden, "'To Send Her to Service,'" *Aboriginal Law Bulletin* 3 (October 1995): 14.

27. "Jennifer," in *Bringing Them Home Report*, Chapter 3, p. 11.

28. See Carla Hankins, "The Missing Links: Cultural Genocide through the Abduction of Female Aboriginal Children, 1883–1969" (Ph.D. dissertation, University of New South Wales, 1982)," 4.5.8–4.5.11; Tucker, *If Everyone Cared*, 124–125.

29. Thom Blake, "A Dumping Ground: Barambah Aboriginal Settlement 1900–1940" (Ph.D. dissertation, University of Queensland, 1991), 210; cited in Haebich, *Broken Circles*, 403.

30. MacDonald, *Between Two Worlds*, 29; Link-Up and Wilson, *In the Best Interest of the Child?*, 111; Ruddick, "'Talking About Cruel Things,'" 16. See also Haebich, *Broken Circles*, 387–393.

31. Anonymous interviewee, quoted in Hankins, 4.3.10–4.3.12.

32. Haebich, *Broken Circles*, 403; Walden, "'To Send Her to Service,'" 14.

33. Woodward B. Skinner, *The Apache Rock Crumbles* (Skinner Publications, 1987), 268–269; Stockel, *Survival of the Spirit*, xxi, 124–136; quote from Stockel, *Survival of the Spirit*, 124; quote from Pratt, *Battlefield and Classroom*, 125.

34. Quoted in Ball, *Indeh*, 146, 147.

35. Recollections, Narrelle Kingsley-Strack (unpublished conversation with Victoria Haskins, Woolgoolga, NSW), May 20, 1993; Rona Mackay (correspondence with author), August 28, 1994, November 7, 1994, January 10, 1995.

36. Jack Davis quoted in Haebich, *Broken Circles*, 393; Wadjularbinna quoted in Rintoul, *The Wailing*, 140–141.

37. Bennett, *Kaibah*, 227, 228; Haskins, "'My One Bright Spot,'" 147; Haebich, *Broken Circles*, 413–4; Walden, "'To send her to service,'" 13.

38. Quoted in Christobel Mattingley and Ken Hampton, eds., *Survival in Our Own Land: "Aboriginal" Experiences in "South Australia" since 1836* (Kew: Australian Scholarly Publishing, 1998), 164.

39. Chenlozite quoted in Stockel, *Survival of the Spirit*, 130–131; Stowe in Pratt, *Battlefield and Classroom*, 159–160.

40. Hazel Hertzberg, *The Search for an American Indian Identity: Modern Pan-Indian Movements* (Syracuse: Syracuse University Press, 1971).

41. Deborah Bird Rose, *Gulaga: A Report on the Cultural Significance of Mt Dromadery to Aboriginal People* (Sydney: Forestry Commission of NSW and NSW National Parks and Wildlife Service, 1990), 45.

42. Father quoted in Haebich, *Broken Circles*, 290; Haebich, *Broken Circles*, 288.

43. F. Maynard, Letter to K——— B———, 14 October 1927, NSW Aborigines Protection Board Archives; letter to premier quoted in Haebich, *Broken Circles*, 317.

44. Nunga men quoted in Haebich, *Broken Circles*, 317; memorial quoted in Haebich, *Broken Circles*, 318–319.

# Chapter Eighteen

# "Baptized in Blood"

## Children in the Time of the Sandino Rebellion, Nicaragua, 1927–1934

### Michael J. Schroeder

Toward the end of 1926, in the verdant Segovian mountains of northern Nicaragua, twelve-year-old Santos López joined the forces of Liberal General Augusto Sandino in the civil war raging between Liberals and Conservatives.[1] The following May the boy-soldier saw that war end and another begin, as General Sandino became Supreme Chief of a guerrilla army that for the next six years waged a struggle of national liberation in the northern mountains against U.S. intervention in Nicaragua. By 1929, the fifteen-year-old had become Colonel Santos López and one of Sandino's most trusted lieutenants. Narrowly escaping assassination alongside Sandino after war's end, he survived more than four decades of dictatorship to become one of the few living links between the Sandino rebellion of the 1920s and 1930s and the Sandinistas of the 1960s and after.

In 1976, the Sandinista Revolutionary Student Front published Santos López's oral account of his years in Sandino's Army. In common with similar testimonies produced after the 1979 Sandinista Revolution, his narrative offers insights into the lives of children in the time of the Sandino rebellion: before the war, crushing poverty, constant toil, and patriarchal oppression; during the war, many dangers, hardships, and opportunities, as well as new forms of community and much violence. Weaving together images of children as victims and children as agents in war, he crafted an ideologically inspired heroic story of national liberation that also captured key aspects of rural Segovian children's lives and experiences in the 1920s and 1930s.

I come from a *campesino* family, my mother originally from Yalacaguina, a village in Las Segovias, my father also Segoviano; that one didn't help my mother sustain our humble home, made up of five children. . . . Since my father completely ignored his obligations to us, my mother had to work to sustain us, she sold corn beer and eggs; and since this wasn't sufficient she sent us to work on neighboring farms from the early age of eight years. Our pay was 20 cents a day, being mistreated physically by the landowners. My mother used to make trips to the San Albino mine and its outskirts to sell more, always looking for the best way to earn a livelihood. On one of these trips . . . we came upon a group from the troops of General Sandino. . . . I approached a group butchering a cow and asked for a piece of meat and asked if they enlisted kids, since I could see among them some of my age, at that time I was twelve.

After recounting many episodes of heroism and hardship among Sandino's "men" (himself included) and after discussing women's roles in the struggle, he returned to the topic of children:

I belonged to a group called the "Chorus of Angels" made up of kids from 13 to 16 years of age, the group numbered fifty kids divided into three smaller groups. . . . these audacious and valiant kids were in the vanguard of the struggle. . . . the children of [Sandinista] women, born in battle camps, baptized with the blood that flowed day after day, had to be doubly patriotic. . . . The Yankees began the repression against the defenseless *campesinos* . . . [raping and] shooting the women, throwing the children back and forth like they were balls, passed from one bayonet to another till they died skewered on them.

In the early 1980s more than a dozen elderly Sandinistas, interviewed as part of a state-sponsored memory project, recalled joining Sandino's Army as boys, remembered the Chorus of Angels (dubbed so by their chants and songs during battle), and told similar stories of children's victimization and agency.[2]

Using fragmentary, ideologically charged evidence, this essay examines the lives and experiences of rural Segovian children in the time of the Sandino rebellion. It focuses on how girls and boys were victimized and acted as agents in this conflict. *Campesino* children's lives and experiences in the war, I suggest, were shaped most profoundly by unrelenting toil, suffering, violence, fear, and loss, and by resilient impulses toward hope, creativity, courage, and variously constituted and deeply affective bonds of family and community.

Before examining this evidence it is necessary to sketch the war's social and historical contexts. From independence in 1821, Nicaragua's strife-torn political history was played out in rural areas in longstanding practices of smuggling, banditry, political bossism, and political violence. The Sandino rebellion, drawing on this rich and complex heritage, found its social base among impoverished *campesinos* (rural folk) of Las Segovias—a rugged, isolated, thickly forested frontier zone bordering Honduras. Unevenly populated by some 100,000 mostly rural inhabitants, the region, like the country as a whole, was marked by extreme divisions: of social class (c. 85–90 percent *campesino*, 8–12 percent "middling," 2–3 percent elite); of social race (c. 33 percent Indian, 66 percent *mestizo*, 1 percent "Spaniard"); of political affiliation (c. 60 percent Liberal, 40 percent Conservative); and of patronage-clientage networks, locale, and patriarchal families.

According to the 1920 census, the population of Las Segovias was weighted toward younger age sets, with children under eleven comprising 34 percent of the total, children under sixteen, 45 percent. The same data yield an average of 2.7 children (age 0–15) for women of childbearing years (age 16–45) and an average life expectancy of 42 years.[3] Perhaps nine-tenths of children were poor *campesinos* living in extended families, with roughly one-third labeled "illegitimate." If many adults engaged in multiple nonmarital sexual relations, patriarchal cultural norms dictated that women bore most responsibility for all children.

The patriarchal family constituted the most important social institution for *campesinos*. In such families, often characterized by strong affections and loyalties, girls and pre-pubescent boys occupied a subordinate legal and social status similar to women. Prized for their labor power especially, *campesino* children older than five worked most of their waking hours. Girls older than three helped with women's domestic and reproductive labor in and around the house, especially food-related work and care of smaller children. Boys five and older generally helped with men's labor in pastures and fields. For *campesinos* there existed no educational or public health institutions. Common forms of structural violence suffered by *campesino* children included poverty, hunger, disease, overwork, racism, sexism, and various types of physical abuse.

Such peace-time patterns continued into the war years. In May 1927, in response to Sandino, the U.S. Marines began an invasion and occupation of Las Segovias that lasted five years. At its height in 1928, nearly two thousand Marines were stationed in the region. Thereafter the Marines slowly withdrew and an increasingly native National Guard (*Guardia*) assumed the state's war effort. The war formally ended in February 1933, a few weeks after the Marines' final departure. A year later the *Guardia* assassinated Sandino and crushed the remnants of his movement.

Throughout the war, and in common with many guerrilla wars in the modern era, the military arm of the state faced an insoluble paradox—an inability to distinguish the civilians it meant to protect from the rebels it meant to destroy. Most Segovian *campesinos* supported the rebels. Most Marines were convinced of their own racial and cultural superiority, well trained in the use of violence, and primed to teach violence-making skills to native *Guardia*, many of whom were eager to learn. The result was extreme levels of state violence against rural folk generally.

The Sandinista narrative of the rebellion accurately conveys the magnitude of state violence against *campesinos*, including children. Dozens of testimonies produced in the early 1980s paint a vivid, detailed portrait of this violence, and suggest some of the ways children experienced it. Emblematic of these patterns, one former rebel recalled: "Lieutenant Lee . . . was the most murderous of them all. Coming into the valleys he'd say, 'We're gonna kill us some bandits!' and he'd gather the people together and kill them. . . . And the children and women, he'd take the children and throw them in the air . . . and stab them." Another recounted: "When [the Marines] came into these mountains, the Yankee named Lee grabbed a baby by its arms and threw it into the air and waited for it with a sword where it landed, and he cut open its chest and pulled out its heart, and he ate it, the heart of that little baby."[4]

Whether Lieutenant Lee or any Marine speared babies on bayonets we cannot know, but these testimonies demonstrate that social memories of extreme Marine and *Guardia* violence in Las Segovias persisted well into the 1980s. Whether accurate in all specifics, these stories point to a larger field of violence, terror, and fear the Marines and *Guardia* created in the northern mountains. This environment of violence saturated everyday life for Segovian *campesinos* during the war, profoundly shaping children's lives.

Marine and *Guardia* (Marine-*Guardia*) violence came from two main sources: from the ground, by roving combat patrols, and from the air. Former rebel Calixto Tercero expressed the essence of the testimonial evidence on ground patrols: "If the [Marines] were going along the road, and someone came along, then paa! they'd shoot them, right in the main road! . . . If for example some little child went near them, 'Oh! I'm going to see if I can hit that little monkey!' and paa! they'd shoot him, a little baby who was crawling around, just for the pleasure of it!"[5] Epitomizing many other testimonies, Tercero portrayed the Marines perpetrating wanton and systematic violence against all Segovian *campesinos,* including children.

This portrayal finds robust corroboration in Marine-*Guardia* records. During the war the Marines and *Guardia* undertook tens of thousands of combat patrols. Despite patrol commanders' reticence on violence against children—certainly none reported spearing babies or shooting children—their reports, read critically, brim with episodes of violence against children and women.

Marked by clinical, objectifying language and a passive voice that worked to mask their authors' agency, these reports provide a chilling portrait of children in war. In a typical report, a group of fifteen to thirty heavily armed men entered a *campesino* house occupied by women and children, often conflated into "a family," and searched thoroughly for evidence of "bandits." Finding such evidence, usually consisting of red cloth—the colors red and black signifying Sandinista—"excessive" amounts of food or medicine, or other "suspicious" items, they evicted the occupants and burned the house. Uncharacteristic only in its use of the active voice, Captain Croka's report epitomizes hundreds: "[Bandit suspect's] house was bountifully stored with ... many articles not appropriate or normally kept by a family living in such an isolated spot. . . . After removing everything from the house I burned it." His terse language leaves to historical imagination the terror and fear children in this "family" experienced. Over the next five days Croka's patrol burned sixteen houses, probably leaving scores of children homeless.[6] "Descended mountainside and surrounded a native shack which was occupied by a large number of women and children," reads another typical report. "While women were being questioned a native was seen in the brush and captured . . . Marines fired at bandits, . . . Fire continued for about 10 minutes. . . . destroyed bandit camp." The report characteristically inflates a small shack into a "bandit camp." Here as elsewhere the reactions and fates of the women and children went unreported, though fear, terror, displacement, destitution, hunger, and sickness probably ranked among the most common consequences.[7]

As one might expect in official documents (and expressing the invaders' self-image as gallant father-figures), Marines and *Guardia* almost always depicted children and women as inappropriate targets. As Lieutenant Brown reported of one attack, "I had a hand grenade in my hand but the presence of two women and several children made it impossible to throw it."[8] Yet reports also demonstrate that attacks injured and killed children and women.

A few days later Lieutenant Brown noted that his patrol "accidentally" killed a woman and "wounded a small boy."[9]

*Campesino* children quickly learned to fear such patrols, as official reports attest. As one Marine reported, "Many women and children who appeared frightened on our appearance sought cover . . . . they stated that they had not seen Marines before and that they were told we killed all we saw."[10] Other reports show entire families sleeping in the bush for fear of attack.[11] Soldiers often forcibly impressed boys as guides. "A boy of about 14 years of age was found, who, after being threatened with death, admitted knowing the position of the bandit camp," reads one unusually frank report.[12] "Impressed as guides two boys" represented more typical phrasing.[13] If they did the same with girls they did not report it. Similarly, no extant report describes Marines or *Guardia* raping girls, though former rebels insisted the practice was common.[14]

Attacks by airplanes comprised the second main source of Marine-*Guardia* violence against children. The gist of the rebel narrative on the air war found apt expression in the recollections of José Ucles: "The planes, when they saw smoke, when they saw someone making food for their children, mothers with families, they bombed them, they killed everybody. When they saw someone, it was a question of dropping bombs."[15] Many recalled the deaths and displacements the air war caused. "In Quilal, the airplanes destroyed us," recounted Juan Sánchez of his fifteenth year. "They killed many people and burned many houses in that invasion. All the people from these villages fled to faraway places . . . many families had to flee to defend themselves against the airplanes."[16]

Marine-*Guardia* records show that while planes neither bombed every house nor killed every *campesino* they saw, they bombed and killed routinely and often. In a typical assault on a "bandit stronghold," for instance, a heavily armed plane "attacked [eight] houses and brush in the vicinity with good effect . . . Bombs were dropped among the horses and cattle, killing a few horses, cattle, and some men." Later that afternoon, "horses and cattle at three different [farms] were bombed and strafed with machine gun fire." Next day, "the places that had been bombed yesterday were fired into, and large numbers of turkey buzzards [feasting on the previous day's carnage] arose from each place." But if *campesinos* soon learned to hide from airplanes, reports consistently noted "smoke and fires, drying clothes," and "small washings" at many "suspicious" places they attacked, clear signs of women's labor and the likely presence of children.[17]

"Village ... was filled with men, women and children," reads one report, "and when the planes approached a near panic occurred among the people. They rushed from place to place, falling over each other, and waving anything they could get. It was evident that ... the villagers were in great fear of an attack by the planes."[18] Two days later another pilot saw three armed men run inside a house in an isolated hamlet. "This house was strafed with machine gun fire but no one appeared. ... the reason [nearby] houses were not bombed [was that] several women and children were present. ... Four bombs ... were dropped close to the houses. No people were seen leaving the houses although several women and children could be seen inside."[19]

Rural folk seem to have soon learned that the obvious presence of women and children could deter deadly air attacks. During one fly-over, in a gesture of courage and defiance, "a woman with a baby and two children came out and stood in front of the house." The gunner fired several bursts but attacked no villagers "on account of the women and children."[20] A month later a plane crew "observed three horses tied up under the porch of a house. Fired a burst into the hill and circled the house. One woman and a child came out and walked around." The firing reportedly ceased.[21]

Despite the state's efforts to create a contrary narrative, its own paper trail demonstrates that Marine-*Guardia* violence against children comprised a fundamental feature of the war. If exact numbers will never be known, thousands of children suffered injury and death in direct consequence of the Marine invasion. Many thousands more suffered trauma, forced migration, and enhanced likelihood of destitution, hunger, and disease. In its insistent emphasis on the victimization of children by the Marines and *Guardia*, the Sandinista narrative is strongly supported by their enemies' own records.

Waging war without quarter against a militarily superior foe, the rebels also committed violence against children, although of a much smaller magnitude overall. Sandinistas frequently robbed and killed other Nicaraguans and sometimes murdered children, usually in retaliation for aiding the enemy.[22] At the same time, most *campesinos* sympathized with and aided the rebels, in large part precisely because their enemies perpetrated the great majority of violence against rural folk, including children.

Yet children in this war were not only victims but agents actively pursuing their own and their families' interests in the face of often extreme adversity. Asención Iglesias, expressing a pattern repeated across Las Segovias, recalled how Marine-*Guardia* violence against his family led him to join the rebels. "I joined the army when I was fourteen, I liked to watch the army's movements and many times the gringos threatened us with death, because we'd see them pass by, bombing our houses for no reason." Predisposed to the rebels, he soon had reason to join their cause. "In my house they shot my brother and took him prisoner . . . they killed two more brothers in a room of the house, slit their throats and cut them to ribbons outside; my mother buried the pieces there." Framing the rebellion as a morally righteous act of self-defense, he acknowledged that larger ideological issues had escaped his comprehension: "We had no idea what it meant politically, we couldn't even read!, but we could see it was a just cause."[23] Jose María Cerro remembered joining as a youth because the Marines-*Guardia* burned his house and machine-gunned and decapitated his uncle; Cosme Castro recalled joining at fifteen because they burned the houses of his mother and brother and shot his sister.[24] Marine-*Guardia* reports corroborate frequent recollections of former rebels that many boys served in Sandino's army. "Several boys between the ages of 12 and 14 were seen with the bandits," reads one.[25] Bountiful further examples show much variation on the theme of wanton Marine-*Guardia* violence provoking boys to become rebels.

Boys' involvement in rebel information flows was even more crucial than their participation as full-time combatants. Acquiring and transmitting information comprised a fundamental feature of the war effort for both sides. Marines-*Guardia* generally controlled the towns, rebels the countryside. By all accounts the Sandinistas constructed an extremely effective "grapevine" system of communication linking both town and country. While patriarchal norms confined girls to domestic spaces, they permitted boys to move with relative ease within and between towns and rural areas. Thus, boys commonly served as rebel spies. Since information was critical to the war effort, since *campesino* culture was an oral culture, and since many children have a great capacity for memorization, it is likely that thousands of boys delivered tens of thousands of oral messages to rebel forces—messages never deposited in any archive. In this way the everyday actions of boys, all but invisible in the documentary record, made the rebellion possible.

Marines-*Guardia* also sought information incessantly, often from children. In their aggressive "hunting" expeditions, ground patrols prized nothing more highly than accurate information on rebel locations.[26] Boys often gave information, accurate and not, thereby becoming key (if often coerced) suppliers of one of the most critical resources in the state's war effort. In a characteristic portrayal, "a native boy finally admitted" information one patrol commander aggressively sought in a hamlet whose inhabitants he described as "afraid," phrasing that leaves to imagination the coercive circumstances under which the boy made the admission and his courage in making it.[27]

Girls' everyday agency, less dramatic and evident in popular memory, more spatially circumscribed, and more dominated by tedium and monotony, was just as critical to the Sandinista war effort. For most *campesinos* the war magnified labor expenditures enormously. Much of this labor fell to children, mostly girls. Domestic labor, especially relating to food—gathering firewood, tending fires, making cheese, pounding tortillas, tending and butchering livestock, cooking and delivering meals—comprised girls' principal contributions to the rebel cause. Making and repairing houses, washing and mending clothes, tending the sick and injured, and untold other daily labors, all but invisible in the documentary evidence, were also key arenas of girls' (and boys') agency. Luisa Cano Arauz's recollections of the war can be reasonably extended to most *campesino* girls: "We helped him [Sandino's army], we brought him food wherever they were, . . . I remember well all those I fed, I gave them food to eat . . . all the foods he ate, this I know about."[28]

Courageous actions of girls rarely found their way into documents produced by men. One report hints at larger patterns: "Surrounded the house and captured . . . a seventeen-year-old girl, dressed in red and black, who announced herself as 'pura [pure] Sandinista.' (She is now locked up at this place.)"[29] This young woman's fierce defiance and assertion of dignity in the face of murderous, rapacious soldiers, her body draped in the symbols of her community and cause, stuns the imagination. If her courage likely found parallels in actions of girls across the region, few archival traces remain.

Overall, extant evidence from both sides underscores children's extraordinary dignity, courage, and commitments to family and community in the face of the horrors and destruction of war. Two vignettes meant to illustrate the invaders' goodwill and paternalism reveal from another angle children's tenacious efforts to recreate war-sundered familial and community bonds. In one, Colonel Robert Denig recorded in his personal diary:

> We have a ten year old kid who sleeps on the back porch and is being trained as a messenger boy and boot-black. He is fitted up as a sergeant, has an old gun and a white pony. He was brought in from an outlying post. His father was killed by bandits. His mother then deserted the kid and ran off with another bandit. When found he was living in a lean-to that he made himself and was rapidly turning into a wild animal.[30]

Painting the Marines-*Guardia* as saviors of an innocent child, institutional repository of moral decency and civilization in a sea of barbarism and moral decrepitude, Denig's account, read against the grain, also highlights the war's profound disruption of *campesino* community and family life, and suggests how children struggled to re-establish relations with kin or fictive kin—ironically, in this case, with those bearing most responsibility for destroying families and communities.

Newspapers told similar tales. One story, "A Little Hero Who Fought For and Against Sandino," told of a boy of thirteen who fought with Sandino in the civil war and later against the Marines. Scooped off the battlefield by the Marine who shot him, the boy reportedly became the faithful aid of his assailant.[31] Like Denig's, the story illustrates both the victimization and agency of children while ironically underscoring their creativity and resourcefulness in reconstituting severed family and community ties.

But in the end, and despite many such tales of agency and resourcefulness, children were more victims than agents in this war. Many died, and many families mourned their deaths. "I came to [a] house . . . where they were holding a religious celebration on account of the death of a child," reads one report. Moments later a firefight with "bandits" erupted.[32]

As an old man, Santos López, with whose story this essay began, vividly expressed the violence and suffering children witnessed and experienced, and their persistent impulses to act with dignity and forge meaningful affective bonds in an often cruel and dangerous world.

> Though we went barefoot, nearly naked and full of pests, with innumerable sufferings, we never complained, and arriving at the General Headquarters our burdens lightened hearing the strumming of guitars and accordions. . . . [We were] to treat each other like brothers, respect the *campesinos*, . . . all the *campesinos* should see each other as brothers helping one another other . . . It's something grand and one ought never forget the great sense of brotherhood Sandino inculcated in everyone in our daily lives. We had a saying we used to repeat all the time: "How are you, brother? Enchanted with life."[33]

Yet despite the truth of López's words and the optimism of his message to a new generation of youth, it is plain that on balance and for the children who lived it, the war destroyed far more love, beauty, and brotherhood than it created. Whether his and his comrades' sacrifices bequeathed a better world to subsequent generations of children, in Nicaragua and beyond, remains a knottier question.

NOTES

Many thanks to Nora Faires for her keen insights and ruthless pencil.

1. Santos López, "Memorias de un Soldado," *Frente Estudiantil Revolucionario*, July 1976, 1. Cf. *Barricada*, February 8, 1986. Evidence and arguments presented here draw from a larger research project; see Michael J. Schroeder, "The Sandino Rebellion Revisited"; "Horse Thieves to Rebels to Dogs"; and "'To Defend Our Nation's Honor.'"

2. Instituto de Estudio del Sandinismo, *Ahora sé que Sandino manda* (Managua: Nueva Nicaragua, 1986), 212–217.

3. Calculated from Oficina Central del Censo, *Censo General de la República de Nicaragua de 1920* (Managua, 1920).

4. Testimonies of Luis Boedeker González, Instituto de Estudio del Sandinismo (Instituto de Historia de Nicaragua, Universidad Centroamericana), document no. 055-1-2, p. 11 (hereafter IES [document no.] : [p. no.]), and Martín Blandón Rodriguez, IES 033:10.

5. IES 097-2-2: 4–5.

6. Patrol Report, Croka, Ocotal, July 18, 1930, Record Group 127, entry 202, box 13, United States National Archives and Records Administration, Washington, D.C. (hereafter NA [entry no.] / [box no.].

7. Patrol Report, Hakala, Somoto, June 18, 1929, NA212/1.

8. Engagement at Potrero, Brown, December 7, 1927, NA212/1.

9. Engagement at Cuje, Brown, December 11, 1927, NA212/1.

10. Report of Patrol, Atkinson, March 5, 1928, NA212/1.

11. Operation and Intelligence Report, Carlson, Jalapa, July 16, 1930, NA202/13.

12. Contact Report, Smith, Esteli, August 8, 1930, NA202/10.

13. Patrol Report, Hakala, Somoto, August 30, 1929, NA202/10.

14. IES 055-1-2: 11: "There were two young girls. 'One for me,' [the Yankee] said, 'and one for the sergeant.' They raped them, and after raping them, *paa! paa!* They killed them."

15. Instituto de Estudio del Sandinismo, *Ahora sé que Sandino manda*, 80–81.

16. IES 104: 6.

17. Reports of Air Missions, Rowell, March 19, 20, 28, 1928, NA220/2.

18. Air Mission #1, Rowell, April 2, 1928, NA220/2.

19. Air Mission, Rowell, April 4, 1928, NA220/2. *Campesino* houses, with walls of spaced poles, sometimes permitted plane crews to "see inside" them.

20. Air Mission, Rowell, April 10, 1928, NA220/2.

21. Air Mission #3, Rowell, May 5, 1928, NA220/2.

22. IES 0-55-1-2: 5; Anastasio Somoza García, *El verdadero Sandino, o el calvario de Las Segovias* (Managua: Robelo, 1936); Schroeder, "To Defend Our Nation's Honor," chap. 11.

23. IES 065: 1, 4, 5.

24. IES 088:1, and IES 049: 1; see also Macario Calderón Salinas, IES 043-2-2: 6; Cosme Castro Andino, IES 049: 13.

25. Bandit Attack, Spotts, León, December 30, 1929, NA202/10.

26. The phrase "to hunt bandits" in Patrol Report, Kelly, El Jacaro, January 6, 1931, NA202/13.

27. Patrol to San Antonio, Lewis, Yalí, May 25, 1929, NA212/1.

28. IES 037: 3.

29. Patrol Report, Broderick, San Juan, January 24, 1931, NA202/14.

30. Robert L. Denig, "Diary of a *Guardia* Officer," Marine Corps Historical Center, Museums Branch, Washington D.C., 11.

31. *La Noticia* (Managua), April 12, 1928.

32. Contact with Bandits, Stevens, León, November 20, 1930, NA202/52.

33. Santos López, "Memorias," 12, 18, 22.

# Chapter Nineteen

# "Too Young for a Uniform"

## *Children's War Work on the Iowa Farm Front, 1941–1945*

### *Lisa L. Ossian*

We'll be little soldiers on the home front
By helping Mother and Dad;
We'll feed the chickens, bring in wood,
And never do anything bad.
—Elois Anderson, "The Voice of Young America" (1944)

The Sunday of December 7, 1941, started like most Sundays for Fred Higginbottom, age seven. His family went to church that morning in nearby Elkhart, Iowa, and when they returned home, his mother served the family dinner. Fred later left with his father to tend and feed their cattle on the Manning land, a newly rented field some distance from their farmhouse. The December afternoon had been cold but sunny, and the daylight was starting to fade as they finished up their work with the cattle when Uncle Harry suddenly arrived to deliver the news of the Pearl Harbor attack. Fred began to worry because his uncle had made such a long trip out to the field to bring his dad this news. Sixty years later, that childhood memory is still frozen for Fred: his father Frank and Uncle Harry, standing in between the feed bunks and the cattle, discussing the news of war.[1]

Pearl Harbor struck during that almost Christmas time, usually a period of hopes and wishes. With Christmas just eighteen days away, U.S. citizens—men, women, and children—suddenly found themselves in a world war. Prime Minister Winston Churchill visited Washington, D.C. that December, and on Christmas Eve he addressed the White House gathering and closed with this comment about the children. "Let the gifts of Father Christmas delight their play. Let us grown-ups share to the full in their unstinted pleasures before we turn again to the stern task and the formidable years that lie before us, resolved that, by our sacrifice and daring, these same children shall not be robbed of their inheritance nor denied their right to live in a free and decent world."[2]

In this fight for a free world, food was a necessary weapon. During World War II, farmers became the soldiers of the soil on the farm front in an all-out battle of production in the federal Food for Freedom campaign. The USDA called upon farmers to market more food for the armed forces, factory workers, and allies, and agriculture broke many production records during 1942, 1943, and 1944. Iowa farmers raised an array of farm products: corn, wheat, hay, hogs, cattle, sheep, chickens, eggs, and milk. Now Midwestern farmers were asked to produce even more pork, beef, soybeans, eggs, and dairy products for the war effort. As the *Iowa Bureau Farmer* proclaimed that spring, "The world's richest land is found in Iowa, and today those who till this soil are called upon to do their utmost to feed the world."[3]

Food for Freedom required intense labor, but older sons and hired men were leaving due to the demands of the draft and the draw of war industries. Agricultural deferments later kept some young men working on their family farms, but never in sufficient numbers. Other men could act as replacements, but outsiders such as underemployed Southern farmers, interned Japanese-Americans, or migrant Mexicans and Jamaicans faced discrimination if hired in the Midwest. Farmers angrily felt these adults were too unreliable and costly. And farmers grew frustrated with the added demands of training and supervision required to develop outside labor sources for mechanized farms. A better solution, as the *Iowa Farm Economist* suggested, became the younger sons as "almost half of the sons living at home fall between the ages of 10 and 20. They're too young to be drafted but are old enough to do much of the work which has been hired."[4]

Sons, and daughters, offered a number of advantages as laborers on the farm front. They were available in ready numbers for seasonal work, and most farm children were trained to work with livestock and machinery. And children were familiar and affordable labor sources—they did not challenge authority as often and were paid in war bonds, if at all, rather than salaries. As one Farmall advertisement proudly summarized, "Too young for a uniform—but on the home fields he did a man-size job this year."[5]

Children had always worked on Iowa family farms, as historian Pamela Riney-Kehrberg has written, and work was "the center of farm children's experience." The farm's needs—not the individual child's—"dictated the balance between work, school, and leisure." Riney-Kehrberg strongly emphasizes the economic role farm children had maintained: "Without their labors, many family farms would have ceased to be." This agrarian work ethic had long been admired by farmers and even social workers because of its outdoor, healthy, and educational nature as contrasted with mines or factories. Sociologist Viviana Zelizer has stated in her economic analysis of turn-of-the-century childhood that as Americans began to condemn industrial child labor, most still believed farming "almost blindly and romantically" to be "good work." "Good" farm work took place on family farms with parents as part of the child's agricultural education. Thus, children's war work on the farm front during World War II continued to be considered "good work" but now necessary for the "Good War."[6]

This sentimental vision of children's farm work continued throughout the war years but ignored the often tedious and sometimes dangerous work children completed for their family's farm economy. Farm children, before and during the war, performed a long list of chores: sawing wood, pulling weeds, collecting eggs, slopping hogs, planting corn, husking corn, cultivating beans, cutting grain, making hay, harvesting wheat, milking cows, watering calves, driving tractors, repairing fences, threshing oats, plowing fields, tending gardens, and spreading manure as well as indoor chores such as washing dishes and canning fruits and vegetables.

But during the Second World War, children's labor, according to historian Robert Kirk, took on an added dimension because of the great national economic need for children as workers. This work was continuously and creatively symbolized through the guise of "small soldiers" as Americans would not view children as possible victims of the war effort machine. As Iowa farmer Fred Higginbottom recalled, the public emphasis was always "patriotism, patriotism, patriotism."[7]

However, Kirk's research focuses mostly on children's war contributions in urban areas, where adults debated childrearing techniques and girls completed supportive tasks through stricter gender roles during the Second World War. However, for rural children, few people argued that increased farm work during wartime would be detrimental because this valued work had historical rural roots. And farm girls were not confined to the sidelines but drawn to the center as "soldiers," especially when older brothers left for the actual fronts. For example, a headline read, "Typical Madison County

Family Gives Total Effort to Total War—Father, Mother and Daughters All Work." The Jobsts were trying their best "to see that every acre and every animal on the farm makes a maximum contribution to feeding Carl Jobst and millions of other men like him who are doing the actual fighting."[8]

Young people who remained on the farm were increasingly called upon to work longer hours with greater responsibilities despite the physical risks and time away from school. Often they were quite young, preteen or young teenagers. Organizations from the federal government to the local schools deemed this child labor acceptable for the all-out production demands of the war effort. These war workers were not laboring children, but "little adults." In fact, writers such as Dorothy Watt, in her *Iowa Agriculturalist* essay "Children in Wartime," portrayed children's war work as simply an additional fighting front. She wrote, "Farms rapidly are becoming the second front of the war. Boys must be shown that every hour of farm labor at home equals an hour of labor in North Africa."[9]

Rather than expressing concern, most Iowans were tremendously proud of their children's wartime production. Farm children earned respect and perhaps developed character from their war contributions; boys and girls as young as three to five were expected to "row their weight in the boat." Work might relieve older children's war worries, but parents were to cultivate a "weather-eye" for signs of strain and ensure their children slept and ate enough. The *Iowa Farm Economist* conducted three county surveys of farm families' war work, but concluded with the benefits for the entire farm family of added work and responsibility: "Moreover, farm boys and girls have the opportunity to work side by side with their parents and be guided step by step in gaining experience. Because each member of the family can see, understand and share the work of others the war crisis very often promotes greater family unity rather than less."[10]

Propaganda romanticized such children's sacrifices. A May 1942 cover of *Life* showed a determined Iowa teen-age boy driving a tractor, his hands gripped in the ten-two position, his eyes focused grimly ahead. A similar advertisement called this work "His Place in the Sun." The copy stated, "He is old enough to sense that something of grave importance is happening in the world. He felt the urgency of it when Dad gripped his arm hard, the day his big brother marched away. When Dad turned to him and said, "'Now it's up to us, Son,' he understood, and he approached the stature of manhood that day."[11]

This further romanticism of the family farm appeared in the *Iowa Bureau Farmer* that "a good Iowa farm is a great place to raise a fine family of boys and girls." Despite the added war work, Americans still considered the country an ideal setting to raise children. The *Iowa Farm Economist* echoed this sentiment with the phrase that "good land and good living tend to go together on Iowa farms." Perhaps farm children were no longer playing with their puppies or exploring the local creeks or sleeping in the hay mounds as often since Pearl Harbor, but Americans had many advantages compared to children caught in war zones. As "Country Air" columnist Elizabeth Wherry reminded her Iowa readers, "Our children can still have plenty of fresh air, milk, vegetables and meat with no more than the usual amount of labor on our part."[12]

Child experts advised parents to keep the family busy during wartime because idle children might worry about enemy soldiers or bombs. Herbert Agar of *Parents' Magazine* urged mothers and fathers to explain "what we're fighting for" and to give everyone in the family some responsibility. "Even the youngest child can have the feeling that he has an important part to play." Elizabeth Cobb Ellis offered similar advice in her *Successful Farming* parenting column: "Don't let your children get to the point of wishing they had something to do. . . . When every member of the family has a part in the work of the farm it becomes home in the real sense." As the farmer proudly stated for a Phillip 66 Motor Oil ad in its Food Fights for Freedom campaign, "Everybody works at our place except our 2-year-old."[13]

And everyone worked. Girls were not exempt from the farm chores, as an *Iowa Bureau Farmer* cover stated: "Iowa Farm Girls Take their Brothers' Places"—such as Doris Jean Stevenson who planted corn and beans and helped cut grain while her brother was in the army. The earlier stigma of women working in the field was replaced with the idea that every citizen worked for the war effort. Farm daughters were never "dainty bits of femininity" but rather "unsung heroines" as girls joined the "Field Artillery." Still, the farm article lamented, "When modern history is recorded, it isn't likely that it will include the story of the Iowa farm girl who helped her dad in the gigantic Food for Freedom campaign."[14]

Dorothy Dengler, high school president of the Sheridan township club called the "Hustlers," provided an exceptional example of war work as she canned 35 quarts of meat, 215 quarts of fruit, and 148 quarts of vegetables, raised 55 geese, 53 ducks, and 600 chickens in 1942. She worked sixty-hour weeks yet never "watched the clock." She wasn't alone. In a survey of 100 eighteen-year-old Iowa farm girls, most did more housework and farm work in 1942 than in 1941. Chores included canning, gardening, gathering eggs, milking, and haying. Three-fourths said they generally liked farm work, especially tractors, and the number of girls driving tractors doubled in 1942. Only 18 of the 100 girls received money for their efforts in 1942; most believed the privilege of attending college more than paid for their farm work. The editor of *American Farm Youth* suggested we salute the "FUTURE FARMERETTE." He wrote, "GIRLS WORKING ON THE FARMS should hold a place in history equal to that of Florence Nightingale."[15]

The debate over farm girls working in agriculture versus moving to industrial war jobs was aired at the Iowa Farm Bureau Convention in November 1942. Maxine Burch, a Madison County farm girl, stated on the panel that "the place for a farm girl is on the farm" by "freeing the hands of her mother and father for the work of boosting farm production." Economist Carl Malone expressed the counterpoint that girls could better help the war effort in factories since "in those industries a girl often is able to produce as much as a man but on the farm she can't do it." An Iowa farm wife, Mrs. Lee Fredericks, believed otherwise when she told a reporter that "all our boys are girls" as her five daughters did the necessary farm work. She boasted, "Each one has definite responsibilities and they're doing a swell job. I wouldn't trade them for boys if I could." *Successful Farming* advised its young female readers not to be Dizzy Lizzies or Gloomy Gertrudes but Merry Margarets, stating that "it's part of your war job to help keep things running smoothly by doing your share of the work without a grumble!"[16]

The task children most enjoyed was driving tractors, which young Lucille Hoppe declared simply was "fun." Although horses still labored on most Iowa farms, as tractors were limited due to war rationing, mechanization could relieve some labor shortage concerns, and tractor advertisements emphasized children's skills with these tanklike machines. The Oliver tractor company promised that either "a boy or a girl can handle it." Ford joined in with the comment that "even a child's finger tips can do a strong man's work."[17]

Youth farm organizations acted during the war as effective war mobilization units. These groups continued to emphasize responsibility and leadership as "wholesome outlets" but now added production demands. The oldest group was 4-H. Its clover symbolized a peaceful devotion to the development of head, hands, heart, and health, but during the war 4-H declared itself a "Victory Army." Since Pearl Harbor, 4-H clubs had created war programs which emphasized production, conservation, and service. The first year 15,055 Iowa 4-H boys and girls raised products worth $2,618,133, and almost 7,000 members raised livestock valued at $1,350,000. In 1944,

Iowa's 4-H club members signed Victory Pledge cards with the slogan, "Feed a fighter or more in forty-four."[18]

National and state leaders noted 4-H children's contributions. Iowa's Governor Hickenlooper stated, "Now when we are at war to protect these heritages, all rural youth of Iowa have a grave responsibility to do their part. No generation of youth has had such opportunity and challenge to serve their country and their world as have the girls and boys of today." And 4-H'ers did have stunning production records. Their national achievements in 1943 "boosted America's food arsenal" by 5 million bushels of Victory Garden products; 90,000 head of dairy cattle; 600,000 head of livestock; 9 million fowl; 12 million pounds of legumes as well as 12 million pounds of scrap and $14 million worth of war bonds. And President Roosevelt paid tribute to the children's war work: "We know that you, like your brothers and sisters in the service, have the spirit and perseverance that will bring victory in the fight for human freedom and a world at peace."[19]

Another farm youth group that mobilized for the war effort was the Future Farmers of America, which started in 1928 as a high school boys' organization and by 1944 had more than 200,000 FFA members in 6,745 local chapters. In combination with vocational agricultural high school courses, the FFA trained farm and town boys to replace labor shortages on the nation's farms with its stated war purpose of "the training of young farmers who can work shoulder to shoulder with Dad in the mutual problems of the farm."[20]

Still, farmers continued to search for new labor sources from America's children. In 1942, an estimated 4 million American city boys, between the ages of fourteen and eighteen, were possibly available for work, if "trained and tried." Des Moines officials at the Tall Corn Council of the Boy Scouts of America initiated one such program, and 150 boys watched farm implement motion pictures at the first meeting and later participated in an instructive program with safety lessons from March to June which ended with a plowing field day. More than 500 Boy Scouts in seven Iowa counties spent at least one week from June to September helping on farms.[21]

Another mobilization was the Victory Farm Volunteers, a national program where town teenagers, aged fourteen to eighteen, participated in "day haul" programs to local farms, especially for harvest needs. Each state provided transportation for the children from town to fields and back at day's end, and local schools provided full cooperation. The total number of Iowa children involved in the day haul program along with a live-in program amounted to 14,385 in 1943; 16,942 in 1944; and 23,404 in 1945.[22]

Clubs and schools not only encouraged children to work on local farms but to contribute to the national scrap drives as well. In September 1942, the Treasury Department and Office of Education started their "Schools at War" program with the children's motto "SAVE, SERVE, CONSERVE." The War Production Board needed scrap iron, brass, tin, rubber, rags, paper, and waste cooking fats. During the first half of 1943, children collected 13 million tons for the "Salvage for Victory" program. International Harvester offered prize money to boys and girls, especially 4-H'ers and Future Farmers, who collected the "biggest load of scrap during a drive." The campaign praised the children's contributions at the end of its first drive: "A million and a half tons—but don't stop now!" Its motto was "Children Understand and Act!"[23]

Scrap drives contributed needed war materials and involved long hours and extreme dedication. For example, Iowa chapters of the Future Farmers of America collected an impressive amount of scrap for the war effort in 1942 as listed in their "Special Report of Wartime Activities": 665,975 pounds of scrap metal; 171,750 pounds of paper; 1,400 pounds of rags; and 61,202 pounds of rubber. The Winterset FFA chapter provided one success story as their instructor, S. A. Ossian, described the boys' salvage work in military terms: "They worked like troopers, never giving up until they had combed ditches, junk piles, and other remote places to find scrap metal and rubber." The boys collected 20.8 tons of metal along with 400 pounds of rubber which netted $155.12 for war bonds. Their high school yearbook called it "one big achievement."[24]

Younger children also expressed the desire to help out as best they could. For example, some rural elementary children sent letters once a month, as "dues," to the "Play House," a children's section of poems and puzzles in *Successful Farming*. The editor Ruth Elaine suggested children watch younger siblings or find other jobs "to help along with the war effort." She wrote in August 1943 that "I'm sure your brothers, uncles, and friends must be very proud of you. When you multiply what you have been doing by what thousands of girls and boys all over the country have been doing, it must be bad news for the Axis!" From their letters, editor Elaine described the children's participation as "grand helpers around the farm" with their "patriotic deeds." She advised her readers to "do everything possible to be helpful. If we all work hard together it will help shorten this war." After the war, Elaine praised the Playhouse children for filling "Big Brother's shoes" as they "truly helped to fill the nation's breadbasket."[25]

Despite the praise, one farming worry was the possibility of accidents, especially from corn pickers and tractors. *Wallace's Farmer* advised adults to teach tractor safety as children were trying to be helpful and running machines for perhaps the first time. Children were also susceptible to farm accidents with livestock, especially bulls and hogs. Iowa clubs distributed a booklet "4-H to the Safety Front," and other youth groups contributed to a safety poster campaign, "Don't Help the Axis."[26]

Parents and educators also expressed concern over plans of a shortened school year to provide for farmers' labor needs. *Wallace's Farmer* editors argued that high school boys were needed on the farm from spring plowing until fall corn husking, and another proposal suggested high school boys attend school for half-days with corn husking "vacations." Only a minority of Iowa farm parents (34 percent men, 28 percent women) approved. The majority of Iowans wanted "big boys" to stay in school and take the regular high school course—"even tho the farm is short-handed and the old folks have to work extra hours." The *Iowa Farm Economist* agreed: "Careful planning will help keep educational standards up despite wartime difficulties."[27]

Many adults believed farm front production not only supported the military effort but ensured their children's future. Vice President Henry A. Wallace, born and raised in rural Iowa, wrote that Americans were fighting this war "for the right of every child to a quart of milk a day." "It is for these little folks we gladly face war's responsibility," echoed *Successful Farming*.[28]

The European war ended in May 1945, but the U.S. war effort continued through the summer on the Pacific front. The chief of the Agricultural Education Service broadcast a radio speech that June in which he saluted the children: "To American farm youth, together with a large number of over-age farm operators, farm women, and girls who have worked long hours, day in and day out, must go a great share of the credit for our tremendous agricultural production during these war years."[29]

Farm work, of course, continued throughout the summer, never stopping even though the war was almost over. Fifteen boys in Greene County called their weed-pulling team the "Cocklebur Battalion." Fred Higginbottom was also pulling cockleburs in a cornfield with his father and brother that hot, muggy Iowa August. Fred, now eleven, did not recall celebrating the end of World War II, but he remembered working toward that carrot his father dangled before them: If the two boys worked hard, Dad promised to take them to the town swimming pool that evening. That was a reward worth all the hard, hot work.[30]

The war was finally over. School started soon after, and autumn turned into early winter. Children could look forward to a peaceful Christmas that year. A little girl from Gladbrook, Iowa, named LaRue Wrage described her days before that 1945 Christmas in "Christmas is Coming":

> All these signs are saying
> That Happy CHRISTMAS DAY
> With all its joys and gladness,
> Can't be far away.

The war disrupted almost Christmas time of 1941 seemed a long, long time ago.[31]

NOTES

1. Interview with Fred Higginbottom, April 2001. Child historians William Tuttle and Robert Kirk have noted that Pearl Harbor was memorable for children not because they recognized the significance of the event but because of the confusing and sometimes frightening actions of the adults around them. Tuttle, *"Daddy's Gone to War,"* and Kirk, *Earning Their Stripes.*

2. Kenneth S. Davis, *FDR: The War President, 1940–1943* (New York: Random House, 2000), 368.

3. "Homemaking Department," *Wallaces' Farmer* 18 (September 1943): 26; "Prices of Iowa Farm Products," *Iowa Farm Economist* (April 1942): 6; *Iowa Bureau Farmer,* March 1942.

4. "The Farm Lookout," *Successful Farming* 41 (January 1943): 4; *Iowa Farm Economist* 3 (May 1942): 7, 9.

5. *Wallaces' Farmer* 2 (October 1943): 2.

6. Pamela Riney-Kehrberg, "Helping Ma and Helping Pa: Iowa's Turn-of-the-Century Farm Children," *The Annals of Iowa* 59 (Spring 2000): 126, 136, and 140; Zelizer, *Pricing the Priceless Child,* 77–79, 97–98; and Studs Terkel, *The Good War: An Oral History of World War Two* (New York: The New Press, 1984), 9–10.

7. Kirk, *Earning Their Stripes,* 60.

8. Ibid., 3–4; and Winterset (Iowa) *Madisonian,* 25 (November 1942): 3.

9. Barbara M. Tucker, "Agricultural Workers in World War II: The Reserve Army of Children, Black Americans, and Jamaicans," *Agricultural History* 68 (Winter 1994): 63; "Children in Wartime," *Iowa Agriculturalist* 42 (February 1943).

10. *Iowa Farm Bureau Spokesman,* June 12, 1943; July 3, 1943; and July 29, 1944.

11. *Life* 25 (May 1942): cover; *The Prairie Farmer* 115 (February 6, 1943): 9.

12. *Iowa Bureau Farmer*, May 1941, cover; "Living is Tops on Iowa Farms," *Iowa Farm Economist* 4 (December 1943): 8; "Country Air," *Wallaces' Farmer* 67 (May 2, 1942): 15.

13. "Our Parents' Forum," *Successful Farming* 41 (July 1943): 55; "Of All Things—A Food Surplus," *Successful Farming* 42 (October 1944): 41.

14. *Iowa Bureau Farmer*, August 1942, cover; October 1942; and September 1942.

15. *Iowa Bureau Farmer*, November 1942; "Farm Girls are Doing Their Part," *Iowa Farm Economist* 4 (August 1943): 2; "Look Out! Girls at Work," *Successful Farming* 41 (April 1943): 96; "Editor's Column," *American Farm Youth* 8 (September 1943): 28.

16. "Successful Homemaking," *Successful Farming* 42 (July 1944): 34; Des Moines *Tribune*, 27 (November 1942): 7; and 28 (June 1943): 11.

17. "Homemaking Department—Plowshares into Swords," *Wallaces' Farmer* 67 (September 5, 1942): 20; *Successful Farming* 40 (May 1942): 6; (September 1942): 45; 42 (January 1944): 9; and (May 1944): 33.

18. Wolf, *Our Children Face War*, 83; *Iowa Farm Bureau Spokesman*, January 9, 1943; August 21, 1943; April 8, 1944; and September 2, 1944. Also, "News for Homemakers" (radio transcript), March 10, 1945, and October 4, 1944.

19. *Iowa Farm Bureau Spokesman*, January 30 and February 20, 1943; "Successful Farming Goes to the 4-H Club Congress," *Successful Farming* 42 (February 1944): 88.

20. *Successful Farming* 42 (April 1944): 46.

21. "Training Town Boys to Farm," *Farm Journal and Farmer's Wife* 67 (February 1943): 26.

22. "How About Manpower Supplies?" *Successful Farming* 42 (February 1944): 19; Wayne D. Rasmussen, *A History of the Emergency Farm Labor Supply Program, 1943–1947*, Agricultural Monograph No. 13 (Washington, D.C.: U.S. Department of Agriculture, September 1951), 120–130.

23. Tuttle, *"Daddy's Gone to War,"* 121, 123; *Successful Farming* 40 (August 1942): 35; *Wallaces' Farmer* 67 (April 18, 1942): 2, 28; and (July 11, 1942): 3.

24. Kirk, *Earning Their Stripes*, 57–60; "Special Report of Wartime Activities of the Future Farmers of America," *American Farm Youth* 7 (December 1942): 25; Winterset *Madisonian*, December 23, 1942; Winterset *Boomerang* (1943).

25. "The Play House," *Successful Farming* 41 (March 1943): 74; (April 1943): 94; (June 1943): 74; (August 1943): 70; 42 (February 1944): 82; (April 1944): 100; 43 (July 1945): 50; and (September 1945): 92.

26. "Editorials," *Wallaces' Farmer* 67 (April 18, 1942): 7; *Iowa Bureau Farmer*, June 1942 and July 1943.

27. Werner, *Through the Eyes of the Innocents*, 211; "The Iowa Community Faces War," *Iowa Farm Economist* 3 (January 1942): 15; "Editorials," *Wallaces' Farmer* 67 (September 19, 1942): 7; (October 3 1942): 6; and 68 (April 3 1943): 5.

28. "Explaining the War to Our Children," *Parents' Magazine* 17 (February 1942): 17; Wolf, *Our Children Face War*, 198; "The Farm Outlook," *Successful Farming* 40 (December 1942): 4.

29. *American Farm Youth* 10 (September 1945): 17.

30. *Iowa Farm Bureau Spokesman*, August 11, 1945.

31. "The Play House," *Successful Farming* 43 (December 1945): 104.

# Chapter Twenty

# Against Their Will
## The Use and Abuse of British Children during the Second World War

## Penny Elaine Starns and Martin L. Parsons

Prior to the outbreak of war in 1939, 1,500,000 British children were moved from their homes in the cities to rural areas over a period of three days. Subsequent large-scale evacuations also took place in 1940 and 1944. Yet despite the uniqueness of this mass child migration, traditional accounts of British wartime history have failed to include the experiences of these evacuated children. Any analysis of the evacuation process has been viewed primarily in terms of how the process affected the lives of adults. Thus, the views of government officials, billeting officers, host parents, teachers, and health workers have been considered, but the evacuee voice has been strangely excluded from evacuation history. The overriding debate has concentrated on whether evacuation served to challenge existing class boundaries within British society or merely served to reinforce them.

However, while historians have debated the evacuation process in terms of social class structures and subsequent postwar policy, they have failed to confront more fundamental issues, such as the varied motivations which prompted government evacuation schemes and the diverse treatment of those children involved. Conventional accounts of evacuation history have portrayed the British government as one which initiated evacuation schemes merely in order to protect children from the horrors of war.[1] Yet despite this assumption, there were other, more pressing concerns which directed evacuation policy. Children also became an integral part of the British war effort, and far from being protected, many suffered widespread physical, emotional, and sexual abuse at the hands of the very people who were responsible for their welfare. This chapter will expose just some of the ways in which British children were used and abused during the Second World War.

## Planning

Prior to 1939, the British government divided the country into "Evacuation," "Reception," and "Neutral" areas (the latter areas did not evacuate or receive children under the evacuation scheme but as the name suggests remained neutral), and decided that children should be evacuated with their schools, under the guidance of teachers. These children and their teachers would then be billeted in individual homes in the countryside.

Billeting was made compulsory. Therefore, if people had spare rooms they were forced to take in evacuees regardless of their circumstances. In the beginning there were exceptions; the disabled, elderly, chronically sick, and those who were at work all day did not have to be hosts. However, when the war actually started, pressure to find billets meant that even these categories found themselves having to look after lively young children. In early 1939, billeting officers toured the countryside recording the number of rooms available in each area, but no checks were ever made on the suitability of the receiving hosts. Furthermore, although billeting was compulsory, evacuation was voluntary. Consequently, individual villages never knew how many evacuees to expect, since numbers were always based on dubious estimates. For instance, Hungerford in Berkshire was expected to receive no evacuees at all, yet over 800 turned up. Over the whole of Britain all counties received a different number of evacuees to the number for whom plans had been made.[2]

Moreover, despite the fact that advisors from the Air Ministry had warned government officials of the dangers of evacuating children to the east coast, since the main thrust of air and sea attack would be targeted on this area, this advice was ignored. Many children were evacuated to the eastern counties and consequently saw far more of the war during the first few months of the conflict than if they had stayed in London. Most were later re-evacuated several times.

Why then, in view of previous advice, was a decision taken to send children into known danger areas? The answer to this question was quite simple, and underpinned the whole of the government's evacuation policy.

Evacuation was not simply about moving civilians from dangerous areas to places of relative safety; it was about "the dispersal of the population," and meeting essential wartime demands. The evacuation of children liberated more women for work in munitions factories. Propaganda played on the fears of parents and argued that children would be healthier and stronger in the country. Mothers in particular were portrayed as being irresponsible if they did not consent to the evacuation of their children. They were also made to feel guilty and told to "Remember, there are others, actively engaged in the service of our country, whose troubles may be much graver."[3]

Evacuation was also considered to be a vital component in lifting military morale. During a debate in the House of Commons, Colonel Wedgewood proclaimed that inadequate evacuation procedures would have a detrimental effect on the fighting forces. This view was underpinned in propaganda films which supposedly included the views of ordinary British soldiers stating that "If we know or children are safe we will fight better."[4]

Both the need to utilize women in essential war industries and the need to maintain military morale were driving forces behind the evacuation of children. Therefore, the whole evacuation process was not merely about providing safe areas for civilians. Clearly, dispersal of the population did not equate with the safety of the population, and most politicians had already recognized that in a country as small as Britain it was impossible to provide any guarantee of safety.

Certainly government officials did not consider the safety of children to be of prime importance. This attitude was highlighted not only by the absence of character checks on host families in the reception areas, but also in their handling of the overseas evacuation scheme which included children between the ages of five and fifteen. Overseas evacuation became known as the "useless mouths" policy. A shortage of food and supplies had prompted some government officials to adopt a rigorous and unfeeling attitude to "useless mouths." They argued that people who were either too old or too young to fight needed to be evacuated to other countries for the duration of the war, in order to conserve supplies for those who were able to take part in the war effort. Children naturally fell into this category of "useless mouths."[5]

There was also a feeling in some quarters that the plight of evacuee children might persuade some of the host countries to enter the war on the side of the allies. Lord Lothian, British Ambassador in Washington, felt that America was out of touch with British war aims and was therefore reluctant to provide armaments of financial contributions to the war effort, but that

American opinion might be swayed by the arrival of evacuees. All evacuees were given a stern talk before they set sail for foreign lands with regard to their behavior.

> If you behave well, people will say "What splendid children these are! We must do everything we can to help their parents win the war." When things go wrong, remember you are British and grin and bear it![6]

In addition to "tugging the heart strings of other nations," overseas evacuation was also considered to be a means of preserving the British race. Eugenicists were keen to send suitable stock abroad and shared a common belief that by sending children abroad these same children would, as the next generation, return to reclaim Britain from Germany should Hitler manage to invade. According to the Canadian Liaison Officer involved in the program, the scheme's participants were "not just evacuees, transferred from the range of menace, but part of Britain's immortality, part of the greatness of her past and part of all the hope for the future."[7] In 1940, the *Eugenics Review* described the ways in which certain eugenically important groups would be transported overseas. Children were to be selected by a committee of doctors who would ensure that these children were intelligent, healthy, and of sound hereditary background.[8]

But not all politicians were in favor of using children as pawns to tug the heart strings and breeding stock for the future. Churchill had spoken out several times against overseas evacuation, claiming that the policy was essentially defeatist. Moreover, the overseas scheme was only endorsed because Churchill was absent at a crucial moment. During a meeting of the War Cabinet, Churchill was interrupted to be informed of the fall of France to the Germans. In his absence a civil servant merely ticked the paper giving the go-ahead to the scheme without Churchill's consent. More importantly, the decision was taken without the advice of the Admiralty.[9]

Nevertheless, although the Admiralty had not been consulted in the initial planning of the overseas evacuation scheme, they subsequently warned the government that the navy could not provide adequate protection for these children. Furthermore unknown to parents, a few ships carried troops and war material along with evacuees and were obvious targets for enemy action. Most convoys of ships carrying evacuee children were torpedoed at some point during their journey, most of these were towed back to Britain. Three ships sank with the loss of life. The most famous casualty of the overseas evacuation scheme was the *SS City of Benares*. The ship was torpedoed on September 17, 1940, and seventy-seven children were killed.

Forty-six of the surviving children spent eight days in life boats before their rescue.[10]

## The Reality of Evacuation

The initial evacuation, code named "Operation Pied Piper," was frantic, emotional, and chaotic. None of the children or their teachers were told of their destinations and were only able to carry bare essentials. Some children were even prevented from taking their dolls and teddy bears to the countryside for fear that they would take up too much room on the trains. Many of the trains carrying the children from the cities to their rural destinations did not have toilets and in some cases there were no seats. Consequently, a lot of children had soiled their clothing before they reached the reception areas and were tired and hungry on arrival.

On reaching the reception areas, children were subjected to a "cattle market" scenario, whereby host families chose evacuees primarily according to their potential usefulness. Thus, farmers chose strong, healthy-looking lads to help them with their work on the land, while many women chose young girls whom they considered able enough to carry out domestic chores. In some areas such as North Wales, children were stripped of their clothes, bathed in antiseptic, and had their heads shaved. Host families took the view that all city children were young criminals who wet their beds and would arrive in reception areas covered in fleas and lice. The pervasive wartime stereotype of the "dirty evacuee" quickly developed, despite substantial evidence to the contrary. Children in host communities by contrast were considered to be clean and well mannered. In North Oxfordshire a nurse suggested that, "if any of the village children were found to be Verminous, it would be due to London children."[11]

Medical inspections of children were increased, but the constant migration of evacuees made continuity difficult and many children were excluded from any form of inspection. There was no national systematic medical inspection for any children and it was far easier for local authorities to blame evacuees for medical problems than to confront the inadequacies of social care systems. Moreover, the blame for poverty and illness was laid not at the door of the medical service but firmly at the door of working-class mothers who were considered to be slovenly. Government and local officials argued that working-class mothers needed to be educated with regard to better habits, though just how educating working-class mothers in better habits was supposed to cure their poverty was never fully explained.

Medical records, however, showed that lice infestation was already a problem in the countryside long before the arrival of city children. Host families also exaggerated the incidence of bed wetting among evacuees in an effort to obtain an extra laundry allowance. Such claims for laundry allowance more than trebled between 1940 and 1942, and officials began an investigation into the abuses of the system. The fact that many evacuees were clean, did not wet the bed, and were disease-free, however, did not deter the makers of "Lifebouy" and "Lifeguard" soap from launching a whole advertising campaign based on how to get evacuees clean! In reality, many evacuees were middle-class children who were shocked to find that their new countryside homes had earthen floors, no running water, and outside toilets. Middle-class children evacuated to South Wales, for instance, were horrified when working-class miners came home in the evening from the coal pit, took out a tin bath, and proceeded to wash in front of the living room fire. There was never any attempt by billeting officers to record the availability of indoor or outdoor facilities, and in most country areas toilets were located outdoors. Indeed, this was one reason why some children wet their beds. Many of them were frightened of venturing out in the middle of the night to use the outside facilities. They were deterred by the strange noises of the countryside and the potential appearance of animals which were previously unknown to them and perceived as threatening.[12]

Middle-class children constituted at least 45 percent of all children evacuated in some areas, such as those children who left Kent for South Wales and Somerset. In areas serving children evacuated from London and Liverpool, they formed a smaller percentage, ranging from 15 to 30 percent.[13]

Traditional accounts of evacuation history have virtually ignored the fact that middle-class children were also evacuated, perhaps because scholars have been unable to fit them into the stereotyped version of the supposedly average evacuee. But while host families claimed that evacuees had no manners, could not even hold a knife and fork, and were responsible for all the petty thieving and vandalism in the reception areas, middle-class children were equally unimpressed by the habits of country people. One woman who was evacuated from Liverpool to North Wales recalled:

> I'd been brought up not to drink after anybody and to make sure the cup was always scalded, because in Liverpool before the war there was always this terrible fear of catching tuberculosis. One of the boys drank from the cream jug which was set on the table for tea and I was reluctant to drink the milk from that jug afterwards.[14]

In addition to stereotyping, evacuees also had to deal with deep-seated religious and cultural prejudices. For example, children frequently found themselves in reception areas where none shared their religious beliefs. Thus, it was not uncommon for Jewish children to come down to farm kitchens in the morning to be confronted by a breakfast of bacon and pork sausages! Farmers and their wives did not always understand religious customs and labeled such children ungrateful when they refused meals on religious grounds. In North Wales, there was a particular problem for the Catholic evacuees who had arrived in Protestant and Welsh Methodist areas; some were made to walk as many as eight miles to attend Mass on Sunday mornings.[15] A priest in Liverpool even advised parents to bring their evacuated children back home to Liverpool from Wales despite the serious risk of bombing, arguing that German bombs posed a lesser threat than that of moral and spiritual corruption.[16]

However, given the numerous other problems which were confronting evacuees on a daily basis, spiritual concerns were probably the least of their worries. According to recent research, which is based on the oral history testimonies of over 500 evacuees, at least 15 percent of these children were subjected to sexual abuse and a further 20 percent to physical and mental abuse.[17] One woman experienced horrific treatment at the hands of her host parent when she was only three years old. As a lonely, frightened little girl, Mrs. Williams cried for her mother and wet the bed. As a punishment for this behavior, the host mother brought the family dog up to the little girl's bedroom, put the dog collar around her neck, dragged the little girl outside into the backyard, and made her sleep in the dog kennel.

> I was left there all night screaming and crying. She done that every time I wet the bed. It became a regular thing. I hated it. I hated it when I went to bed and I would be saying in my prayers "Oh God, don't let me wet the bed, don't let me wet the bed."[18]

Another woman remembered her sister's sexual abuse:

> The teacher that brought my sister home from school had noticed when my sister was in the shower she was obviously pregnant. The doctor confirmed

she was pregnant and she was sent off to what was called a workhouse. As for us at home, we were told nothing. All we knew was that these people were going to come and question us. The questions were quite strange because we didn't understand what they were trying to get at. They asked us if we had seen anything strange occur between our sister and any man. I could say that I had never seen anything, but my younger sister had witnessed this farmer having sex with my sister in one of the barns. Because she was afraid of the repercussions, and she knew in her heart and mind that we would have to stay there, she dare not name this farmer. I hate the thought that this man got away with it, because no charges were ever brought.[19]

Boys were also abused. "She had this horse whip with a crook handle and about 6 or 7 inches of leather on the end," John Abbot recalled.

She walloped me all over. I had bruises from my neck right down to my ankles on both sides and on my left hip all my clothes were stuck to my hip where it was bleeding. My mother, who turned up on a surprise visit, took me straight to the police station.

At the police station, John's bruises and weeping wounds were photographed. The host mother was eventually fined £5![20]

Evacuees were by no means the only children to be abused (it should also be noted that many children escaped an abusive home life in the cities to find caring host parents in the countryside), but their circumstances made abuse easier for the perpetrators. The teachers who had accompanied their pupils on their journeys were often billeted miles away from their charges. In some instances, teachers cycled over a hundred miles a week to check on children and their host families. There were even cases where teachers initially lost children altogether, only to find them weeks later roaming the countryside. The changing pattern of evacuation also complicated the situation. By early 1940, over 80 percent of evacuated children had returned to the cities. The "Phony War" had lulled everyone into a false sense of security and evacuees drifted back just in time for the Blitz! A second evacuation began in the summer of 1940 and a third in 1944. However, while there were only three major evacuation trends, children were constantly travelling back and forth across Britain throughout the war.[21]

In order to try and stem the flow of children back to the cities, government propaganda desperately tried to convince parents that children were not only safer in the country but also healthier, stronger, and more alert. But there was no evidence to support this rhetoric. More alarmingly, some evidence showed that evacuees in the reception areas actually displayed retarded growth rates when compared to children who had remained in the cities. This trend was extremely disconcerting to government officials, who needed mothers in the city workplace and children out of the way. Studies of children throughout the war, which were largely conducted by social workers and school medical officers, stressed the individual child's capacity to remain emotionally stable even through bombing raids as long as they were accompanied by their parents. However, if bombing resulted in the evacuation of the child and a break with the family, then severe emotional problems ensued. Yet it was not until after the war that a link was established between emotional deprivation and retarded growth rates.[22]

The later waves of evacuation produced further problems in the reception areas. Central government had failed to equip rural areas for the large influx of children, and the numbers of destitute children shocked individual communities. Appeals were made to Mr. Ramsbottom, as president of the Board of Education, to take action with regard to the plight of needy children, but action was not forthcoming. Teachers working in the countryside also voiced concerns with regard to the number of children employed in agriculture. They had accepted that children over the age of eleven would be absent from school during harvest periods, but most farmers pushed the boundaries of this acceptance by employing children on their farms all year long. Children as young as seven were kept away from school to help with farm duties. Accidents involving farm equipment and children were frequent. Eventually the Board of Education intervened and threatened to withhold funds from local education authorities if children did not attend school. Some authorities such as Herefordshire and Shropshire ignored this warning, however, and continued to use child labor on their farms, arguing that children were urgently needed to contribute to the war effort.[23]

In some respects farmers could be forgiven for not following the advice of the Board of Education, since the latter's policies were often conflicting. On the one hand, the Board argued against the use of children in the war effort on the grounds that this effort had a detrimental effect on their education; while on the other hand the Board sanctioned all manner of dubious schemes whereby children helped in the war effort during school hours. A lack of school premises in the reception areas had given rise to a shift system in most schools, and teachers took their pupils on frequent "nature rambles" to alleviate the pressure on school buildings. Initially these rambles were intended to be educational, but they were quickly used as a means to employ children to gather wool, berries, or plants for the war effort. Children were expected to gather wool from barbed wire fences, trees, and hedges and pack them in bags of fifty pounds to send to the Gathered Wool Officer. In one county children collected 627 pounds of wool in a few weeks.[24]

The Board also sanctioned a far more dangerous practice, that of collecting Colchicum (*Colchicum Autumnale L.*) for the Ministry of Health, for use in the preparation of medicines. The collection of this herb was a complicated and dangerous process. As the Board stated in its request for child labor, "Children should be warned that Colchicum is a deadly poison." By 1941 the school curriculum had been totally taken over by the war effort. The "Dig for Victory" campaign resulted in the loss of nearly all school playing fields, as they were taken over in order to grow more vegetables.[25]

But although the war effort infiltrated their school life, most children acknowledged that teachers generally attempted to protect them from the harsher realities of war. "We knew there was a war on," one former evacuee recalled:

> The only time that we realized that it was very serious was when the teachers came in one afternoon and said we'd all got to pray because all our soldiers were coming home from a place called Dunkirk, and we would have ten minutes prayer for them, to get them home safely. So we realized it was very serious then, because the look on the teacher's face, you would have thought that Hitler was standing outside the classroom door waiting to take her away![26]

The protection offered to evacuees by their original city teachers did not last. The constant upheaval caused by re-evacuations, teachers being called up for military service or being recalled to the cities disrupted pupil-teacher relationships. A large proportion of evacuees claimed that once their original teachers had left reception areas, they were subjected to frequent scapegoating and neglect. Evacuees were increasingly blamed by villagers and local authorities for petty crimes and vandalism, much of which had been caused by local children. The regular weekly home checks of evacuees, which had been conducted by their original teachers, lapsed and the evacuee was left wide open to abuse. Host families were not always concerned about the welfare of their evacuees, and many stole their food rations which lowered the immunity levels of evacuees, thus making them more susceptible to infections. The evacuee frequently had no way of voicing his or her distress. Correspondence sent home to parents was often censored by teachers in order not to worry parents unduly and to underpin the government view that children should remain in the country.

Those children who had returned to the cities received no education at all for some time, since the Board of Education had closed all city schools and was reluctant to reopen them. In some areas, a curfew was imposed on children as members of the police force became increasingly concerned about the rise of juvenile crime. The breakdown of the education system, the compulsory blackout, and a lack of adult supervision had all contributed to this trend.[27]

The experience of evacuees, and indeed all children during the Second World War, cannot be generalized. It is clear, however, that both domestic and overseas evacuees suffered in ways that are yet to be revealed. They were used as political pawns, advertising campaigns, farm laborers, domestic servants, and collectors of poison plants. They were abused by some host parents, village workers, priests, and in some cases even teachers. They were subjected to radical changes in their culture and surroundings, inadequate diet, education, and medical care, accompanied by social exclusion and scapegoating. Some will never regain any semblance of emotional equilibrium.

An assessment of the whole process can be summed up in the reflections of one evacuee:

> It's never been easy to talk about the events of the evacuation but I feel now that it needs to be recorded, needs to be spoken about to try to dispel a lot of myths that have been woven around evacuation, how wonderful and splendid the whole thing was. It may have been founded on very good notions, trying to save children from the blitz. Quite frankly, the trauma it caused them, by being torn away from their families and their parents at a very young age, scarred them for life. It didn't really work out as well as everyone thought it was going to.[28]

## Notes

1. For examples, see A.J.P. Taylor, *English History, 1914–39* (Oxford: Oxford University Press, 1992; A. Calder, *The Myth of the Blitz* (London: Jonathan Cape, 1991).

2. Parsons, *"I'll Take That One,"* 54–57, 189.

3. Statements in the press and via radio broadcasts by the majority of MPs to mothers underpinned the government stance that all children were likely to be safer and healthier if they were evacuated from the cities or those areas considered to be vulnerable. For an example, see the statement by Herbert Morrison, printed in all newspapers in August 1939. Parsons, *"I'll Take That One,"* 261.

4. *Parliamentary Debates, Commons, 5th Series*, vol. 362 1939–40, cols. 5–6, June

18, 1940. Parliamentary debates on the issue of evacuation took place throughout the war and can be found in *Hansard, 5th Series, HMSO*. For a more detailed list of Government Papers relating to evacuation see Parsons, *"I'll Take That One,"* 278–280. See also *Westward Ho* (1940), one of many propaganda films made by the Ministries of Information and Health designed to underpin the government line on evacuation. Others include *Living with Strangers* (1941) and *Village School* (1941). They can now be found together on a video collection produced by the Imperial War Museum, London, under the generic title *Keep the Wheels Turning*.

5. *Parliamentary Debates, Commons, 5th series*, vol. 363, 1939–40, col. 358, June 17, 1940; Document Number 65/7/170, June 17, 1940, Cabinet Documents (CAB), Public Record Office (PRO), London; 65/8/179, July 1, 1940, PRO.CAB. Documents pertaining to the Children's Overseas Reception Board can be found in the Dominion Office File Series (DO), notably PRO.DO 131/29, PRO.DO 35/259/B277/4, PRO.DO 35/529/B305/8, and PRO.DO 35/529/B305/4.

6. Fethney, *The Absurd and the Brave*, 89.

7. See PRO.DO 131/45 for the establishment of the Children's Overseas Reception Board and the concerns of eugenicists.

8. *Eugenics Review* 32 (April 1940–Jan. 1941), in PRO.DO.131/45. See also Parsons and Starns, *Evacuation*, 161–162. The *Eugenics Review* outlined basic guidelines on how children should be selected for overseas evacuation. The Eugenics Society also funded several evacuation schemes.

9. Churchill was known to be against overseas evacuation and spoke out against such a policy on several occasions during Parliamentary Debates, June 21, 1940, PRO.CAB65/7/174. See also Parsons, *"I'll Take That One,"* 160–163.

10. The sinking of the *S.S. City of Benares* effectively put an end to government overseas evacuation schemes, although some children were still evacuated overseas privately. September 23, 1940, PRO.CAB 79/6, folio 323. See also Ralph Barker, *Children of the Benares: A War Crime and Its Victims* (London: Grafton Books, 1990), 28.

11. Documents 113/4, 78, 10, County Record Office, Chipping Norton, Oxfordshire. (There are no reference numbers.) See also Parsons, *"I'll Take That One,"* 119.

12. Parsons and Starns, *Evacuation*, 71–74.

13. None of the original central government statistics for this period are entirely reliable, and the social class pattern of children in all areas varied greatly throughout the war. The statistics quoted here, therefore, are based on recent documentary research conducted in county as well as government record offices, oral history testimonies conducted with over 500 evacuees, and 850 letters from other evacuees. Copies of oral history testimonies are held at the Centre for Evacuee Studies, Bulmershe Court, University of Reading, Reading, UK. A list of some of the contributors can be found in Parsons, *"I'll Take That One,"* 286–289.

14. Interview with A.J., June 8, 1998. Oral History Testimonies. See also Parsons and Starns, *Evacuation*, 74.

15. April 23, 1940, Evacuation File, Caernarvon County Record Office, Caernar-

von, North Wales. Correspondence pertaining to evacuation procedures is held in the evacuation files, which are not identified by reference numbers.

16. R. Padley and M. Cole, *Evacuation: A Report to the Fabian Society* (London: Routledge, 1940), 236–237.

17. John Macnicol's excellent study of health and evacuation reveals that there was a huge rise in the number of child guidance clinics established both during and after the war to deal with the increase in emotional deprivation experienced by evacuees. "The Effect of the Evacuation of Schoolchildren on Official Attitudes to State Intervention," in Smith, ed., *War and Social Change*, 3–28.

18. Interview with Mrs. Williams, July 1, 1999. Oral History Testimonies.

19. Interview with G.B., February 2, 1999. Oral History Testimonies.

20. Interview with John Abbot, February 1, 1999. Oral History Testimonies.

21. Parsons, "*I'll Take That One*," 276–277.

22. Macnicol, "The Effect of the Evacuation of Schoolchildren," 5.

23. Parsons, "*I'll Take That One*," 96.

24. Ibid., 81.

25. Document CA771/1/1, Board of Education Files, Sheffield County Record Office. Sheffield was an unusual city in terms of evacuation procedures because half of the city was designated an evacuation zone while the other half was designated a "neutral" evacuation zone. This resulted in very confusing policy initiatives.

26. Interview with A.S., October 2, 1998. Oral History Testimonies.

27. For more information on the effect of evacuation on education and the pressure on teachers, see Parsons, "*I'll Take That One*," 70–101. It is important to note that the initial planning of the evacuation scheme was undertaken by the Home office. In practical terms, however, it was the Board of Education who administered the evacuation procedures and it was not particularly powerful in the early stages of the war. The Board of Education only gained prominence after the Butler Education Act in 1944. Consequently, the Board had little impact when it came to child protection and was frequently at odds with the more powerful ministries when it came to issues of child labor.

28. Interview with Marlene Heselden, June 15, 1999. Oral History Testimonies.

# Chapter Twenty-One

# Innocent Victims and Heroic Defenders
## *Children and the Siege of Leningrad*

*Lisa A. Kirschenbaum*

By the fall of 1941, as the German army closed its blockade of Leningrad and the German air force began its campaign to bomb the city into submission, only a small fraction of the city's 400,000 children had been evacuated.[1] Few children escaped the city during the first months of the siege, when the daily bread ration for dependents fell to 125 grams. No official figures count the number of children who died during the terrible winter of 1941–1942, when thousands of Leningraders died of starvation every day. The city lacked the capacity to bury, let alone identify, all of them. When the so-called "Road of Life" opened across frozen Lake Ladoga in late 1941, children were among the first evacuated. However, some remained in the blockaded city, which was often subject to heavy air and artillery attack until the siege was finally broken in January 1944.

In official Soviet parlance, Leningrad was a "city front," a place where the distinction between front and rear, soldier and civilian, disappeared. With most of its adult male population in the army or evacuated with the war industry, the city of Leningrad was a front "manned" largely by women and children. Wartime accounts tended to emphasize that children not only withstood the siege but also that they played a vital role in defending the city. In these accounts the most visible representative of the young generation was the Young Communist teenager (*Komsomol*), often a girl, digging anti-tank trenches, extinguishing incendiary bombs in buckets of sand before they set fire to rooftops, or delivering food, water, and even the mail to Leningraders struggling against starvation and isolation.

While wartime accounts emphasized child heroes, the emerging "cult" of World War II in the 1960s made an innocent child victim a prominent state-sanctioned symbol of the city's wartime experience.[2] The rituals, heroes, and memorials of the "cult" worked to turn the war into the Soviet state's chief legitimizing myth. In the case of Leningrad, the cult of the war made an eleven-year-old girl the most visible victim of the siege. Tania Savicheva's laconic nine-sentence "diary" chronicling the deaths of six members of her family during the famine winter and spring of 1941–1942 became an emblem of the "Leningrad epic." Soviet, post-Soviet, and Western accounts used the diary as a means of evoking the horrors of the blockade.

Tania's brief diary and stories about hard-working, spirited Young Communist girls and boys define the city's children in wartime as at once innocent victims and heroic defenders. The publicity these images received, both during and after the war, illuminates the political uses of children's wartime experiences. That these images continue to shape the memory of the war in post-Soviet Russia suggests the difficulty of separating the "raw" memory of people who lived through the siege as children from the Soviet "myth" of innocence and heroism.

## Wartime Images of Children in Leningrad

In wartime accounts, two sorts of children inhabited besieged Leningrad: those receiving excellent care in state institutions and those doing adult work to "defend" the city. Newspapers praised Leningrad's women for their protection and rehabilitation of the youngest survivors of the siege. The press pictured teenage boys and girls as fighting for their mothers and the motherland by caring for children, the sick, and the old. The wartime story of Leningrad's children can thus be understood as of a piece with propaganda that made devotion to family and hometown key markers of Soviet patriotism.[3]

What remained largely invisible in these Soviet wartime accounts was the failure to evacuate children and the fatal effects of starvation. During the war, telling the story of the youngest victims of Nazi aggression proved difficult for the Soviet state. Images of threatened and wounded children often functioned in Soviet wartime propaganda as a means of generating hatred of the invader and of inspiring sacrifice. A wartime photograph of Leningrad's main street shows a bombed-out building decorated with a two-story version of a frequently reproduced poster that featured a woman with a child in her arms and the caption "Death to the child-killers!"[4]

At the same time, the failure to evacuate or feed hundreds of thousands of children hardly constituted the sort of fact that the Soviet state liked to publicize. The Soviet press did not cover experiences like those of historian Andrei Dzeniskevich, who as a nine-year-old in 1941 was part of a group of children evacuated from Leningrad directly into the path of the advancing Germans. Trainloads of children that came under German bombardment had to be returned to Leningrad, and not all could be re-evacuated in a safer direction before the blockade closed.[5]

Instead, wartime accounts detailed the extraordinary acts performed predominately by women to save children. Typical of the genre is a 1944 account, published in English for Allied consumption, that described a nurse at a children's home who led her charges to the shelter during an air raid, all the while restraining her motherly impulse to leave and check on her own children. When the immediate danger had passed and the nurse returned home, she found that her own children had been taken to safety by the neighbors.[6]

Unable to raise uncomfortable questions about the state's failure to respond effectively to the emergency, the wartime press emphasized measures taken to protect children, and in general downplayed starvation as a cause of death in the besieged city—favoring instead stories about heroic efforts to combat the deadly effects of German bombs and artillery.[7]

Recognizing the profoundly damaging effects of war on children, wartime accounts maintained that for Soviet youngsters the trauma was short-lived. The credit went both to dedicated women and to the Soviet state. Writing in the newspaper *Komsomol'skaia pravda* in May 1943, novelist Aleksandr Fadeev emphasized the speed with which Leningrad's children recovered from the famine winter of 1941–1942. "In April [1942], when I first saw Leningrad children, they had already passed through the most difficult period of their lives, but the imprint of that terrible winter remained on their faces and was expressed in their games. Many children played by themselves. Even in collective games, they played silently, with serious faces." Yet by July, according to Fadeev, "the majority of children appeared completely normal and healthy," the only exceptions being recently orphaned children.[8] In an extended version of his Leningrad observations published in 1944, Fadeev provided a detailed catalog of physical and emotional injury fully healed by the "sacred work of Leningrad's women."[9]

Wartime accounts traced children's resilience to the upbringing provided by the Soviet state. A 1944 account of the siege acknowledged that Leningrad "[p]arents worried over the psychological effect of such abnormal times, remembering stories of embittered, gnome-like children and maladjusted, unhealthy adults, the spawn of warfare. What actually happened," according to the authors, "was that most of the children who remained in Leningrad developed a sardonic and simple humor that was indestructible." They traced these happy results to the fact that "[m]ost of these children had received splendid training as members of the Young Pioneers," and, at a still younger age, as Little Octobrists.[10]

The "steadfastness" (*muzhestvo*), patriotism, and determination attributed to children made it possible to picture them as "heroic defenders" on par with the adults. Moving from his description of the speed with which Leningrad's orphans "had become completely normal children" to his account of Leningrad schoolchildren, Fadeev emphasized that while "the people of Leningrad can be proud of having saved the children" it was also true that "the children of school age can be proud of having defended Leningrad together with their fathers, mothers, elder brothers and sisters."[11] The official newspaper of the Young Communist League, *Komsomol'skaia pravda*, routinely carried stories of schoolchildren and *Komsomols*, usually teenagers finishing or just out of school, who, in addition to their studies, waited in line for bread for the family, worked in defense factories, brought food and firewood to the homebound, stood watch on rooftops, put out incendiary bombs, and caught spies and speculators.[12] In a glowing account of an industrial trade school, the school's director attributed the remarkable survival rates among his pupils to the teachers' commitment to preserving discipline and to the teenagers' work in war industries.[13] The school provided an inspirational story not only of survival but of survival made possible by participation in the heroic defense of the city.

The story of the haven of the trade school, as well as accounts of infants saved from bombed buildings, diverted attention from the thousands of children who died in the blockaded city. Women's heroic protection of children during air raids could not change the fact that in Leningrad the primary killer of children was starvation, not German bombs and artillery. With regard to teenagers, later Soviet accounts admitted that some of the highest death rates in the city could be found in the industrial trade schools, where children, who worked like adults but received only the dependent's ration, were among the first to die. The memoir literature and archival documents suggest that many starving teenagers resorted to stealing ration cards and bread. Other teenagers, both pupils in the factory schools and those who, as early as age fourteen, had entered the work force, tried to defect to the German lines. One memoir documents a demonstration of several hundred people, mainly children between the ages of ten and fourteen, demanding that Leningrad be declared an open city.[14]

None of which is to deny that both adults and children displayed remarkable courage and fortitude in withstanding the siege and trying to save others. As Richard Bidlack notes in his study of political attitudes in blockaded Leningrad, many people "demonstrated considerable heroism and self-sacrifice and pride in their native city."[15] The point is that despite the best efforts of parents and officials alike, death by starvation was everywhere in Leningrad—a simple and painful reality downplayed or ignored in wartime accounts of the city's children.

## Children and the "Cult" of the War

With the emergence in the 1960s of the state-sponsored "cult" of World War II, increasingly graphic accounts of innocent victims of starvation became a part of the official story of the siege of Leningrad.[16] This reworking of the story of the children of the siege parallels "the forty-year evolution of Soviet war literature" that critic Boris Gasparov has characterized as involving "the revelation of the war's human aspect: personal suffering, individualized characters, social and ethical problems."[17] In the 1960s, the "human aspect" of the blockade came to be embodied in Tania Savicheva, whose diary became an indelible icon of the siege. Such individual accounts humanized the war and were, therefore, well suited to one of the chief aims of the state-sponsored war cult: impressing upon the postwar generation the sacrifices and heroism of their elders as well as the legitimacy of the Soviet state that engineered victory.

The fame of Tania's diary, at least in the Soviet Union, suggests comparisons with the legendary status of the diary of Anne Frank. While Tania's brief account offers none of the intimate details that have made it possible to read Anne's diary as "an uplifting and not a harrowing experience," her matter-of-fact log has been similarly represented as a testament to "sustaining strength rather than debilitating weakness."[18] By the early 1980s, Tania's diary had opened the way to the publication of other, much fuller, children's diaries and oral histories.

Tania Savicheva's diary went on display in Leningrad before the war ended. In its totality, the diary, written in a child's notebook, reads:

Zhenia died 28 December, 12:30 in the morning, 1941.
Babushka [Grandmother] died 25 January, 3:00 in the afternoon, 1942.
Leka died 17 March, 5:00 in the morning, 1942.
Dedia [Uncle] Vasia died 13 April, 2:00 at night, 1942.
Dedia Lesha, 10 May, 4:00 in the afternoon, 1942.
Mama, 13 May, 7:30 in the morning, 1942.
Savichevs died. All died. Only Tania remains.[19]

In 1944, Tania Savicheva's terse log of the deaths of her mother, grandmother, sister, brother, and two uncles constituted one small piece of a massive museum in Leningrad that filled over 20,000 square meters of space and featured impressive displays of Soviet and captured German military hardware. Tania's sister Nina, who had been evacuated from Leningrad, found the diary in 1944 and turned it over to the museum. At the time of the museum's opening, the diary attracted little official attention. It is not mentioned in the 1945 guidebook to the exhibition, although it does appear briefly in the 1948 guidebook, where Tania is identified as a nine-year-old. The many press reports announcing the opening of the exhibition and later the museum did not mention the diary. The press and the exhibition's guidebook focused on the military displays and on the mock-up of a Leningrad bakery where the visitor could look through an icy window to see scales with the 125-gram bread ration of late 1941 and a sign describing its adulterated contents.[20]

In more recent accounts of the museum, the diary is mentioned as a key exhibit. When, in the early 1980s, one of the museum's founders looked back on the establishment of the museum, Tania's diary assumed a prominent place in his narrative. Vasilii Kovalev remembered the diary as a central exhibit in the room that displayed the 125-gram bread ration. "This little book," he recalled, "made an incredible impression. . . . I remember Lady Churchill standing before the case containing Tania Savicheva's diary. When the contents were translated to her, her eyes filled with tears."[21]

The retrospective importance of the diary stemmed in part from its prominent display, along with a prewar photograph of Tania, in the small museum at Piskarevskoe Memorial Cemetery fifteen years after the end of the war. Opened on Victory Day (May 9) 1960, Piskarevskoe Cemetery honors the hundreds of thousands of nameless dead buried in mass graves—and one girl with a name and a face, who recorded the deaths of her family.

Tania, who was evacuated but died as a result of prolonged malnutrition suffered in Leningrad, became a "symbol of the blockade."[22] In 1968, the diary itself became part of a memorial to "the young heroes of Leningrad" that consisted of a gigantic "flower of life" and Tania's diary, each page rendered in larger-than-life stone.[23]

The children's memorial suggests the conflation of heroism and victimization that became central to the war cult's use of the stories of children. Historian Nina Tumarkin explains the emergence of the war cult in the 1960s, and particularly in the years after Leonid Brezhnev took power in 1964, as "a kind of counter-campaign against the international youth culture" that "tried to shame young people into feeling respect for their elders or, as a minimum goal, into behaving obediently in their presence."[24] Stories about children who gave their lives to "defend" Leningrad—even if that "defense" consisted only of going to school during the blockade—offered a means of reaching the postwar generation.[25] Sergei Smirnov's 1971 poem "Heart and Diary" takes Tania's diary as its point of departure and imagines Tania's siblings and uncles as dedicated young people expending their last reserves of strength working in the war industry and Tania herself as a dutiful Young Pioneer struggling to survive. The poem's homey details—such as the family's preparations for summer vacations—is bracketed by notes emphasizing that Tania's diary served as evidence of Nazi war crimes at Nuremberg.[26] The framework allows identification with a fellow child while underscoring the historic significance of her story and the war.

Persuading survivors to share personal and painful stories of the siege, Ales Adamovich and Daniil Granin, editors of an important collection of siege diaries and oral histories, made the need to reach youngsters explicit. They told one reluctant informant "that it was very important for the younger readers to know more about the life of a teenager during the blockade."[27]

One of the central accounts included in Adamovich and *Granin's Blokadnaia kniga* (A Book of the Blockade) is the diary of Iura Riabkin, who turned sixteen shortly after the blockade closed. *Blokadnaia kniga* begins with the iconic image of Tania, but its real child hero is Iura, whose lengthy diary records the inner life of a teenager in blockaded Leningrad. Typical of the diary's perspective is the first entry on the outbreak of war. Having gone to the Pioneer Palace—a kind of youth club—to play chess, Iura heard the announcement of the German invasion. Iura's account recognizes the immensity of the news—"My head was spinning. I just couldn't think straight"—but also notes that despite the shock he managed to win three straight games of chess.[28] Iura recorded his involvement in all sorts of war work from helping to build bomb shelters to putting out incendiary bombs at school. He thus fits the stereotype of the young heroic defender. At the same time, he emerges as a very real boy, whose motives and reactions were not self-consciously "heroic," but included the desire to be with friends, to keep busy, and to participate in the great adventure of war.

Iura's diary, unlike Tania's, provides insight into the child's experiences and understandings of the blockade. As food rations diminished in the winter of 1941, Iura chronicled a painful struggle between, in the editors' phrase, "conscience and hunger." In December 1941, the starving Iura recorded his "degradation . . . dishonor and shame": "like a bastard I sneak their last morsels" from his mother and thirteen-year-old sister Ira.[29] In early January, Iura described the advanced stages of starvation—"I'm bloated . . . I can't force myself to move about, can't make myself get up from a chair and walk a step or two"—and expressed his soon-realized fears that his sister and mother would leave him behind when they were evacuated.[30]

The power of Iura Riabkin's diary, like other diaries and oral histories published in the years of the war "cult," stems in part from the moving, personal descriptions of previously taboo subjects: the inadequacy of efforts to evacuate children, the effects of starvation, the strain and breakdown of family relations.[31] In his diary, fifteen-year-old Misha Tikhomirov told the story of December 1941 and early January 1942 by detailing his daily food intake, the often "hellish cold" inside and out, the increasing difficulty of reading and preparing lessons, and the numbers of corpses encountered on the way to school.[32] A child survivor interviewed by Adamovich and Granin recounted that she remembered the children's New Year's party in January 1942 because it was the day her father died. A woman who was twelve during the siege remembered that her four-year-old sister, who never asked for food "because she understood that it couldn't be got," coped by incessantly cutting and tearing paper. Many mothers, like Iura's, had to choose which child to save. Others abandoned their children altogether. A woman who had been in charge of evacuating children told of a once "tender mother," who threw her child out of the house when he lost a ration card. The child died, and sometime after the war, the mother committed suicide.[33]

Collections of documents published in the years of the war cult represented the words of children and child survivors as providing direct access to the reality of the siege. Explicitly in Adamovich and Granin's collection, and implicitly in others, children's diaries became privileged repositories of the "true" story of the siege. The editors of *Blokadnaia kniga*, who collected large numbers of oral reminiscences, argued that the diaries provided the truest picture of life in blockaded Leningrad. While oral histories might be distorted by contact with published accounts, diaries constituted the pure "bedrock" of truth. At the same time, of all the oral histories, they most trusted the words of child survivors, deeming the child's memory "clear and exact."[34]

What such claims about the authenticity of the child's words ignored was the degree to which the diaries themselves reflected not just the child's truth but also the child's internalization of the official version of the war and the siege. Many in Leningrad kept diaries during the war, often for the first time. Convinced that they were living through epic events, diarists created personal accounts for the historical record. Iura Riabkin, for instance, wrote that on the first day of the war, "A really serious battle is beginning, a clash between two antagonistic forces—socialism and fascism! The wellbeing of mankind depends on the outcome of this historic struggle." Iura may well have shared this view of the war, but it was clearly one that he had encountered in school or in the press, which he read avidly.[35] Nonetheless, the diary's emotional authenticity softens and sometimes conceals its ideological content. The war cult capitalized on the "truth" of children's diaries and recollections, presenting them as unmediated proofs of the sacrifice and heroism at the center of the mythic telling of the war.

That the mythic story of Leningrad's stoic and heroic children persisted after the fall of communism suggests that it was more than a means of maintaining the authority of the Soviet state. Even at its most hackneyed, the war cult recognized and represented the suffering of individuals, while offering a larger meaning for their sacrifices. Since the dissolution of the Soviet Union in 1991, the war cult has in part been unmasked as a manipulative effort to invent heroes of mythic status.[36] Still, many of the heroes and monuments created by the cult remain compelling, particularly for the generation that fought the war. One child survivor, telling her story eight years after the demise of the Soviet Union, prefaced her account with the story of Tania Savicheva.[37] Similarly, a recent book of reminiscences of the siege compiled by survivors who relocated to Stalingrad (now Volgograd) opens with the images of the Soviet-era memorials commemorating the siege of Leningrad and the battle of Stalingrad.[38] The Tania Savicheva memorial graces the cover of a post-Soviet collection of poetry by child survivors of the siege.[39] Moreover, the collection itself contains nothing that would directly challenge the official story of innocent and heroic children. Adamovich and Granin cautioned readers looking for the "truth" that

survivors often "substituted well-known facts for their personal stories."[40]
That "truthful" children and child survivors often did the same suggests that
the "substitution" or interleaving of the personal and the public functioned
as a key means of endowing the experience and the memory of a wartime
childhood with meaning.

NOTES

1. Dmitri Pavlov, in charge of food distribution for the city, provides the figure
of 400,000 children in the city at the start of the siege, September 8, 1941. Pavlov,
*Leningrad 1941: The Blockade, Translated by John Clinton Adams* (Chicago: University of Chicago Press, 1965), 48. He does not specify the age range included in the
category "children."

2. On the "cult" of World War II, see Tumarkin, *The Living and the Dead*, 3, 188,
and Weiner, *Making Sense of War*, 17, n. 18.

3. Kirschenbaum, "'Our City, Our Hearths, Our Families,'" 825–847.

4. The photograph is reproduced in Boris Skomorovsky and E. G. Morris, *The
Siege of Leningrad: The Saga of the Greatest Siege of All Time as Told by the Letters,
Documents, and Stories of the Brave People Who Withstood It* (New York: E. P. Dutton, 1944), 45.

5. Andrei R. Dzeniskevich, "The Social and Political Situation in Leningrad in
the First Months of the German Invasion: The Social Psychology of the Workers,"
in Thurston and Bonwetsch, eds., *The People's War*, 73–74.

6. Skomorovsky and Morris, *The Siege of Leningrad*, 83–84.

7. Lydia Ginzburg, *Blockade diary*, Translated by Alan Myers (London: Harvill
Press, 1995), 31; Ol'ga Berggol'ts, "Iz dnevnikov," *Zvezda* no. 5 (1990), 190. The press
mentioned "hunger" in Leningrad only in 1943, well after the period of starvation
had passed.

8. A. Fadeev, "Deti geroicheskogo goroda: Iz leningradskikh zarisovok," *Komsomol'skaia pravda* (hereafter *KP*), May 12, 1943.

9. A. Fadeev, *Leningrad in the Days of the Blockade*, Translated by R. D. Charques
(London: Hutchinson and Co., [1946]), 40–45. The Russian original is A. Fadeev,
*Leningrad v dni blokady* (Moscow: Sovetskii pisatel', 1944).

10. Skomorovsky and Morris, *The Siege of Leningrad*, 42. *KP*'s coverage of the
war routinely explained young peoples' heroism as stemming, at least in part, from
their training as Young Communists.

11. Fadeev, *Leningrad in the Days of the Blockade*, 45, 46.

12. Fadeev, "Deti geroicheskogo goroda"; K. Filatova, "Chasovye goroda-geroia:
Komsomol'tsy okhraniaiut revoliutsionni poriadok," *KP*, July 10, 1942; K. Filatova,
"V povestke dnia—voprosy vospitaniia," *KP*, February 20, 1943.

13. Fadeev, *Leningrad in the Days of the Blockade*, 47–48.

14. Ales Adamovich and Daniil Granin Adamovich, *A Book of the Blockade* (Moscow: Raduga, 1983), 46, 82; Richard Bidlack, "Survival Strategies in Leningrad," in Thurston and Bonwetsch, eds., *The People's War*, 100–101.

15. Richard Bidlack, "The Political Mood in Leningrad during the First Year of the Soviet-German War," *Russian Review* 59 (January 2000), 112.

16. A discussion of why the "cult" of the war emerged in the 1960s lies beyond the scope of this chapter. See Tumarkin, *The Living and the Dead*.

17. Boris Gasparov, "On 'Notes from the Leningrad Blockade,'" *Canadian American Slavic Studies* 28 (Summer–Fall 1994): 217.

18. Alvin H. Rosenfeld, "Popularization and Memory: The Case of Anne Frank," in Hayes, *Lessons and Legacies*, 250, 260.

19. I have used the photographs of the diary included in Sergei Simonov, *Serdtse i dnevnik* (Moscow: Izdatel'stvo "Sovremennik," 1971). Harrison Salisbury provides a translation in *900 Days: The Siege of Leningrad* (New York: Harper and Row, 1969), 484.

20. *Vystavka "Geroicheskaia Oborona Leningrada": Ocherk-putevoditel'* (Leningrad and Moscow: Iskusstvo, 1945); *Muzei oborony Leningrada* (Leningrad and Moscow: Iskusstvo, 1948), 54. Press accounts include: L. Rakov, "Vystavka "Geroicheskaia oborona Leningrada," *Leningrad* no. 8 (June 1944): 14–15; S. Avvakumov, "Pamiatnik muzhestvy i stoikosti," *Leningradskaia pravda*, August 22, 1944; L. Rakov, "Pamiatnik geroiam nashego goroda: K godovshchine so dnia otkrytiia vystavki "geroicheskaia oborona Leningrada," *Leningradskaia pravda*, April 30, 1945; D. Khrenkov, "Po znakomomu adresu," *Literaturnaia gazeta*, January 25, 1964.

21. V. P. Kivisepp and N. P. Dobrotvorskii, "Muzei muzhestvo, skorbi i slavy," *Leningradskaia panorama* no. 8 (August 1991): 24. Adamovich and Granin, *A Book of the Blockade*, 12–13. In her telegrams from Leningrad, Churchill mentioned her visit to a children's hospital, but not the museum. Mary Soames, ed., *Winston and Clementine: The Personal Letters of the Churchills* (Boston: Houghton Mifflin, 1998), 525.

22. Adamovich and Granin, *A Book of the Blockade*, 13. Gennadi Petrov, *Piskarevskoe kladbishche* (Leningrad: Lenizdat, 1971), 35–36; Iu. Alianskii, "Tanets v ogne," in *Deti voennoi pory* (Moscow: Izdatel'stvo politicheskoi literatury, 1984), 181.

23. Viktor Golikov, ed., *Podvig naroda: Pamiatniki Velikoi Otechestvennoi voiny, 1941–1945* (Moscow: Izdatel'stvo politicheskoi literatury, 1980), 120; Iu. A. Lukíianov, *Rubezhi stoikosti muzhestva* (Leningrad: Lenizdat, 1985), 127–135.

24. Tumarkin, *The Living and the Dead*, 133.

25. Adamovich and Granin, *A Book of the Blockade*, 454.

26. Smirnov, *Serdtse i dnevnik*, 4, 91.

27. Adamovich and Granin, *A Book of the Blockade*, 486. A. Aleksii, "Detiam-planetu bez voin," in *Deti voennoi pory*, 6.

28. Adamovich and Granin, *A Book of the Blockade*, 236.

29. Ibid., 411, 410.

30. Ibid., 414–415. Iura himself was later evacuated, but did not survive.

31. *A Book of the Blockade*, 247, 255; E. Maksimova, "Vtoraia pobeda," in *Deti voennoi pory*, 92–102.

32. Ia. Kamernetskii, "Dnevnik Mishi tikhomirova," in *Deti voennoi pory*, 79–91. The introductory material states that Misha died in an artillery attack. Similar accounts may be found in *Deti goroda-geroia* (Leningrad: Lenizdat, 1974).

33. Adamovich and Granin, *A Book of the Blockade*, 192, 163, 21.

34. Ibid., 234, 25, 134, 177.

35. Adamovich and Granin, *A Book of the Blockade*, 236–237.

36. Elena S. Seniavskaia, "Heroic Symbols: The Reality and Mythology of War," *Russian Studies in History* 37 (Summer 1998): 61–87; Rosalinde Sartori, "On the Making of Heroes, Heroines, and Saints," in *Culture and Entertainment in Wartime Russia*, ed. Richard Stites (Bloomington: Indiana University Press, 1995), 176–193.

37. Interview at the Russian National Library, June 1999.

38. *Blokadniki: Volgogradskoe oblastnoe dobrovol'noe obshchestvo "zashchitniki i zhiteli blokadnogo Leningrada"* (Volgograd: Komitet po B70, 1996).

39. *Blokadnoi pamiati stranitsy* (St. Petersburg: ROO "Iunie uchastniki oborony Leningrada," 1999). See also Sankt-Peterburgskii Gosudarstvennyi Universitet. *Universitet v blokadnom i osazhdennom Leningrade 1941–1944: Sbornik ofitsial'nykh dokumentov, pisem, fotografii i drugogo fakticheskogo materiala* (St. Petersburg: TOO "Gippokat," 1996).

40. Adamovich and Granin, *A Book of the Blockade*, 25.

# Epilogue
## *The Girl in the Picture*

### *James Marten*

Perhaps the most famous image of a twentieth-century child marked by war is the photograph taken on June 8, 1972, during North Vietnam's so-called "Easter Offensive." When a South Vietnamese pilot accidentally bombed a temple in the little village of Trang Bang in Hau Nghia province, just north-west of Saigon, a number of South Vietnamese civilians were killed and in-jured. The napalm splashed over the back and side of nine-year-old Phan Thi Kim Phuc, burning off her clothes and searing her skin. She ran scream-ing down a road leading away from town, where she was photographed by an Associated Press photographer, Nick Ut. Within forty-eight hours the picture had appeared in newspapers all over the world. Ut would later win the Pulitzer Prize; Kim Phuc would become a poster child for the young vic-tims of war.

But Kim's experience of war preceded her accidental rise to fame and lasted far longer than the immediate pain from the tragic bombing. After snapping her picture, Ut had helped get Kim to a Saigon hospital; other journalists got her transferred to a Western-sponsored burn clinic, where she made a slow recovery and was released several months later. Although they felt fortunate that their daughter had survived, Kim's parents had nev-ertheless suffered greatly from the war. Comfortably middle class despite the long years of conflict, they owned land, a house, and a noodle stand along the highway running through their little village. Although the family had little interest in politics, the war was a constant presence in Kim's child-hood. Her sister was the widow of a South Vietnamese soldier; Viet Cong guerillas frequently visited their house, demanding food and information. When the North Vietnamese finally overran South Vietnam in 1975, the family lost everything and was reduced to a level of poverty it had not experienced for generations.

Kim suffered along with her parents and siblings, but her life changed forever when the Communist government turned her misfortune into propaganda against Vietnam's enemies. She became an example of the hardy Vietnamese, scarred by American bombs, who nevertheless overcame adversity and prospered under the new order in a unified, Communist Vietnam, and she became the subject of numerous articles and documentaries by foreign journalists. She became accustomed to the attention, but never felt in control of her own destiny. Although she had dreamed since childhood of becoming a doctor, the government forced her to give up a place in medical school. Her propaganda work made her feel like a pawn to a cynical government that did not really care about her.

Of course, her image was used for many purposes outside Vietnam, too. It became a symbol for anti-war protesters, and since her wounds were inflicted by a misdirected South Vietnamese attack on Viet Cong positions, as an example of the incompetence of the South Vietnamese government. People from the West sent her gifts and money, perhaps as a way of relieving their own guilt and anger for the way the war in Southeast Asia had turned out. She inspired a German campaign to create a modern burn center for children in Saigon and was the subject of renewed interest—as a symbol for the world of the wartime victimization of all Vietnamese—during the commemoration of the tenth anniversary of the war's conclusion in 1985.

Mostly unaware of the extent to which she had become an icon in other parts of the world, and resentful of her manipulation by Communist handlers in the government, Kim also had to come to grips with her own war experiences. She converted to Christianity, which gave her hope that her life would improve; she took advantage of her special status to spend several years studying Spanish in Cuba; and she accepted an invitation to go to Germany for treatment of her still painful injuries. Finally, in 1992, she and her husband defected during a layover in a Canadian airport and settled in Toronto. In Canada, Kim finally was able to carve out her own meaning from her experiences, as the Canadian representative to the United Nations Educational, Scientific, and Cultural Organization (UNESCO), for whom she now travels the world. She also heads up the Kim Foundation, devoted to helping child victims of war.

Kim's experiences during the war—chronicled most recently in Denise Chong, *The Girl in the Picture: The Story of Kim Phuc, the Photograph, and the Vietnam War* (New York: Viking, 1999)—match the three threads running through this anthology. She was, in her own way, a central actor in the war in Vietnam, not only as a victim, but also as a participant in the political and cultural aftermath of that unhappy conflict. She became a part of the imagery created during the war. Her picture transcended the specifics of her own experiences, coming to represent every child in every war and providing a reference point to whatever lessons could be gleaned from them. While her example helped others articulate the meanings they drew from the war in Southeast Asia, Kim's experiences of course came to mean specific things to her as well. With courage, perseverance, and luck, Kim built a new life from the ruins of her old, shattered existence, illustrating the complex outcomes that can emerge from the unholy and inseparable link between children and war.

# Bibliography

Adams, David Wallace. *Education for Extinction: American Indians and the Boarding School Experience, 1875–1928*. Lawrence: University Press of Kansas, 1995.

Apfel, Roberta J. and Bennett Simon, eds. *Minefields in Their Hearts: The Mental Health of Children in War and Communal Violence*. New Haven, CT: Yale University Press, 1996.

Ball, Eve. *Indeh: An Apache Odyssey*. Norman: University of Oklahoma Press, 1988.

Baruch, Dorothy. *You, Your Children, and War*. New York: D. Appleton-Century, 1943.

Baumel, Judith Tydor. *Unfulfilled Promise: Rescue and Resettlement of Jewish Refugee Children in the United States 1934–1945*. Juneau, AK: Denali, 1990.

Benjamin, Thomas. "A Time of Reconquest: History, the Maya Revival, and the Zapatista Rebellion in Chiapas." *American Historical Review* 105 (April 2000): 417–450.

Black, Maggie. *The Children and the Nations: The Story of Unicef*. New York: Unicef, 1986.

Boltansky, Luc. *Distant Suffering. Morality, Media and Politics*. Cambridge: Cambridge University Press, 1999.

Bond, Brian. *War and Society in Europe, 1870–1970*. Montreal: McGill-Queen's University Press, UK, 1998.

Boyer, Paul. *By the Bomb's Early Light: American Thought and Culture at the Dawn of the Atomic Age*. New York: Pantheon Books, 1985.

Breen, Rodney. *Claiming Rights for Children. The Drafting of the Declaration of the Rights of the Child*. London: Save the Children Fund, 1994.

Brown, Ian. *Khomeini's Forgotten Sons: The Story of Iran's Boy Soldiers*. London: Grey Seal, 1990.

Brown, Joanne. "A is for Atom, B is for Bomb: Civil Defense in American Public Education." *The Journal of American History* 75 (June 1988): 68–90.

Brown, Kenneth D. "Modelling for War? Toy Soldiers in Late Victorian and Edwardian Britain." *Journal of Social History* 24 (1990).

Brown, Mike. *A Child's War: The Home Front, 1939–1945*. Phoenix Mill: Sutton Publishing, 2000.

Brunk, Samuel. "Remembering Emiliano Zapata: Three Moments in the Posthumous Career of the Martyr of Chinameca." *Hispanic American Historical Review* 78 (1998): 457–490.

Buxton, Dorothy F. and Edward Fuller. *The White Flame: The Story of the Save the Children Fund.* London: Longmans, Green and Co., and The Weardale Press, 1931.

Child, Brenda J. *Boarding School Seasons: American Indian Families, 1900–1940.* Lincoln: University of Nebraska Press, 1998.

Cochrane, Peter. *Simpson and the Donkey: The Making of a Legend.* Carlton: Melbourne University Press, 1992.

Coe, Richard N. *When the Grass Was Taller: Autobiography and the Experience of Childhood.* New Haven, CT: Yale University Press, 1984.

Coles, Robert. *The Political Life of Children.* Boston: Houghton Mifflin, 1986.

Cunningham, Hugh. "The Rights of the Child from the Mid-Eighteenth to the Early Twentieth Century." *Aspects of Education* 50 (1994): 2–16.

Davey, Thomas. *A Generation Divided: German Children and the Berlin Wall.* Durham, NC: Duke University Press, 1987.

Davis, Charles T. and Henry Louis Gates Jr., eds. *The Slave's Narrative*, ed. New York: Oxford University Press, 1985.

Dawidowicz, Lucy S., ed. *A Holocaust Reader.* West Orange, NJ: Behrman House, 1976.

Dickson, Maxcy Robson. "The War Comes to All: The Story of the United States Food Administration as a Propaganda Agency." Ph.D. dissertation, George Washington University, 1942.

Dodge, Cole P. and Magne Raundalen. *Reaching Children in War: Sudan, Uganda, and Mozambique.* Bergen, Norway: Sigma Forlag; Uppsala, Sweden: Scandinavian Institute of African Studies, 1991.

Dower, John W. *Embracing Defeat: Japan in the Wake of World War Two.* New York: W. W. Norton, 1999.

———. "Sensational Rumors, Seditious Graffiti, and the Nightmares of the Thought Police." In Dower, ed. *Japan in War and Peace: Selected Essays.* New York: The New Press, 1993.

———. *War without Mercy: Race and Power in the Pacific War.* New York: Pantheon, 1986.

Dulles, Foster Rhea. *The American Red Cross: A History.* New York: Harper and Brothers, 1950.

Eisen, George. *Children and Play in the Holocaust: Games among the Shadows.* Amherst: University of Massachusetts Press, 1988.

Eth, Spencer and Robert Pynoos, eds. *Post-traumatic Stress Disorder in Children.* Washington, DC: American Psychiatric Press, 1985.

Fethney, Michael. *The Absurd and the Brave: The True Story of the British Government's World War II Evacuation of Children Overseas.* Lewes, England: Book Guild, 1992.

Fraser, M. *Children in Conflict*. New York: Basic Books, 1973.

Freeman, Michael and Philip Veerman, eds. *The Ideologies of Children's Rights*. Dordrecht/Boston/London: Martinus Nijhoff Publishers, 1992.

Freud, Anna and Dorothy Burlingame. *War and Children*. New York: Ernst Willard, 1943.

Garbarino, James, Nancy Dubrow, Kathleen Kostelny, and Carole Pardo. *Children in Danger: Coping with the Consequences of Community Violence*. San Francisco: Jossey-Bass Publishers, 1992.

Garbarino, James, Kathleen Kostelny, and Nancy Dubrow. *No Place to Be a Child: Growing Up in a War Zone*. Lexington, MA: Lexington Books, 1991.

Gilbert, Dennis. "Rewriting History. Salinas, Zedillo and the 1992 Textbook Controversy." *Mexican Studies/Estudios Mexicanos* 13 (Winter 1997): 271–297.

Gillis, John, ed. *The Militarization of the Western World*. New Brunswick, NJ: Rutgers University Press, 1989.

Gilman, Sander. *Jewish Self-Hatred: Anti-Semitism and the Hidden Language of the Jews*. Baltimore, MD: Johns Hopkins University Press, 1986.

Graham, Jeanine. "Childhood Experiences." *Proceedings of the "Taranaki Odyssey 2001" Conference of the New Zealand Society of Genealogists, 1–4 June 2001* (New Plymouth: New Zealand Society of Genealogists): 171–181.

———. "Towards a History of New Zealand Childhoods." *Historical Review* 48 (November 2000): 89–102.

———. "My Brother and I . . .": *Glimpses of Childhood in Our Colonial Past*. Dunedin: Hocken Library, University of Otago, 1992.

———. "Disrupted Lives: An Exploration of the Impact of Armed Conflict on Children's Lives in Nineteenth Century Aotearoa/New Zealand." *Historical News* 65 (October 1992): 8–11.

Haebich, Anna. *Broken Circles: Fragmenting Indigenous Families 1800–2000*. Fremantle: Fremantle Arts Centre Press, 2000.

Hall, R. and Winter, J. *The Upheaval of War: Family, World and Welfare in Europe, 1914–1918*. New York: Cambridge University Press, 1988.

Halls, W. D. *The Youth of Vichy France*. Oxford: Clarendon Press, 1981.

Harbison, J. J., ed. *Children of the Troubles: Children in Northern Ireland*. Belfast: Stranmillis College Learning Resources Unit, 1983.

Havens, Thomas. *Valley of Darkness: The Japanese People and World War Two*. New York: University Press of America, 1986.

Hayes, Peter, ed. *Lessons and Legacies: The Meaning of the Holocaust in a Changing World*. Evanston, IL: Northwestern University Press, 1991.

Heathorn, Stephen. *For Home, Country and Race: Constructing Class, Gender and Englishness in the Elementary Classroom*. Toronto: University of Toronto Press, 2000.

Higgins, James and Joan Ross. *Fractured Identities: Cambodia's Children of War*. Lowell: Loom Press, 1997.

Horne, J. *State, Society and Mobilization in Europe during the First World War*. New York: Cambridge University Press, 1997.

Hoxie, Frederick. *A Final Promise: The Campaign to Assimilate the Indians, 1880–1920*. Lincoln: University of Nebraska Press, 1984.

Humphrey, John. *Human Rights and the United Nations: A Great Adventure*. Dobbs Ferry, NY, 1984.

Hurt, J. S. *Elementary Schooling and the Working Classes*. London: Routledge, 1979.

Hutchinson, John F. *Champions of Charity: War and the Rise of the Red Cross*. Boulder, CO: Westview Press, 1996.

Inglis, Ken. *Sacred Places: War Memorials in the Australian Landscape*. Carlton: Miegunyah Press at Melbourne University Press, 1998.

Inglis, Ruth. *The Children's War: Evacuation 1939–1945*. London: William Collins Sons, 1989.

Iriye, Akira. *Cultural Internationalism and World Order*. Baltimore, MD: Johns Hopkins University Press, 1997.

Jahn, Hubertus. *Patriotic Culture in Russia during World War I*. Ithaca, NY: Cornell University Press, 1995.

Jones, B. and Howell, B. *Popular Arts of the First World War*. New York: McGraw-Hill, 1972.

Kestenberg, Judith S. and Ira Brenner, eds., *The Last Witness: The Child Survivor of the Holocaust*. Washington: American Psychiatric Press, 1996.

Kestenberg, Judith S. and Eva Fogelman, eds. *Children during the Nazi Reign: Psychological Perspective on the Interview Process*. Westport, CT: Praeger, 1994.

Kilbourn, Phyllis, ed. *Healing the Children of War: A Handbook for Ministry to Children Who Have Suffered Deep Traumas*. Monrovia, CA: MARC Publications, 1995.

Kirk, Robert William. *Earning Their Stripes: The Mobilization of American Children in the Second World War*. New York: Peter Lang, 1994.

Kirschenbaum, Lisa A. "'Our City, Our Hearths, Our Families': Local Loyalties and Private Life in Soviet World War II Propaganda." *Slavic Review* 59 (Winter 2000): 825–847.

Koven, Seth. "Remembering and Dismemberment: Crippled Children, Wounded Soldiers, and the Great War in Great Britain." *American Historical Review* 99 (October 1994): 1167–1202.

*Liberian Civil War through the Eyes of Children*. Monrovia: Education Secretariat, Catholic Archdiocese of Monrovia, 1992.

Lindsey, Donal. *Indians at Hampton Institute, 1877–1923*. Urbana: University of Illinois Press, 1995.

Link-Up (NSW) and Tikka Jan Wilson. *In the Best Interest of the Child? Stolen Children: Aboriginal Pain/White Shame*. Canberra: Link-Up NSW and Aboriginal History, 1997.

Lowenthal, David. *The Past Is a Foreign Country*. Cambridge: Cambridge University Press, 1985.

Mackenzie, J. M. *Propaganda and Empire: The Manipulation of British Public Opinion, 1880–1960*. Manchester: Manchester University Press, 1984.

Mangan, J. A., ed. *Making Imperial Mentalities*. Manchester: Manchester University Press, 1990.

———. *Benefits Bestowed?* Manchester: Manchester University Press, 1987.

Mann, Henrietta. *Cheyenne-Arapaho Education, 1871–1982*. Niwot: University Press of Colorado, 1997.

Marshall, Dominique. "The Formation of Childhood as an Object of International Relations: The Child Welfare Committee and the Declaration of Children's Rights of the League of Nations." *International Journal of Children's Rights* 7 (1999): 103–147.

———. "Canada and Children's Rights at the United Nations, 1945–1959." In Greg Donaghy, ed. *Canada and the Early Cold War. 1943–1957*. Ottawa, Department of Foreign Affairs and International Trade, 1998: 183–214.

———. "Reconstruction Politics, the Canadian Welfare State and the Ambiguity of Children's Rights, 1940–1950." In Ed Montigny and Lori Chambers, eds., *Family Matters: Papers in Post-Confederation Family History*. Toronto: Canadian Scholars' Press, 1998: 135–156.

Marten, James. *The Children's Civil War*. Chapel Hill: University of North Carolina Press, 1998.

McCann, Phillip, ed. *Popular Education and Socialization in the Nineteenth Century*. London: Methuen, 1977.

McEnaney, Laura. *Civil Defense Begins at Home: Militarization Meets Everyday Life in the Fifties*. Princeton, NJ: Princeton University Press, 2000.

Mitchell, Mary Niall. "Raising Freedom's Child: Race, Nation, and the Lives of Black Children in Nineteenth-Century Louisiana." Ph.D. dissertation, New York University, 2001.

Morehead, Caroline. *Dunant's Dream*. London: Harper, 1999.

Morris, Ivan. *The Nobility of Failure: Tragic Heroes in the History of Japan*. New York: The Noonday Press, 1975.

Mosse, G. *Fallen Soldiers: Reshaping the Memories of the World Wars*. New York: Oxford University Press, 1990.

Oakes, Guy. *The Imaginary War: Civil Defense and American Cold War Culture*. New York: Oxford University Press, 1994.

Ofer, Dalia and Lenore J. Weitzman, eds. *Women in the Holocaust*. New Haven, CT: Yale University Press, 1998.

Parker, Peter. *The Old Lie: The Great War and the Public School Ethos*. London: Constable, 1987.

Parsons, Martin L., *"I'll Take That One": Dispelling the Myths of Civilian Evacuation 1939–45*. London: Beckett-Karlson, 1998.

Parsons, Martin L. and Penny Starns. *Evacuation: The True Story*. London: DSM, 1999.

Patri, Angelo. *Your Children in Wartime*. Garden City, NY: Doubleday, Doran and Company, 1943.

Penn, Alan. *Targetting Schools: Drill, Militarism and Imperialism*. Manchester: Manchester University Press, 1999.

Reader, Ian and Tony Walter. *Pilgrimage in Popular Culture*. Houndmills: Macmillan, 1993.

Riney, Scott. *The Rapid City Indian School, 1898–1933*. Norman: University of Oklahoma Press, 1999.

Riseborough, Hazel. *Days of Darkness: Taranaki 1878–1884*. Wellington: Allen and Unwin/Port Nicholson Press in association with Historical Branch, 1989.

Rosenblatt, Roger. *Children of War*. Garden City, NY: Anchor Press/Doubleday, 1983.

Scates, Bruce. "'From a Brown Land Far Away'": Australian pilgrimages to Great War cemeteries." *Locality* 9 (1998): 6–13.

Scates, Bruce and Raelene Frances. *Women and the Great War*. Cambridge: Cambridge University Press, 1997.

Schroeder, Michael J. "The Sandino Rebellion Revisited: Civil War, Imperialism, State Formation, and Popular Nationalism Muddied Up Together in the Segovias of Nicaragua, 1926–1934." In Gilbert Joseph, Catherine LeGrand, and Ricardo Salvatore, eds., *Close Encounters of Empire*. Durham, NC: Duke University Press, 1998.

———. "Horse Thieves to Rebels to Dogs: Political Gang Violence and the State in the Western Segovias, Nicaragua, in the Time of Sandino." *Journal of Latin American Studies* 28 (October 1996): 383–434.

———. "'To Defend Our Nation's Honor': Toward a Social and Cultural History of the Sandino Rebellion in Nicaragua, 1927–1934." Ph.D. dissertation, University of Michigan, 1993.

Sinclair, Keith. *Kinds of Peace: Maori People After the Wars, 1870–85*. Auckland: Auckland University Press, 1991.

———. *The Origins of the Maori Wars*. Wellington: New Zealand University Press, 1957.

Skolnick, Arlene. *Embattled Paradise: The American Family in an Age of Uncertainty*. New York: Basic Books, 1991.

Smith, Harold L., ed. *War and Social Change: British Society in the Second World War*. Wolfeboro, NH: Manchester University Press, 1986.

Smith, Kate Darian and Paula Hamilton. *Memory and History in Twentieth Century Australia*. New York and Melbourne: Oxford University Press, 1996.

Smith, Leonard. *Between Mutiny and Obedience*. Princeton, NJ: Princeton University Press, 1994.

Steedman, Carolyn. *The Tidy House: Little Girls Writing*. London: Virago, 1982.

Stockel, H. Henrietta. *Survival of the Spirit: Chiricahua Apaches in Captivity*. Reno: University of Nevada Press, 1993.

Thurston, Robert W. and Bernd Bonwetsch, eds. *The People's War: Responses to World War II in the Soviet Union.* Urbana: University of Illinois Press, 2000.

Trennert, Robert. *The Phoenix Indian School: Forced Assimilation in Arizona, 1891–1935.* Norman: University of Oklahoma Press, 1988.

Tumarkin, Nina. *The Living and the Dead: The Rise and Fall of the Cult of World War II in Russia.* New York: Basic Books, 1994.

Turner, Victor and Edith Turner. *Image and Pilgrimage in Christian Culture: Anthropological Perspectives.* New York: Columbia University Press, 1978.

Tuttle, William M., Jr. *"Daddy's Gone to War": The Second World War in the Lives of America's Children.* New York: Oxford University Press, 1993.

United Nations. *Promotion and Protection of the Rights of Children: Impact of Armed Conflict on Children.* New York: United Nations, 1996.

Vaughan, Mary Kay. *Cultural Politics in Revolution.* Tucson: University of Arizona Press, 1997.

Veerman, Philip E. *The Rights of the Child and the Changing Image of Childhood.* Dordrecht/Boston/London: Martinus Nijhoff Publishers, 1991.

Wall, Richard and Jay Winter, eds. *The Upheaval of War: Family, Work, and Welfare in Europe, 1914–1918.* Cambridge: Cambridge University Press, 1988.

Weiner, Amir. *Making Sense of War: The Second World War and the Fate of the Bolshevik Revolution.* Princeton, NJ: Princeton University Press, 2001.

Werner, Emmy E. *Through the Eyes of the Innocents: Children Witness World War II.* New York: Westview Press, 2000.

Whitfield, Stephan J. *The Culture of the Cold War*, 2nd ed. Baltimore, MD: Johns Hopkins University Press, 1996.

Willinsky, John. *Learning to Divide the World: Education at Empire's End.* Minneapolis: University of Minnesota Press, 1998.

Winkler, Allan M. *Life under a Cloud: American Anxiety about the Atom.* New York: Oxford University Press, 1993.

Winter, Jay. *Sites of Memory, Sites of Mourning: The Great War in European Cultural History.* Cambridge: Cambridge University Press, 1995.

Wolf, Anna W. M. *Our Children Face War.* Boston: Houghton Mifflin, 1942.

Zelizer, Viviana A. *Pricing the Priceless Child: The Changing Social Value of Children.* New York: Basic Books, 1985.

Zimand, Gertrude Folks. *Child Workers in Wartime.* New York City: National Child Labor Committee, 1942.

# Contributors

*Benita Blessing* is assistant professor for European women's and gender history at Ohio University. She received her Ph.D. from the departments of history and educational policy studies at the University of Wisconsin–Madison. Her research interests include antifascism, memory, and youth culture, particularly in postwar Germany and Italy.

*Thomas Cardoza* holds a Master's degree in military history from Purdue University, and a Ph.D. in French history from the University of California at Santa Barbara. He teaches history at Eleanor Roosevelt College at the University of California at San Diego.

*Aaron J. Cohen* received his Ph.D. at Johns Hopkins University in 1998 and completed an M.A. at the University of Oregon in 1992. He is currently assistant professor in the Department of History at California State University, Sacramento.

*Robert Coles*, a child psychiatrist and James Agee Professor of Social Ethics at Harvard University, is the author of over 1,300 articles, reviews, and monographs. He won the 1973 Pulitzer Prize for his five-volume series, *Children of Crisis*, and received the Presidential Medal of Freedom in 1998.

*Guillaume de Syon* is an associate professor of history at Albright College and a research associate at Franklin & Marshall College. He is the author of *Zeppelin! Germany and the Airship, 1900–1939* (Johns Hopkins University Press, 2001).

*Cynthia B. Eriksson* is currently an adjunct assistant professor of psychology in the Graduate School of Psychology at Fuller Theological Seminary, where she co-leads the Headington Program in International Trauma. She has done trauma training and research in Liberia, Japan, Cambodia, and Los Angeles, California. Her research examining the traumatic exposure and re-entry distress of international relief and development workers was published in the *Journal of Traumatic Stress*.

*Jeanine Marie Graham* is a senior lecturer in history at the University of Waikato, New Zealand. Most of her publications relate to nineteenth- and early twentieth-century New Zealand social history and reflect her particular research interest in the history of children's experiences. She is currently endeavoring to write the findings of her Colonial Childhoods Oral History Project, which involved recorded interviews with 166 New Zealanders, the majority of whom were born before 1903.

*Owen Griffiths* received his Ph.D. from the University of British Columbia, where he wrote a dissertation titled "Reconstruction of Self and Society in Early Postwar Japan, 1945–1949." He is now an assistant professor in the Department of Asia Pacific Studies at San Diego State University, San Diego, California. He has lived and studied in Japan for more than seven years.

*Victoria Haskins* is a lecturer in the history department of Flinders University of South Australia. She teaches Australian history, specializing in the history of gender, class, and indigenous and non-indigenous race relations. She has published a number of articles on Aboriginal domestic workers and is currently working on a book about historical relationships between indigenous and non-indigenous women.

*Stephen Heathorn* is associate professor of British History at McMaster University, Ontario, Canada. He is the author of *For Home, Country and Race: Constructing Class, Gender and Englishness in the Elementary Classroom* (Toronto, 2000), and several articles on the relationships among nationalism, imperialism, social prescription, and educational provision in nineteenth- and twentieth-century Britain. He is currently researching a monograph on the commemoration of martial figures in modern British culture.

*Margaret D. Jacobs* is an assistant professor of history at New Mexico State University, where she teaches American Indian history and women's history. Her 1999 book, *Engendered Encounters: Feminism and Pueblo Cultures, 1879–1934*, won the Gaspar Perez de Villagra from the Historical Society of New Mexico and the Sierra Prize from the Western Association of Women Historians.

*Lisa A. Kirschenbaum* is associate professor in the Department of History,

West Chester University of Pennsylvania. She has published a book entitled *Small Comrades: Revolutionizing Childhood in Soviet Russia, 1917–
1932.* She is currently researching the memory of the siege of Leningrad,
1941–1991.

*Stephen E. Lewis* is assistant professor of Latin American history at California State University, Chico. He is currently co-editing an anthology on
Mexican national identity and is finishing his own book on state- and
nation-building through education in Chiapas, Mexico.

*Dominique Marshall* is associate professor of history at Carleton University.
She is working on a history of the Child Welfare Committee of the
League of Nations and on a history of humanitarian aid on behalf of
African children, with a special study of Canada as a country of donors.

*James Marten* is professor of history at Marquette University. He is the author of *The Children's Civil War*, editor of *Lessons of War: The Civil War
in Children's Magazines*, and director of the Children in Urban America
Project, a digital archive on the history of Milwaukee children funded by
the National Endowment for the Humanities.

*Molly Mitchell* is assistant professor of history at the University of New Orleans. She is completing a cultural history of African American childhood in the nineteenth-century South. Her published work includes articles on free children of color and African American migration movements, and freed children and abolition.

*Chris O'Brien* is an independent scholar living in New Jersey. He received his
Ph.D. from the University of Kansas and has taught at Johnson County
Community College and at the University of Kansas.

*Lisa L. Ossian* completed her doctorate in agricultural history and rural
studies at Iowa State University in 1998 with a dissertation titled "The
Home Fronts of Iowa, 1940–1945." She is currently researching the depression in rural Iowa and is English and history instructor at South-
western Community College in Creston, Iowa.

*Martin L. Parsons* is Deputy Head of the School of Education at the University of Reading and is the author of many publications on British society
and on the evacuation of civilians in the UK during World War II, including *"I'll Take That One!" Dispelling the Myths of Civilian Evacuation
in the UK during World War Two.*

*Elizabeth A. Rupp* is pursuing her Ph.D. in clinical psychology at Fuller Theological Seminary's Graduate School of Psychology. She credits a 1999
stay in Sarajevo, Bosnia-Herzegovina with propelling her interest in
cross-cultural psychology into the area of international trauma response
and trauma associated with war. Studying with the Headington Program
in International Trauma remains central to her interests in the effects,
treatment, and healing of war-related trauma.

*Bruce C. Scates* teaches history at the University of New South Wales and
is the author of *A New Australia: Citizenship, Radicalism and the First
Republic*, and is co-author of two other books. His school text *Australian Women and the Great War* won the NSW Premier's History Prize
in 1998.

*Michael J. Schroeder* received his Ph.D. in history from the University of
Michigan in 1993 and currently teaches U.S. and Latin American history
at Eastern Michigan University. He received an Honorable Mention in
the 1997 prize competition from the Conference on Latin American History for "Horse Thieves to Rebels to Dogs: Political Gang Violence and
the State in the Western Segovias, Nicaragua, in the Time of Sandino,
1926–1934," which appeared in the *Journal of Latin American Studies*. He
is currently completing a book manuscript, *Tragedy, Redemption, Power:
The Sandino Rebellion in Las Segovias and Nicaragua, 1926–1934*.

*Diana Selig* received her Ph.D. from the University of California at Berkeley
and is an assistant professor of history at Claremont McKenna College,
where she teaches twentieth-century U.S. history. She is completing a
study of education against prejudice in the Unted States between the
wars.

*Penny Elaine Starns* is a research fellow at the London School of Hygiene
and Tropical Medicine (England) and a historical consultant to the BBC.
She is the author of *Nurses at War: Women on the Frontline, 1939–1945*,
and, with Martin L. Parsons, of *Evacuation: The True Story*.

*Eric J. Sterling* is Distinguished Research Professor of English at Auburn
University–Montgomery (Alabama). He has published widely on drama
and poetry, and has completed a book manuscript called *Holocaust
Drama: Social Responsibility During the Shoah*. He was the 1996 winner
of the College English Association's national Robert E. Hacke Scholar-
Teacher Award.

*Elizabeth McKee Williams* is completing her Ph.D. in the Program in American Culture at the University of Michigan. Her dissertation studies autobiographical accounts of childhood during the era of the American Revolution.

# Index